*A***FALCON**GUIDE®

TRAVELING

the

Lewis and Clark Trail

THIRD EDITION

Julie Fanselow

FALCON®

GUILFORD, CONNECTICUT
HELENA, MONTANA
AN IMPRINT OF THE GLOBE PEQUOT PRESS

To the memories of:

Meriwether Lewis (1774–1809)
William Clark (1770–1838)
and Ruth Fanselow (1925–1987)

A FALCON GUIDE®

All photos by Julie Fanselow unless otherwise noted.

Text design by Lesley Weissman-Cook

ISBN 0-7627-2589-3

Manufactured in the United States of America
Third Edition/First Printing

Contents

Acknowledgments

When I first researched this book in 1993, I was only dimly aware that the United States would mark the Lewis and Clark Expedition's bicentennial in a decade. Now the bicentennial is here, and I hope this book will help travelers take an active part in exploring firsthand one of history's most compelling adventure stories.

Many people have contributed their time and expertise to make this book what it is. For this edition I am thankful for advice, counsel, and logistical assistance from Doug Arnold, Mary Boyle, Katie Bump, Daphne Richards Cook, Dell Courtney, Pete Donatucci, Mary Ethel Emanuel, Larry Epstein, Calvin Grinnell, Alan Hansen, Mary Hendron, Jim Holmberg, Mimi Jackson, Clay Jenkinson, Stan Lawson, Steve Lee, Sharon McCoy, Diane Norton, Dennis O'Connell, Harlan and Barb Opdahl, Diane and Orville Oster, Keith Petersen, Don Peterson, Rachel Retterath, Carol Ryan, Don Striker, Cindy Tryon, Steve Wang, Phyllis Yeager, and Carol Zahorsky. Dozens of other people at local museums and visitor bureaus also provided valuable information. Thanks to you all, and my apologies to those I forgot to list and those who helped so much on earlier editions. I haven't forgotten you!

Stephen Ambrose did me a big favor when he picked up the first edition of this book while researching his own ode to the Corps of Discovery, *Undaunted Courage,* and later when he told my publisher what a help it had been. Professor Ambrose, who died the day before I finished this edition, did more than any other person to generate modern interest in the Lewis and Clark story. I wish he had lived long enough to enjoy the bicentennial.

Dayton Duncan's *Out West* served as my own inspiration to hit the trail. He, too, has proven an advocate for my work, and I thank him. I also value the staff, past and present, of the National Council of the Lewis and Clark Bicentennial and of the many publications and other companies that—through their assignments—help me underwrite my continual Lewis and Clark research. Some of these businesses are cited in this book, including River Odysseys West and Lindblad Expeditions, both of which I've served as a paid on-river interpreter.

Thanks, too, to Falcon Publishing and The Globe Pequot Press for their ongoing support.

My husband, Bruce Whiting, is my partner in all things. My daughter, Natalie Fanselow Whiting—born just after the first edition of this book came out—often joins me on voyages of discovery. My father, Byron Fanselow, is a great friend to me and grandfather to Natalie. My in-laws are terrific, too; I am especially thankful to Kay Phillips and her family for helping out with child care.

Much will be said and written about the Lewis and Clark Bicentennial over the next few years. Many towns, tribes, and organizations along the route hope that the anniversary will not be simply a short-term commemoration but the beginning of a new era of communication, preservation, and legacy-building. On a personal level, I am grateful that this ongoing project has given me a chance to experience many days of paddling, hiking, cycling, and driving along the expedition's path, as well as many nights filled with the same sort of campfire conversations, brilliant stars, and coyote choruses the explorers enjoyed. It's my wish that everyone interested in the United States—its past, present, and future—will get the chance to experience these wonders for themselves. Let's get started.

Preface

These days, travelers think little of crossing a continent in a matter of hours. But 200 years ago, a small group of Americans undertook a journey so complex and so potentially dangerous that their president and benefactor, Thomas Jefferson, and their fellow citizens half expected they would never return. In less capable hands, the mission surely would have failed. But Meriwether Lewis and William Clark had the intelligence, the bravery, and the generous spirit to see it through.

The trip was the Lewis and Clark Expedition of 1803–1806, and it ranks among the world's greatest journeys of exploration. This guidebook aims to help travelers—both actual and armchair—relive the expedition's excitement and drama. In these pages, you will find details about the major historic sites all along the Lewis and Clark Trail, along with information on modern recreational and scenic attractions, activities, and visitor amenities along the way. In short, this is a guide for people who want to retrace Lewis and Clark's route while finding some adventures of their own.

It is true that we can whip across our nation in mere hours or days. But these are journeys of expedience, not experience. Today we must give ourselves the luxury of taking time to linger and learn, even dawdle and drift.

Few artifacts of the Lewis and Clark journey remain along the route, and in many areas interpretation is minimal. A trip along the trail today is very much a journey of imagination. But there are many places visitors can well imagine what it was like to be Lewis and Clark; this book aims to guide you to the best of those places.

Map Legend

Interstate Highway	15	Outward Bound 1804–1805	....
U.S. Highway	12 101	Homeward Bound 1806	- - - - - - - - - - -
State Highway	94 220	Town	○ **LEWISTON**
Forest Road	220	Airport	✈
River or Stream	~~~	Point of Interest	⬛
Peak	▲ **Mt. Hood** 11,239 ft.	Lewis and Clark Campsites/Landmarks	**Camp River Dubois**
Boundary	▬ ▬ ▬ ▬ ▬	Interpretive Center	ℹ
Trail	....	River and Scenic Boat Trips	
		Hiking	🚶
Compass	N W E S	Bicycling	🚲
		Native American Site	
Scale	0 5 10 miles	Equestrian	

How to Use This Book

By the time its travels were completed, the Lewis and Clark Expedition had logged more than 7,500 miles paddling, hiking, and riding across the continent and back.

Obviously, it would be difficult to duplicate such a journey today. But it is possible to take a great Western vacation focusing on the Lewis and Clark Trail. What's more, the historical aspects of a Lewis and Clark vacation can easily be combined with your favorite leisure activities, be they camping, canoeing, sightseeing, fishing, golf, hiking, or just plain taking it easy.

There are two ways to travel. Some travelers would like to see the whole trail in one trip, and it's possible to retrace the route in your vehicle in just under two weeks using the itinerary below. But many people would rather take their time discovering the route, covering one section one year and another the next.

SUGGESTED ITINERARIES

The following is a suggested Lewis and Clark trip designed to fit within a two-week vacation period. The main itinerary is for travelers who prefer sight-seeing and visiting historical sites. In-depth alternatives are offered for adventure-oriented travelers or others seeking to spend more time in fewer places.

These itineraries assume a starting point in the St. Louis area, where final trip preparations were made and the full expedition got under way in May 1804. But many Lewis and Clark buffs may want to begin farther east, visiting such sites as Monticello, the Falls of the Ohio, and the river forts where the Corps of Discovery filled its ranks. These places and others are covered in Chapter 2, The Eastern Legacy. The Louisville, Kentucky—Clarksville, Indiana, area makes an especially good alternative starting point, since it's only a half day's drive from St. Louis and was where Lewis picked up Clark on his way down the Ohio River in October 1803.

Day 1: The St. Louis—St. Charles Area, Missouri

Start with a visit to the **Lewis and Clark State Historic Site** near the banks of the Mississippi River in Illinois (just off Illinois Highway 3 south of Alton). Next tour the **Museum of Westward Expansion** and **Gateway Arch**; **William Clark's grave** in St. Louis's Bellefontaine Cemetery; and the **Lewis and Clark Boathouse and Nature Center** in St. Charles. Overnight in St. Charles.

■ *Approximate driving time/distance:* not applicable; all sites in St. Louis metropolitan area.

Day 2: St. Charles to Kansas City, Missouri

Drive west along the Missouri River. Possible stops include the Daniel Boone Home; the German-style town of Hermann; **Jefferson City**, where a relief on the capitol grounds depicts the signing of the Louisiana Purchase; **Arrow Rock**; and **Fort Osage,** a trading post Clark helped build after the expedition. Missouri Highways 94 and 100 parallel the river from St. Charles to Jefferson City. From there, follow U.S. Highway 63 to Columbia; Interstate 70 to Boonville; MO 41 through Arrow Rock to Marshall; and U.S. Highways 65 and 24 to Fort Osage and the Kansas City area. Overnight in Kansas City.

■ *Approximate driving time/distance:* six hours, 275 miles.

■ *In-depth alternative:* Spend a few hours—or days—bicycling or hiking along the Katy Trail. For Lewis and Clark buffs, the best stretches are those closest to the Missouri River, such as the portion near Rocheport in central Missouri. Overnight in a riverside town, or drive on to the Kansas City area.

Day 3: Kansas City, Missouri, to Sioux City, Iowa

Travel north on Interstate 29 to the Omaha—Council Bluffs area, possibly stopping for side trips to **Lewis and Clark State Park** (northwest of Kansas City on Missouri 45) and nearby **Atchison, Kansas,** where the expedition spent July 4, 1804. Continue on to Council Bluffs, Iowa, via I–29 and visit the Western Historic Trails Center and the **Lewis & Clark Monument Park** on the bluffs overlooking the Missouri. Cross into Omaha, Nebraska, and visit the Joslyn Art Museum to see its Karl Bodmer collection or **Fort Atkinson State Park.** Take either U.S. Highway 75 or I–29 to Onawa, Iowa, where a replica of the Corps of Discovery's keelboat is on display at Iowa's **Lewis and Clark State Park.** Continue north to Sioux City and see the **Lewis and Clark Interpretive Center** and the **Sergeant Floyd Monument.** Overnight in Sioux City.

■ *Approximate driving time/distance:* seven hours, 340 miles.

Day 4: Sioux City Iowa, to Pierre, South Dakota

Take I–29 north to Vermillion, South Dakota, and visit **Spirit Mound.** Next, see the **Lewis and Clark Visitor Center** at Gavins Point Dam west of Yankton,

South Dakota. Have lunch in one of the many nearby park areas. Take South Dakota Highways 46 and 50 to Platte, then SD 45 to Interstate 90. Follow the interstate to Chamberlain (where the South Dakota Visitor Information Center features exhibits on Lewis and Clark); then take SD 50 and SD 34 north and west to Pierre. Visit **Farm Island State Recreation Area** and the **Teton Council Site.** Overnight in Pierre.

■ *Approximate driving time/distance:* seven hours, 325 miles.

■ *In-depth alternative:* Rent a canoe or book a guided trip and paddle the free-flowing stretches of the Missouri River near Ponca or Niobrara State Park.

Day 5: Pierre, South Dakota, to Bismarck/Mandan, North Dakota

Drive north to Mobridge on U.S. Highways 83 and 12. Visit the **Sacagawea and Sitting Bull** monuments west of town, and continue north on South Dakota 1806, which changes to North Dakota 24 at the border. Follow ND 24 and ND 6 north to **Fort Abraham Lincoln State Park** and visit its On-A-Slant Indian Village. If time permits, take a cruise on the *Lewis and Clark* riverboat. Overnight in Bismarck or Mandan.

■ *Approximate driving time/distance:* four and a half hours, 225 miles.

Day 6: Bismarck/Mandan to Williston, North Dakota

Take U.S. Highway 83 north to Washburn. Visit the **North Dakota Lewis and Clark Interpretive Center** and **Fort Mandan** replica; then take North Dakota Highway 200 to the **Knife River Indian Village National Historic Site.** ND 200 loops back to U.S. 83. Drive north to North Dakota 37. Follow ND 37 and ND 1804 north of **Lake Sakakawea,** stopping for a picnic lunch at one of the parks en route. Overnight at Williston.

■ *Approximate driving time/distance:* five and a half hours, 260 miles.

■ *In-depth alternatives:* Take a canoe trip near Washburn, either on your own or with a local outfitter. Sign up for the annual "Heritage Outbound" midwinter campout in the Fort Mandan—Knife River area, or arrange for a personal tour of tribal lands from a local historian.

Day 7: Williston, North Dakota, to Fort Benton, Montana

Start the day with a visit to the Missouri-Yellowstone confluence and nearby **Fort Union National Historic Site.** Take U.S. Highway 2 across northern Montana to Havre, and then follow U.S. 87 south to **Fort Benton.** Explore Fort Benton's riverfront. Overnight in Fort Benton or Great Falls.

■ *Approximate driving time/distance:* seven hours, 385 miles (to Fort Benton); 420 miles (to Great Falls).

■ *In-depth alternative:* Plan a multiday canoe trip on the Wild and Scenic Upper Missouri downriver from Fort Benton.

Day 8: Fort Benton to Dillon, Montana

Take U.S. Highway 87 from Fort Benton to Great Falls. Visit the **Great Falls of the Missouri** and the **Lewis and Clark National Historic Trail Interpretive Center.** Drive south on Interstate 15 to exit 209, and take the **Gates of the Mountains** boat tour. If time permits, visit the Montana Historical Society in Helena; then drive southeast on U.S. 287 to Three Forks and Missouri Headwaters State Park. From Three Forks, take Montana Highways 2, 55, and 41 to Dillon, watching for **Beaverhead Rock** en route. Overnight in Dillon.

■ *Approximate driving time/distance:* Five hours, 250 miles (from Great Falls).

■ *In-depth alternative:* Take a naturalist-led boat trip on the Jefferson River near the Missouri headwaters.

Day 9: Dillon to Missoula, Montana

Visit Clark's Lookout in Dillon and the **Camp Fortunate Overlook** at Clark Canyon Reservoir southwest of town. Continue over **Lemhi Pass,** following the directions given in Chapter 7. (This road may not be suitable for large RVs or vehicles towing trailers; check locally for current road conditions.) Pick up Idaho Highway 28 at Tendoy, Idaho, and continue north to Salmon. Follow U.S. Highway 93 over **Lost Trail Pass** and down to **Ross' Hole** and the Bitterroot Valley. Stop in Lolo, site of **Travelers' Rest State Park.** Overnight in Missoula.

■ *Approximate driving time/distance:* Five hours, 200 miles.

■ *In-depth alternatives:* Stay a few days at a guest ranch near Lemhi Pass, or spend some time rafting the Salmon River—the river Lewis and Clark could not conquer.

Day 10: Missoula, Montana, to Lewiston, Idaho

Retrace U.S. Highway 93 south to Lolo and take U.S. 12 west to Lewiston, Idaho, allowing plenty of time for the 108-mile stretch between Lolo Pass and Kamiah, Idaho. Possible stops include the **Lolo Pass Visitor Center,** Powell Ranger Station (the site of **"Colt Killed Creek"**) and—if your vehicle has high clearance—part of the rugged **Lolo Motorway,** which traces the Lewis and Clark route more closely than U.S. 12 does. (See precautions and directions in Chapter 7 and inquire locally for road conditions and permit requirements; permits to the Lolo Motorway will be necessary during the bicentennial.) If time permits, also visit the Nez Perce National Historic Park sites at Kamiah, Weippe, Orofino, and Spalding. Overnight in Lewiston and see the Lewis and Clark exhibits at **Hells Gate State Park.**

■ *Approximate driving time/distance:* Five hours, 225 miles (allow more time for exploration of the Lolo Motorway).

■ *In-depth alternatives:* Take a horse-packing or mountain-biking trip over the Lolo Trail, or book a canoe voyage on the Clearwater River.

Day 11: Lewiston, Idaho, to The Dalles, Oregon

Drive west of Lewiston/Clarkston on U.S. Highway 12, stopping briefly at the **Lewis and Clark Timeline** in Clarkston and **Lewis and Clark Trail State Park** near Dayton. Pick up Washington Highway 124 at Waitsburg, and continue west to **Sacajawea State Park** near Pasco. Reconnect with U.S. Highway 12 and follow it to U.S. 730 across the Oregon border. Visit **Hat Rock,** named by Captain Clark. From Umatilla, Oregon, take either WA 14 or Interstate 84 (via I–82) west to The Dalles, Oregon, gateway to the Columbia Gorge. Overnight in The Dalles.

■ *Approximate driving time/distance:* five and a half hours, 270 miles.

Day 12: The Dalles, Oregon, to the Pacific Ocean

Cross the Columbia River and continue west on Washington Highway 14. Stop at **Beacon Rock,** named by the expedition. Hike to the top or drive to the state park lookout/picnic area. Other activities might include a visit to Bonneville Dam or a cruise on the stern-wheeler *Columbia Gorge* at Cascade Locks. From the Portland–Vancouver area, proceed west to the ocean via one of the routes described in Chapter 8 (U.S. Highway 26 from Portland is fastest). Overnight on the coast.

■ *Approximate driving time/distance:* three and a half hours, 180 miles (using U.S. 26 to coast).

■ *In-depth alternative:* Go kayaking on the Lower Columbia near Skamokawa, Washington, or book a small-ship cruise on the Columbia.

Day 13: On the Pacific Coast, Oregon–Washington

Visit **Fort Canby State Park** and its Lewis and Clark Interpretive Center on Washington's Cape Disappointment. Return to Oregon and visit **Fort Clatsop National Memorial,** the **Saltworks,** and **Ecola State Park.**

■ *Approximate driving time/distance:* about 35 miles; sites all located on the Pacific Coast.

■ *In-depth alternative:* Hike over Tillamook Head, either as a day trip or as an overnight backpacking expedition.

The main thirteen-day itinerary is tailored to fit into a two-week vacation, which, including weekends, typically encompasses sixteen days. But most people will need to factor in several travel days at each end of the trip to drive from home to St. Louis and from Astoria back home. Add a few more days to your vacation, if possible, or see a part of the trail this time, saving the remainder for another year. Another option might be flying to St. Louis, renting a vehicle, driving the trail to Oregon, and flying home from there.

WHEN TO GO

Much of the Lewis and Clark Trail lies in the High Plains and mountains of the West, where weather is typically unpredictable and sometimes extreme. The best period for travel is mid-July through mid-September. Fortunately, the trail has plenty of indoor interpretive centers and attractions to help travelers pass the time should inclement weather strike.

Modern explorers may want to plan their trip to coincide with one of the annual Lewis and Clark festivals held along the trail. From 2003 through 2006, a series of national Signature Events planned and organized by the National Council of the Lewis & Clark Bicentennial will commemorate the expedition's journey. Details on the Signature Events and other major Lewis and Clark festivals can be found at the back of the book.

TOURING WITH A GROUP — OR ON YOUR OWN?

When the first edition of this book first came out in 1994, very few package tour operators had Lewis and Clark offerings. That has changed; many top tour companies now lead travelers to trail highlights, and more are joining the field every year. Guided tours are the priciest way to travel the Lewis and Clark route, but most everything—from meals to lodgings to interpretation—is included. Here's a sampling:

American West Steamboat Company runs seven-night cruises year-round aboard the 163-passenger *Queen of the West* and the *Columbia Queen,* authentic paddle-wheel boats plying the Columbia, Snake, and Willamette Rivers. Trips feature shore excursions and nightly showroom-style entertainment. American West Steamboat Company, 1200 Northwest Naito Parkway, Suite 500, Portland, OR 97209; (800) 434–1232; www.queenofthewest.com.

Cruise West offers small-ship cruises on the Columbia and Snake Rivers. The eight-day, seven-night trips are scheduled each spring and fall on vessels carrying eighty-four to ninety-six passengers. Of note to shutterbugs: Some trips include the presence of a Kodak photography expert to offer tips on getting great photos. Cruise West, 2401 Fourth Avenue, Suite 700, Seattle, WA 98121-1438; (800) 580–0072; www.cruisewest.com.

Elderhostel has many Lewis and Clark–themed programs in locations along the trail. Some are active, including cycling Missouri's Katy Trail or sea kayaking on the Columbia River in the Pacific Northwest. Other programs focus on certain aspects of the expedition: mapmaking, Native American encounters, or geology. Programs are for people age fifty-five and over; younger spouses or adult companions can enroll, too. Elderhostel, 11 Avenue de Lafayette, Boston, MA 02111-1746; (877) 426–8056; www.elderhostel.org.

History America Tours, in conjunction with The History Channel, has a "Lewis and Clark in the Shadows of the Rockies" tour. Typically offered in August, the tour visits major sites in Montana and Idaho, including a hike along part of the Lolo Trail. Gary Moulton, editor of the Lewis and Clark journals, has served as historian on several trips. History America Tours, P.O. Box 797687, Dallas, TX 75379; (800) 628–8542; www.historyamerica.com.

Lindblad Expeditions runs annual trips up the Columbia, Snake, and Palouse Rivers. Titled "In the Wake of Lewis and Clark," the one-week trips sail on a seventy-passenger vessel and take place in late spring and early fall. Lewis and Clark historians are on most sailings. Lindblad Expeditions Inc., 720 Fifth Avenue, New York, NY 10019; (800) 397–3348; www.expeditions.com.

Moki Treks specializes in active "journeys into Native North America." One Montana trip blends the Blackfeet perspective on the Two Medicine River fight—the expedition's only fatal encounter with Indians—and canoeing on the Upper Missouri River. The "Rocky Mountain Challenge" trek features the Lemhi Pass–Lost Trail Pass areas in Montana and Idaho, including a visit to Big Hole National Battlefield. Another tour visits key expedition and Native American sites in the Columbia Gorge and on the Pacific coast of Washington and Oregon. Moki Treks, P.O. Box 162, Moab, UT 84532; (886)352–6654; www. mokitreks.com.

Odyssey Tours offers a wide range of Lewis and Clark-themed adventures in Western Montana and Idaho. The small-group tours feature noted humanities scholar and historical actor Clay S. Jenkinson, who faithfully re-creates both Thomas Jefferson and Meriwether Lewis in trailside living history programs. Options range from luxury bus tours to multisport packages featuring hiking, mountain biking, horseback riding, and kayaking along the Lewis and Clark route. Odyssey tours, P.O. Box 1573, Lewiston, ID 83501; (208) 791–8721; www. hibek.com.

Off the Beaten Path offers a small-group journey, "Lewis and Clark's Trail Across Montana." No more than eighteen people take part in these tours, which travel in a minibus with an expert guide. Highlights include canoe trips on the Jefferson and Missouri Rivers and a trek over Lemhi Pass. Off the Beaten Path, 7 East Beall Street, Bozeman, MT 59715; (800) 445–2995; www. offbeaten-path.com.

RiverBarge Excursion Lines offers four-to-ten-day trips on several rivers traveled by Lewis and Clark, including the Ohio, Mississippi, and Missouri. The ninety-eight-stateroom barge is like a floating hotel, with frequent stops for shore excursions. A few trips each year include special interpretation of the Lewis and

Bike It or Boat It

Many freewheeling travelers believe that bicycles are the best way to experience the Lewis and Clark Trail. Adventure Cycling Association, America's largest not-for-profit recreational bicycling organization, has been busy plotting a 3,975-mile Lewis & Clark Bicycle Trail spanning the route from Illinois to Oregon—and it has maps and a new guidebook to prove it.

The guidebook, *Bicycling the Lewis & Clark Trail,* was written and researched by *Adventure Cyclist* magazine field editor Michael McCoy. It offers plenty of bike-specific advice to discovering the explorers' route. The Association also offers waterproof maps that are divided into eight sections covering both the westbound and eastbound routes taken by the corps, with details on everything from easy road rides to challenging treks in Montana's Upper Missouri Breaks National Monument. The maps include listings of bike shops, food and water sources, and cyclist-friendly accommodations. Maps cost $11 each or $76 for the entire set, with discounts for Adventure Cycling members. The guidebook is $16.95 and will be published by The Globe Pequot Press in Spring 2003. Check book and bike shops; call (800) 755–2453; or order online at www.adventurecycling.org.

There's also been an upsurge of interest in paddling the explorers' river routes. Dams and locks make this a challenging proposition, but several resources are available to ease boaters' journeys. *A Guide to Canoeing the Missouri River* by Keith Drury outlines the 2,320-mile route from Three Forks, Montana, all the way to St. Louis, with lots of valuable information on gear, routes and the river's best sections. The book is available from amazon.com or online at www.indwes.edu/tuesday/guide.html.

In the Northwest a coalition of individuals representing many agencies and groups plans to identify a 355-mile water trail from Canoe Camp near Orofino, Idaho, down the Clearwater, Snake, and Columbia Rivers to Bonneville Dam. The coalition is developing a *Northwest Discovery Water Trail Traveler's Guide and Journal* with information on campgrounds, launch ramps, cultural resources, and more, which will be available in summer 2003. To get a copy, write to U.S. Army Corps of Engineers, P.O. Box 2946, Portland, OR 97208-2946; Attn: Patti Williams.

Beyond Bonneville, the 146-mile Lower Columbia River Water Trail is taking shape, too. Visit www.columbiariverwatertrail.org to learn more about the trail and to find ordering information for maps and for the *Lewis*

(continued)

& Clark Columbia River Water Trail guidebook, with information on more than 260 sites along the Corps' final approach to the Pacific. You can also order the book by contacting author Keith Hay, 15775 Northeast Ribbon Ridge Road, Newberg, OR 97132, or by calling (503) 538–0924.

Clark Expedition. RiverBarge Excursion Lines, 201 Opelousas Avenue, New Orleans, LA 70114; (888) 282–1945; www.riverbarge.com.

Rocky Mountain Discovery Tours specializes in eight-day Rocky Mountain motorcoach tours along the expedition's routes, as well as six-to-eighteen-day "Plains to Pacific" tours covering longer stretches of the trail. Rocky Mountain Discovery Tours, PMB 520, 248A North Higgins Avenue, Missoula, MT 59802; (888) 400–0048; www.rmdt.com.

Stephen Ambrose Historical Tours feature a ten-day itinerary in Montana and Idaho that was personally planned by the *Undaunted Courage* author before his death. Highlights include a three-day canoe trip on the Wild and Scenic Upper Missouri River and a horseback ride on the Lolo Trail. Stephen Ambrose Historical Tours, 1515 South Salcedo, New Orleans, LA 70125; (888) 903–3329; www.stephenambrosetours.com.

In addition to these offerings, many companies offer small-group, adventure-oriented trips focused on river running, horseback rides, hiking, or a combination of these activities. Because adventure trips tend to center on a specific area, I list them in the chapters as we work our way west. Bear in mind that these trips are not just for hard-core adventurers; most are fully accessible to people with little or no experience in wilderness settings. They're excellent alternatives for people who would like an interpreted, outdoors-oriented trip.

·I have established a Web site, www.lewisandclarktravel.info, featuring updated trail information and news of activities and events along the route—information that might surface once this edition goes to print. In addition, I am available to help travelers pick a guided trip or plan custom itineraries for vacations along the Lewis and Clark Trail. For details, visit www.lewisandclarktravel.info, or write to Julie Fanselow, P.O. Box 1593, Twin Falls, ID 83303-1593.

HOW TO TRAVEL

There are two schools of thought on how to drive across America. Some folks like to take the major, limited-access highways and get where they are going as fast as possible. Others prefer the scenery and slower pace of secondary roads.

After tens of thousands of miles spent researching American historic trails,

I've come to the conclusion that it's best to mix secondary roads and major highways. I take secondary highways and backroads most of the time, but every once in a while—when I get tired of dodging farm machinery and watching for dogs and children by the roadside, or if I need to make a little time, having dawdled a little too long—I get on an interstate.

But remember: The joy of discovery most often comes far from the interstates and large cities, and that is what a modern–day journey along the Lewis and Clark Trail is all about. You won't see many chic boutiques, trendy restaurants, or tourist traps along this route. What you will find is land, water, wind, mountains—and people who stubbornly find ways to live where life isn't too easy.

Of the 7,500 miles traveled by Lewis and Clark, nearly 6,000 miles were spent on water. For that reason, modern explorers should attempt to include at least one (and preferably more) river trips on their own journey. Many scheduled pleasure boat rides—such as those at Bismarck, North Dakota; the Gates of the Mountains near Helena, Montana; and the sternwheeler *Columbia Gorge* at Cascade Locks, Oregon—last just a few hours and are easily worked into most travel itineraries. Others, notably excursions on Montana's Wild and Scenic Missouri River, require at least a full day and can take up to a week. However much time you can give to river exploration will be time well spent.

In many cases, two or more roads parallel the waterways followed by Lewis and Clark. When planning a trip, write in advance to the state transportation departments and request free highway maps and state visitor guides (see addresses near the end of this chapter). Use a highlighter pen and, with the help of this book and the visitor guides, map out the route that looks most interesting.

Most of the areas described in this book are easily accessible with any passenger car or truck in good working condition. In a few locations, however, it is wise to inquire locally before setting out. Roads can be closed part of the year, and some roads, notably Lemhi Pass and the Lolo Motorway, are not suitable for RVs or vehicles towing large trailers. It's also smart to outfit your vehicle with the following: dashboard compass, working odometer, full-size spare tire and jack, gasoline can, shovel, ax, and a basic emergency kit including flashers. Once on the road, pay attention to the gas gauge: It's a long way between filling stations in many parts of the West.

WHERE TO STAY, WHAT TO EAT

The Lewis and Clark Trail primarily runs through small-town and rural America. Lodging options are limited along a few stretches, so it pays to plan ahead. The trip outlined above recommends overnight stops in places where motels and campgrounds are fairly plentiful.

Because of its distance from urban America, a Lewis and Clark Trail vacation is quite affordable. Larger cities along the route typically offer a mixture of chain motels and mom-and-pop inns. Smaller towns usually have at least one locally owned motel. These can be a great bargain, often less than $45 a night for a double. Reservations are a good idea in some areas, especially the Oregon–Washington coast and Montana's larger towns. In general, however, finding a room before 6:00 P.M. or 7:00 P.M. shouldn't pose much trouble. If you plan to arrive later, call ahead to save a room.

Consider camping along at least part of the trail. Aside from being economical, camping affords a better taste of what travel was like for the Corps of Discovery—after all, Lewis and Clark and company sure didn't have their choice of motels in 1804. Camping options range from RV parks to primitive, pick-your-own sites in the national forests. You might even choose to sleep in a tepee or fire lookout.

Quite a few small towns along the Lewis and Clark route have municipal parks that offer free or very-low-cost camping to tourists passing through. Many are well posted at the entrances to town. As much as possible, I've noted the presence of these parks throughout the text of this book.

Travelers who want to slow down and spend a few days in one place may want to look into a stay at a Western-style guest ranch or bed-and-breakfast inn. Accommodations of these sorts abound along the Lewis and Clark route. Be aware, however, that many guest ranches may require a minimum stay of anywhere from two nights to a week. Rates at guest ranches can be high—up to several hundred dollars a day per person—but they usually include all meals and activities.

Travelers can save money by packing a cooler full of sandwiches, drinks, and snacks. But part of the fun of traveling is eating in restaurants at least once in a while. When the time comes, consider sampling some regional cuisine: catfish in Missouri, buffalo burgers on the Great Plains, huckleberry pie in western Montana and Idaho, and seafood in the Northwest. Keep an eye open for farmers' markets, too; most towns of at least a few thousand people have them during summer and fall, often on Saturday morning.

Each of the travel chapters ends with a list of lodging options, campgrounds, and restaurants for areas along the trail. The chapters and the listings follow Lewis and Clark's route generally from east to west (with a few variations for the homeward-bound trips). In most cases, establishments mentioned are simply representative of those available in each town; listing in this book does not imply endorsement of any kind. Hotel, motel, and bed-and-breakfast rates listed are generally for double occupancy during the summer travel season and are accurate as of 2002. The text lists direct numbers to each lodging, including toll-free numbers when available, but the following chainwide toll-free reservation numbers may come in handy: Best Western, (800) WESTERN; Budget Host,

Treading Lightly

Interest in the Corps of Discovery has risen exponentially in recent years, and while many people are content to follow the explorers' route from their armchairs, others are eager to see at least part of the route for themselves. This has put added pressure on the trail, particularly the stretches that remain much the same as the explorers found them. In some cases, sites are sacred to Native Americans, who lived in these places long before the explorers' arrival. Some portions of the trail are ecologically threatened; many simply will not survive unless visitors take care to tread gently. That's why, especially over the coming few years, it's important for trail visitors to learn about and practice low-impact recreation.

Here are a few guidelines for treading lightly along the trail:

- Pack out all garbage.
- Check locally for travel and fire restrictions
- Indian reservations welcome visitors, but it's important to respect these sovereign nations' customs and regulations. Check with the local tribal office if you plan to camp, fish, or hunt on reservation land. Request permission before taking photographs at powwows or other tribal gatherings. It's especially important to leave cultural artifacts and sites (rock cairns, tepee rings, etc.) undisturbed.
- Get permission before walking or driving on private land.
- Keep noise to a minimum and be respectful of other travelers
- In heavily used areas, concentrate activities in areas already affected by previous use. Stay on established trails; use existing campsites away from water, main trails, and other campers; use existing fire rings but only build fires if wood is abundant and if regulations allow wood fires, pack out all human waste or bury it in a hole at least 200 feet from surface water; and leave a clean campsite for others.
- In lightly used areas, disperse impact to minimize damage to any one site. Travel in a small group. When no trails are available spread out or follow routes over such durable surfaces as sand, exposed bedrock, or gravel. Move camp nightly, if possible. If a fire is necessary, build it in a fire pan. Disperse human waste away from water sources; or—if human discovery is likely—bury it in a hole. When you leave, try to disguise any signs of your camp by ruffling trampled-down grass and picking up even the smallest pieces of litter.

It's critically important that we preserve the Lewis and Clark Trail's wildest places for generations to come. To learn more about minimum-impact outdoor recreation, consult *Leave No Trace* by Will Harmon (Falcon) a quick-reference guidebook packed with practical information on this topic.

(800) BUD–HOST; Choice Hotels (Comfort/Quality/Sleep Inn/Clarion/Main Stay Suites/EconoLodge/Rodeway Inn), (877) 424–6423; Days Inn, (800) 432–9755; Hilton (Hilton/Doubletree/Embassy Suites/Hampton Inns/Homewood Suites), (800) HILTONS; Holiday Inns, (888) 632–5465; Marriott (Marriott/Courtyard/Fairfield/Residence Inn/Spring Hill Suites), (866) 211–4607; Microtel, (888) 771–7171; Motel 6, (800) 4–MOTEL6; Red Lion (800) RED–LION; Shilo Inns, (800) 222–2244; Super 8, (800) 800–8000; Travelodge, (800) 578–7878; WestCoast (800) 325–4000.

More-complete lists of hotels, motels, campgrounds, and restaurants are available from state and local tourism bureaus. State tourism offices are listed later in this chapter, and many local offices are noted throughout the book.

WHAT TO PACK

Bearing in mind that Western weather can be unpredictable and fast changing, even in midsummer, it's best to be prepared with a variety of clothing. On hot days lightweight, light-colored clothing will be most comfortable. But pack a sweater, jacket, and rain gear for when the weather turns cold or wet. Sneakers or walking shoes are best for touring historic sites, but toss in a pair of lightweight hiking boots and sport sandals. Casual clothing is appropriate everywhere along the trail. Don't forget a swimsuit, sunblock, and a wide-brimmed hat.

Campers should make sure their gear is waterproof and able to stand up to high winds. A ground cloth and extra tent stakes are good ideas. Other camp essentials include a simple tool kit with a hammer, ax, and pocketknife; a reliable camp stove and fuel (wood campfires are prohibited in some locations); cooking and eating utensils; a can opener; insect repellent; a bucket for hauling water and washing dishes; biodegradable dish soap; rope (for clothesline and other uses); first-aid and snakebite kits; a camp lantern and flashlight; matches; trash bags (along with separate space for recyclables); and a bag for dirty laundry.

Travelers hoping to preserve their trip in pictures should include a wide-angle lens and polarizing filter for the high, wide horizons and beautiful skies. Binoculars might come in handy, as will books and travel games. And don't forget a good atlas or state highway maps—the maps in this book are general and should always be used in conjunction with a more-detailed local highway map.

TRAVELING WITH KIDS

To children, all of life is an adventure, with new discoveries made every day. Seen from this perspective, a trip along the Lewis and Clark Trail makes an ideal family vacation. It's interesting, educational, and informal and can easily be combined with a more traditional Western vacation, say, to Yellowstone National Park or the Oregon coast. Moreover, it is an economical vacation choice, since most historic sites are free or inexpensive, and since nearly all of Lewis and Clark's route lies far from expensive big cities and traditional tourist attractions.

Still, it's always a challenge to keep kids happy and occupied. Here are a few ideas on how to do it:

Have them keep a journal like Lewis and Clark did, describing their trip in words and pictures. (Journaling is a great way to develop writing skills, and this is a grand time to start.) Although long-winded recitations from the captains' journals may prove ponderous to young ears, look for short passages to read at picnic stops or around the campfire. Or buy a children's-book version of the Lewis and Clark story, and let your kids read along as they go.

Plan a Lewis and Clark scavenger hunt, making a list of items the kids can look for along the way. Such "treasures" might include a keelboat, dugout canoe, Native American earth lodge, river, animals, and statues of Lewis, Clark, Sacagawea, York, and Lewis's dog, Seaman. You might want to provide an inexpensive or disposable camera so your child can take photos as the discoveries are made. President Jefferson asked Lewis and Clark to describe and, where possible, get samples of the flora and fauna they encountered along their way. Your children can do the same thing on a smaller scale. Young naturalists might enjoy a small bug-catching box, sketch pad, or leaf and wildflower press. (**Note:** Picking flowers and other plants is against the law in national parks and in some state parks.)

If you're camping, consider packing a separate tent for the children (if they're old enough). Most kids love having a tent of their own, and it will give the grown-ups some rest and privacy. Kids also enjoy having a bit of their own money to spend on vacation. Help them learn financial responsibility and decision-making by giving each child a special trip allowance. Make sure they know this money should cover any souvenirs or extras they want to buy—and that it should last the whole trip.

WHAT TO READ, WATCH, AND HEAR

Many travelers will want to learn more about Lewis and Clark before, during, or after tracing the captains' route. For sure, you'll want a copy of the Lewis and Clark journals to read as you cross the continent. The University of Nebraska Press recently released *The Lewis and Clark Journals: An American Epic of Discovery,* a 544-page abridgment of Gary E. Moulton's definitive, thirteen-volume edition of the journals. It is easily the best one-volume version of the journals you'll find, but the hardbound book may be a bit hefty to toss in your backpack. For a less expensive, less weighty edition, try the mass-market paperback edition edited by John Bakeless or the classic one-volume reference edited by Bernard DeVoto—though bear in mind that Moulton's work corrected some mistakes made in the earlier editions on which DeVoto, Bakeless, and others relied.

Aside from the journals themselves, my all-time-favorite book about Lewis and Clark is Dayton Duncan's *Out West: A Journey Through Lewis & Clark's America.* Originally written in the 1980s after Duncan traced the explorers' route in a camper van, it's the book that first made me want to travel the trail and is still a gem. Other good reads include *The Way to the Western Sea* by David Lavender; *Undaunted Courage: Meriwether Lewis, Thomas Jefferson, and the Opening of the American West* by Stephen Ambrose; *Lewis & Clark: Historic Places Associated with Their Transcontinental Exploration* by Roy E. Appleman; *The Character of Meriwether Lewis* by Clay Straus Jenkinson; *Backtracking: By Foot, Canoe, and Subaru Along the Lewis & Clark Trail* by Benjamin Long; and *Voyages of Discovery: Essays on the Lewis & Clark Expedition,* edited by James Ronda.

Travelers seeking a comprehensive visual introduction to the expedition will want to pick up a copy of Ken Burns's fine PBS documentary *Lewis & Clark— The Journey of the Corps of Discovery.* For shorter, more kid-friendly fare, check out National Geographic's film *Lewis & Clark—Great Journey West.* Shot as a large-format film, it will be showing at many IMAX theaters along the trail throughout the bicentennial, but it's also available on video and DVD.

CarTours is working with the National Park Service to prepare a ten-volume series of driving tours to the Lewis and Clark Trail. The tapes blend interviews with historians, park rangers, Native American elders, and others, along with period music, sight-seeing tips, and a map in every package. They're coming out one by one, with plans for all ten to be released by spring 2004 on both audiotape and enhanced CD. To order or get updates on the project's progress, visit www.cartours.org.

There are many other resources. In fact, don't be surprised if you wind up wanting to read, watch, and listen to everything you can about the expedition. "Once you get interested, you become a buff, and there's constant controversy about why they did this, how they did this, what that looked like, what they were wearing" says Butch Bouvier, a Lewis and Clark aficionado from western Iowa. "It's constant. It's exciting."

TENDING THE TRAIL

Since it is a federally designated National Historic Trail, the 3,700-mile Lewis and Clark route is administered by the National Park Service in cooperation with other federal, state, and local agencies; the Lewis and Clark Trail Heritage Foundation and other private organizations; and private landowners along the route. Together, they work to identify, preserve, and interpret sites important to the expedition. The Park Service publishes and distributes a general information brochure and map of the trail. It's widely available along the route, or you can request a copy by writing to Lewis and Clark National Historic Trail, 1709 Jackson Street, Omaha, NE 68102; calling (888) 237–3252; or sending an e-mail to Midori_Raymore@nps.gov. Thirty-two agencies involved in preserving and promoting the trail have established a Web site (www.lewisandclark200.gov) that traces the expedition's path, with links to most major sites, including those in the eastern United States.

People interested in learning more about the Corps of Discovery and trail preservation may want to join the Lewis and Clark Trail Heritage Foundation. This not-for-profit organization holds an annual convention with seminars, field trips, and social activities each August. The foundation publishes *We Proceeded On,* a scholarly yet entertaining quarterly journal dedicated to the Lewis and Clark Expedition and related topics. Many members also take part in local and state chapter activities. For information, write the Lewis and Clark Trail Heritage Foundation, P.O. Box 3434, Great Falls, MT 59403; or access the group's Web site at www.lewisandclark.org.

The National Council of the Lewis & Clark Bicentennial is the main organization coordinating the 200th anniversary commemoration of the Corps of Discovery. For more information on the national effort, visit www.lewisandclark 200.org.

American Rivers is the nation's foremost river conservation organization. One of its main initiatives is the "Voyage to Recovery" effort aimed at revitalizing the Missouri River before the Lewis and Clark Bicentennial. For more information on American Rivers and its work, call (202) 347–7550; write American Rivers, 1025 Vermont Avenue NW, Suite 720, Washington, D.C. 20005; or visit www.americanrivers.org.

The Sierra Club also has undertaken an ambitious effort to mark the expedition's bicentennial by conserving and restoring some of the wildest areas along and near the route—fifty-six million acres in all. Many local Sierra Club chapters are holding day hikes, backpacking trips, and other events along the trail in their respective states. For more information, visit www.sierraclub.org/lewisand clark/.

STATE TOURISM OFFICES

Illinois Bureau of Tourism
State of Illinois Center
100 West Randolph Street
Chicago, IL 60601
(800) 223–0121
www.enjoyillinois.com

Missouri Division of Tourism
Truman Office Building
P.O. Box 1055
Jefferson City, MO 65102
(800) 877–1234
www.missouritourism.com

Kansas Travel & Tourism Division
700 Southwest Harrison, Suite 1300
Topeka, KS 66603
(800) 252–6727
www.travelks.com

Iowa Division of Tourism
200 East Grand Avenue
Des Moines, IA 50309
(800) 345–4692
www.traveliowa.com

Nebraska Tourism Office
P.O. Box 98907
Lincoln, NE 68509-8907
(877) NEBRASKA
www.visitnebraska.com

**South Dakota Department of
    Tourism**
711 East Wells Avenue
Pierre, SD 57501
(800) 732–5682
www.travelsd.com

North Dakota Tourism
604 East Boulevard
Bismarck, ND 58505
(800) 435–5663
www.ndtourism.com

Travel Montana
1424 Ninth Avenue
P.O. Box 200533
Helena, MT 59620-0533
(800) 847–4868
www.visitmt.com

Idaho Travel Council
700 West State St., Second Floor
Boise, ID 83720
(800) 847–4843
www.visitid.org

Washington State Tourism Division
P.O. Box 42500
Olympia, WA 98504
(800) 544–1800
www.tourism.wa.gov

Oregon Tourism Division
775 Summer Street Northeast
Salem, OR 97310
(800) 547–7842
www.traveloregon.com

A Note on Spelling

Modern readers always wonder how Lewis and Clark, who were certainly among the smartest people of their day, could be such terrible spellers. Their journals contained, for example, twenty-seven different spellings of Sioux and twenty-four different versions of Charbonneau, the French interpreter who joined the party during its 1804–1805 winter stay in North Dakota. And proper names weren't the only object of such mangling; Lewis, Clark, and their men had a way of garbling even simple words.

The reality was that in the early nineteenth century, even the most learned Americans used wildly irregular spellings. Noah Webster, who published his pioneering dictionaries in the late 1700s and early 1800s, advocated such variants as "wimmen," "groop," and "bilt." Many historians insist on preserving the captains' misspellings in journal quotes. I appreciate the argument behind such preservation, but for the sake of readability, I have rendered all journal quotes into modern, standard English. In the case of the Native American woman who accompanied the expedition, I use the spelling "Sacagawea," generally considered to be most accurate, unless a different spelling is used in a proper name (as in North Dakota's Lake Sakakawea or Washington's Sacajawea State Park).

Is This Book Out of Date?

All across the United States, communities and organizations are finalizing plans for the 200th anniversary of the Lewis and Clark Expedition during its bicentennial of 2003–2006. New attractions and activities celebrating the Lewis and Clark legacy are planned nearly everywhere along the route. Many will be in place by the time you read this book; I've offered as many details as I could find on these. Other things may change, too. Restaurants and motels may open, close, or take new names, and visitor attractions may alter operating schedules.

If you find an error, omission, or change, please write to me, Julie Fanselow, in care of P.O. Box 1593, Twin Falls, ID 83303. I will use your input in future editions of *Traveling the Lewis & Clark Trail.*

Thanks, and happy travels!

The Corps of Discovery: A Brief History and Overview

From his youth, Thomas Jefferson was fascinated with the West. Not so much the West as he understood it, for even as president he never traveled far from his Virginia home, but the West as he imagined it: a land of mystery and revelation, a land where the United States could stretch its boundaries and grow into a preeminent world power.

In his inaugural address of 1801, Jefferson described America as "kindly separated by nature and a wide ocean from the exterminating havoc of one-quarter of the globe, possessing a chosen country with room enough for our descendants to the thousandth and thousandth generation." With these blessings, he asked, "what more is necessary to make us a happy and prosperous people?" Jefferson expected it would take the passing of a full forty generations just to explore the whole of the United States. Remarkably, it took only four years to chart a large measure of the continent.

For years Europeans and Americans believed that by following the Missouri River to its headwaters, they would discover a Northwest Passage to the Pacific Ocean. French, British, and Spanish explorers had long tried to prove this theory, and when the United States was born in 1776, the contest for domination of the Western frontier became a four-way race.

The power struggle continued for another quarter century, with the young American nation siding first with one European power, then another. Ultimately, France's desire to limit English influence in North America made possible the United States' acquisition of the Northwest via the Louisiana Purchase. For $15 million—less than four cents an acre—the United States bought more than 800,000 square miles of land.

The Louisiana Purchase had an incalculable effect on the future of the United States. With its boundaries set by the Missouri and Mississippi River drainages, the deal doubled the country's area, giving the young nation access to a wealth of valuable natural resources. Assessing the agreement's impact, noted historian Bernard DeVoto wrote: "There is no aspect of national life, no part of our social and political structure, and no subsequent event in the course of our history that it has not affected." And what a bargain it proved to be: Even by the time the interest was paid, the Louisiana Purchase cost America a total of just $23 million.

The Louisiana Purchase is often viewed as the event that precipitated the Lewis and Clark Expedition, but plans for the trek were already well under way by the time the deal was signed. In fact, Jefferson had long wished for an expedition, particularly after he read Scotsman Alexander Mackenzie's account, published in 1801, of his 1793 explorations across the Continental Divide and to salt water at the mouth of British Columbia's Bella Coola River. Mackenzie's efforts—and those of Simon Fraser, who in 1808 explored the river now bearing his name—strengthened British claims to the Northwest, but it was an American, Robert Gray, who in 1792 had sailed into the mouth of the Columbia River from the west. Jefferson knew there had to be a way to reach the Columbia overland from the Missouri. With Lewis he began laying groundwork for the mission in fall 1802.

At that time he asked the Spanish minister, the Marques de Casa Yrujo, whether Spain would object if the United States sent a small party to explore the Missouri River to seek the Northwest Passage. (Spain was to transfer the land in question to France under an 1800 treaty, but the move hadn't yet taken place.) The Spaniard wrote back that he saw no need for the exploration, since the European powers had already sought and disproved the notion of a Northwest Passage. He also warned Jefferson that Spanish authorities would be notified if he proceeded with the idea.

Undaunted, Jefferson sent a secret message to Congress in January 1803. He asked for an appropriation of $2,500 for an expedition to seek the source of the Missouri River and, upon finding it, follow the best course westward to the Pacific Ocean, "for the purpose of extending the external commerce of the United States."

Jefferson had hired Meriwether Lewis as his private secretary, at least in part with an eye to the possible expedition. As DeVoto wrote in his edition of the Lewis and Clark journals, "Lewis was a family friend, but Jefferson had many friends better qualified by background and education to be secretary to the President. He was, however, uniquely qualified for a project which Jefferson had cherished for many years, the exploration of the Missouri River and the lands west of its source." In his letter offering employment to Lewis, Jefferson wrote, "Your knowledge of the Western country, of the army and all its interests and relations have rendered it desirable for public as well as private purposes that you should be engaged in that office."

Lewis was born August 18, 1774, just a few miles from Jefferson's home in Virginia, the second of three children of plantation owners William and Lucy Meriwether Lewis. His father died when Meriwether was just five years old. Lucy soon married again, and the family moved to Georgia. Early on, Lewis showed great intellect but also much moodiness.

By age 13 Lewis was sent back to Virginia to continue his education and learn how to run the plantation, which was still in his family. After his stepfather, John Marks, died in the early 1790s, young Lewis traveled to Georgia to bring the rest of his family back to Virginia. Soon after, he joined the Army. He had served six years and risen to the rank of captain by the time Jefferson sought his help in Washington, D.C. Lewis, just twenty-six years old when he received the job offer of secretary in March 1801, readily agreed. A year and a half later, he was working at Jefferson's behest to draw up plans for the Western expedition.

Originally Lewis was to select a second-in-command from the party's ranks after the expedition had gotten under way. But as preparations progressed, Jefferson and Lewis—aware of the trip's significance—decided it might be best to select Lewis's right-hand man before the journey started. The man they chose was William Clark, under whose command Lewis had served several years earlier.

Clark was born August 1, 1770, in Virginia, the younger brother of George Rogers Clark (who became a hero in the Revolutionary War). William followed in his family's military footsteps and by 1795 was put in command of an elite company of riflemen at Fort Greenville, Ohio. It was there he met Meriwether Lewis, and the men quickly became friends. Clark soon left the Army to take care of his older brother, who was battling alcoholism and debt in Indiana. But he and Lewis stayed in touch by mail and visits.

On June 19, 1803, Lewis wrote to Clark, told him of the mission, and said, "If therefore there is anything … in this enterprise, which would induce you to participate with me in its fatigues, its dangers, and its honors, believe me there is no man on earth with whom I should feel equal pleasure in sharing them with as yourself." He further noted that Jefferson would promise Clark—who had resigned as a lieutenant—a full captain's commission and all the attendant benefits. "Your situation will in all respects be precisely such as my own," Lewis concluded.

When weeks went by with no word from Clark, Jefferson and Lewis prepared to ask Lt. Moses Hooke, their second choice, if he would accept the role. But Clark's reply finally came on July 29. "My friend I do assure you no man lives with whom I would prefer to undertake such a trip as yourself," Clark wrote to Lewis, thus ending any thoughts of what history might have come to call the "Lewis and Hooke Expedition."

The coleaders set about choosing the men to accompany them. In Lewis's

Bronze relief depicting signing of the Louisiana Purchase, Missouri State Capitol grounds, Jefferson City.

words, they looked for "good hunters, stout, healthy, unmarried, accustomed to the woods and capable of bearing bodily fatigue in a pretty considerable degree." Some members of the expedition were recruited for special skills they possessed: Lewis wanted Patrick Gass along as a carpenter and boatbuilder, for example. Gass had grown into manhood with the young nation, ever moving west with the frontier, and he turned out to be one of the most interesting members of the expedition.

George Drouillard was selected as an interpreter and hunter, and the importance of his latter task can't be underestimated: It took four deer and an elk or one deer and a buffalo to feed the entire group for twenty-four hours. John Shields, a relative of Daniel Boone, hired on as gunsmith, and Clark later wrote: "The party owes much to the ingenuity of this man by whom their guns are repaired when they get out of order, which is very often."

One recruit had no say in the matter. Ben York, a Clark family slave, had been William Clark's constant companion since early childhood, and there was no question that he would accompany Clark on the trip west. York became the first black man to join a military expedition, cross the Continental Divide, and reach the Pacific Ocean. He was a large, strong, and good-natured man. The Indians considered York "great medicine" and would travel long distances to see and touch him.

The recruits sensed they were embarking on a journey of great importance. On April 8, 1804, John Ordway wrote, "Honored parents: I am now on an expedition to the westward with Captain Lewis and Captain Clark to the western ocean. This party consists of 25 picked men, and I am so happy as to be one of them." Even Seaman, Lewis's Newfoundland dog, proved a valuable member of the expedition. He retrieved game and, with his barking, alerted the party to the presence of grizzly bears and buffalo.

Many of us spend hours agonizing over what belongings to take on a two-week vacation, so it is hard to imagine what it might be like trying to pack for a trip of undetermined length. The food alone weighed seven tons. Other items selected included a blacksmith's forge, a mill for grinding corn, carpenters' tools and axes, surveying and navigational instruments, medical supplies, cooking utensils, an iron boat frame, fifty-two lead canisters weighing 420 pounds for sealing 175 pounds of gunpowder, six kegs—or thirty gallons—of brandy, and canvas for tarpaulins.

Congress's $2,500 appropriation purchased the following: mathematical instruments, $217; provisions, $224; materials for portable packs, $55; pay for hunters, guides, and interpreters, $300; pay for members' moving expenses, $100; weapons, $81; camp equipment, $255; medical supplies, $55; boats, $430; and $87 for contingencies. The largest single budget item, $696, paid for presents for Native Americans. That amount purchased 47.5 yards of red flannel, 12 dozen pocket mirrors, 73 bunches of beads, 2,800 fishhooks, and 4,600 needles.

Even back then, the federal government occasionally had a tough time living within its means. Although only $2,500 was originally allocated, the corps carried a letter of credit from Jefferson, and actual expenditures wound up totaling about $38,000. Still, few people would dispute that the investment was worth it. Aside from strengthening American claims to the West, the expedition had an immeasurable impact on scientific, anthropological, and geographic knowledge.

The Corps of Discovery—a nickname given to the expedition by Jefferson—finally left Camp River Dubois, in what is now Illinois, on May 14, 1804. The men returned on September 23, 1806, two years, four months, and ten days after they had departed. In the interim, they lived one of the greatest examples of exploration and cooperation the United States—or the world, for that matter—has ever seen ... a trip we shall examine in much greater detail as we follow the corps' progress west.

2

The Eastern Legacy

The object of your mission is to explore the Missouri River and such principal stream of it, as by its course and communication with the water of the Pacific Ocean, may offer the most direct and practicable water communication across this continent for the purposes of commerce. —THOMAS JEFFERSON, JUNE 3, 1803, INSTRUCTIONS TO MERIWETHER LEWIS

MONTICELLO

Lewis and Clark aficionados like to debate where the expedition began. Many say it started when Meriwether Lewis arrived at the Falls of the Ohio at present-day Louisville, Kentucky, in mid-October 1803 to renew his partnership with William Clark. Others feel it got under way when the expedition left Camp River Dubois near the confluence of the Mississippi and Missouri Rivers on May 14, 1804.

Still others believe that it truly launched from Monticello, President Thomas Jefferson's mountaintop home near Charlottesville, Virginia. It was at Monticello, after all, that Jefferson and his young secretary Lewis began earnestly preparing for the expedition in 1802 and 1803. Here Lewis prepared preliminary cost estimates for the trip, studied botany in Jefferson's gardens, and spent hours poring over maps and books in the president's private library. Later it was at Monticello that Jefferson proudly displayed items sent back to him by Lewis and

Clark on the expedition: specimens of plants and animals previously unknown to science and Native American artifacts documenting the continent's mix of indigenous cultures and traditions.

Monticello itself is a richly historic place—the only house in the United States on the United Nations' World Heritage List of natural and cultural sites of outstanding universal value.

Jefferson called the house his "essay in architecture," designing, building, and tinkering with it for decades. The Monticello plantation of 5,000 acres had four farms and was home to about 150 people, including as many as 130 enslaved African-Americans.

In January 2003, Monticello served as the site for the inaugural signature event of the Lewis and Clark Bicentennial. Throughout 2003 the site is featuring "Framing the West at Monticello: Thomas Jefferson and the Lewis and Clark Expedition," an exhibition re-creating the home's Entrance Hall as it looked circa 1807–1809, when Jefferson showcased artifacts from Lewis and Clark's travels. Some of them are original items (including a set of elk antlers); others are historically inspired re-creations made by modern-day Native American artists from North Dakota. These latter items will remain on view at Monticello after 2003.

The Monticello Visitor Center on Virginia Highway 20 near Interstate 64 in southeast Charlottesville is a good place to begin a visit. It's open from 9:00 A.M. to 5:30 P.M. daily March through October and 9:00 A.M. to 5:00 P.M. daily the rest of the year, except Christmas Day. The permanent exhibition, "Thomas Jefferson at Monticello," explores Jefferson's life at Monticello. There's also a film, *Thomas Jefferson: The Pursuit of Liberty,* shown at 11:00 A.M. and 2:00 P.M. daily (hourly in summer). Admission to the visitor center and film is free.

Admission to the Monticello grounds costs $13.00 for adults and $6.00 for children ages six to twelve. Guided half-hour tours of Jefferson's house run continuously from 8:00 A.M. to 5:00 P.M. March through October and 9:00 A.M. to 4:30 P.M. the rest of the year, except Christmas. If the wait to tour the house is longer than forty-five minutes, visitors receive cards that release them from standing in line until a designated time, often more than an hour later. There are plenty of things to do at Monticello if you have to wait for a house tour: See Jefferson's grave, tour the gardens and grounds, or even have a picnic. (Food and tables are available at the Little Mountain Luncheonette near the ticket office.) Families with kids may want to plan their visit between June 15 and August 15, when family-focused tours are held on the hour between 10:00 A.M. and 3:00 P.M.

For more information call (434) 984–9822 or visit www.monticello.org. Monticello's Web site is an excellent source of background on the expedition—from essays on earlier efforts to explore the West to Jefferson's letter of instructions and Lewis's packing list.

Charlottesville may someday also be home to a Lewis and Clark Exploratory Center, a site intended to explain Virginia's contributions to the expedition. (As we've noted, both Lewis and Clark were sons of the state.) Meanwhile, the site's planners have been holding annual festivals in May. For project updates, visit www.lewisandclarkeast.org. For more information on visiting Charlottesville, call (877) 386–1102 or check out www.charlottesvilletourism.org.

WASHINGTON, D.C.

As secretary to Thomas Jefferson, Meriwether Lewis actually lived, worked, and dined with the president at his two homes—Monticello and what was then known as the President's House. Today we call it the White House, standing at 1600 Pennsylvania Avenue in Washington, D.C.

Construction at the White House started in 1792, on a site selected by President George Washington and city planner Pierre L'Enfant. Its architect was James Hoban, who topped eight others in a competition to determine its design. It took almost a decade to complete the house, and president John Adams and his wife, Abigail, were its first residents. The mansion became known as the White House after it was repainted following an 1814 fire set by the British during the War of 1812.

Lewis lived in the cavernous quarters known as the East Room. Today the room is marked by a full-length portrait of George Washington, the only known object that's been continuously in the White House since 1800. President George W. Bush used the East Room as a backdrop when he formally declared 2003–2006 the Lewis and Clark Bicentennial on July 3, 2002. Lewis and Jefferson likely ate together—and frequently entertained guests—in the Green Room, adjacent to the East Room.

Public tours of the White House were canceled after the terrorist attacks of September 11, 2001, and haven't been resumed at this book's press time. Tours are still available to organized school, military, and veterans' groups. Call (202) 456–7041 or visit www.whitehouse.gov to check current policies. It is still possible to tour the White House Visitor Center, a National Park Service site located in the north end of the Department of Commerce Building between Fourteenth and Fifteenth Streets on Pennsylvania Avenue Northwest, where you'll see six permanent exhibits related to the White House and its history. Other Washington sites of interest to Lewis and Clark buffs include:

■ **The Library of Congress.** The world's largest library was begun in 1800 when President John Adams authorized the purchase of "such books as may be necessary for the use of Congress." But Thomas Jefferson is its real father. He

Eastern Legacy Region

regularly recommended books for its collections during his two terms as president; and when the library's collections were lost to fires set by the British in 1814, Jefferson offered to sell his personal collection of nearly 7,000 volumes (twice the number that had burned) to rebuild the library's holdings. Today the library has more than 120 million items on about 530 miles of shelves in three buildings on Capitol Hill. Guided tours are offered Monday through Saturday; the library is closed Sunday and federal holidays. Visit www.loc.gov for information on the many exhibits, concerts, lectures, and other events at the library. The Web site also has an online collection of Jefferson's papers, including many documents related to the Lewis and Clark Expedition.

■ **The National Museum of American History.** This arm of the Smithsonian normally displays several items from the Lewis and Clark Expedition, including William Clark's pocket compass—but that will be on loan through the bicentennial years to the Missouri Historical Society for its national exhibition. (See Touring St. Louis in Chapter 4.) Still, there's plenty to see here, including a stunning bison hide in the Hands On History room painted by contemporary Native American artist Dennis R. Fox Jr., who also created a similar hide for Monticello's "Framing the West" exhibit. The museum, open daily except Christmas, with free admission, is located on the National Mall, Fourteenth Street and Constitution Avenue, NW. Call (202) 357–2700 or visit www.americanhistory.si.edu for more information.

■ **The United States Capitol.** The Capitol is at the east end of the National Mall, and guided tours are available Monday through Saturday. Visitors must obtain free tickets for tours on a first-come, first-served basis at the Capitol Guide Service kiosk located along the curving sidewalk southwest of the Capitol (near the intersection of First Street, SW, and Independence Avenue). Ticket distribution begins at 8:15 A.M. daily. The Architect of the Capitol office handles tours; for information call (202) 225–6827 or visit www.aoc.gov.

■ **Thomas Jefferson Memorial.** This lovely tribute to the third president includes Rudolph Evans's 19-foot statue and a museum of Jefferson's life, located in the basement. The monument is open from 8:00 A.M. to midnight daily, except on Christmas. Visit www.nps.gov/nama for more information on all the monuments on the National Mall.

No matter where you go in Washington, D.C., it's best to take public transportation. Parking is hard to find, and the region's excellent Metro system has stops near all the major attractions. For help in planning a visit to Washington, call (202) 789–7000 or check out www.washington.org.

HARPERS FERRY

In February 1803 Congress approved Jefferson's request to fund an expedition. By mid-March, Lewis was on his way from Washington, D.C., to the U.S. Armory and Arsenal at Harpers Ferry, in present-day West Virginia, to gather military hardware for the trip. Lewis brought with him a letter from Secretary of War Henry Dearborn for Joseph Perkins, the armory superintendent, which read: "You will be pleased to make such arms and ironwork as requested by the Bearer Captain Meriwether Lewis and to have them completed with the least possibly delay." Lewis ordered fifteen rifles, fifteen powder horns, thirty bullet molds, thirty ball screws, extra rifle and musket locks, gunsmith's repair tools, several dozen tomahawks, and two dozen large knives.

Lewis also wanted the arsenal workers to do him a special favor. He asked them to build a collapsible iron-framed boat he designed himself. Lewis referred to this as "my darling project," but the armory workers had difficulty executing Lewis's design for the boat, and the endeavor wound up keeping Lewis in Harpers Ferry for more than a month. When it was finished, however, Lewis was pleased. The frame weighed just 100 pounds but the completed craft would be capable of carrying about 1,700 pounds.

Harpers Ferry National Historical Park recently dedicated a Meriwether Lewis exhibit detailing the armory's role in the expedition. The exhibit features hands-on discovery stations on such themes as "The Object of Your Mission," "Preparing for the Unexpected," "Supplied for Survival," and "Why Harpers Ferry?" Other park features interpret Harpers Ferry's role in the abolitionist movement (antislavery leader John Brown conducted his famous 1859 raid at the armory here) and the Civil War. Harpers Ferry is located along U.S. Highway 340 at the confluence of the Potomac and Shenandoah Rivers, approximately 65 miles west of Washington, D.C. For more information, call (304) 535–6298 or visit www.nps.gov/hafe.

Jefferson visited Harpers Ferry in 1783 and later wrote in *Notes on the State of Virginia:* "The passage of the Potomac through the Blue Ridge is perhaps one of the most stupendous scenes in Nature." Indeed, the area is known for great outdoor activities. The Appalachian Trail and C&O Canal towpath run through Harpers Ferry, and white-water rafting and horseback trips are available. For more information on the Harpers Ferry area, contact the Jefferson County (West Virginia) Convention & Visitors Bureau at (800) 848–TOUR or visit www.jeffersoncountycvb.com.

Lewis left Harpers Ferry for Pennsylvania on April 18, 1803, but returned in July to pick up his supply order. On July 8 he wrote Jefferson that he'd test-fired the guns and examined the other "articles which had been manufactured for me at this place; they appear to be well executed."

PREPARATIONS IN PENNSYLVANIA

Pennsylvania's nickname is "the Keystone State," originally intended to signify the commonwealth's status at the geographical center of the thirteen original states that formed the union. But Pennsylvania also proved a keystone in preparations for the Lewis and Clark Expedition.

Jefferson had arranged for Lewis to call on many of Jefferson's friends in the scientific community to help him learn skills he'd need while commanding the expedition, and most of them lived in the greater Philadelphia area. On April 19, 1803, Lewis arrived in Lancaster, Pennsylvania, to meet with Andrew Ellicott, who would instruct him in wilderness surveying and celestial observation. Ellicott was noted as a designer and builder of scientific instruments, and—although he is not as well known as Pierre L'Enfant for his role in laying out Washington, D.C.—he was actually the one who completed the job. The home where Lewis and Ellicott met still stands at 123 North Prince Street in Lancaster. There's little interpretation of Lewis's visit, but a historic marker in front of the house mentions the encounter. Tours of the house are available from 9:00 A.M. to 3:00 P.M. Monday through Friday. Call (717) 291–5861 for more information.

From Lancaster, Lewis went to Philadelphia, where he remained May 10 through June 17, meeting with mentors (doctors and scientists) and visiting with more than two dozen merchants to buy 3,500 pounds of supplies for the expedition. Finally, he arranged for a wagon and driver to haul all this stuff to Pittsburgh, where it would be loaded onto a keelboat Lewis had ordered built for the expedition.

Philadelphia also played a prominent role in the disposition of material brought back by the Corps of Discovery. The American Philosophical Society, founded by Benjamin Franklin in 1743 and located at 105 South Fifth Street, became the repository for the journals kept by Lewis and Clark as well as by Sgt. John Ordway. The society doesn't generally have the journals on display, but several volumes will appear at major expeditions during the bicentennial. Call (215) 440–3400 for more information.

Hundreds of pressed plants collected by the expedition are at home in the Lewis & Clark Herbarium at the Academy of Natural Sciences, 1900 Ben Franklin Parkway, Philadelphia. Although they're preserved in strict, climate- and pollution-controlled cabinets, a few specimens will join the journals and other expedition artifacts for the Missouri Historical Society's national bicentennial exhibition. (Selected plants and journals also will be on exhibit during the Lewis & Clark Trail Heritage Foundation's meeting in Philadelphia in August 2003. Visit www.lewisandclark.org/aboutmeet.htm for details.) The plants are also featured on an Academy-produced CD that includes digital images of every specimen as well as of the labels Lewis put on each in the field. It can be ordered by calling the academy's scientific publications office at (215) 299–1050.

The academy itself has evolved into a twenty-first-century, hands-on science museum open daily except major winter holidays. Call (215) 299–1000 or visit www.acnatsci.com for general information. Although the academy focuses on natural history (dinosaurs, butterflies, and the like), the Franklin Institute Science Museum at 222 North Twentieth Street is packed with four floors of high-tech, interactive exhibits. Other top attractions in Philadelphia include Independence National Historic Park (home to Independence Hall and the Liberty Bell), the Philadelphia Art Museum, the Philadelphia Zoo, and Eastern State Penitentiary, a former prison that's now open for tours. For information on visiting Philadelphia, call (888) GO–PHILA or visit www.gophila.com.

From Philadelphia Lewis returned to Washington, D.C., from mid-June through July 5, 1803. While back in the capital city, he wrote to Clark to invite him to join the expedition. Lewis then paid a repeat visit to Harpers Ferry before traveling on to Pittsburgh, where he planned to pick up the keelboat he had ordered built for the voyage. The boat was supposed to be ready July 20, 1803, but when Lewis arrived a few days before that, he found it nowhere near completion. The boatbuilder hired for the task had a penchant for drink, and it was all Lewis could do to keep the man at his task.

The boat was finally finished on August 31. It measured 55 feet in length, was 8 feet wide at its center, and could carry about ten tons of cargo. Within hours of the boat's completion, Lewis set out down the Ohio River with at least eleven other men, including several expedition recruits (probably including George Shannon and John Colter, although some historians believe that the latter joined at Maysville, Kentucky), and a single pirogue, or large dugout canoe. Another member of the party probably came aboard in Pennsylvania, too: Seaman, Lewis' big black Newfoundland dog. Lewis made the first entry in his expedition journal: "Left Pittsburgh this day at 11 o'clock with a party of 11 hands 7 of which are soldiers, a pilot and three young men on trial."

The Senator John Heinz Pittsburgh Regional History Center plans a full menu of activities and exhibits in summer 2003 to commemorate Lewis's time in Pittsburgh, and some material will be on permanent display in the museum's "Points in Time" exhibit. The center, open daily except major holidays from 10:00 A.M. to 5:00 P.M., is at 1212 Smallman Street in the city's Strip District. Call (412) 454–6000 or visit www.pghistory.org for more information.

DOWN THE OHIO, TO THE FALLS

It wasn't easy going on the Ohio that summer. The river was unusually low that year, and the crew frequently had to unload the keelboat cargo to get the craft past shallows, riffles, and other obstructions in the channel. The party stopped

This replica of the 1803 cabin where William Clark stayed before the start of the expedition can be seen at Falls of the Ohio State Park in Clarksville, Indiana.

in Wheeling, in present-day West Virginia, on September 7, 1803, to get additional supplies and a second pirogue to help carry the keelboat's heavy load. In a letter to Jefferson, Lewis wrote: "I have been compelled to purchase a pirogue at this place in order to transport the baggage which was seny by land from Pittsburgh, and also to lighten the boat as much as possible." Just north of Wheeling, Wellsburg is the hometown of expedition member Patrick Gass, who built a home there after the trip and who is buried in town.

The party moved on downriver to Marietta, the oldest town in Ohio, and Cincinnati, where Lewis picked up two letters sent by Clark, one reporting on his success in recruiting for the voyage. Near Cincinnati, Lewis explored the vicinity of what is now Big Bone Lick State Park in Kentucky, collecting mammoth and mastodon bones to send to President Jefferson. Lewis reached the Falls of the Ohio at Clarksville, Indiana, and Louisville, Kentucky, in mid-October 1803. Here he was finally reunited face to face with his friend and compatriot Clark on October 14.

The fledgling expedition spent nearly two weeks in the area, during which Lewis and Clark had long conversations with Clark's oldest brother, George Rogers Clark, who knew much about the personalities and places on the frontier from his Revolutionary War career. (To this day, the elder Clark is by far the better-known brother in the Louisville area. Recent publicity for the Lewis and

Clark Bicentennial may help matters, but there are probably still locals who think that George Rogers is the Clark who went west with Lewis!) When the corps left the Falls of the Ohio on October 26, it include the two leaders; Clark's slave, York; Lewis's earlier recruits; and the men Clark had collected to make the trip, including William Bratton, Joseph and Reubin Field, Charles Floyd, George Gibson, Nathaniel Pryor, and John Shields.

Since this is where Lewis and Clark actually joined forces, the Louisville area is a great spot to begin a modern-day retracing of the expedition's route. Highlights include:

■ **Falls of the Ohio State Park.** Here on the Indiana side of the river, you can see a furnished replica of the cabin where William and George Rogers Clark (and probably York) were living in 1803. Nearby, Lewis and Clark Plaza overlooks the expedition's actual departure point at Mill Creek. It's about a 1.5-mile hike or 2-mile drive from the cabin area to the park's interpretive center, at the west end of Riverside Drive in Clarksville. See the "Men of Discovery" exhibit and view the film telling the local perspective on the expedition. The center also interprets the 400-million-year-old limestone fossil reef in the riverbed outside. The park is open daily from dawn to dusk, and the interpretive center ($4.00 for adults; $1.00 for children) is open from 9:00 A.M. to 5:00 P.M. Monday through Saturday and 1:00 to 5:00 P.M. Sunday. For more information call (812) 280–9970.

In 1806, after the expedition had ended, Lewis and Clark visited Clark's family at Locust Grove in Louisville, Kentucky.

■ **Louisville Waterfront.** When he arrived October 14, 1803, Lewis probably met Clark at what is now the Fourth Street Wharf on the Ohio River in downtown Louisville. Today there's interpretive signage and a new statue of York by Ed Hamilton. This is also the place to catch a ride on the paddle wheelers *Belle of Louisville* and *Spirit of Jefferson,* which run daily sight-seeing cruises late May through October. Call (866) 832–0011 or visit www.belleoflouisville.com for schedules.

■ **Filson Historical Society.** A true treasure trove for Corps of Discovery buffs, the Filson's collections include a half dozen expedition-related letters written by William Clark (and one by Lewis), a bighorn sheep horn, and the diary kept by Clark's brother Jonathan, who noted on October 26, 1803, that "Cap Lewis and Cap Wm Clark set off on a Western tour." There's also a fine collection of early printed accounts of the expedition—including the October 9, 1806, edition of the *Frankfort Palladium,* with the first detailed news report of the corps' successful return. Although the Filson is headquartered in the stately Ferguson Mansion at 1310 South Third Street in Louisville, it will have many of its expedition-related materials on view from spring 2003 through late 2004 or 2005 at 626 West Main Street in downtown Louisville. Hours for the special exhibit are 9:30 A.M. to 5:00 P.M. Monday through Saturday and noon to 5:00 P.M. Sunday. For more information call (502) 635–5083 or visit www.filsonhistorical.org.

■ **Locust Grove.** Lewis and Clark visited and relaxed here in November 1806 after returning from the West. Locust Grove, built around 1790 and now a national historic landmark, was at the time the home of Clark's sister Lucy, as well as of George Rogers Clark, who spent the last nine years of his life here. Tours are available from 10:00 A.M. to 3:30 P.M. Monday through Saturday and from 1:30 to 3:30 P.M. Sunday; admission is $4.00 for adults, $3.00 for seniors, and $2.00 for children ages six through twelve. A small log cabin houses a Hands-on History Center with activities for children; it's usually open Tuesday through Saturday in summer. Locust Grove is at 561 Blankenbaker Lane in Louisville. Call (502) 897–9845 or visit www.locustgrove.org for more information.

■ **Mulberry Hill/George Rogers Clark Park.** William Clark lived here as a teenager after his family moved from Virginia to the Kentucky frontier. The farmstead's original buildings were razed in 1917, but visitors can still see a cypress tree dating to the Clarks' time. The park also has picnicking, a playground, and a splash pool. It's on Poplar Level Road south of the Eastern Parkway.

Ask locally for a copy of the *Lewis and Clark at the Falls of the Ohio* brochure, which lists even more sites associated with the expedition, its members, and their kin. Each October Louisville and Clarksville team for an annual Lewis & Clark River Festival—a bicentennial Signature Event in 2003—commemorating the corps' stay in the area.

Local Lewis and Clark aficionado Phyllis Yeager or a family member is available to guide visitors to local expedition-related sights as well as such landmarks as the Kentucky Derby Museum (the Derby was actually founded by William Clark's grandson, Meriwether Lewis Clark Jr.) and the Louisville Slugger Museum. Cost is $50 an hour in your vehicle or $65 per hour in Yeager's. Call (812) 923–3822 or e-mail yeager@win.net to arrange a tour or plan a customized itinerary. The Yeager family also owns the Days Inn Sellersburg/Louisville North in Sellersburg, Indiana, which offers special Lewis and Clark packages including lodging, continental breakfast, and family admission to the Falls of the Ohio State Park interpretive center. Visit www.daysinnlouisville.com, or call (812) 246–4451.

For more information on Lewis and Clark–related activities and attractions, see www.fallsoftheohio.org. For help planning a trip to the area, contact the Greater Louisville Convention & Visitors Bureau (888–568–4784; www.goto louisville.com) and the Southern Indiana Clark-Floyd Counties Convention & Tourism Bureau (800–552–3842; www.sunnysideoflouisville.org).

PRESSING ON TOWARD ST. LOUIS

From Louisville/Clarksville, it's a 260-mile, half-day drive to the St. Louis area via interstate 64. But some purists may want to continue to trace the river route, down the Ohio and up the Mississippi, between the two cities. Lewis and Clark interpretation is minimal, but a few sites are noteworthy.

At Fort Massac in Illinois on November 11–12, 1803, the captains recruited several more expedition members, including George Drouillard, son of a Shawnee Indian mother and French-Canadian father. There's a small museum at what's now Fort Massac State Park, but as of 2002, there was scant mention of Lewis and Clark (though there are plans for a November 2003 event to mark the expedition's visit). The park does offer good camping, hiking, fishing, and a boat ramp. Call (618) 524–9321 for more information.

Fort Massac sits across the Ohio from Paducah, Kentucky, and outside the small town of Metropolis, Illinois. Metropolis bills itself as the "Hometown of Superman," and many people stop to get their photo taken with the giant Superman statue in front of the Massac County Courthouse. Of course the local newspaper is called *The Metropolis Planet.* A Superman Days festival is held each June, and Fort Massac State Park hosts an encampment in October. Both events draw tens of thousands of visitors.

The expedition left Fort Massac on November 13 and reached the mouth of the Ohio that evening. At what is now Cairo, Illinois, the expedition camped for about a week before moving on to the mighty Mississippi. Here, too, they practiced using their navigational instruments to fix latitude and longitude and met

Native Americans from the Delaware and Shawnee nations. One of the Indians tried to buy Seaman from Lewis, but the captain refused.

There wasn't much to see in the Cairo area in 2002, but local Lewis and Clark buffs plan a variety of improvements by the fall of 2003. Look for a new memorial atop the hill overlooking the river confluence, just outside Fort Defiance State Park (the monument was placed outside the park because the actual confluence area is under water several months of the year). As you stand here facing south, the Ohio comes in from the left, joining the Mississippi on the right. Other plans call for Lewis and Clark–related displays in the former Toll House restaurant (now a visitor center), the Cairo Public Library, and the Custom House Museum, as well as several new interpretive signs throughout Alexander County.

The expedition made it to Fort Kaskaskia on November 28 and spent about a week in the area. The upriver journey on the Mississippi had convinced Lewis and Clark that they'd need more men for similarly arduous travel on the Missouri; they recruited about a dozen more people, including the estimable Patrick Gass and John Ordway, both of whom would become sergeants in the Corps of Discovery.

Fort Kaskaskia State Historic Site near Chester, Illinois, has camping, picnicking, and a scenic overlook of the Mississippi River; there are plans to add interpretation about the expedition members recruited here. Kaskaskia, Illinois's first state capital, from 1818 to 1820, was once located on the opposite bank of the river, but an 1881 flood isolated the village. The former village site is now on a 14,000-acre island that's still part of Illinois but is accessible only via a bridge from St. Mary, Missouri. It's home to the "Liberty Bell of the West," rung by Father Pierre Gibault when George Rogers Clark and his "Long Knives" marched from Fort Massac to Fort Kaskaskia to capture it from the British on July 4, 1778. Another area landmark, the Pierre Menard Home State Historic Site, is a French Colonial home built in the early nineteenth century for Illinois's first lieutenant governor.

The expedition reached the Camp River Dubois site on December 12, 1803. Originally Lewis had hoped to be 200 or 300 miles up the Missouri River before making the first winter camp. But the lateness of the season, combined with the fact that the territory up the Missouri had not yet been transferred to the United States, meant that the expedition would have to resume its westward trek the next spring.

3

Illinois, Missouri, and Kansas

I set out at 4 o'clock P.M., in the presence of many of the neighboring inhabitants, and proceeded on under a gentle breeze up the Missouri.

—WILLIAM CLARK, MAY 14, 1804, UPON LEAVING CAMP RIVER DUBOIS.

CAMP RIVER DUBOIS AND CAHOKIA

Our journey continues at a monument on the banks of the Mississippi River. There, surrounded by a gauntlet of rocks, sits a ring of substantial stone pillars commemorating the start of the Lewis and Clark Expedition.

The actual site of Camp River Dubois—or Camp Wood, as it is sometimes known—has long since disappeared, swallowed up by urban development, industrialization, and the shifting channels of the Mississippi, Missouri, and Wood Rivers. Historians believe the camp sat about 3 miles northwest of the monument, an area dredged by oil companies operating in the vicinity. The approximate location is about 2.5 miles north of the present north bank of the Missouri River at its mouth.

But it was in this general area that the expedition planned and trained for its mission. The party camped here from December 12, 1803, through May 14, 1804, mostly under the command of Clark, who whipped the corps into a disciplined band while Lewis gathered supplies and information elsewhere in the St. Louis area.

Lewis and Clark weren't the first white visitors in the vicinity. Jacques Marquette and Louis Joliet reached the confluence in 1673, and other early European explorers followed. Their impressions of the site blended horror and delight. Describing a thicket of dead trees clogging the river, Marquette wrote that he "had seen nothing more dreadful." But Father Pierre Francois de Charlevoix called it "the finest confluence in the world. The two rivers are much the same breadth, each about half a league; but the Missouri is by far the most rapid, and seems to enter the Mississippi like a conqueror."

The corps' Camp River Dubois winter is detailed in full at the Lewis & Clark State Historic Site in Hartford, Illinois. Built near the longstanding monument described below, the new-in-2002 facility features a full-size replica of the expedition's keelboat, but with a twist: It's cut in half lengthwise so that visitors can see what the party took and how the material was organized and packed. Other exhibits lay the background for the expedition and show how the winter layover gave the corps time to galvanize as a unit.

Future plans call for a reconstruction of the expedition's 1803–1804 winter quarters. Also look for a 0.75-mile trail from the interpretive site to the riverside monument, which features eleven stone pillars—one for each present-day state Lewis and Clark passed through once they'd left Camp River Dubois. (For now you can drive to the monument after visiting the center.)

Lewis & Clark State Historic Site can be found at the intersection of Illinois Highway 3 and New Poag Road, 3 miles north of Interstate 270 (the major beltway around St. Louis). Hours are 9:00 A.M. to 5:00 P.M. Wednesday through Sunday; budget permitting, the center may also open Monday and Tuesday starting in summer 2003. For updates or more information, call (618) 251–5811 or visit www.campriverdubois.com.

Mindful of the Missisippi River's lessons in the difficulties of traveling upriver, Lewis and Clark continued to recruit during the winter. Once enlisted, the high-spirited young soldiers had to be trained. At first discipline was quite a problem. Drinking and fighting were rampant, and there also were instances of insubordination, refusal to stand guard, theft of government property, and men going AWOL. Author Roy E. Appleman wrote, "At one time or another, practically all the men in camp engaged in some wrongdoing. Yet some of the rowdiest and most undisciplined, such as (John) Colter and Reuben Field, were later to number among the most reliable in the command." Clark used a mixture of punishment and incentive to handle the men, and discipline had improved greatly by the time the corps left Camp River Dubois.

Over the winter the party also made numerous refinements to the keelboat to promote more efficient loading. Lockers were built to protect supplies, with lids that could be lifted to serve as defensive breastworks in the event of attack.

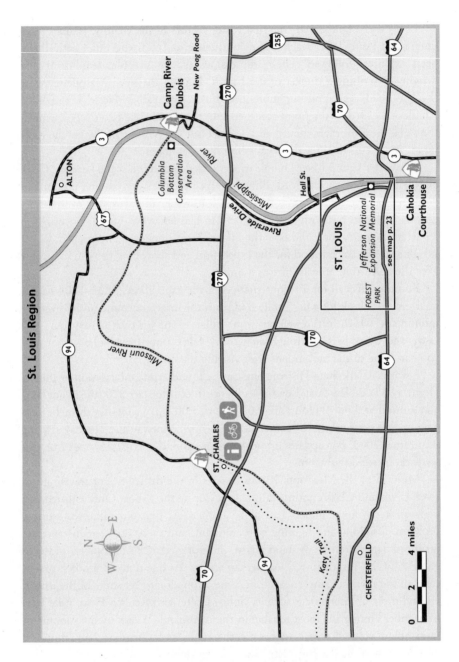

St. Louis Region

Clark also outfitted both the keelboats and the pirogues with weapons, including a small cannon (for the keelboat) and swivel guns.

Shortly before the expedition's departure, Clark received some bad news: The War Department had denied his commission as captain in the Corps of Engi-

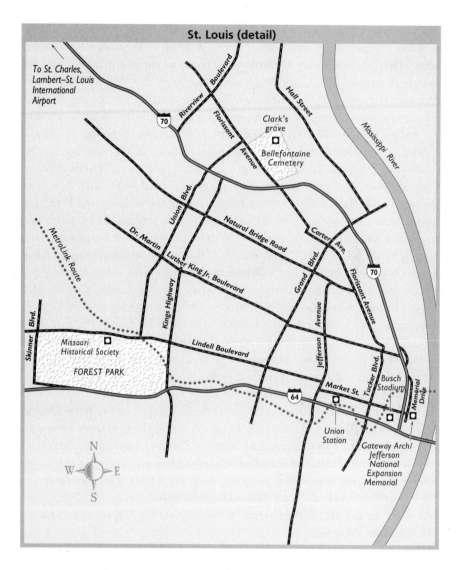

St. Louis (detail)

neers. In a letter including Clark's commission as a second lieutenant in the Corps of Artillerists, Lewis explained to his friend that in the peacetime Army, officer vacancies were scarce, and the Corps of Artillerists position was all that was available. But as he had promised earlier, Lewis swore to Clark that—in his mind, if not that of the government—Clark was his cocaptain. It was a secret kept safely between the friends for the duration of the two-and-a-half-year mission.

IL 3 is also known as The Great River Road. A few miles upriver from the Lewis & Clark State Historic Site sits Alton, Illinois, a city well known for riverboat gambling and an antiques district. Both are located near the riverfront area.

The seventh and final Lincoln-Douglas presidential debate was held at the intersection of Broadway and Market Streets here in 1858. Bridge fanciers will want a look at Clark Bridge, the striking cable stay suspension span over the Mississippi River here. The Clark Bridge also is the route to U.S. Highway 67 and Missouri Highway 94. Although these highways roughly parallel the Missouri River, most travelers will want to move west via St. Louis (see below).

Alton's Spencer T. Olin Community Golf Course, designed by Arnold Palmer, is considered among the best public courses in the metropolitan St. Louis area. The Piasa Bird, located on a limestone bluff along Illinois Highway 100, re-creates the flying-monster pictograph discovered in 1673 by Pere Marquette. IL 100 also parallels a 20-mile bike trail between Alton and Pere Marquette State Park, one of Illinois's largest and most popular parks. Grafton, a riverside town near the state park, is a main outfitting spot for area recreation. Stop by Grafton Canoe & Kayak in front of the town boat ramp to rent canoes, kayaks, bikes, and more. The Grafton Ferry Boat Company offers service across the Illinois and Mississippi Rivers between Grafton and St. Charles County, Missouri. The ferry runs daily from 5:00 A.M. to 10:00 P.M. and carries cars, bicycles, pedestrians, and motorcycles at a one-way cost of $6.50. Call (618) 786–3373 for more information. Call (800) 258–6645, visit www.Visit Alton.com, or stop by the Alton visitor center (kitty-corner to the Alton Belle Casino parking lot) for more information on activities and events in southwestern Illinois.

To proceed west via St. Louis, retrace IL 3 south to Interstate 270. Just over the Mississippi River, the state of Missouri runs a comprehensive statewide visitor center at the Riverview Drive exit. Head 2 miles north on Riverview from the welcome center turnoff to reach the Columbia Bottom Conservation Area, with its view of the confluence of the Mississippi and Missouri Rivers. Or turn south for the most direct route to the St. Louis riverfront. After a few miles Riverview Drive bears left into Hall Street. When Hall Street dead-ends at a "T," turn right and watch for the signs for Interstate 70 East. Get on the freeway and watch for the Riverfront/Arch exit.

Travelers with time to spare may want to spend a few more hours exploring expedition-related sites on the Illinois side. Lewis spent considerable time during the winter of 1803–1804 at Cahokia, the first European settlement on the Mississippi River. At the time of the expedition, the Cahokia Courthouse State Historic Site, built about 1740, served as the federal building for a huge area that extended north to the Canadian border. It's now open for visits Wednesday through Saturday at 107 Elm Street in Cahokia; call (618) 332–1782.

In his journals Clark reported trekking to an ancient, abandoned mound village. He hadn't reached what's now been designated as Cahokia Mounds State Historic Site in present day Collinsville, but what he saw was probably similar. The Cahokia Mounds area, one of the most significant of its kind in the United

States, was home to a civilization from about A.D. 700 to 1400. At its peak, the village may have supported as many as 20,000 residents. An interpretive center and trails, open Wednesday through Sunday, explain the area's past. The site is located along Collinsville Road; take I–70 exit 6 or I–255 exit 24. For more information call (618) 346–5160.

ST. LOUIS

At the time of the Lewis and Clark Expedition, St. Louis was a mere forty years old but already on its way to becoming one of the most important cities in the United States. Its location made St. Louis the ideal hub of transportation, exploration, mercantile activity, and culture. Consequently, the city attracted everyone from fur traders to scientists, military agents to missionaries. It was here Captain Lewis gathered much of the intelligence essential to the expedition's success, as well as where he witnessed the March 9–10, 1804, ceremonies marking the transfer of Upper Louisiana from Spain to France and from France to the United States.

Any visit to St. Louis should begin at the Jefferson National Expansion Memorial, best known for its graceful stainless-steel centerpiece, the 630-foot Gateway Arch. The Arch is America's tallest monument, topping the 555-foot Washington Monument and the 305-foot Statue of Liberty. It is a marvel of engineering and design.

The Museum of Westward Expansion beneath the Arch celebrates the vision of Thomas Jefferson and offers one of the nation's best overviews of why the Lewis and Clark Expedition took place. Exhibits are arranged in a wagon-wheel fashion, with each decade radiating off a hub. In the center stands a life-size statue of Jefferson, who stood 6-foot-3. He is seen gazing out toward an ocean mural on the far wall, and strategic lighting ensures Jefferson's shadow is cast in all directions, just as his influence looms formidably even today.

Central to the museum's Lewis and Clark interpretation are the large, floor-to-ceiling photographs of sites along the expedition route. These beautiful images serve as a backdrop for everything else on display. Smaller photos show plants and animals seen by the corps, and a map of the Louisiana Purchase illustrates how that event nearly doubled the size of the United States.

Other exhibits pay tribute to later great American explorers, from the Oregon Trail pioneers to Charles Lindbergh and the Apollo astronauts. The museum features an "animatronic" representation of Captain Clark as he appeared in 1832, by then Superintendent of Indian Affairs, explaining why early explorers gave peace medals to the Native Americans they met. The museum also offers fine interpretive programs, including talks by rangers who sometimes discuss the

William Clark's grave at Bellefontaine Cemetery, St. Louis, Missouri.

Lewis and Clark Expedition. And no visit would be complete without a ride to the top of the Arch. After a four-minute ride up the monument's innards in a podlike tram car, the visitor is treated to outstanding views reaching 30 miles both east and west on a clear day.

The museum is open from 8:00 A.M. to 10:00 P.M. Memorial Day through Labor Day and 9:00 A.M. to 6:00 P.M. the rest of the year. Admission to the Arch tram and museum is $8.00 per person age seventeen and up, $5.00 for students ages thirteen through sixteen, and $3.00 for children ages three through twelve. Also worthwhile are movies in the Arch Odyssey Theatre, with its four-story screen, and another theater showcasing the *Monument to the Dream* documentary, which describes the building of the Arch. (Each showing carries an additional charge.) There may be a wait of an hour or more to take the tram, so buy your tickets as soon as you arrive, and then enjoy the museum and other activities. All facilities are closed Thanksgiving, Christmas, and New Year's Day. For more information, call (877) 982–1410 or visit www.gateway arch.com. The Jefferson National Expansion Memorial also includes an expansive park surrounding the Arch and the Old Courthouse. The latter features exhibits on early St. Louis, including a diorama showing the transfer of the Louisiana Territory.

St. Louis Travel Tips

Lambert–St. Louis International Airport (STL) is served by most major and Midwest regional airlines. The airport is undergoing a major expansion, so allow extra time. Rental cars are available from numerous companies.

The Amtrak station is at 550 South Sixteenth Street; the Greyhound terminal is at 1450 North Thirteenth Street.

St. Louis's MetroLink light-rail system is an easy way to get around town. Although parking is plentiful and fairly cheap at the riverfront, savvy travelers will hop the MetroLink at Laclede's Landing to explore other area sites such as Union Station and Forest Park. It's also possible to take the train from several convenient stops near the airport and Interstate 70 (though you'll want to leave early if it's the night of a Cardinals home game, when the park-and-ride lots are jammed). Look for a Metro Link route map at your hotel, or call (314) 231–2345 from 6:00 A.M. to 8:00 P.M. weekdays or 8:00 A.M. to 5:00 P.M. weekends.

The St. Louis area is developing a good network of bicycle and pedestrian trails along the Mississippi and Missouri Rivers. For information on the 40-mile Confluence Greenway network, visit www.trailnet.org, or call (314) 416–9930.

Touring St. Louis

As the largest city along the Lewis and Clark route, St. Louis offers a full menu of urban attractions. Once you've seen the Arch, take time to explore the bustling riverfront area. Visitors can choose from a scenic riverboat cruise, casino gambling, a Cardinals game at Busch Stadium, or explorations of the shops, restaurants, and nightlife of Laclede's Landing, the restored historic area just north of the Arch. Stop in the Drury Plaza Hotel at Fourth and Market Streets to see the 3-D Lewis and Clark exhibit in the lobby.

South of the Arch, the Soulard area thrives on live musical entertainment, with more than thirty restaurants and pubs, many offering jazz and blues. Soulard is also home to the Anheuser-Busch Brewery, where free tours (complete with product samples) are offered daily. Union Station, west of the riverfront along Market Street, has been transformed from a train station to a major shopping, dining, and entertainment destination.

The Missouri Historical Society in Forest Park plans a major Lewis and Clark exhibition to commemorate the bicentennial. Billed as a reunion of expedition artifacts and documents not seen together since 1806, the exhibition will be on view here January 22–September 6, 2004, before traveling to Philadelphia (November 2004–March 2005), Denver (May–September 2005), Portland (November 2005–March 2006), and Washington, D.C. (May–September 2006). Visit www.lewisandclarkexhibit.org for more information.

Other Forest Park attractions include the St. Louis Zoo, with more than 3,400 animals; the Muny, an outdoor performing arts center; and the St. Louis Art Museum. The St. Louis Science Center, in an impressive building straddling Interstate 64 adjacent to the park, has great shows in its OMNIMAX Theater and McDonnell Planetarium. It's worth noting that there is free basic admission to all Forest Park attractions. Forest Park also offers bicycle rentals, bike/jog walk paths, fishing, boating, skating, golf courses, and tennis courts.

Six Flags Over Mid-America, one of the nation's biggest amusement parks, is located about 30 miles southwest of downtown, near the Allenton exit off Interstate 44. Raging Rivers, a water park, is in Grafton, Illinois. For more information about St. Louis–area attractions, call the convention and visitors commission at (800) 916–8938, visit www.explorestlouis.com, or write to One Metropolitan Square, Suite 1100, St. Louis, Missouri 63102.

Although Lewis spent the most time in St. Louis the winter before the expedition, it was Clark who eventually made the city his home. After the expedition, Clark owned several buildings—none still standing—in the general vicinity of what is now the Gateway Arch. These included various Clark residences; his museum of Indian curiosities (an early St. Louis tourist attraction); and storehouses and offices he used in dealing with the Native Americans. Late in life, Clark lived mainly at his farm on Bellefontaine Road about 3.5 miles north of the city, but he died at the downtown home of his son, Meriwether Lewis Clark.

Clark is buried at the mammoth Bellefontaine Cemetery, 5 miles north of downtown on Florissant Avenue. The grave is situated on an elaborate stone plaza featuring an obelisk and bust of the explorer, along with a buffalo's head and gargoyle. Clark is described here as a "soldier, explorer, statesman and patriot. His life is written in the history of his country." No one would dispute that. Some may, however, question the Biblical quote also prominently displayed: "Behold, the Lord thy God hath set the land before thee. Go up and possess it." Certainly, that was what Lewis and Clark did. But these captains, along with their boss the president, envisioned a United States where the Native Americans and the more recently arrived whites could exist in harmony. The notion that the continent was somehow ours to plunder with no thought given to consequence came largely after the time of Jefferson, Lewis, and Clark.

To find the grave from the Florissant entrance, take Willow Avenue to Vine Avenue, bear left then right onto Althea Avenue, then left onto Aspen Avenue. Aspen runs into Meadow Avenue, where the Clark family plot is located. Better yet, stop at the office for a map to Clark's grave and a look at a chart of the Clark family tree, with branches hailing from St. Louis, Louisville, and Michigan. Guided tours are available by appointment. The cemetery is open to visitors from 8:00 A.M. to 5:00 P.M. daily.

ST. CHARLES

Although Camp River Dubois has a strong claim as the expedition's starting point, St. Charles was where final preparations were made, last-minute supplies obtained, and the boatload readjusted. Moreover, as we have seen, the expedition was shy one captain upon its arrival in St. Charles May 16, 1804. Lewis caught up with the corps May 20, and they formally got under way the next day.

In his journal Clark described St. Charles in this way: "This village is about one mile in length, contains about 100 houses and about 450 inhabitants, chiefly French. Those people appear poor, polite, and harmonious." Founded in

1769 as a fur-trading post by Louis Blanchette, a French-Canadian hunter, St. Charles was the first permanent white settlement on the Missouri River. Early white inhabitants called the area Les Petites Cotes ("The Little Hills") because of the surrounding terrain.

After the United States took over the Louisiana Territory, St. Charles's influence grew. Its location near the confluence of the Mississippi and Missouri Rivers made it an ideal outfitting port for land and water routes to the West. The city also was the eastern terminus of the Boonslick Road, which led to the Boone brothers' saltworks in Howard County. St. Charles served as Missouri's first state capital from 1821 to 1826.

The Lewis and Clark Boathouse and Nature Center, open in Spring 2003 at 1050 Riverside Drive, is the new home of the former Lewis and Clark Center and the Discovery Expedition of St. Charles. (The latter is a group of Lewis and Clark buffs who are authentically re-creating Lewis and Clark's journeys in keelboat and pirogue replicas. For more information on the expedition and its scheduled appearances along the route, visit www.lewisandclark.net.) The first floor of the building features a flow-through design that protects the Discovery Expedition's watercraft and allows easy access to the river. Upstairs, exhibits focus on the natural history of the Missouri River and the Corps of Discovery's time in St. Charles. A walk-through Lewis and Clark campsite, hands-on nature displays, and a terrifically detailed diorama by artist Evangeline Groth are among the highlights.

The center has a trading post and offers a variety of classes and programs for school and youth groups. It also sells a handy booklet telling about Lewis and Clark in St. Charles, complete with a map that pinpoints sites known to the expedition. The center is open daily (except major holidays) from 10:00 A.M. to 5:00 P.M. Admission is $2.00 for adults and $1.00 for children ages three through seventeen. For more information, call (636) 947–3199.

After visiting the center, take some time to explore the riverfront and St. Charles's South Main Street historic district, with its cobblestone streets and charming little parks. (Self-guided walking tour brochures are available at most businesses.) The building at 719 South Main Street, now Karen's River Cabin, was built in the 1790s and stood when Lewis and Clark were in town.

Lewis and Clark Heritage Days, staged the third weekend each May, includes a reenactment of the corps' 1804 encampment. Other activities include a parade, crafts and foods of the period, a fife and drum corps muster, and military reenactment groups demonstrating eighteenth- and nineteenth-century drill tactics.

St. Charles serves as a major access point to the Katy Trail, one of America's most unusual state parks. See the Katy Trail section later in this chapter for more information. This may also be the honeymoon capital of the Lewis and Clark Trail, with several wedding chapels and many bed-and-breakfast inns ready to serve romantic couples. For more information on things to see and do in St. Charles, stop by the visitors bureau at 230 South Main Street, or call (800) 366–2427.

THE SHAKEDOWN CRUISE

Interstate 70 cuts a wide, straight swath across Missouri, allowing motorists to traverse the state in about four hours. But travelers who stay on I–70 miss some of the most beautiful hill country and the quaintest small towns in the Midwest—reason enough to consider following the meandering Missouri River and the route of Lewis and Clark across at least part of the Show-Me State. Good roads parallel the river on both sides to Jefferson City—Missouri Highway 94 to the north and MO 100 to the south. Drive these for a while until you grow tired of the relentless roller-coaster hills and curves; then return to I–70 to make up some time. Note that, unlike most other states, Missouri marks many of its secondary roads with letters, not numerals—a system started in 1932.

Start southwest from St. Charles on MO 94 and see suburban St. Louis disappear in your rearview mirror as the road becomes a panorama of wildlife areas, wineries, and access points to the Katy Trail, the longest rails-to-trails conversion in the United States. Once the site of one of the world's largest munitions plants, the Weldon Spring area is now laced with fishing ponds (with boat rentals and bait available at Busch Lodge off of Missouri Highway D) and trails, including two named for our heroes. Past the junction with MO D, watch on your left for the Lewis and Clark trailhead parking lot. The 8.2-mile Lewis Trail takes about five hours to hike, while the 5.3-mile Clark Trail takes about three hours. A few miles farther west, the rugged Lost Valley Trail is open to both hiking and mountain biking.

This is also Daniel Boone country, where the famous American frontiersman spent the last two decades of his life, from about 1799 through 1820. In other words, the aging pioneer was living here when Lewis and Clark trekked through the area in 1804 and again in 1806, but no record exists of an encounter between the parties. For an in-depth look at Boone's life, visit the Daniel Boone Home on Missouri Highway F near Defiance. One of Missouri's most popular attractions, the dwelling was completed in 1810 and still houses many Boone family heirlooms. The grounds also include "The Judgment Tree," a large elm under which Boone settled disputes between white men and local Indians. Other important Boone family sites in Missouri include Daniel's grave at Marthasville and the Boone's Lick State Historic Site north of Boonville.

More important for our explorations, this country also served as the shakedown cruise section for the Lewis and Clark Expedition, the area where the men became intimate with the river on which they would do most of their traveling over the next couple of years. Of the 7,500-plus miles covered by Lewis and Clark, roughly three-quarters of them were on the Missouri River. Rising in southwest Montana where the Madison, Gallatin, and Jefferson Rivers join, the Missouri drains one-sixth of the land in the contiguous United States. Hundreds of rivers and creeks join the Missouri over its 2,315-mile course to the Mississippi.

For tens of thousands of years, the Missouri was free and wild. But as the nation expanded, the demand for hydroelectric power and desire for flood control resulted in one of history's largest public works efforts, the Pick-Sloan Project of the 1940s and 1950s, which created six huge dams in the Dakotas and Montana. Combined with dredging and channelization farther downriver, the dams changed the Missouri into a river far different from the one Lewis and Clark saw.

Indeed, the Missouri of 1804 was considered to be the most unruly river in America, and it didn't take the corps long to find out why. Keelboats were pulled along by hand with a 1,000-foot line called a cordelle tied to the mast. The keelboat often had to be towed against a strong current, and it typically took at least twenty men to cordelle a keelboat along most sections of the Missouri. At times, sandbars made cordelling impossible. In those instances, the boat would be poled or even rowed upstream. A small mast sail was sometimes used if winds were favorable, yet snags were another constant hazard. Blistering summer heat, thundering rainstorms, mosquitoes, gnats, and ticks made matters still more difficult all across Missouri and onto the Plains.

The expedition had other matters to address as well. Jefferson had compiled a long list of duties and objectives, chief among them keeping journals. Along with noting latitude, longitude, and landmarks, the captains were to record extensive details of any Indian nations encountered; "the soil and face of the country, its growth and vegetable productions, especially those not of the U.S."; animals; minerals, "volcanic appearances"; and climate.

Both Lewis and Clark kept journals, and their versions of the trip are the best known today. But other expedition members also contributed written accounts. Joseph Whitehouse's was one of the most detailed; Clark frequently fed him information in the hope that if the captains' journals were lost, another comprehensive account might survive. Others who kept journals were Patrick Gass, Charles Floyd, and John Ordway. Gass, perhaps the most unlikely journal writer, was the first to hit print. He'd had only nineteen days of schooling, but he wrote faithfully during the expedition, and his work, edited afterward by Pittsburgh print shop owner David McKeehan, came out in 1807—the first book to be published about the expedition. Nathaniel Pryor probably also kept a journal, but it has never been found.

Mapmaking was another of the expedition's primary duties. In an 1805 letter Jefferson wrote, "The work we are now doing is, I trust, done for posterity in such a way that they need not repeat it. We shall delineate with correctness the great arteries of this great country. Those who come after us will extend the ramifications as they become acquainted with them and fill up the canvas we begin."

Clark did most of the mapmaking. Using simple navigational instruments and his own estimates, he measured the length and direction of each bend of the rivers and the distance they had traveled, scribbling these courses and distances next to his sketch maps. In most instances, his "guesstimates" were remarkably accurate. Clark's maps recorded a wealth of other information, too, including campsites, creeks and rivers, Native American villages, and bad rapids.

And as instructed, the captains made note of the plants and animals they encountered. More than 120 animals and 170 plant species, many new to science, were described in the journals. Consequently, two entire plant categories—*Lewisia* and *Clarkia*—were named after the explorers, and their names also were freely assigned to landmarks and natural features across the land. When the corps members published their work, readers were fascinated to hear for the first time of such beasts as grizzly bears, bighorn sheep, and pronghorn antelope.

With all these duties, it would seem Lewis and Clark had scant time for adventure. But barely under way, Lewis had a close brush with death on May 23, 1804. On that day, the captains stopped to explore an area known as Tavern Cave, located east of present-day Washington, Missouri. "The challenge was too much for Lewis," David Lavender wrote in his book *The Way to the Western Sea*. "While Clark was adding his name to the register inside the cavern, Meriwether found a break in the precipice, ascended it, and began working his way along the edge. A foothold crumbled. He slid and bounced downward about 20 feet. Just short of disaster, Clark wrote in his journal, 'He saved himself by the assistance of his knife,' driving it wildly one assumes, into some crevice that held. Just how he extricated himself from the dizzy perch does not appear."

Tavern Cave is about 2 miles north down the railroad tracks from the village of St. Albans, an upscale housing and golf development. St. Albans is located off Missouri Highway T, which makes a hilly loop north of MO 100, the main road east of Washington (on the opposite side of the river from MO 94, with a crossing via MO 47 at Dutzow). Several interpretive markers stand in front of the village's Chesterfield Day School, but hiking to the cave itself isn't recommended, since it's on private land and accessible only by walking the railroad tracks. The state of Missouri may improve access to the cave by the time the bicentennial ends; check locally for updates. For now it's not really worth backtracking to St. Albans unless you really want to sneak a peek at the lifestyles of Missouri's rich and famous.

Washington is a town of about 10,000 people, with a good selection of interesting shops and restaurants and a mile-long riverfront park. Lewis and Clark camped in the vicinity two days after the episode at Tavern Cave. From Washington, continue west on MO 100 or MO 94, through Missouri's scenic and hilly wine country. New Haven and Hermann are two other communities worth exploring on the MO 100 side.

First settled around 1805, New Haven was originally called Miller's Landing for pioneer Philip Miller. The Missouri-Pacific Railroad reached here in 1855, and the present town was laid out and renamed the next year. Today's New Haven begins up on MO 100 and tumbles down the river bluffs to a pleasant landing district with an antiques mall, a year-round Christmas store, a 1930s movie theater, and dining. A stairclimb from the downtown district leads to a viewpoint.

John Colter, one of the most famous members of the Lewis and Clark Expedition, settled a few miles east of New Haven in 1810. (The Missouri Department of Conservation has a fishing access area named for him east of town on MO 100.) After the expedition, Colter went on to great fame as the first white man to discover what is now Yellowstone National Park. He was probably buried in the New Haven area, although the location is uncertain. His grave was likely never marked and may have disappeared when the local river bluffs were reshaped to construct a levee—one of a handful that was able to withstand the floods that wracked the Midwest during summer 1993.

Hermann, sometimes called Little Germany, is reminiscent of Rhine Valley towns with its distinctive architecture. White settlers had arrived in the area by the early 1800s, and a town historical marker notes how the returning Lewis and Clark Expedition "joyfully hailed the sight of cows along the riverbank here."

Hermann was founded by the German Settlement Society of Philadelphia in 1836 as a place where German customs and language could be preserved "amid the benefits of America." The town was laid out on part of an 11,300-acre parcel purchased by Society agent George F. Bayer for $15,612. The society disbanded in 1839, but a steady stream of Germans continued to arrive for years afterward.

The year 1843 was a momentous one in Hermann history. That year, many newly arriving German emigrants died when a steamboat exploded. In 1843 Hermann also became the fourth town to serve as seat of Gasconade County— a title it retains today. The present courthouse was built in 1898. At one point, the town also boasted a German-language newspaper known for its antislavery views and a German school. River shipping and winemaking became big industries.

Hermann is a fairly touristy place, but one can understand why city slickers from St. Louis and Kansas City might want to head here for a weekend. Wine and beer tasting are big activities; fortunately, there are also plenty of accommodations available for anyone who samples a bit too much.

Hermann has a nice campground in its city park, with spots designed for tents as well as RVs. In addition to rest rooms with showers, the park also has plenty of picnic tables, tennis courts, great playground equipment, and a pool.

Check the weather report before pitching a tent here, however: Signs warn visitors that the area is subject to flash flooding.

Cross the Missouri again at Hermann and proceed west on MO 94 (or I–70, 13 miles north via MO 19) to Jefferson City. The highlight here is a bronze relief on the State Capitol grounds depicting the signing of the Louisiana Purchase. Robert R. Livingston (seated) and James Monroe are seen witnessing French Marquis Francois de Barbois Marbois signing the purchase agreement, one of the most momentous events in American history. With their pen strokes, these men nearly doubled the size of the United States.

Bike or walk close to the river on the Katy Trail.

Other sights on the Capitol grounds include several lovely fountains and an imposing statue of President Jefferson. The Capitol itself hasn't had the greatest luck. First built in 1826, it was destroyed by fire in 1837. The second building, started that year, burned in 1911 after being struck by lightning. The present Capitol was built in 1918.

Inside, the Missouri Museum features historical and contemporary displays. Thomas Hart Benton's mural, *A Social History of the State of Missouri,* is painted on all four walls of the House Lounge, located on the west wing of the third floor. You'll also find statues of Lewis, Clark, and Sacagawea in its halls. The statehouse is open and free tours are available daily except Easter, Thanksgiving, Christmas, and New Year's Day.

Jefferson City's other attractions include the Jefferson Landing State Historic Site, with several buildings dating from the 1830s to the 1850s; the Governor's Garden, where outdoor drama is sometimes held; and the Runge Nature Center at 2901 West Truman Boulevard, featuring a large aquarium and hands-on nature exhibits. The Missouri Department of Natural Resources recently received a thirteen-acre donation for a landmark near Jefferson City known as Clark's

The Katy Trail

I n 1986 the Missouri-Kansas-Texas (MKT) Railroad decided to end operations on a trans-Missouri route from near St. Charles to Sedalia. The decision paved the way for creation of the Katy Trail, at 185 miles the
longest biking, hiking, and handicapped-use rails-to-trails project in the
United States. ("Katy" is the popular abbreviation for MKT.)

The Katy Trail parallels the Missouri River across much of eastern Missouri,
affording Lewis and Clark buffs and opportunity to see the river "trail" up
close in several areas. Scenic wonders abound. Lewis and Clark noted the
limestone bluffs south of Rocheport (on U.S. Highway 40 west of Columbia),
known as the Manitou (or Moniteau) Bluffs for the Indian word for Great
Spirit. These bluffs once had many pictographs, which Clark noted in his journal entry of June 7, 1804: "A short distance above the mouth of a creek is several curious paintings and carving on the projecting rock of limestone inlaid
with white, red and blue flint of a very good quality . . ." To see the area now
known as Lewis and Clark Cave, ride east 4 miles from the Rocheport trailhead. The cave itself is full of bats and is off-limits to exploration, but this is
a lovely riverside ride that's among the Katy Trail's nicest stretches.

Katy Trail users wheel or walk past an array of wildflowers, and
the trail's location along the Missouri River Flyway means mi-
grating bird and waterfowl sightings are common. But the Katy Trail experience also means visits to small Missouri towns far from the interstates, where
a slower way of life is still savored. If you can, come in fall when it's cooler
and much of the route is ablaze in color. But no matter what the season, anyone who enjoys easy cycling or hiking through pastoral settings should plan
to spend at least a day on the Kay Trail.

Katy Trail State Park was designed for bicyclists and hikers. Wheelchairs
are welcome, too, but other motorized vehicles (except official and emergency vehicles) are prohibited. Users should stay on the trail, as the areas immediately outside trail boundaries are often on private property. Pets should
be kept on a leash.

Businesses catering to cyclists and hikers are springing up all along the
route. Bike rentals are widely available, starting at about $5.00 an hour or
$20.00 a day for a standard bike—more for tandems, recumbent bikes, and
high-performance models. The listing below is but a sample; for detailed information on the route, its history, and amenities along the way check out
The Complete Katy Trail Guidebook by Brett Dufur, widely available along the
route or from www.pebblepublishing.com.

The Touring Cyclist, with several St. Louis–area locations, including St. Charles (636–949–9630; www.touringcyclist.com), rents bicycles and runs an annual Katy Trail end-to-end tour. This ride, covering 30 to 50 miles a day, usually takes place mid-September.

Scenic Cycles in Marthasville (636–433–2909; www.scenic-cycles.com) has bike rentals of all sorts, including tandem cycles, trailers, and Trailabikes, which attach to the back of an adult bike and are great for preschoolers. Its Web site has a Katy Trail section with lots of good trip-planning information.

Parsons House Bed & Breakfast (636–798–2222) in Defiance is one of several bed-and-breakfasts close to the Katy Trail. Bike rentals and trailside meals are also available in Defiance.

Trailside Cafe & Bike Rental (573–698–2702) in Rocheport is the closest bike shop to the portion of trail nearest Lewis and Clark Cave, described above. Before or after your ride, stop in for a buffalo burger or homemade baked goods. **Katy O'Neil** (573–698–BIKE, a "bed-and-bikefest" nearby, features a hot tub and accommodations in a converted boxcar.

Several companies run shuttle services along the Katy Trail, including **Cyclehaulics** in Boonville (660–882–3338) and **Roadrunner Shuttles/Ride-MeRecycles** (888–274–4626). Amtrak also serves several cities along the Katy Trail route, including Washington, Hermann, and Jefferson City; you can park your car in one of these towns, ride to the next, and take the train back. The Missouri Department of Natural Resources also has an annual Katy Trail Ride that covers the whole route in five days. The cost in 2002 was $200 (or $600 per family), which included campsites and showers, gear shuttle, daily breakfasts and dinners, a support wagon, and souvenirs; optional transportation to or from the starting or ending point was $40.

For more information on the Katy Trail, contact the Missouri Department of Natural resources, P.O. Box 176, Jefferson City, Missouri 65102, call (800) 334–6946, or visit www.katytrailstatepark.com.

Hill, overlooking the confluence of the Missouri and Osage Rivers. Clark wrote on June 1, 1804, that he found "a delightful prospect from this hill which commands both rivers." Inquire locally for directions to the Clark's Hill/Norton State Historic Site, which will offer a trail and interpretive information.

From Jefferson City, the traveler once again has a choice of routes. U.S. Highway 63 provides speedy access to Columbia and I–70 to the north, while MO 179 takes a more leisurely approach, reaching the interstate west of Columbia. MO 179 stays somewhat closer to the river; a popular attraction en route is Croy's River Hills Farm at Marion. Lewis and Clark camped nearby on

June 4, 1804, and the farm now features a zoo, trail, gift and snack shops, and pick-your-own produce.

Columbia sits several miles from the Missouri, but what it may lack in location, it more than makes up in culture and recreation. Columbia is home to the main University of Missouri campus, Columbia College, and Stephens College, which together add some 27,000 students to Columbia's population of about 70,000. Campus highlights include the Francis Quadrangle at MU, where six ionic columns are all that remain of Academic Hall, destroyed by fire in 1892; Stephens College's Firestone Baars Chapel, designed by Eero Saarinen, the same architect responsible for the Arch in St. Louis; and the Chinese Pavilion at Columbia College. Interestingly, Thomas Jefferson's original grave marker is on Columbia Quad at MU, in recognition of the school's being the first state university in the Louisiana Territory.

Cultural attractions include the Shelter Insurance Gardens; Maplewood Barn Theatre, where outdoor dramas are presented in a converted barn Memorial Day through Labor Day; and a variety of art galleries. (Columbia College is considered one of the nation's top fine and commercial art schools; its gallery is located on North Tenth Street.) Recreational possibilities range from swimming, golf, and tennis to cycling on the nearby Katy Trail. Columbia Mall at Stadium and Bernadette Streets is the city's largest, but Columbia also has a thriving downtown district centered near Providence Road and East Broadway. For more information on area attractions, call (573) 875–1231 or visit www.visitcolumbia mo.com.

ARROW ROCK AND FORT OSAGE

Boonville, located near I–70 and Missouri Highway 87, is one of the oldest towns in central Missouri and has more than 400 buildings on the National Register of Historic Places. The town has a good selection of food and lodging, along with a full calendar of festivals and tours of the historic districts. Stop by the Katy Depot at 320 First Street for more information.

From Boonville, the river flows west then north to Arrow Rock, long a major stopping point for people headed west. Lewis and Clark reached the area June 9, 1804, and Clark noted "several small channels running out of the river below a bluff and prairie (called the Prairie of Arrows)." Even at that time, the area had already received its name.

In the mid–nineteenth century, many emigrants passed through the area on their way to the western trailheads leading to Santa Fe, Oregon, and California. The town's population peaked around 1860 but dropped off after the Civil War and the decline of traffic on the nearby Missouri River.

Arrow Rock, Missouri.

Today, Arrow Rock looks much as it did in the mid-1800s. An interpretive center (open daily in summer and Friday through Sunday in winter) explains the town's history, and visitors can see the past up close by walking through town. Historic buildings include the Old Tavern (dating to 1834) and a home occupied by famed frontier artist George Caleb Bingham from 1837 to 1845.

About two dozen merchants and innkeepers are doing their best to keep Arrow Rock alive, and the town enjoys thriving tourism, especially in summer and fall. Major events include an arts festival the third weekend of May and a crafts festival the second weekend each October. The Lyceum Theatre presents a half dozen different dramas each summer, with performances usually set Wednesday through Sunday. The town has several bed-and-breakfasts, and camping is available at Arrow Rock State Park.

Arrow Rock State Historic Site is located 17 miles from Boonville and 15 miles from Marshall. To get there, take I–70 exit 98 to MO 41. For more information, call (660) 837–3330.

From Arrow Rock, it's a short drive to one of the most extraordinary natural locations along the lower Missouri River. The 1993 floods created a side channel, or chute, in an area known as Lisbon Bottoms. Instead of sealing off the chute as it normally would, the Army Corps of Engineers has allowed the river to take its natural course, or nearly so. (Although engineers have erected a rock

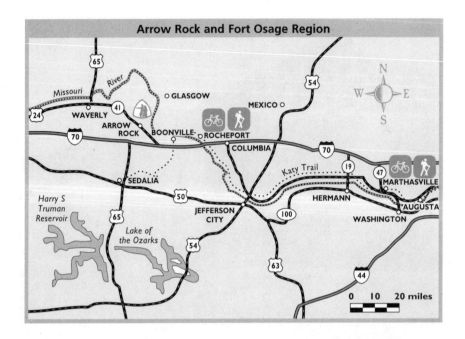

wall at the north end of the chute, this barrier is notched to allow the river to continue flowing through, while still maintaining the main channel for barge traffic.) The result: Lisbon Bottoms and adjacent Jameson Island make up one of the only stretches south of Sioux City, Iowa, where visitors can see a Missouri River that resembles the waterway seen by Lewis and Clark.

Lisbon Bottoms and Jameson Island are now designated part of the Big Muddy National Fish and Wildlife Refuge. Eventually river advocates hope to establish many free-flowing areas like this all along the Lower Missouri. Lisbon Bottoms is located downriver from Glasgow, which is 19 winding miles north of Boonville via Missouri Highway 87. There's a boat ramp at Glasgow for people who would like to travel downriver to Lisbon Bottoms. Small crafts like canoes or kayaks can usually negotiate the chute through the notch at its north end, though it's smart to call the refuge office at (573) 876–1826 to assess river conditions before setting out. Larger boats could run up the chute from its south end. You can also get a view from the riverbanks by following MO 87 then Highways Z, 328, and 319 to the nearly abandoned community of Lisbon. The vista is actually best a bit south of Lisbon; look for signs announcing the wildlife refuge in this area.

From Arrow Rock, continue northwest on MO 41 to Marshall, the seat of Saline County and gateway to Van Meter State Park, an area featuring ancient Indian burial sites and ceremonial mounds (12 miles northwest on MO 41 and MO 122). At Marshall, pick up U.S. Highway 65 going west; it turns into U.S. 24 at the small crossroads of Waverly.

U.S. 24 proceeds west through an area filled with orchards offering everything from asparagus to blackberries to Christmas trees, depending on the season. The rural vistas blend with picturesque small-town scenes: young men working on a souped-up yellow car, complete with painted red flames streaking across its side, and older folks porch sitting into the twilight. Sweetly scented fruit blossoms replace diesel fumes, and a hawk may be spotted soaring above the trees. Best of all: almost no billboards. These roads have character.

Many small towns along the Lewis and Clark route have annual summer festivals or community picnics, usually advertised with signs posted near the village limits. If you happen to be in the right place at the right time, by all means stop and investigate. Anticipate a good meal, friendly conversation, and maybe some sight-seeing tips, too.

Lexington, Missouri, was settled in 1822 by former residents of Lexington, Kentucky. The town became a busy riverport and was the site of a three-day Civil War battle won by the Confederates. The battlefield is now a state historic site, and a cannonball fired during the September 1861 event may still be seen lodged in a column at the courthouse.

Lewis and Clark reached the present site of Fort Osage National Historic Landmark in late June 1804 and named it Fort Point, noting its suitability for a military installation. In 1808 Clark returned to supervise the construction of a fortified trading post to sway the Indians from Spanish and British influence. Fort Osage was operated by the government until 1822 and played an active and important part in the earliest development of the Louisiana Territory.

Interest in Fort Osage was revitalized during Missouri's statehood centennial in the 1920s. Restoration started in 1941 and was completed in 1962. To get to the site, take U.S. 24 to Buckner; then turn north on Sibley Street (Missouri Highway BB). Directional signs point the rest of the way to the park.

Fort Osage was run by George Sibley, and he seemed to enjoy his post, noting in his diary: "I am very comfortably fixed." A household inventory done in 1813 included a cherry dining table, ten Windsor chairs, a walnut cupboard, and brass candlesticks. In his diary Sibley noted his typical daily meals: coffee and unbuttered toast for breakfast; beef, pork, or venison and potatoes for midday dinner; and a dish of tea and milk and hominy for supper. "Frequently, we are honored with an Osage chief or war captain to dine or sup with us," he added, "and very often are favored with the company of the princesses and young ladies of rank, decked out in all the finery of beads, red ribbons and vermillion, silver ornaments and scarlet blankets."

Start your visit with a walk through the museum, which outlines the post's operations. A showcase displays items recovered during archaeological excavations at the site, including building materials, tools, household furnishings, and personal items. There's also an exhibit detailing the history of the U.S. Army at Fort Osage. A new education center will debut at the fort in 2004.

Fort Osage, Missouri.

Next stroll the grounds and visit some of the restored buildings. Authentically attired living-history interpreters are frequently on hand to describe what life was like during Fort Osage's heyday. Reproductions of trade-era goods, including tin wear, beads, buttons, tin whistles, lanterns, and more, are available for purchase in the factory.

Fort Osage stages several special events each year, including the Spring Flint Knap-In (held in mid-May), Independence Day festivities on the Fourth of July, Children's Day in midsummer, a rendezvous and trade fair in early September, and a Christmas Frontier Open House in early December. An annual calendar of events is published each March. For more information call (816) 650–5737 or visit www.historicfortosage.com.

The Fort Osage admission fee is $3.00 for adults and $2.00 for youth and seniors; children under five are admitted free. The site is open from 9:00 A.M. to 4:30 P.M. Wednesday through Sunday mid-April through mid-November and weekends only the rest of the year. Stop at the visitor center to buy tickets before proceeding onto the actual fort reconstruction.

Picnic grounds are available both at Fort Osage and at nearby Hayes Park, which also has a playground. A honey farm and several orchards in the vicinity welcome visitors.

KANSAS CITY

Lewis and Clark didn't spend a lot of time in what is now Kansas City. They reached the area on June 26, 1804, camping near the confluence of the Missouri and Kansas Rivers, and returned on September 15, 1806, just days before arriving back in St. Louis. Kansas City's tribute to the Corps of Discovery rests high atop a bluff at Eighth and Jefferson, at a small park known as Lewis and Clark Point.

The park may be small, but the monument unveiled there in 2000 is impressive indeed. Sculptor Eugene Daub's tribute to Lewis, Clark, Sacagawea (her infant Pomp sleeping on her back), and York is rich in detail: Check out the compass in Clark's hand and Sacagawea's basket of roots. At about 18 feet high, this is the largest monument to the expedition now in existence.

Another spot worth a visit is the Discovery Center, a joint project of the Missouri Department of Conservation and the Missouri Department of Natural Resources. This urban nature learning center has Lewis and Clark and the Corps of Discovery as its "hosts." Small groups can schedule time in any of six workshop rooms featuring specific outdoors-oriented activities. For example, corps carpenter Patrick Gass is the emblem for "Woodworking for Wildlife," where bird feeders and nesting boxes can be built, while Lewis presides over "Nature's Palette," where workshop participants learn to interpret nature through art and journal-keeping. But even drop-in visitors can enjoy such sights as Michael Haynes's mural of Kaw Point (the confluence of the Missouri and Kansas Rivers), thirty-seven acres of gardens, and the environmentally friendly building itself, built largely from recycled materials. The center, located at 4750 Troost, is open from 8:00 A.M. to 5:00 P.M. Monday through Saturday (Thursday until 9:00 P.M.) and 1:00 to 5:00 P.M. Sunday. Call (816) 759–7300 for more information.

Kansas City Travel Tips

Kansas City International (MCI), sometimes called KCI, is the main airport for Kansas City. It's located 17 miles northwest of downtown via Interstate 29 or 435 and is served by most major airlines. Visit www.kcairports.com for more information. The local Amtrak station is at 2200 Main Street, and the Greyhound bus depot is at 1101 Troost.

For information on routes served by The Metro, Kansas City's local bus service, check www.kcata.org, or call (816) 221–0660.

Kansas City–Area Attractions

With its fine architecture, broad boulevards, and European-style gardens and fountains, Kansas City often surprises visitors who expect little more than an overgrown cow town. In fact, Kansas City is one of the Midwest's largest and most progressive metropolitan areas. Kansas City has plenty of great gathering spots. One of the hottest is the developing River Market area along East Fifth Street near downtown. Local boosters say the Saturday farmers' market here is the Midwest's largest. Nearby at 400 Grand, the *Arabia* Steamboat Museum features more than 200 tons of sunken treasure recovered from the nineteenth-century vessel. South of downtown, Union Station Kansas City features interactive fun at Science City.

Sports-crazy Kansas City doesn't limit itself to spectator events. The city hosts an abundance of recreational activities, including golf, swimming, horseback riding, boating, hiking, and tennis. Much of the activity centers around 1,772-acre Swope Park. Worlds of Fun and Oceans of Fun, two popular theme parks, are located 13 miles north of Kansas City on Interstate 35.

Culture plays in equally strong role in Kansas City. The Nelson-Atkins Museum of Art (Forty-fifth and Oak Streets) includes fifty-eight galleries and the largest collection of Henry Moore sculptures in the United States. Kansas City was home to artist Thomas Hart Benton, whose home may be toured at 3616 Belleview Avenue. Kansas City is world famous for its jazz scene, now documented at the American Jazz Museum at 1616 East Eighteenth Street and still going strong at clubs all around town.

Top shopping areas include Westport, where Kansas City began and where, westward-bound emigrants frequently outfitted themselves for their trips, and Country Club Plaza, the first planned shopping center in the United States. Antiques fans flock to Forty-fifth Street and State Line Road, a district with more than fifty antiques, arts, and crafts dealers. Crown Center, just south of downtown, is yet another place to shop, eat, and party

History buffs may also want to pay a visit to Kansas City's suburban neighbor to the east, Independence. The town served as a primary jumping-off spot for the Oregon Trail, the California Trail, and the Santa Fe Trail. All are described in detail at the National Frontier Trails Center, 318 West Pacific Avenue, which also has a major exhibit called "Blazing the Way West: From Lewis and Clark to Fur Traders and Trappers." The center is open 9:00 A.M. to 4:30 P.M. Monday through Saturday and 12:30 to 4:30 P.M. Sunday. Call (816) 325–7575 for more information.

Every Labor Day weekend, Independence stages Santa-Cali-Gon Days, a festival marking the city's role as "Queen City of the Trails." Independence was also the hometown of President Harry S Truman, and tours are available at several important sites, including the Truman Library and the home at 219 North Delaware Street, where Harry and Bess lived from their marriage in 1919 to his death in 1972.

For more information on Kansas City, write the Convention and Visitors Bureau of Greater Kansas City at 1100 Main Street, Suite 2550, Kansas City, Missouri 64105, call (800) 767–7700, or visit www.visitkc.com.

LEWIS AND CLARK STATE PARK AND WESTON BEND STATE PARK (MISSOURI)

From Kansas City, take Interstate 29/U.S. Highway 71 north to Missouri Highway 45 (exit 5), the route closest to the Missouri River. Lewis and Clark camped in the vicinity of Leavenworth, Kansas, on July 1, 1804, and September 13, 1806. Leavenworth is also known as the first incorporated town in the Kansas Territory and as site of Fort Leavenworth, an outpost traversed by branches of the Oregon and Santa Fe Trails in the mid-1800s. The town remains a major military community, and the Frontier Army Museum at the post offers a bit of Lewis and Clark interpretation, including a handsome mural of the White Cliffs section of the Missouri River in Montana. Leavenworth also is home to one of the most famous prisons in the United States.

Lewis and Clark State Park, Missouri.

A short way upriver back on the Missouri side, the Show-Me State has two good riverside state parks, both accessible off MO 45. Weston Bend State Park mostly occupies the bluffs high above the Missouri River. A scenic overlook offers a fine vantage point for sunsets. Farther north on MO 45, Lewis and Clark State Park ranks as one of Missouri's smaller state parks. Nevertheless, it is blessed with the presence of a sandy beach and a 365-acre lake popular for fishing, swimming, boating, and water-skiing.

Sugar Lake—called Gosling Lake by Lewis and Clark—is a good example of an oxbow lake, a phenomenon seen up and down the banks of the Missouri River. Oxbow lakes are formed by abandoned floodplain meanders. A thousand or more years ago, the river meandered over a wide valley, creating vast wetlands. Constant riverbed erosion during flooding deepened the main channel, gradually isolating bends, or oxbows. Eventually the oxbows lost all but flood-level contact with the river, creating shallow lakes. Modern-day flood-control measures continue to isolate these oxbow lakes.

Lewis and Clark State Park has a seventy-site campground, with facilities that include hot showers, a laundry room, dump station, and playground. Sugar Lake is known for its bass, bluegill, channel catfish, carp, and buffalo fish. For more information call (816) 579–5564.

The town of Weston was a thriving port town from its founding in 1837 until a flood moved the Missouri River a mile away in the late nineteenth century. Weston went through some tough times, its 1853 population of 5,000 dropping to 1,000 by 1890. But in recent years Weston has made a new name for itself through historic preservation and a charming little downtown shopping district. A Lewis and Clark campsite marker at the foot of Main Street shows where the river once ran.

Weston is also noted for its excellent limestone springs. Lewis and Clark paused to enjoy the water in 1804, and by the 1830s the springs were a popular stopping place for wagons heading west. One of those who stopped was Benjamin J. Holladay, who settled in the area in 1838. Realizing that the limestone water, free of acid and iron, was perfect for making whisky, Holladay opened a distillery in 1856. The McCormick Distilling Company, as it is known today, is still in operation.

INDEPENDENCE CREEK (KANSAS)

From Lewis and Clark State Park, it's a short drive to Atchison, Kansas, where the Corps of Discovery spent the first of three Fourth of Julys on their two-and-a-half-year trip. The town of Atchison marks the occasion at Independence Park on the city's riverfront. A sign there reads: "The Lewis and Clark Expedition passed this area on July 4, 1804. They camped north of here at the mouth of a

Independence Creek Region

IOWA

MISSOURI

AUBURN

136

75 67

73

NEBRASKA

KANSAS

159

Brownville State Recreation Area

Indian Cave State Park

29

Missouri River

Independence Creek

ST. JOSEPH

59

ATCHISON

Lewis & Clark State Park

45

35

Fort Osage

TOPEKA

KANSAS CITY

BUCKNER

70

LAWRENCE

0   10   20 miles

creek which they named Independence Creek, in honor of the day. They cele-brated 'by an evening gun and an additional gill of whisky to the men.'" Lewis and Clark also named Fourth of July Creek in present-day Atchison. Clark, in his journal, remarked that "as we approached this place the prairie had a most beautiful appearance, hills and valleys interspersed with copses of timber gave a pleasing diversity of the scenery."

Atchison will mark both the Lewis and Clark Bicentennial and its own sesquicentennial in 2004 and plans to have several new attractions in place by then, including a riverfront plaza and a designated biking/hiking/driving route to Independence Creek. Due to channelization, the creek is no longer where the expedition saw it in 1804, but you can get close. From the center of town, take Second Street north for about 4 miles, then turn right on 314th Road and drive east about 1 mile until you reach Independence Creek. The designated loop between Atchison and Independence Creek will also have a spur to Benedictine Bottoms, a wetlands area used by Benedictine College as a biodiversity laboratory.

For more local directions stop at the Atchison Visitor Information Center in the restored Santa Fe rail depot at 200 South Tenth Street, where you'll also find some Lewis and Clark displays. The depot is also the departure point for the Atchison Trolley, which offers forty-five-minute narrated tours of the city during the summer. The cost is $4.00 per person ($2.00 for children ages four to twelve). Or you can pick up the visitor guide and self-guiding map brochure that features the city's impressive Victorian-era architecture—more than twenty sites in all, including the Amelia Earhart Birthplace Museum at 223 North Terrace Street.

The International Forest of Friendship is another popular attraction, honoring people from all over the world who have contributed to aviation and space travel. The park's centerpiece is a tree grown from a sycamore seed taken to the moon on Apollo 14. Atchison has a community theater, outdoor downtown shopping mall, hiking trails, and more than twenty-five city lakes. For more information call (800) 234-1854 or visit www.atchison.org.

From Atchison, cross the Missouri River back to Missouri and follow U.S. Highway 59 to St. Joseph, where the Pony Express was headquartered during its brief existence, 1860–1861. Two main sites interpret the "lightning mail" system: the Patee House Museum at Twelfth and Penn and the Pony Express Museum at 914 Penn Street. Other popular museums include the St. Joseph Museum at Eleventh and Charles (which has Lewis and Clark exhibits) and the Albrecht-Kemper Museum of Art at 2818 Frederick Boulevard. Get back on Interstate 29 (via I–229 out of St. Joseph) to head north into Iowa.

Alternatively, head north from Atchison on Kansas Highway 7 or U.S. 73. These scenic routes run north into Nebraska, traversing the Sac, Fox, and Iowa Indian reservations and a lot of pretty prairie country.

Lodging

Lodgings, campgrounds, and restaurants listed below are a representative sampling of what is available. Listing in these pages does not imply endorsement, nor is this a complete listing of all reputable businesses. For more complete listings contact the visitor information bureau or chamber of commerce in each town. Room rates were accurate as of summer 2002 but are subject to change.

ALTON, ILLINOIS
Comfort Inn, (618) 465–9999, 11 Crossroads Court; $75–$85.
Super 8 Motel, (618) 465–8885, 1800 Homer Adams Parkway; $60–$70.

GREATER ST. LOUIS/ST. CHARLES, MISSOURI
Adams Mark St. Louis, (314) 241–7400, Fourth & Chestnut Streets; $150–$200.
Baymont Inn, (636) 946–6936, 1425 South Fifth Street (St. Charles); $75–$85.

(continued)

Independence Creek, north of Atchison, Kansas, is a beautiful spot along the trail.

Best Inns of America, (618) 397–3300, I–64 and IL 157 (Caseyville, Illinois); $60–$80.

Boone's Lick Trail Bed & Breakfast, (636) 947–7000, 1000 South Main Street (St. Charles); $105–$175.

Drury Plaza, (314) 231–3003, 14 South Fourth Street; $135–$175.

Hampton Inn—St. Louis Airport, (314) 427–3400, I–70 exit 236; $90–$120.

Holiday Inn—Forest Park, (314) 645–0700, 5915 Wilson Avenue; $120–$150.

Hostelling International—The Huckleberry Finn Youth Hostel, (314) 241–0076, 1904-08 South Twelfth Street; $15/bed.

Lococo House II Bed & Breakfast, (636) 946–0619, 1309 North Fifth Street (St. Charles); $80–$95.

Travelodge at the Airport, (314) 890–9000, 9645 Natural Bridge Road; $65–$75.

WASHINGTON, MISSOURI

Lewis and Clark Inn, (636) 239–0111, 500 Highway 100 East; $60–$70.

Schwegmann House Bed & Breakfast Inn, (800) 949–2262, 438 West Front Street; $110–$175.

DEFIANCE, MISSOURI

Parsons House Bed & Breakfast, (800) 355–6878, on the Katy Trail; $95 and up.

HERMANN, MISSOURI

Captain Wohlt Inn Bed & Breakfast, (573) 486–3357, 123 East Third Street; $70–$150.

Hermann Motel, (573) 486–3131, 112 East Tenth Street; $65–$75.

JEFFERSON CITY, MISSOURI

Best Western Inn, (573) 635–4175, 1937 Christy Drive; $65–$75.

Hotel DeVille, (573) 636–5231, 319 West Miller Street; $80–$110.

Ramada Inn, (573) 635–7171, 1510 Jefferson Street; $70–$80.

COLUMBIA, MISSOURI

Best Western Columbia Inn, (800) 362–3185, 3100 I–70 Drive Southeast; $60–$90.

Drury Inn, (573) 445–1800, 1000 Knipp Street; $95–$115.

Eastwood Motel, (573) 443–8793, 2518 Business Loop 70 East; $38–$45.

Red Roof Inn, (573) 442–0145, 201 East Texas Avenue; $50–$70.

ROCHEPORT, MISSOURI

School House Bed & Breakfast, (573) 698–2022, 504 Third Street; $95–$225.

Katy O'Neil Bed & Bikefest, (573) 698–2453, 101 Lewis Street, on the Katy Trail; $40–$105.

NEW FRANKLIN, MISSOURI

Rivercene Bed-and-Breakfast, (660) 848–2497, 127 County Road 463; $95–$160.

BOONVILLE, MISSOURI

Comfort Inn, (660) 882–5317, I–70 exit 101; $65–$75.

Morgan Street Repose Bed & Breakfast, (660) 882–7195, 607 East Morgan Street; $75–$110.

ARROW ROCK, MISSOURI

Borgman's Bed & Breakfast, (660) 837–3350; $55–$60.

Down Over Inn Bed & Breakfast, (660) 837–3268; $65–$95.

GREATER KANSAS CITY, MISSOURI/KANSAS

American Inn, (800) 905–6343, 4141 South Noland Road (Independence); $40–$70.

Budget Host Inn, (816) 373–7500, 15014 East Highway 40 (Independence); $50–$55.

Holiday Inn Citi Centre, (816) 471–1333, 1215 Wyandotte Street; $130–$150.

Homestead Studio Suites, (816) 531–2212, 4535 Main Street; $70–$80.

Hyatt Regency Crown Center, (816) 421–1234, 2345 McGee; $140–$275.

Quarterage Hotel, (800) 942–4233, 560 Westport Road; $120–$180.

Sleep Inn, (816) 224–1199, I–70 exit 20 (Blue Springs); $55–$80.

Woodstock Inn Bed & Breakfast, (816) 833–2233, 1212 West Lexington Avenue (Independence); $75–$190.

LEAVENWORTH, KANSAS
Prairie Queen Bed & Breakfast, (913) 758–1959, 221 Arch Street; $125–$140.

WESTON, MISSOURI
Benner House Bed & Breakfast, (816) 640–2616, 645 Main Street; $90–$120.

ATCHISON, KANSAS
Comfort Inn, (913) 367–7666, 509 South Ninth Street; $45–$60.

St. Martin's Bed & Breakfast, (877) 367–4964, 324 Santa Fe Street; $75–$95.

ST. JOSEPH, MISSOURI
Days Inn, (816) 279–1671, I–29 exit 47; $55–$70.

Drury Inn, (816) 364–4700, I–29 exit 47; $65–$95.

Pony Express Motor Inn, (816) 233–3194, I–29 exit 47; $37–$47.

ROCK PORT, MISSOURI
Rock Port Inn, (660) 744–6282, I–29 exit 110; $45–$55.

Camping

GREATER ST. LOUIS, MISSOURI/ILLINOIS
Babler Memorial State Park, (636) 458–3813, 20 miles west via MO 100 and MO 109.

North Greater St. Louis KOA, (618) 931–5160, 3157 West Chain of Rocks Road (Granite City, Illinois).

St. Louis RV Park, (800) 878–3330, 900 North Jefferson Avenue (downtown).

ST. CHARLES, MISSOURI
Sundermeier RV Park, (636) 940–0111, 111 Transit Street.

HERMANN, MISSOURI
Hermann City Park, (573) 486–5953, junction of MO 19 and MO 100.

COLUMBIA, MISSOURI
Finger Lakes State Park, (573) 443–5315, 10 miles north via U.S. 63.

NEW FRANKLIN, MISSOURI
Katy Roundhouse, (660) 848–2232, 1893 Katy Drive.

ARROW ROCK, MISSOURI
Arrow Rock State Historic Site, (660) 837–3330.

MARSHALL, MISSOURI
Van Meter State Park, (660) 886–7537, 12 miles northwest of Marshall via MO 122.

GREATER KANSAS CITY, MISSOURI/KANSAS
Basswood Country RV Resort, (816) 858–5556, 15880 Interurban Road (Platte City).

Kansas City East KOA, (816) 690–6660, I–70 exit 28 (Oak Grove).

Trailside Campers Inn of K.C., (816) 229–2267, I–70 exit 24 (Grain Valley).

WESTON, MISSOURI
Weston Bend State Park, (816)
640–5443, MO 45.

RUSHVILLE, MISSOURI
Lewis and Clark State Park, (816)
579–5564, 801 Lake Crest Boulevard.

ATCHISON, KANSAS
Warnock Lake, (913) 367–4179, City of
Atchison.

ST. JOSEPH, MISSOURI
Walnut Grove Campground, (816)
233–1974, I–29 exit 53.

ROCK PORT, MISSOURI
KOA—Rock Port, (660) 744–5485, I–29
exit 110.

Restaurants

ALTON, ILLINOIS
Don & Penny's, (618) 465–9823, 306
State Street. Mexican, Italian, and Cajun
fare.
Tony's Restaurant and Lounge, (618)
462–8384, 312 Piasa. Steaks, chops, and
Italian specialties.

GRAFTON, ILLINOIS
The Loading Dock, (618) 786–3494, on
the Grafton riverfront. Open mid-April
through October.

**GREATER ST. LOUIS/ST. CHARLES,
MISSOURI**
Cardwell's, (314) 726–5055, 8100 Mary-
land Avenue (Clayton). Creative upscale
food. Closed Monday.
Eckert's Tavern, (636) 947–3000, 515
South Main Street (St. Charles). Dine in
historic building.
Imo's Pizza, (314) 644–5480, 1000
Hampton, near Forest Park. Local
favorite, with many locations.
Jake's Steaks, (314) 621–8184, 708
North Second Street. Steaks with a
Southwestern flair.
Lewis and Clark's, (636) 947–3334, 217
South Main (St. Charles). Contemporary
menu, open-air dining on upper floors.

Meriwether's, (314) 361–7313, in the
Missouri History Museum. Daily lunch,
Sunday brunch.
Norton's Cafe, (314) 436–0828, 808
Geyer. Cajun and Creole specialties.
Trainwreck on the Landing, (314)
436–1006, 720 North First Street. Ostrich
burgers, sweet potato fries, other un-
usual pub fare.

WASHINGTON, MISSOURI
American Bounty Restaurant, (636)
390–2150, 430 West Front Street. Casual
fine dining with river view.
Char-Tony's Ristorante, (636) 239–2111,
116 West Front Street. Local favorite for
steaks, seafood, pasta.
Creamery Hill Cafe/Basket Case Deli,
(636) 239–7127, 323–A West Fifth Street.
Deli by day, fine dining at night.

NEW HAVEN, MISSOURI
Raymond's of New Haven, (573)
237–7100. 129 Front Street. Upscale dining.

HERMANN, MISSOURI
Vintage Restaurant, (573) 486–3479, at
Stone Hill Winery. Casual dining with
scenic hilltop view.

JEFFERSON CITY, MISSOURI
Das Stein Haus, (573) 634–3869, 1436 Southridge Drive. German food.
Madison's Cafe, (573) 634–2988, 216 Madison. Casual dining featuring homemade pastas.

COLUMBIA, MISSOURI
Boone Tavern & Restaurant, (573) 442–5123, 811 East Walnut. Outdoor dining, Sunday brunch.
Flat Branch Pub & Brewing, (573) 499–0400, 115 South Fifth Street. Handcrafted beer and full restaurant menu.
Jack's Gourmet Restaurant, (573) 449–3927, 1903 I–70 Business Loop 70E. Dinner club featuring steak and seafood.
Shakespeare's Pizza, (573) 449–2454, 225 South Ninth Street. Local favorite.

ROCHEPORT, MISSOURI
Abigail's, (573) 698–3000, 206 Central Street. Lunch (11:00 A.M.–2:00 P.M.) and dinner (by reservation) Wednesday through Sunday.
Les Bourgeois Winegarden & Bistro, (573) 698–2300. Blufftop dining overlooking Missouri River.
Trailside Cafe, (573) 698–2702, Katy trailhead. Sandwiches and baked goods.

ARROW ROCK, MISSOURI
The Evergreen Restaurant, (660) 837–3251, MO 41. Fine dining in restored 1840s home.
Schoolhouse Cafe, (660) 837–3331, Eighth and Main. Homemade breakfast and lunch specialties.

GREATER KANSAS CITY, MISSOURI/KANSAS
Gates Barbecue, (816) 753–0828, 3201 Main and five other locations. Often voted KC's best.

Grand St. Cafe, (816) 561–8000, 4740 Grand Street. Seafood specials, contemporary cuisine.
Milano, (816) 426–1130, 2450 Grand Avenue in Crown Center. Casual Italian dining.
Ophelia's, (816) 461–4525, 201 North Main (Independence). Fine dining.
Stephenson's Apple Farm Restaurant, (816) 373–5400, I–70 exit 14 (Independence). Country atmosphere.
Union Cafe at Union Station, (816) 300–2233, 30 West Pershing. Pizza, seafood, Sunday brunch.

WESTON, MISSOURI
America Bowman Restaurant, (816) 640–5235, 520 Welt. Traditional Irish dishes.

ATCHISON, KANSAS
Jerry's Again, (913) 367–0577, 125 North Fifth Street. Ribs, steak, catfish.
The River House, (913) 367–3330, 101 Commercial Street. Casual fine dining with a river view.
Paolucci Restaurant and Lounge, (913) 367–6105, 113 South Third Street. Italian-American cuisine.

ST. JOSEPH, MISSOURI
Frederick Inn Steak House, (816) 364–5151, 1627 Frederick Avenue. Casual dining. Closed Sunday.
Sunset Grill, (816) 364–6500, 4012 River Road. Pasta, seafood, steaks.

ROCK PORT, MISSOURI
Trail's End Restaurant, (816) 744–6389, I–29 exit 110. Open twenty-four hours.

4

Nebraska, Iowa, and South Dakota

This scenery already rich pleasing and beautiful was still further heightened by immense herds of buffalo, deer, elk, and antelopes which we saw in every direction feeding on the hills and plains. I do not think I exaggerate when I estimate the number of buffalo which could be (comprehended) at one view to amount to 3,000.

—MERIWETHER LEWIS, SEPTEMBER 17, 1804, NEAR PRESENT-DAY CHAMBERLAIN, SOUTH DAKOTA.

INDIAN CAVE STATE PARK — BROWNVILLE STATE RECREATION AREA

Summer on the Missouri River can be an unpredictable time, as the Corps of Discovery learned in July 1804. One day the men would be in danger of sunstroke. The next they'd be shivering through a thunderstorm. Clark described a typically atypical summer day, July 14, like this: "Some hard showers of rain this morning prevented our setting out until 7 o'clock. At half past seven, the atmosphere became suddenly darkened by a black and dismal-looking cloud . . . in this situation the storm which passed over an open plain from the northeast struck the (our) boat on the starboard quarter, and would have thrown her up on the sand island dashed to pieces in an instant, had not the party leaped out

The Missouri River from Indian Cave State Park, Nebraska.

on the leeward side and kept her off with the assistance of the anchor and cable until the storm was over. . . . In this situation we continued about 40 minutes when the storm suddenly ceased and the river became instantaneously as smooth as glass."

The episode Clark described took place near present-day Indian Cave State Park in southeast Nebraska. This heavily wooded park offers a smorgasbord of pursuits, with something to interest everyone. Twenty miles of trails wind through the park, with many backpacking campsites and nine Adirondack-style shelters with three sides and a roof. These are first-come, first-serve. Other activities include RV camping, guided hour-long horseback rides, weekend living history programs, bison barbecues, and boat rides. There's a fine Missouri River view from the park's scenic overlook. The park is especially stunning in fall, when the trees blaze with color. Indian Cave State Park is east of Nebraska Highway 67 via Nebraska South 64 East north of Shubert. For more information call (402) 883–2575.

Moving upriver, the corps approached present-day Brownville, Nebraska. Brownville has a population of only about 150 people, but it frequently has several times that many visitors. Many come to trace the past at Brownville State Recreation Area. A historical marker at the site notes that on July 15, 1804, Lewis and Clark camped south of here on the northeast side of the river after traveling about 10 miles. The next morning the keelboat caught on a snag in the river; despite the delay, the corps made 20 miles that day. Clearly, the men were becoming expert boatmen.

The recreation area's centerpiece is the Meriwether Lewis Museum of Missouri River History and the *Meriwether Lewis,* a steam-powered U.S. Army Corps of Engineers vessel that is dry-docked within sight of the river. In its heyday, the *Meriwether Lewis* helped stabilize the Missouri for navigation starting in the 1930s. The boat remains pretty much as it was during its active career, and anyone who served on a similar craft would find it especially interesting. Tours are available, and there are plenty of exhibits, including a Missouri River Rat Hall of Fame and a former cabin filled with Lewis and Clark lore. Admission is $3.00 for adults and $1.00 for kids ages six through twelve. (Younger children are admitted free.) Hours are 10:00 A.M. to 5:30 P.M. daily June through August, with the same hours but on weekends only May and September.

Brownville State Recreation Area has a pleasant primitive campground in a grove of trees not far from the steamboat. (Some sites even command views of the old vessel through the trees.) There are only fourteen sites, and they tend to go quickly. The *Spirit of Brownville* paddle-wheel boat runs Memorial Day through Labor Day, with a variety of cruises. One-hour trips leave at 3:00 P.M. Saturday and Sunday and cost $6.95 for adults, $5.95 for senior citizens, and $3.95 for children. These feature a bit of Lewis and Clark lore plus compli-

Meriwether Lewis Museum of Missouri River History at Brownville, Nebraska.

mentary ice cream. Longer trips are available, including lunch and dinner trips and full-day runs to Indian Cave State Park. Call (402) 825–6441 for more information or reservations.

Brownville was settled in 1854, making it one of Nebraska's oldest communities. It's an interesting little town with its own concert hall and something happening almost every weekend all summer long, from the big flea market Memorial Day Weekend to repertory theater. The Brownville Methodist Church, oldest of its kind in Nebraska, still holds services every Sunday. Another local landmark, the Muir House, has a third-floor observatory. Several other fascinating buildings may be seen in the town's historic district, an area roughly bounded by First, Seventh, Nemaha, and Richard Streets.

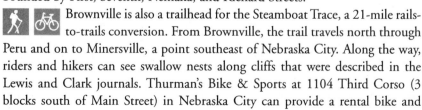 Brownville is also a trailhead for the Steamboat Trace, a 21-mile rails-to-trails conversion. From Brownville, the trail travels north through Peru and on to Minersville, a point southeast of Nebraska City. Along the way, riders and hikers can see swallow nests along cliffs that were described in the Lewis and Clark journals. Thurman's Bike & Sports at 1104 Third Corso (3 blocks south of Main Street) in Nebraska City can provide a rental bike and

transportation to and from the trailhead for $25 per person, which includes use of a cell phone. Bike rentals without the shuttle also are available for $12 per half day and $15 for a full day. For more information call (402) 873–7509.

From Brownville, travelers can cross the Missouri to access Interstate 29. Or continue west on U.S. Highway 136 to Auburn, known as southeast Nebraska's antiques capital with about thirty dealers. From Auburn, U.S. 75 heads north through the southeastern corner of the Cornhusker State, with lush, rolling green hills and prosperous-looking farms. Twenty-five miles north of Auburn, the highway reaches Nebraska City. This area is especially lovely in springtime when the apple trees are decked out in blossoms. By July 2004 the Missouri River Basin Lewis & Clark Interpretive Center will be open along Nebraska Highway 2 south of Nebraska City. Situated on seventy-nine acres of wooded bluffs above the river, the center will focus on the scientific discoveries made by the expedition. There will be a life-size keelboat replica and a "Great Hall of Animals" featuring mounts of species encountered by the corps. Plans also call for a connection to the Steamboat Trace trail as well as a separate walking trail that will tell—in microcosm—of the explorers' journey from the Mississippi River to the Pacific Ocean. For updates on the center's progress, contact the Nebraska City Chamber of Commerce at (800) 514–9113, ext. 400, or visit www. nebraskacity.com. Nebraska City's other attractions include Arbor Lodge State Historical Park and the Morton Orchard and Tree Farm, both of which commemorate the life of J. Sterling Morton, the founder of Arbor Day.

OMAHA, COUNCIL BLUFFS, AND FORT ATKINSON

Lewis and Clark conducted their first council with a Native American tribe at a Nebraska site called Council Bluffs, not to be confused with the Iowa city of the same name. Early in August 1804, the captains met with a group of Oto and Missouri Indians at the site about 15 miles north of downtown Omaha. Fort Atkinson State Historical Park marks the site today, but before heading there, visitors may want to stop to see several points of interest in the Omaha–Council Bluffs area.

The Western Historic Trails Center, located about 0.5 mile south of Interstate 80 exit 1-B in Council Bluffs, ranks among the most inventive interpretive sites along the Lewis and Clark Trail. Unusual painted three-dimensional aluminum sculptures detail the Lewis and Clark Expedition as well as the Mormon, Oregon, and California Trails. A short film in the museum theater contrasts nineteenth-century travel with the road trips of today. Before departing, visitors are asked to send the center a postcard later from their own travels along any of

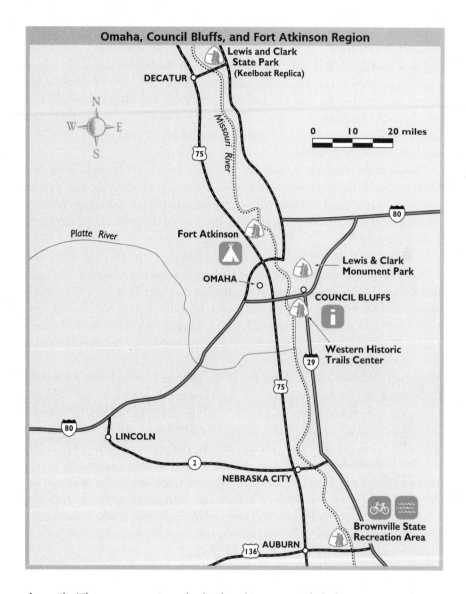

Omaha, Council Bluffs, and Fort Atkinson Region

the trails. These are prominently displayed in a two-sided glass case near the entrance, and they're lots of fun to read.

A 0.5-mile path leads to the nearby Missouri River banks. In addition, trails lead to Lake Manawa, near the site of the expedition's July 22–26 "White Catfish Camp," reenacted at a living-history festival each July, and to the Wabash Trace (see Touring Omaha–Council Bluffs). The trails center also includes a very good gift shop and Iowa travel information center. Hours are 9:00 A.M. to 6:00 P.M. daily from May 1 through September 30, and 9:00 A.M. to 5:00 P.M. daily the rest of the year except Thanksgiving, Christmas, and New

Year's Day. Admission is free, but donations are welcome. Call (712) 366–4900 for more information.

Next visit Lewis & Clark Monument Park on the hillside north of Council Bluffs. The stone-plaza monument offers an outstanding view of the Missouri River and Omaha; the city of Council Bluffs is all but obscured by the lush woods cascading down the hillsides. The site is a favorite with red-tailed hawks, which are often seen riding the thermals above the bluffs. It's a splendid place for a picnic, especially at sunset.

To get to the overlook, take North Sixteenth Street and turn right at the sign for Big Lake Park. Drive beneath a railroad trestle into the park and skirt its edges on the road. Past a second railroad trestle, turn left on North Eighth Street. After about 0.3 mile, turn left again. The entrance to the park is 0.7 mile up the hill on the left.

Omaha's N. P. Dodge Park also pays tribute to the corps' first encounter with a native people. A small plaque in the parking lot near the camping area notes that the expedition camped just across the river. Dodge Park has plenty of big grassy areas for a variety of sports, as well as a bridle trail, horse camping area, boat ramp, and RV dump station. To get to Dodge Park from Council Bluffs, take I–29 north, then I–680 west over the Mormon Bridge, and then follow the signs to the park.

Fort Atkinson is located just east of the town of Fort Calhoun, a few miles north of Omaha along U.S. 75. Archaeological crews from the Nebraska Historical Society conducted digs at the site during the 1950s, hoping to establish the location of the fort's walls, gates, and outbuildings. All records at the fort indicated it was the site of the Indian council. But sometime after 1827, when the fort was decommissioned, the Missouri River shifted course and is now about 3 miles east of the original bluff. Moreover, the face of the land is much different now than it was nearly 200 years ago, with scrub trees and brush covering the face of the bluffs, and it is impossible to tell exactly where the council was held. Still, one can walk the grounds secure in the knowledge it was near here the first momentous encounter took place.

For a while it looked as though the council was not to be. In late July, camped to the south near the Platte River, Drouillard and Cruzatte went out in search of the Indians, only to learn the Otos had moved onto the plains for their annual buffalo hunt. Dejected, the explorers moved upriver. But just a few days later, Drouillard located a Missouri Indian who said that while most of the Otos were off on the buffalo hunt, a hundred or so Indians were camped nearby. On July 29, the captains sent one of the French boatmen, Liberte, with the Missouri Indian to locate the Indians and invite them to council.

The Corps of Discovery moved upriver, arriving at the bluff on July 30. Captains Lewis and Clark walked up the bluff together and marveled at a landscape far different from any they'd yet seen. "This prairie is covered with grass of 10 or

Touring Omaha–Council Bluffs

With a population of about 700,000 people, Omaha–Council Bluffs is the last major metropolitan area near the Lewis and Clark Trail until Portland, Oregon. It offers quite a lot in the way of recreation, visitor attractions, culture, and shopping.

The Joslyn Art Museum, 2200 Dodge Street, is one of the Midwest's best. Housed in a marble Art Deco building, the Joslyn's collections include works from ancient Greece and Egypt and from the European masters. It may be best known, however, for its outstanding collection of art depicting the American West, especially the work of Swiss artist Karl Bodmer.

Bodmer's work is of great interest to Lewis and Clark buffs chiefly for its depiction of the Upper Missouri, a region the artist traversed with his boss, Alexander Phillip Maximilian, Prince of Wied, on the steamboat *Yellow Stone*, in the 1830s. Bodmer's paintings depict in image much of what Lewis and Clark noted in their journals thirty years earlier. The museum also holds a set of maps that William Clark had copied for Maximilian's use.

The Henry Doorly Zoo, another popular Omaha attraction, is located at Deer Park Boulevard and South Tenth Street. Zoo highlights include a huge open-air aviary and the Lied Jungle, stocked with rain forest plants, animals, birds, and fish from Asia, Africa, and South America. A children's petting zoo, aquarium, educational center, and steam train ride are also among the exhibits and activities.

Omaha is at its liveliest in the Old Market area, which is centered around Howard and Eleventh Streets downtown. The area throngs with people every evening after work and on the weekends. Incidentally, the National Park Service's Lewis & Clark National Historic Trail's office is at 1026 Dodge Street near the Old Market, and visitors are welcome during regular business hours (8:00 A.M. to 4:30 P.M. weekdays except federal holidays).

North and east of the Old Market, the Gene Leahy Mall and Heartland of America Park are downtown Omaha's main outdoor gathering spots. The *General Marion* tour boat offers fifteen-minute rides around the 300-foot Heartland of America Fountain for $1.00, with sailings May through September. The Omaha–Council Bluffs area is developing an ambitious "Back-to-the-River" trail system that will ultimately offer bicycle and pedestrian access up and down the Missouri River. There already are many miles of paths in place along area creeks. Ask at area visitor centers for a copy of the *Paths of Discovery* map and brochure.

(continued)

Council Bluffs has several riverboat casinos and greyhound racing. Other Bluffs attractions include the RailsWest Railroad Museum at Sixteenth Avenue and South Main Street; the Golden Spike Monument at South Sixteenth Street and Ninth Avenue; and the Grenville M. Dodge Home at 605 Third Street, erected in 1869 by the Civil War general and railroad builder.

Council Bluffs is the northern terminus of the Wabash Trace Nature Trail, a 63-mile route through the Loess (pronounced "Luss") Hills of rural western Iowa, a rare land formation found only here and in China. The trailhead is behind Lewis Central School along U.S. 275 south of Iowa 92 in south Council Bluffs. For more information call Southwest Iowa Nature Trails at (712) 328–6836.

Annual events in the area include the Renaissance Faire of the Midlands, held the second weekend each June at Iowa Western Community College in Council Bluffs; the Phantasmagoric Arts Festival, held each August in Council Bluffs' Bayliss Park; and the Omaha Summer Arts Festival, also held each June. The Omaha Royals minor-league baseball team plays Pacific Coast League ball at Rosenblatt Stadium, which also is home to the NCAA College World Series each spring. For more information about Omaha, call (866) YES–OMAHA, visit www.visitomaha.com, or stop by the visitor center near I-80's Thirteenth Street exit. To learn more about Council Bluffs, stop by 7 North Sixth Street, visit www.councilbluffsiowa.com, or call (712) 325–1000.

12 inches in height, soil of good quality and at the distance of about a mile still farther back the country rises about 80 or 90 feet higher, and is one continued plain as far as can be seen," Clark wrote. "From the bluff on the second rise immediately above our camp, the most beautiful prospect of the river up and down and the country opposed presented itself which I ever beheld."

Back at camp, the men waited. The Indians finally arrived late on August 2, and the captains suggested they meet the next morning. Lewis, aided by Clark, stayed up late that night writing the first speech he would make to the Indians. It was an important occasion, the first instance in which the party would attempt to fulfill one of the principal orders set forth by President Jefferson. "In all your intercourse with the natives treat them in the most friendly and conciliatory manner which their own conduct will admit," Jefferson wrote. "Allay all jealousies as to the object of your journey, satisfy them of its innocence, make them acquainted with the position, extent, character, peaceable and commercial dispositions of the U.S., of our wish to be neighborly, friendly and useful to them, and of our dispositions to a commercial intercourse with them."

The next day Lewis told the Otos all that and more. In a long speech, he explained how the Missouri River was now controlled by the United States—the

Great Father in Washington—and that if the Indians honored that sovereignty, there would be good trading for all. The Indians followed with a speech of their own, "promising to pursue the advice and directions given them that they were happy to find that they had fathers which might be depended on," Clark wrote. The speeches were accompanied by gifts to the Otos, and by a demonstration of the corps' airgun, an example of new American technology that never failed to amaze the natives. It is true the captains were disappointed that they were unable to meet with the main chiefs of the Otos and Missouris. On the other hand, this first encounter with the Indians had gone smoothly. All in all, the council had to be considered a success.

Omaha Travel Tips

Omaha's Eppley Airfield (OMA) is served by about a dozen airlines. Rental cars are available from all the major companies. Omaha is on Amtrak's Chicago–to–West Coast California Zephyr line, with the station at 1003 South Ninth Street. Long-distance bus service is available form Greyhound at 1601 Jackson Street in Omaha.

Metro Area Transit runs extensive bus service in Omaha and a handful of routes in Council Bluffs. For schedule information call (402) 341–0800.

Soon visitors to Fort Atkinson will be greeted by a sculpture garden featuring statues of the captains, the Oto and Missouri chiefs, and the French interpreter who helped them communicate. Inside the visitor center, there's a videotape on the Louisiana Purchase and Lewis and Clark Expedition that can be shown on request. Another video details the fort's military history. Fort Atkinson served as an important outpost for frontier exploration and trapping until it was abandoned in 1827, replaced by Fort Leavenworth, which was better situated to protect traffic on the Santa Fe Trail.

A walking trail leads from the visitor center to the fort's reconstruction. The fort consisted of a rectangular formation of one-story barracks built from horizontal logs. The barracks opened out upon an enclosed parade ground. Other buildings included a large council house for negotiating with the Indians, a gristmill, a schoolhouse, and a brick kiln.

Fort Atkinson's visitor center is normally open daily Memorial Day weekend through Labor Day weekend from 9:00 A.M. to 5:00 P.M. During late April, May, September, and October, the visitor center is open weekends from 10:00 A.M. to 5:00 P.M. Living history days take place the first weekend of every month May through October. For more information call (402) 468–5611.

Fort Calhoun is a tiny town of small, neat houses and a few home-style restaurants. In addition to Fort Atkinson, Fort Calhoun is home to the Washington County Historical Museum. Three miles east of town, check out the hiking and biking trails and canoe access at Boyer Chute National Wildlife Refuge, which is adjacent to the bluff where the council was held. Another short drive north, you'll reach DeSoto National Wildlife Refuge, noted for great fishing and an exhibit on the wreck of the steamboat *Bertrand* in 1865. From the Omaha–Council Bluffs area, travel north on U.S. 75 (in Nebraska) or I–29 (in Iowa) to Onawa, Iowa, home of the Hawkeye State's version of Lewis and Clark State Park.

LEWIS AND CLARK STATE PARK (IOWA)

Although it is located along the Corps of Discovery's route, nothing really remarkable happened at the site Iowa's Lewis and Clark State Park. The expedition camped in the vicinity on August 10, 1804, on the far side near the present-day KOA campground. The site is worth a visit, however, because it is home to a full-scale replica of the expedition's keelboat, as well as its two pirogues.

The keelboat replica was designed and constructed by a group called the Friends of Discovery under the supervision of Butch Bouvier, a local woodwright, history aficionado, and boat buff. To create the replica Bouvier used both William Clark's drawings of the keelboat and his own research into early-nineteenth-century boatbuilding. Its hull was launched in 1987, and its deck, mast, sidewall lockers, and cabins were added later.

Today the full-scale boats are maintained by volunteers. In fact, visitors who stop by the park early in the season may find the "Friends" on the scene, doing maintenance on the project. The boats are usually on view from mid-May through August. The best time to visit, however, may be during the Lewis and Clark Festival the second weekend each June. Events include music and dancing, historical presentations, a buffalo burger feed, a black powder shoot, an art show, a fire-starting contest, and more.

Over the next few years, Lewis and Clark State Park hopes to build a visitor center to shelter and interpret the boats year-round. For now there's a temporary visitor center in a yurt near the waterfront. In addition, Bouvier frequently leads boat tours and boatbuilding classes. Visit his Web site at www.keelboat.com for more information.

Like its Missouri neighbor, Iowa's Lewis and Clark State Park rests on the shore of an oxbow lake. Blue Lake was part of the river in 1804 and now serves as nucleus of a state park that offers a campground with boat access, a beach, and good fishing opportunities. Picnic areas and hiking trails make the park a nice spot for day use, too. For more information call (712) 423–2829.

The town of Onawa is just east of the park. It boasts what is supposed to be the widest Main Street in America, a claim to fame celebrated the third Saturday

A keelboat replica brings the expedition to life at Lewis and Clark State Park near Onawa, Iowa.

in June with an old-fashioned dance, car show, and "cruise." Onawa also lures visitors with Casino Omaha, a twenty-four-hour gaming emporium stocked with hundreds of slot machines and a variety of tables.

BLACKBIRD HILL

From Onawa cross the toll bridge over the Missouri River into Nebraska and rejoin U.S. 75 at Decatur. Somewhere between here and Macy, 10 miles to the north, is Blackbird Hill, grave of the chief of the Omahas.

After the meeting at Council Bluffs, the Corps of Discovery once again started up the Missouri. It wasn't long before one of the privates, Moses Reed, requested permission to go back and retrieve a knife he said he'd left at the council site. Soon, however, it became apparent that Reed had deserted, the second man to do so in one week. Liberte, sent earlier to call the Otos to council, had also disappeared.

The captains sent a four-man search party to bring the deserters back. Meanwhile, the main party moved farther upriver in hopes of meeting the Omahas. On August 11, 1804, they came upon a mound about 300 feet high, marked at the top with a post. It was Blackbird's grave. Lewis, Clark, and ten of their men decided to climb up, have a look, and pay their respects—even if Blackbird was the sort of man who won tribute out of fear, not admiration. For a brief time the Omahas had enjoyed great power under Blackbird. He frequently used arsenic to poison his rivals, and by this and other means he and his tribe waged a war of terror over any party trying to pass through their country. Blackbird's reign was cut short when a smallpox epidemic swept through the Omaha village, reducing its population from 700 to no more than 300.

In Blackbird's day, and in the time of Lewis and Clark, Blackbird Hill offered a commanding view up and down about 70 miles of the Missouri River. These days timber growth has obscured what once was a fine view, and the site on the Omaha Indian Reservation is off-limits to the general public. But a road wayside area about 3.5 miles southeast of the actual site provides a similar hilltop view of the Missouri, along with interpretation of Omaha history. The overlook is situated along U.S. 75 about 2.5 miles north of Decatur.

View of Missouri River from Blackbird Hill wayside, Decatur, Nebraska.

The Omahas' earliest known home was the Ohio River Valley. Like Lewis and Clark after them, the Omaha people knew how tough it was to battle the Missouri upstream, and their name means "against the current." By 1700 the tribe had migrated to the Blood Run site about 100 miles north of the Blackbird Hill area and moved several more times around the vicinity before building their "Big Village" about 20 miles north of Blackbird Hill in 1775. Creation of this village (called "Tonwontongathon" in the Omaha language) coincided with Blackbird's rise to power.

A shelter at the site re-creates the look of an Omaha earth lodge, although, at just 30 feet in diameter, it would have been considered small. Many lodges spanned up to 60 feet in diameter, able to accommodate large families and their horses. The exhibit notes how two men of the Lewis and Clark Expedition—Pierre Cruzatte and Francois Labiche—were sons of Omaha mothers and thus began the tribe's long history of U.S. military service.

The Corps of Discovery located the main Omaha village August 14 and hoped for a council, but, again, the village was nearly deserted. Finally, on August 17, the search party returned with Reed in tow, accompanied by three Indian chiefs who had been traveling with Reed and who hoped to make peace with the Omahas. Liberte had been caught but got away.

Found guilty of desertion the next day, Reed was sentenced to run four times through a gauntlet of his peers, who beat him with willow switches. This shocked the visiting Indian chiefs, who "petitioned for pardon of this man," Clark wrote. But after the captains explained the necessity for such punishment, "they were all satisfied with the propriety of the sentence," Clark added. Afterward, the mood turned merrier as everyone celebrated Captain Lewis's thirtieth birthday with an extra measure of whisky and dancing.

Continue north on U.S 75 through some very pretty hill country. The Omaha Nation runs a bingo and casino hall located south of Macy, and the town is the site of the annual Omaha powwow the weekend nearest the full moon of August. Winnebago, 10 miles to the north, serves as headquarters for the Winnebago Indian Reservation. Its powwow takes place the last full weekend in July. Dakota City, just south of South Sioux City, Nebraska, has an aptly named park at Cottonwood Cove, with riverside picnic tables and a boat launch amid the tall trees.

SIOUX CITY AND SERGEANT FLOYD

It seems almost unbelievable that during twenty-eight months in the wilderness, facing everything from grizzly bears to rattlesnakes to extreme weather, only one member of the Lewis and Clark Expedition died. The Sergeant Floyd Monument in Sioux City pays tribute to that man.

The Omahas never returned to their village during the corps' brief respite there, so a council was held with the visiting Oto and Missouri chiefs on August 19. "We showed them many curiosities and the airgun which they were much astonished at," Clark wrote. But by the end of the day, the captains' attention had turned to Sergeant Charles Floyd, who was clearly very ill with what the captains believed was a bilious colic. "We attempt to relieve him without success as yet, he gets worse and we are much alarmed at his situation," Clark wrote. Modern doctors and historians believe Floyd actually suffered from an infected appendix—an ailment no doctor of the time could have cured.

On the morning of August 20, 1804, the corps proceeded upriver as usual. But by noon, Floyd had taken a turn for the worse. The party halted to prepare a warm bath for their colleague. But before it was ready, Floyd turned to Clark and said, "I'm going away. I want you to write a letter." Those were the sergeant's last words.

The corps saw another riverside bluff a mile or so away and decided it would be a fitting final resting place for their comrade. Floyd was wrapped in a blanket and carried to the hilltop. "We buried him with all the honors of war, and fixed a cedar post at his head with his name, title and day of the month and year," Clark wrote. "Captain Lewis read the funeral service over him." The bluff on which Floyd was buried was named after him, as was a small stream in the vicinity.

Over the next few decades, Sergeant Floyd's grave became something of a nineteenth-century tourist attraction. The corps visited on its way home in

View from the Sergeant Floyd Memorial at Sioux City, Iowa.

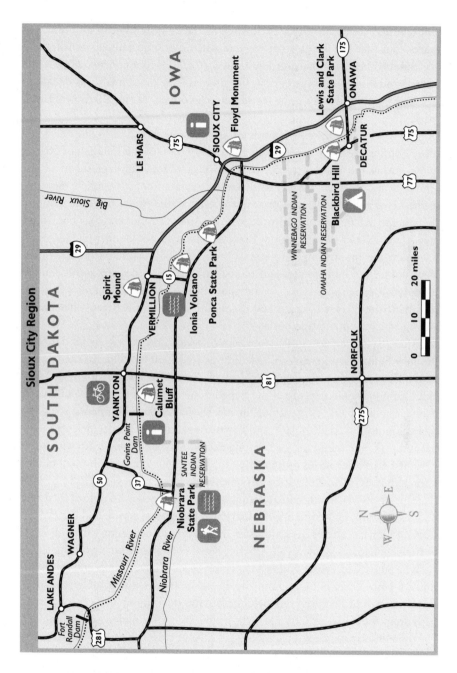

1806; later visitors probably included artists George Catlin and John Audubon and Prince Maximilian. According to Roy Appleman, author of a National Park Service guide to Lewis and Clark sites, an 1857 flood swept away part of the bluff, reportedly exposing some of poor Floyd's bones. The remains were rescued and reburied about 200 yards back from the face of the bluff in an unmarked grave—but that site was nearly forgotten when dirt from railroad construction was dumped nearby. Finally, in 1900 the current 100-foot concrete obelisk was erected and Floyd's remains once again interred. The monument was dedicated in 1901, the first site ever to be registered as an official National Historic Landmark.

To visit the site, travel 0.5 mile east and 0.5 mile north of I–29 exit 143. A plaque on the monument reads: "In commemoration of the Louisiana Purchase made during the administration of Thomas Jefferson, third president of the United States, April 3, 1803; of its successful exploration by the heroic members of the Lewis and Clark Expedition; of the valor of the American soldier; and of the enterprise, courage and fortitude of the American pioneer, to whom these great states west of the Mississippi River owe their secure foundation."

Below the monument, a rock wall provides a panoramic overlook. Today's view, dominated by highways and railroad tracks, isn't especially scenic, but an interpretive panel points out several spots of historic note, including the approximate site of Floyd's death and the mouth of the Floyd River, where Lewis and Clark camped after the burial.

After paying respects to Sergeant Floyd, head to the riverfront for a look at the new Sioux City Lewis & Clark Interpretive Center, which opened in fall 2002. This fine new center, with a theme of "Soldiering and Serving with Lewis and Clark: A Day in the Life of the Expedition," is a great stop for families and people who like hands-on history. Outside, check out the monumental sculpture by Pat Kennedy of Lewis, Clark, and Lewis's dog, Seaman. Inside, pick up a journal and make the rounds of the opening exhibit hall, where you learn what skills were necessary for various jobs on the expedition. The outer exhibit hall has interpretive areas on nineteenth-century medicine, Floyd's illness and its impact on the expedition (it's worth remembering that no one knew when Floyd died that he'd be the corps' only casualty), military life, the natural world, and the expedition's aftermath. There's also a theater showcasing a short film where an actor portraying Captain Clark recalls Charles Floyd's life and untimely death.

The Sioux City center is also notable for its impressive murals and for its admission cost: There is none. (You can thank local riverboat gamblers for that, since casino boat boarding fees help underwrite the center.) The center is open daily from 9:00 A.M. to 6:00 P.M. year-round except for major winter holidays. For more information call (712) 224–5242. Just across the parking lot from the center, look for the Sergeant Floyd Riverboat Museum and Welcome Center, where you can get more information on river history and area attractions. Both the Sioux City Lewis & Clark Interpretive Center and the Sergeant Floyd Welcome Center are located along Larsen Park Road (exit 149 off I–29).

Baseball fans may want to take in a game of the minor-league Sioux City Explorers, who play at Lewis and Clark Park on the city's south side. The Sioux

City Public Museum, located in a former mansion at 2901 Jackson Street, includes displays on anthropology, archaeology, natural history, science, and military memorabilia. In spring 2003, Sioux City's Southern Hills Mall at 4400 Sergeant Road unveiled *Lewis & Clark: An American Adventure.* This huge permanent mural, covering 296 feet, is located above the mall's center court and depicts the expedition from start to finish. For more information on area events and attractions, stop by the welcome center, call (800) 593–2228, or visit www.siouxlandchamber.com.

From Sioux City, continue north on I–29 to Vermillion, South Dakota, home of Spirit Mound. Somewhere near the town of Elk Point, the Corps of Discovery chose Patrick Gass to replace Charles Floyd as sergeant. A marker in the town's Heritage Park commemorates that event. A Lewis & Clark Heritage Days festival is held in Elk Point each August with living history reenactments, children's activities, and a buffalo supper. Also in this area, the Adams Homestead and Nature Preserve offers several miles of hiking and biking trails near the Missouri River. Take the I–29 McCook exit and follow the signs. The South Dakota Information Center at I–29 milepost 26.6 near Vermillion rents CD or audiotape travel tours of Lewis and Clark's route through the state.

SPIRIT MOUND

Day after day of upriver travel was hard enough, but sometimes the explorers couldn't resist the chance to take a hike away from the Missouri. By late August Lewis and Clark had heard the story of a hill much feared by the region's Native American tribes, who believed it was the residence of little spirit beings. "They are in human form with remarkable large heads, and about 18 inches high, that they are very watchful and armed with sharp arrows with which they can kill at a great distance; they are said to kill all persons who are so hardy as to attempt to approach the hill. . . . So much do the Omaha, Sioux, Otos and other neighboring nations believe this fable, that no consideration is sufficient to induce them to approach the hill," Clark wrote on August 24, 1804.

Of course Lewis and Clark figured they had to see the place for themselves, and they hiked to the mound on August 25. It was an oppressively hot day, and it took nearly three hours to reach the landmark. Lewis's dog, Seaman, collapsed on the way; he was almost joined by his master, who two days earlier had mildly poisoned himself while tasting the minerals of a bluff the party had encountered near Sioux City. But they finally made it and were rewarded not by death but by an inspiring view of the surrounding plains. Clark described it thus: "From the top of this mound we beheld a most beautiful landscape; numerous herds of buffalo were seen feeding in various directions; the Plain to the north-northwest and northeast extends without interruption as far as can be seen."

Spirit Mound near Vermillion, South Dakota.

The explorers concluded that it must have been the swirl of birds and insects on the mound that produced the Indian legends—that and the fact the mound did stand out quite remarkably from the surrounding landscape. They soon retreated to the Vermillion River where, hungry and thirsty, they found water and a variety of delicious fruits including grapes, plums, and currants.

Spirit Mound is still visible today, located along South Dakota 19 north of Vermillion. An interpretive sign is placed in view of the mound, but the landmark is well worth a closer look, mainly because it is one of just a few places along the Lewis and Clark Trail that today's traveler can know with certainty he or she is standing in the exact spot the explorers stood.

Long on private land, Spirit Mound was recently acquired by South Dakota Game, Fish and Parks, with help from the National Park Service. The site is being replanted with native grasses to restore it to its 1804 appearance. For years the mound was being eroded by a cattle feedlot, but preservation efforts are now ensuring that Spirit Mound will be an important site for the Lewis and Clark Bicentennial. Climb to the top and enjoy the beautiful view, and take care to leave this lovely spot as you find it.

Before heading to Spirit Mound, consider a stop at the W. H. Over Museum at 1110 Ratingen Street on the University of South Dakota campus in Vermillion, next to the Dakota Dome. The museum's Spirit Mound Learning and Information Center includes a mural of the expedition's trek to the hill and display cases with several early editions of the corps' journals. Interactive computer terminals tell of the expedition's travels in the region and help give Native American perspective on Spirit Mound. The museum is open daily except major holidays, with admission by donation.

Every August Vermillion holds a Spirit Mound Festival that's marked by a communal 6-mile reenactment of the hike from Vermillion to the landmark. Other festival highlights include historic food vendors, craft demonstrations, boat trips, and a Native American village. For more information on the event, call the Vermillion Area Chamber of Commerce at (800) 809–2071.

Vermillion is a pleasant college town of about 10,000 people. The South Dakota state legislature named Vermillion the site of the university in 1862, but classes weren't held until twenty years later. Vermillion was originally located closer to the river, but a big flood in 1881 forced the town to move atop the bluffs.

The local Lions club has established a public campground right along the business route on the edge of town; in addition to RV space, the park offers lots of shade trees and a playground for kids. Another park, Prentice Park, has a swimming pool with a water slide and a disc golf course. From Vermillion it's about a half-hour drive to Yankton on South Dakota Highway 50.

RIVERS AND LAKES: THE NEBRASKA–SOUTH DAKOTA BORDER

Two stretches of river along the Nebraska–South Dakota border still bear some resemblance to the river seen by Lewis and Clark. The river flows free from below Gavins Point Dam to near Sioux City and again from Fort Randall Dam to the mouth of the Niobrara River. Snags, sandbars, islands, eroding banks, and a merrily meandering channel all still exist in this area.

Public river access points are available at several places along these stretches. Nebraska ramps include those at Niobrara, Cedar County northeast of Wynot, and Ponca State Park. In South Dakota, public ramps can be found at Riverside Park in Yankton and Clay County Park near Vermillion. If you don't have watercraft of your own, several area outfitters stand ready to help you get out on the river.

Marlin Roth is a local boatman who grew up on the Mighty Mo and has been paddling the waterway for many years. His business, Missouri River Tours, rents canoes for $50 a day and can tailor trips and shuttle service to your needs. Roth also offers hour-long motorized "johnny boat" tours for $20 per person; highlights include a look at what Roth believes are giant prehistoric turtle fossils and beautiful chalk bluffs mentioned in the Lewis and Clark journals. Longer guided trips are available, as is free riverside RV or tent camping to anyone who books a boat trip. For information contact Roth (pronounced "Roath") at (402) 985–2216 or visit www.missouri-river-tours.com.

Stone Outdoor Adventures, a family-run business based in Yankton, runs a variety of short-term trips that are great for travelers who don't have much time or money but want to get at least a taste of canoeing the Missouri. Excursions include a one-hour paddle ($10.00 adults; kids ages five to ten $5.00); a half-day outing ($40; kids $20); a full-day float ($100 including lunch; $50 kids); and the overnight Discovery Journey ($150; kids $100). All trips go out in a 29-foot canoe that's a replica of the birch-bark boats used by the early fur traders. Longer trips and custom itineraries (including river weddings) are possible; ask for details. For more information call (603) 665–4169 or send e-mail inquiries and messages to stoneoutdoor@dtgnet.com.

Vermillion-based Missouri River Expeditions specializes in three-day sea kayaking trips May through September, covering 39 miles from Fort Randall Dam to Running Water, South Dakota. Paddlers enjoy gourmet-style meals and spend nights camped out along the river. Each year, several trips cater to special interests, including a bird-watching excursion in June and a stargazers' expedition in August during the Perseid meteor showers. Rates in 2002 were $230 per person ($150 for kids seventeen and under), which includes the paddling gear, guide service, and two meals a day. (Participants are asked to bring their own lunch and snacks, as well as some gear including a sleeping bag and camp chair.) For people who like paddling but prefer sleeping indoors, two-night bed-and-breakfast trips are available, as are dinner paddles; these all include gourmet meals and wine tasting. For more information and current prices, call (605) 360–2646 or visit www.missriverexp.com.

Nebraska's Niobrara State Park runs history and nature float trips regularly during the summer months. These two-and-a-half-hour trips feature easy paddling and plenty of interpretation on the area's human and natural history. Cost in 2002 was $12 for ages twelve and up and $10 for children ages six to twelve. Reservations are suggested; call (402) 857–3373 to sign up.

There's plenty of good land-based recreation and sight-seeing in the area, too. Upriver from Gavins Point Dam, the Missouri becomes Lewis and Clark Lake. The expedition camped from August 28 to September 1, 1804, on the bottomlands below Calumet Bluff on the Nebraska side and held a council with the friendly Yankton Sioux. (Pierre Dorion, who had joined the expedition on June 12, interpreted.) Today the area's shores teem with one campground, beach, and boat ramp after another. Most of the two million or so annual visitors have recreation on their minds, but it's also possible to find a healthy dose of history, notably at the Lewis & Clark Visitor Center, located on the Nebraska side of the river.

The center sits atop Calumet Bluff, and its focus is on the history of the Mis-

Missouri River bluffs near Wynot, Nebraska.

souri River. This is a great stop for kids, who can pull a rope to hear a steamboat whistle, try their hand at spinning a pilot wheel, examine natural specimens with a magnifying glass, or just pull up a big floor pillow and read awhile. Other exhibits share the story of the U.S. Army Corps of Engineers, which helped build everything from the Panama Canal to the six main stem dams of the Pick-Sloan project. Together, these dams—Gavins Point, Fort Randall, Big Bend, Oahe, Garrison, and Fort Peck—make up the nation's largest dam system, with storage capacity of about 22.5 trillion gallons. Gavins Point Dam was completed in 1957, and if all its spillway gates opened wide at once, the total flow would be 4.5 million gallons a second—enough to cover a football field in 14 feet of water in one second.

Slide presentations are shown daily, and tours of the dam are also available daily through the summer and by appointment the rest of the year. The visitor center is open seven days a week from 8:00 A.M. to 6:00 P.M. Sunday through Thursday and 8:00 A.M. to 9:00 P.M. Friday and Saturday Memorial Day through Labor Day. Hours vary the rest of the year. For more information call (402) 667–7873; ext. 3246. Picnic tables and several hiking trails are available outside on the bluff.

There are probably a thousand or more campsites surrounding Lewis and Clark Lake, but since they manage to fill up fast on many summer weekends, it's important to stake a place early. The campgrounds all look quite inviting, but in wet years they can be abuzz with annoying gnats and small black flies. The usual insect repellents seem to have little power over these cursed critters, but local park personnel say a dab of vanilla extract or a fabric-softener dryer sheet pinned to your clothing may ward them off for a while. Try that, or play it safe and find indoor accommodations.

Other than the insect swarms, this is a splendid area, flanked by heavily treed, rolling hills. A nature foot trail in the Gavins Unit of South Dakota's Lewis and Clark State Recreation Area leads to a commanding view of the Missouri River bluffs. An interpretive shelter imparts information on the expedition's travels through the area.

Yankton, South Dakota, is a good-sized town with many hotels and restaurants. Be sure to stop at 119 West Third Street downtown, where you'll find the national headquarters of LewisAndClarkTrail.com and a superb selection of Lewis and Clark–related souvenirs and bicentennial memorabilia in all price ranges. This is also a good spot to get updated information on traveling the trail as well as free Internet access.

Yankton has more than 30 miles of trails in and around town, including a paved 8-mile route out to the Lewis & Clark Lake recreation areas. Most of the trail is fairly flat, aside from a formidable hill just west of town. Lewis and Clark Marina just west of Gavins Point Dam rents and services boats for do-it-yourself sailors. Cottonwood Corral west of Yankton on South Dakota 52 also rents canoes and bicycles. The Yankton area's biggest annual events include Riverboat Days in mid-August and a Lewis & Clark Festival later in the month.

Lewis and Clark Lake on the Nebraska–South Dakota border.

It's a half-day's drive from Yankton to Pierre—South Dakota's capital and site of Lewis and Clark's fearsome confrontation with the Teton Sioux. Cross-country travelers in a hurry will probably want to make a beeline for Pierre via U.S. Highway 81, Interstate 90, and U.S. 83. Dawdlers, on the other hand, will relish some time on Nebraska 12, accessed by driving west from Sioux City or south via either South Dakota/Nebraska Highway 15 south from Vermillion or U.S. 81 south from Yankton. This route, once a favorite haunt of ne'er-do-wells including Jesse James, is also known as Nebraska's "Outlaw Trail" scenic byway. From east to west, towns along the way include:

■ **Ponca.** The Missouri National Recreational River Resource and Education Center is set to open in 2003 at Ponca State Park. The interpretive site focuses on the natural and cultural history of the Missouri River, which it overlooks from a bluff. Ponca State Park also has many weekend interpretive programs and activities, campsites and cabins (the latter can be—and often are—reserved up to a year in advance), a swimming pool, trail rides, a boat ramp, and more than 20 miles of trails for hiking and bicycling. Full-moon hikes are held April through October on the Saturday closest to the lunar event. Contact the park at (402) 755-2284 for more information.

■ **Newcastle.** An interpretive sign in the city park here tells of the

Where's Shannon?

Twelve communities in northeast Nebraska have developed a "Shannon Trail" to honor Private George Shannon, the youngest member of the expedition (until Sacagawea and her infant son joined in 1805, anyway).

Shannon was born in Pennsylvania in 1787. In late August 1804, he and George Drouillard were dispatched near present-day Yankton, South Dakota, to round up the expedition's pack horses, but Drouillard returned the following day saying that he could find neither the horses nor Shannon. Several men—including John Colter—were sent to look for him, to no avail. Shannon thought he had fallen behind the main party, but in fact he was traveling ahead and was reunited with the group more than two weeks later. Shannon may have been young, but he was an expert woodsman. Although he ran out of ammunition, he was able to survive on berries, grapes, and a rabbit he shot with a bullet made from a stick.

Modern travelers in the region can get a Shannon Trail passport and look for the dozen life-size, chainsaw-carved statues of the teenage explorer in these towns: Wynot, Hartington, Crofton, Lindy, Santee, Niobrara, Verdigre, Center, Winnetoon, Creighton, Bloomfield, and Wausa. Each statue sighting is worth a stamp from area businesses, and passports with all twelve stamps earn a prize. For more information visit shannontrail.cjb.net.

Ionia Volcano. Clark reported that a bluff near here felt hot to the touch, and later fur traders frequently noticed dense smoke and fire in the vicinity. Scientists later learned the heat was generated by oxidation of shale.

■ **Crofton.** This is the nearest Nebraska town to Gavins Point Dam and its Lewis & Clark Visitor Center, already described. Check out the Corps of Discovery Welcome Center along U.S. Highway 81, where you'll find a scenic overlook and interpretive displays, along with plenty of information on local activities and attractions.

■ **Niobrara.** In addition to the raft trips noted above, Niobrara State Park offers rental cabins atop the river bluffs (reserve well ahead), camping and picnicking, and excellent fishing. The Cramer interpretive shelter includes information on Lewis and Clark; from there a path leads to a pedestrian bridge crossing the Niobrara River and access to the Missouri River bottomlands. Other activities at the park include bicycling and guided trail rides.

■ **Lynch.** Near here on September 7, 1804, the expedition had its first encounter with the curious "barking squirrels," today known as prairie dogs. Private John Shields killed the first one they saw, and the captains ate it for dinner. But capturing another example to send back to President Jefferson proved much more difficult. Telling of the incident in his book *Lewis & Clark: Pioneering Naturalists,* Paul Russell Cutright wrote: "Having no further luck with their guns, they resorted to digging. After going down six feet and finding the runways seemed bottomless, they gave that up and tried flooding. This became a full-scale operation, with all members of the corps participating except a guard left with the boats. They spent a major portion of the day carrying water from the river and pouring it into the subterranean passageways. Though they persisted until nightfall, they succeeded in capturing only one, flushing it out alive. Clark had better luck a few days later. 'I killed four,' he reported, 'with a view to have their skins stuffed.'"

Clark called the place where all this happened "the Steeple"; later names have included the Tower and Baldy. The site is now on private land but can be seen along the county road north of Lynch, about 7 miles out of town. Plans call for more interpretation of the site to be in place by 2004. For now Lynch is capitalizing on the incident with soft, cuddly Lynch Dawgs—handmade plush prairie dogs, *not* the stuffed sort Clark envisioned! The Dawgs are the brainchild of an informal group of local women called the Lynch Ladies. They get together at least once a week to craft a new crop of critters, with proceeds supporting the local Lewis and Clark Bicentennial commemoration. Look for Dawgs for sale at local businesses (including Ponca Valley Oil Company at Fourth and Ponca Streets, which doubles as an informal local information center), or order one by mail for $23.25, including shipping, by calling (800) 337–2706.

From this area, there are two ways to cross the river back into South Dakota. Chief Standing Bear Memorial Bridge spans the river east of Niobrara, linking

Nebraska 14 and South Dakota 37. An interpretive area on the South Dakota side explains how the expedition, returning downriver in September 1806, met a group of Yankton Sioux whom they'd encountered two years before. Realizing they were old friends, the parties exchanged news and smoked pipes together before Lewis and Clark resumed their homeward journey. From the rest area, SD 37 heads north about 20 miles to meet SD 50 at Tyndall.

Alternatively, travelers can continue west from Lynch to U.S. Highway 281, which leads across Fort Randall Dam then winds north to I–90 west of Mitchell, South Dakota. Right over the border, pause a few minutes to see the former site of Fort Randall, built in 1856 as a military outpost. Fort Randall Dam impounds 101-mile-long Lake Francis Case. The Fort Randall Casino and Hotel deals up gambling, entertainment, and dining twenty-four hours a day, 10 miles west of Wagner on South Dakota 46. The Snake Creek Recreation area, 14 miles west of Platte on SD 44, is another major access to Lake Francis Case.

Near here, the corps enjoyed a reunion with its missing member. "In the morning we observed a man riding on horseback down toward the boat," Clark wrote on September 11, 1804. "We were much pleased to find that it was George Shannon, one of our party, for whose safety we had been very uneasy."

CHAMBERLAIN—OACOMA AND THE CIRCLE OF TEPEES

Interstate 90 and the Missouri River meet at the two small towns of Chamberlain and Oacoma. The Lewis and Clark Information Center at milepost 264.4 features a 55-foot keelboat replica that doubles as a Missouri River overlook. One exhibit tells how, while camped nearby September 16–18, 1804, the corps enjoyed wild plums and the captains decided to wait until spring to send the keelboat back to St. Louis laden with specimens, journals, and a report for Jefferson. Other displays depict daily camp life on the expedition, the flag flown by the Corps of Discovery, and the expedition's attempts to make peace among the tribes. One sign reads: "All the Indians they talked to agreed peace would be a good idea, but a few hours of talk cannot resolve grievances between old enemies, and Lewis and Clark had to keep moving. They were actually more like tourists than long-term diplomats." It was also near here that Lewis wrote of the amazing number of bison the expedition was encountering on the plains, noting, "I do not think I exaggerate when I estimate the number of buffalo which could be comprehended at one view to amount to 3,000." The information center is open daily from mid-May to mid-October, and the rest area next door remains open year-round.

The Akta Lakota Museum & Cultural Center in Chamberlain is known for its impressive collection of Sioux art and artifacts. Located 2 miles north of the interstate on the St. Joseph's Indian School campus, it's open daily Memorial Day through Labor Day and weekdays the rest of the year. Not far west at Oacoma (exit 260), seven Native American nations have established a Circle of Tepees information area. Travelers can stop here to watch tribal dancers and drum groups, sample native cuisine, and even arrange guided tours into Indian country. Many options are available, from a trip to a powwow to a trek featuring traditional uses of wildlife and plants. Or ask for a self-guiding tour brochure to the Native American Scenic Byway, which runs between Oacoma and Pierre using roads along the Missouri River. To arrange tribal tours in advance, call the Lower Brule Sioux Tribe's tourism office at (605) 473–0561.

PIERRE AND THE TETON COUNCIL SITE

The expedition had a close call on the night of September 20–21, 1804, while camped in the vicinity of what is now West Bend State Recreation Area. "At half past one o'clock this morning the sand bar on which we were camped began to undermine and give way which alarmed the sergeant on guard," Clark wrote. "The motion of the boat awakened me; I got up and by the light of the moon observed that the sand had given away both above and below our camp and was falling in fast. I ordered all hands on as quick as possible and pushed off, we had pushed off but a few minutes before the bank under which the boat and pirogues lay gave way, which would certainly have sunk both pirogues."

This was an unnerving episode, but even more troubling events were yet to come. The expedition entered what is now the Pierre area on September 23, camping near present-day Antelope Creek. That evening, three Sioux boys swam to the camp and told the explorers that two Teton Sioux villages were not far up-river. "We gave those boys two carrots of tobacco to carry to their chiefs, with directions to tell them that we would speak to them tomorrow," Clark wrote.

On the twenty-fourth Lewis and Clark somewhat nervously prepared for their meeting with the Teton (or Brule) Sioux—a tribe other Indians had mentioned with much fear and loathing. The explorers knew the Sioux were now dominating the area; even Jefferson had told them that "on that nation, we wish most particularly to make a favorable impression." The boats moved 13 miles to the mouth of the Bad River, which the explorers renamed the Teton River, perhaps in hopes of placating the Sioux. (It is once again known as the Bad River.) Several chiefs arrived that evening, and arrangements were made for a council the next day.

The meeting took place at noon on September 25 on a sandbar in the mouth

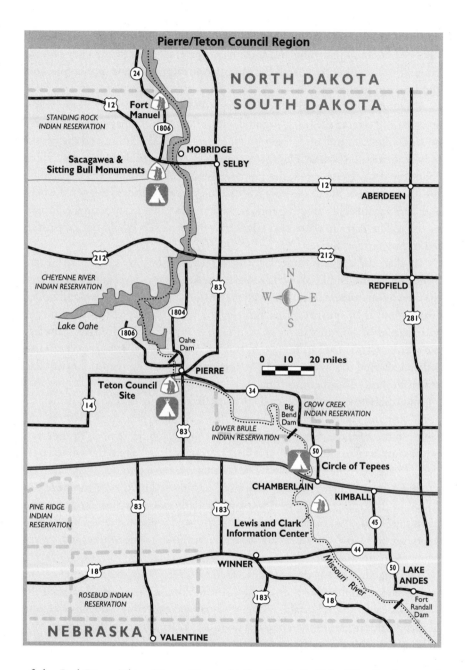

Pierre/Teton Council Region

NORTH DAKOTA

SOUTH DAKOTA

24

12

Fort
Manuel

1806

*STANDING ROCK
INDIAN RESERVATION*

**Sacagawea &
Sitting Bull Monuments**

MOBRIDGE

SELBY

12

ABERDEEN

212

212

*CHEYENNE RIVER
INDIAN RESERVATION*

83

REDFIELD

281

N

W   E

S

Lake Oahe

1804

1806

Oahe
Dam

0   10   20 miles

**Teton Council
Site**

PIERRE

14

34

83

Big
Bend
Dam

*CROW CREEK
INDIAN RESERVATION*

*LOWER BRULE
INDIAN RESERVATION*

50

Circle of Tepees

CHAMBERLAIN

KIMBALL

*PINE RIDGE
INDIAN
RESERVATION*

83

183

**Lewis and Clark
Information Center**

45

44

WINNER

Missouri River

18

50

LAKE
ANDES

*ROSEBUD INDIAN
RESERVATION*

183

18

Fort
Randall
Dam

NEBRASKA   VALENTINE

of the Bad River. Three Teton Sioux chiefs—Black Buffalo, The Partisan, and Buffalo Medicine—were on hand. But both sides soon found they were barely able to communicate: Pierre Dorion had stayed back with the Yankton Sioux, and no one else in the corps knew enough Sioux to translate. It was finally decided to employ Cruzatte, who knew Omaha, to translate through a member of that tribe made prisoner by the Sioux. Almost immediately, the Sioux showed signs of greediness, laughing and sneering at the gifts given them. They said the explorers must either trade with the Sioux alone or give up one of their pirogues and its cargo in tribute.

The captains attempted to lighten the mood by rowing the chiefs out to the keelboat and staging the usual airgun demonstration, accompanied by a measure of whisky for each Indian. The airgun failed to impress the Sioux, and the whisky only made matters worse: The chiefs pretended to be drunk and started falling about the deck. Exasperated, the captains shipped the Indians back to shore on the white pirogue. But as the boat reached the sand, one Indian hugged the mast and others grabbed its mooring rope—a signal they intended to seize the pirogue by force. The Partisan again told Clark that the explorers would not be permitted to pass farther upriver.

At that, the captains' moods changed from wariness to anger. Clark brandished his sword, and Lewis swiftly loaded the keelboat's swivel guns and ordered the crew to man their rifles. The Indians, in turn, strung their bows and pulled arrows from their quivers. Black Buffalo, the main chief, grabbed the towrope and ordered his warriors to let go, but he repeated that the river was closed to the whites. Clark stood in the water, sure he could not chance a retreat. But he ordered his men to row the pirogue to the keelboat, pick up reinforcements, and return to shore. Together they finally faced down the Sioux.

Incredibly, the captains agreed to Black Buffalo and Buffalo Medicine's request that the chiefs, along with two other Sioux, be permitted to spend the night on the keelboat. No one slept well that night. On September 26 the boats traveled upriver to the second and larger Sioux village. Here, the whites were treated with deference: Lewis and Clark were even carried to the village aloft on a buffalo robe. Much entertainment and feasting followed over the next two days, but the explorers remained wary, particularly since the Sioux continued to insist they be allowed to sleep on the keelboat—and because several Omaha prisoners warned Cruzatte the Sioux were simply biding time while plotting the white men's destruction.

Hearing that news, the captains decided to leave on the morning of the twenty-eighth. But before they could cast off, Sioux warriors again grabbed the keelboat's cable. Black Buffalo, on the keelboat and expecting a ride upriver, said his people demanded more tobacco. Disgusted, Clark tossed tobacco to the men holding the cable and grabbed the rope away from them. The Sioux tried to reclaim the rope, but the boats made a clean getaway.

"The four-day ordeal was over," Roy Appleman wrote. "Against weaker men, the Tetons would have triumphed. Only sleepless vigilance, excellent judgment, and bold determination had saved the day. For the time being at least, the two captains had gained much prestige and established U.S. authority over this stretch of the Missouri. . . . The news spread rapidly up and down the river and promised a peaceful welcome for the explorers among the upriver tribes."

The exact site of the September 25, 1804, encounter with the Sioux has been lost in the mouth of the Bad River, but Fort Pierre's Lilly Park has a sign marking the approximate location. Situated on Fort Pierre's south side where the Bad River meets the Missouri, Lilly Park offers camping for $6.00 a night. The second Sioux encounter site is unmarked, but it probably took place on the west riverbank about 4 miles north of Fort Pierre and 2 miles south of Oahe Dam. A county road leading along the river offers access at several points. Below Oahe Dam, the Missouri again looks much as it did in the early 1800s.

Another site associated with the expedition is Farm Island State Park, located just east of Pierre on SD 34. Expedition member John Colter is said to have hunted here just before the encounter with the Sioux, who may have stolen his horse. Later, other members of the expedition may have stopped on the island to pick up game Colter had shot.

Farm Island is still well worth visiting for its good camping, fishing, boating, and swimming. The island itself has returned to a near-wilderness state, most of it accessible only on foot. A park naturalist conducts guided interpretive hikes in summer. Walkers, joggers, and bird-watchers favor the trail in the warmer months, while cross-country skiers find its flat terrain ideal for easy winter outings.

The town of Pierre is named for Pierre Chouteau, but the name is pronounced "Peer"—no one seems to know why. Fort Teton, built at the present site

South Dakota State Capitol, Pierre.

South Dakota on the Beaten Path

For a state with well under a million people and an off-the-beaten-path location, South Dakota does a remarkably good job of promoting itself. Visitors following the Lewis and Clark Trail will be mostly immune to the relentless public relations campaign that is Interstate 90, but as long as you're in the area, you may want to check out some of South Dakota's myriad claims to fame—some dubious, others divine.

The closest big-name attraction to our route is the Corn Palace in Mitchell, a Moorish-inspired monument to agriculture at Sixth and Main Streets. Built in 1892, the palace is decorated inside and out with thousands of bushels of native corn, grains, and grasses. It's also the site or the inspiration for all of Mitchell's big annual events: the Corn Palace Stampede Rodeo in late July and the Corn Palace Festival and Corn Palace Polka Festival, both in mid- to late September.

Heading west on I-90, Badlands National Park is accessible via exits 131 (Cactus Flat) and 110 (Wall). The Badlands are known for their raw, rugged landscape and some of the world's finest fossil beds, formed about thirty-seven million years ago during the Oligocene epoch. Backcountry adventure abounds, with the Castle Trail particularly acclaimed for its varied prairie to-pography and wealth of wildlife, including pronghorn antelope, bison, bad-gers, coyotes, and prairie dogs.

For a quick look at the Badlands, drive the 40-mile loop road (South Dakota 240) between Cactus Flat and Wall. Primitive camping is available, as are cabins at the Sioux-run Cedar Pass Lodge, located south of Cactus Flat. The White River Visitor Center, on the Pine Ridge Reservation in the park's South Unit, features displays and programs on Sioux history. For a very different look at South Dakota, visit the Pine Ridge Indian Reservation south of the Badlands. This was the site of the 1890 Wounded Knee Massacre, where more than 350 Indians were killed by federal troops.

West of the Badlands, the traveler enters the famous Black Hills region. Wind Cave National Park, adjacent to Custer State Park on South Dakota 87, offers daily subterranean tours during the summer. The excursions range from short candlelight walks to more strenuous spelunking missions. Jewel Cave National Monument, 14 miles west of Custer, South Dakota, on U.S. Highway 16A, is one of the longest caves in the world. It, too, offers tours, as do a num-ber of privately held caves scattered throughout the area. Custer State Park is known for its 18-mile wildlife loop drive and abundant recreation.

The Black Hills were named by the Lakota Sioux for the dark appearance of their coniferous forests. The Sioux considered the land sacred, and their rights to it were assured in a treaty signed in 1868. But the U.S. government broke the pact during the gold rush of the late 1870s. In recent years, the U.S. Supreme Court offered the Sioux $200 million as compensation for loss of their lands, but the Sioux were not interested. They want only the land.

Today's Black Hills are heavily commercialized, but their beauty remains mostly intact. Check with the USDA Forest Service office in Custer for maps and information on the area's many scenic byways (and for restrictions on motor homes and trailers, which may have trouble negotiating the region's roads).

Mount Rushmore is probably the best-known Black Hills attraction. Created under the direction of Gutzon Borglum, it features the 60-foot-high heads of presidents George Washington, Thomas Jefferson, Abraham Lincoln, and Theodore Roosevelt, all bathed in floodlights each night at dusk.

The Crazy Horse Memorial near Custer was started in 1947 by sculptor Korczak Ziolkowski to honor Chief Crazy Horse and the Native Americans. Progress has been slow, but the monument is planned to measure 563 feet high and 641 long, which would make it the largest statue in the world. It, too, is lit nightly at dusk.

Although gambling continues to proliferate throughout the United States, western South Dakota still draws crowds to its small gaming towns, perhaps because visitors feel a bit wilder when they gamble in the West. After all, it was in Deadwood that Bill Hickok was shot in the back while playing poker in 1876. He's buried alongside Calamity Jane (who claimed she was his secret bride) in Mt. Moriah Cemetery overlooking the city.

Nearby, the town of Lead (rhymes with "greed") is famous for its Homestake Gold Mine, largest in the Western Hemisphere. And in early August, Sturgis attracts hordes of Harley-Davidson enthusiasts for the Black Hills Motorcycle Classic. Spearfish is home to the Black Hills Passion Play, presented Sunday, Tuesday, and Thursday from June through August. For more information on South Dakota, write the state Department of Tourism, Capital Lake Plaza, Pierre, South Dakota 57501, call (800) 732–5682, or visit www.travelsd.com.

---

of the town of Fort Pierre, was established in 1817 and is credited with being the state's first continuous settlement. But the white man's history at Pierre dates back before those days, and even before the time of Lewis and Clark. In 1743 Chevalier and Louis La Verendrye, two explorers from French Canada, planted a lead plate on a hill in what is now Fort Pierre, claiming the region for the King of France. Like Lewis and Clark sixty years after them, the Verendryes were looking for a route to the Pacific Ocean. They'd come down the Missouri River and traveled as far west as the Black Hills before returning to present-day central South Dakota.

The plate was covered with rocks and remained hidden for 170 years. In 1913 three students from Fort Pierre High School found the plate. A monument was built to the Verendryes, and Gutzon Borglum—sculptor of Mount Rushmore—was the keynote speaker at its dedication in 1933. The Verendrye Plate was a top historical find, since it provided a key to early white exploration of the region.

The plate is now on display at the South Dakota Cultural Center, located near the State Capitol grounds in Pierre. Built for the state centennial in 1989, the 63,000-square-foot building is completely underground, reminiscent of Arikara earth lodges that used to dot the Missouri River valley. Look for exhibits on Lewis and Clark, as well as excellent displays on Native American heritage.

Pierre and Fort Pierre offer ample cycling, hiking, and boating opportunities. The 30-mile Lewis and Clark Bicentennial Trail runs between the aforementioned Farm Island State Park and Lilly Park, as well as to several other area landmarks and parks (including Griffin Park in Pierre, which offers free camping with electricity for up to three days, and Oahe Dam). No matter how you explore, be sure to visit lovely La Framboise Island, accessed by a causeway from Steamboat Park. The island is a natural area where only foot traffic is permitted. There's great bird-watching and easy hiking; a sign explaining the Teton Sioux encounter can be found here, too.

Trailshead Cycle Rentals (with three locations at Farm Island, Griffin Park, and the Oahe Dam Downstream Campground) offers kid- and adult-sized recumbent bicycles, surreys, tandem cycles, and mountain bikes. They're open daily from noon to dark in summer and weekends in May and September. Call (605) 280–6162 or visit www.trailsheadrentals.com for more details.

Dakota Adventures, also based in Pierre, runs guided canoe and kayak trips on the Missouri River. Take a two-and-a-half-hour sunset paddle for $30 or a full-day trip for $70. Or book a three-day, two-night excursion at $250 for adults, half that for children age twelve and under. (All rates are per person.) The company also rents boats and camping gear and offers shuttle services. For more information or reservations, phone (605) 224–6572, stop by 511 West Dakota Avenue, or visit www.adventuresd.com.

Other Pierre places worth a stop include the beautiful State Capitol grounds and the South Dakota Discovery Center and Aquarium, with hands-on science exhibits. For more information stop in the visitor center at 800 West Dakota Avenue, call (800) 962–2034, or check out www.pierrechamber.com.

Thirty-one miles northwest of Fort Pierre off South Dakota Highway 1806, the Triple U Buffalo Ranch was the setting for the film *Dances With Wolves.* Formerly known as the Houck Ranch, Triple U offers tours to help visitors see the shaggy beasts, as well as sites where the filmmaking took place. You'll also find a bed-and-breakfast, a gift shop, and camping, as well as hunting packages. For more information or to reserve a trip, call (605) 567–3624.

THE LAKE OAHE REGION

Travelers who haven't realized it already will probably note north of Pierre that South Dakota has devised an ingenious way of marking state routes closest to the Lewis and Clark Trail. The road on the east side of the Missouri River is South Dakota Highway 1804 (for the year the corps first passed through), and the one on the west side is SD 1806 (named for the year the expedition returned). North Dakota continues this system, but no other states have adopted it. It's important to note that neither of the routes proceeds in a continuous fashion along the river; each frequently sputters out near the shores of Lake Oahe. The quickest way north is U.S. Highway 83 to Selby, then U.S. 12 to Mobridge.

North-central South Dakota is dominated by Lake Oahe, the massive man-made body of water created by Oahe Dam and the largest of the four Missouri River reservoirs in South Dakota. President John F. Kennedy dedicated the rolled-earth dam north of Pierre in 1963. It is 245 feet high and 9,300 feet long and backs up a lake capable of storing some 23.5 million acre-feet of water. "Oahe" is a Sioux word meaning "foundation" or "a place to stand on."

Lake Oahe offers 2,250 miles of shoreline, and thirty-nine separate recreation areas dot its length from Pierre to Bismarck, North Dakota. Some of them—including those at Okobojo Point, Little Bend, Sutton Bay, Whitlock Bay, Swan Creek, and Indian Creek—are in the vicinity of campsites used by Lewis and Clark. Primitive camping is available at nearly all the sites, and about half have boat ramps. Lake Oahe is known for excellent walleye fishing, with nearly half a million caught each year.

Onida is one of a handful of towns right along U.S. 83. It has a park with a pool and playground on the southeast side of town; a free parking area (with no facilities) just south of town is best suited for self-contained RVs.

Gettysburg was settled by Civil War veterans in 1883. It is home to the Dakota Sunset Museum at 207 West Commercial Avenue, open afternoons daily between Memorial Day and Labor Day. In addition to exhibits of items used by Gettysburg-area pioneers, the museum displays a replica of the Medicine Rock, a huge boulder held sacred by the Sioux. The tribe looked on the rock as an oracle, often praying there for advice and for the safety of their children. The original boulder is now submerged under Lake Oahe, one of many sacred sites in the Dakotas flooded by the Pick-Sloan Project dams.

Located 5 miles east of U.S. 83, Gettysburg has golf, tennis, and swimming

Civil War veterans settled the town of Gettysburg, South Dakota.

facilities, along with free camping in its city park. Gettysburg is also gateway to the popular East and West Whitlock Bay recreation areas on Lake Oahe. West Whitlock State Recreation Area was once a popular Mandan and Arikara campsite, and a replica Arikara earth lodge may be seen—though it is not as impressive as similar dwellings at Fort Abraham Lincoln State Park and Knife River Indian Villages Historic Site in North Dakota.

Selby is at the intersection of U.S. 83 and U.S. 12, and it's here the traveler can turn west for Mobridge. Campers are welcome to stay free at Selby's park near the end of Dakota Street.

It was in this vicinity near the present-day North Dakota border that the expedition was greeted by the Arikara Indians and enjoyed an encounter far different from that with the Teton Sioux. They stayed several days, held a council, and traded gifts with the natives. For the first time on the expedition, some of the men apparently took their hosts up on what Clark termed a "curious custom . . . to give handsome squaws to those whom they wish to show some acknowledgements to." The Indians, for their part, were especially fascinated with York, the first black man they had ever seen. "Those Indians were much astonished at my servant," Clark wrote. "All flocked around him and examined him top to toe."

With about 4,000 people, Mobridge serves as the "big town" for north-central South Dakota. The community reportedly got its name when somebody wired that the Missouri River had been bridged, or "Mobridged," for short. Mobridge is known for its walleye and pike fishing, sailboarding, and the annual Sitting Bull Stampede Rodeo, July 2–4. The Klein Museum on U.S. 12 displays prairie and Native American artifacts and items from local history.

Aside from the lake recreation, Mobridge's big draw is the Sitting Bull Monument on a ridge west of Lake Oahe. To get there, take U.S. 12 west out of Mobridge; then turn left on SD 1806 and drive south 4 miles. You really can't miss it: Just look for a billboard nearly as big as the monument itself.

South Dakotans claim this is the burial place of Sitting Bull, the great Sioux leader killed in the area in 1890. He was originally buried at Fort Yates, North Dakota, just over the border, but Mobridgers maintain that the body was moved to its "rightful" place in 1953. Many in North Dakota disagree, however; they say the South Dakotans got the wrong bones. In any case, a second Sitting Bull gravesite may be seen south of the town of Fort Yates, North Dakota. The Mobridge monument is a seven-ton granite bust carved by Korczak Ziolkowski, the same sculptor who started the Crazy Horse carving near Custer, South Dakota.

Mobridge's Sitting Bull site is also notable for its monument to Sacagawea, the Shoshone woman who would join the Lewis and Clark Expedition during its 1804–1805 winter stay in North Dakota. Although some people believe that Sacagawea lived to be an old woman in Wyoming, most historians agree that she actually passed away at a young age and was buried at Fort Manuel, a Missouri Fur Company trading post. On December 20, 1812, a clerk who compiled the daily journal of events at the fort wrote, "This evening the wife of Charbonneau,

View of Lake Oahe at Mobridge, South Dakota.

a Snake squaw, died of a putrid fever. She was . . . the best woman in the fort, aged about 25 years." Fort Manuel was probably located near what is now the west shore of Lake Oahe a few miles south of the North Dakota border. There is no interpretation of the site, but we will learn much more about Sacagawea as we follow Lewis and Clark west.

Nearby, the Grand River Casino & Resort offers gaming, food, and lodging from the Standing Rock Sioux Tribe. From here it's about a two-hour drive north to the Bismarck-Mandan area.

Lodging

Lodgings, campgrounds, and restaurants listed below are a representative sampling of what is available. Listing in these pages does not imply endorsement, nor is this a complete listing of all reputable businesses. For more complete listings, contact the visitor information bureau or chamber of commerce in each town. Room rates were accurate as of summer 2002 but are subject to change.

AUBURN, NEBRASKA
Auburn Inn, (402) 274–3143, 517 J Street; $45–$60.
Palmer House Motel, (402) 274–3193, 1918 J Street; $45–$50.

NEBRASKA CITY, NEBRASKA
Apple Inn, (800) 659–4446, 502 South Eleventh; $55–$65.
Days Inn, (402) 873–6656, 1715 South Eleventh; $45–$60.

GREATER OMAHA, NEBRASKA/ COUNCIL BLUFFS, IOWA
American Family Inn, (402) 291–0804, 1110 Fort Crook Road (Bellevue); $55–$65.
Ameristar Casino Hotel, (712) 328–8888, I–29 exit 52 (Council Bluffs); $90 and up.
Baymont Inn, (402) 592–5200, 10760 M Street (Omaha); $65–$75.
Embassy Suites, (402) 346–9000, 555 South Tenth Street (Omaha); $135 and up.
Heartland Inn, (877) 334–3277, I–80 exit 5 (Council Bluffs); $65–$80.
Ramada Inn—Airport, (402) 342–5100, 2002 East Locust Street; $80–$90.

Sleep Inn, (402) 342–2525, 2525 Abbott Drive (Omaha); $60–$80.

ONAWA, IOWA
Super 8 Motel, (712) 423–2101, I–29 exit 112; $55–$70.

SIOUX CITY, IOWA
Best Western City Centre, (712) 277–1550, 130 Nebraska Street; $65–$80.
Fairfield Inn, (712) 276–5600, 4716 Southern Hills Drive; $75–$100.
Hilton Sioux City, (712) 277–4101, 707 Fourth Street; $80–$110.
Holiday Inn, (800) 238–6146, 701 Gordon Drive; $70–$80.
Marina Inn, (402) 494–4000, Fourth and B Streets (South Sioux City, Nebraska); $90–$105.
Park Plaza Motel, (402) 494–2021, 1201 First Avenue (South Sioux City, Nebraska); $45–$50.

VERMILLION, SOUTH DAKOTA
Buffalo Run Resort Bed & Breakfast, (605) 624–4117, 1500 West Main Street; $85–$100.
Comfort Inn, (605) 624–8333, 701 West Cherry Street; $70–$120.

YANKTON, SOUTH DAKOTA

Best Western Kelly Inn, (605) 665–2906, East SD 50; $90–$110.

Days Inn, (605) 665–8717, 2410 Broadway Avenue; $65–$75.

Gavins Point Bed & Breakfast, (605) 668–0691, 252 Gavins Point Road; $70–$85.

Lewis & Clark Resort, (605) 665–2680, at Lewis & Clark Lake Recreation Area; $75–$80.

PONCA, NEBRASKA

Ponca State Park (cabins), (402) 755–2284.

CROFTON, NEBRASKA

Argo Hotel Bed & Breakfast, (800) 607–2746, 211 West Kansas Street; $60–$135.

Lewis and Clark State Recreation Area (cabins), (402) 388–4169.

NIOBRARA, NEBRASKA

Hilltop Lodge, (402) 857–3611, 253 Walnut Street; $35–$45.

Niobrara State Park (cabins), (402) 857–3373.

PICKSTOWN, SOUTH DAKOTA

Fort Randall Inn, (800) 340–7801, just east of the dam; $60.

GEDDES, SOUTH DAKOTA

The Barn Bed & Breakfast, (605) 337–2483, 37191 284th Street; $75 and up.

PLATTE, SOUTH DAKOTA

Dakota Country Inn, (605) 337–2607, SD 44; $45–$68.

Kings Inn, (605) 337–3385, SD 44; $45–$70.

CHAMBERLAIN, SOUTH DAKOTA

Alewel's Lake Shore Motel, (605) 734–5566, 115 North River Street; $40–$65.

Cedar Shore Resort, (888) 697–6363, I–90 exit 260; $90–$140.

Oasis Inn, (605) 734–6061, I–90 exit 260; $80–$110.

PIERRE/FORT PIERRE, SOUTH DAKOTA

Best Western Ramkota Inn Rivercentre, (605) 224–6877, 920 West Sioux; $82–$92.

Budget Host State Motel, (605) 224–5896, 640 North Euclid; $40–$50.

Fort Pierre Motel, (605) 223–3111, 211 South First Street; $45–$55.

Governor's Inn, (605) 224–4200, 700 West Sioux; $60–$105.

River Place Inn Bed & Breakfast, (605) 224–8589, 109 River Place; $65–$125.

Spring Creek Resort, (605) 224–8336, 10 miles north of Oahe Dam on SD 1804; $70 and up.

ONIDA, SOUTH DAKOTA

Wheatland Inn, (605) 258–2341, 200 South Main Street; $30–$55.

GETTYSBURG, SOUTH DAKOTA

Bob's Resort, (605) 765–2500, west of town at Lake Oahe; $70–$120.

Harer Lodge Bed & Breakfast, (605) 765–2167, 12 miles north; $50–$150.

South Whitlock Resort, (605) 765–9762, 14 miles west at Lake Oahe; $55.

Trail Motel, (605) 765–2482, 211 East Garfield; $37–$45.

MOBRIDGE, SOUTH DAKOTA

East Side Motel and Cabins, (605) 845–7867, 510 East Seventh Avenue; $32–$36.

Camping

BROWNVILLE, NEBRASKA

Brownville State Recreation Area, 0.5 mile southeast of town. Primitive sites.
Indian Cave State Park, (402) 883–2575, 9 miles south on NE 67, then 5 miles east.

NEBRASKA CITY, NEBRASKA

Riverview Marina State Recreation Area, northeast of town on U.S. 73/75 and NE 2. Primitive sites.

GREATER OMAHA, NEBRASKA/ COUNCIL BLUFFS, IOWA

Bluffs Run Casino RV Park, (712) 323–2500, I–29/I–80 exit 1B (Council Bluffs).
N. P. Dodge Park, (402) 444–4673, I–680 Thirtieth Street exit; follow signs.
Lake Manawa State Park, (712) 336–0220, south of Council Bluffs on IA 192.

ONAWA, IOWA

Interchange RV Campground, (712) 423–1387; from junction of I–29 and IA 175, go 1 block east on IA 175, then 1 block south to campground.
KOA–Onawa, (712) 423–1633, 1 mile west of I–29 on IA 175, then 1.5 miles north on county road.
Lewis and Clark State Park, (712) 423–2829, 1 mile west of I–29 on IA 175, then 1 mile north on IA 324.

SIOUX CITY, IOWA

KOA–North Sioux City, (605) 232–4519, on west side of I–29 between exits 2 and 4 (North Sioux City, South Dakota).
Scenic Park, (402) 494–7531, Fourth and D Streets (South Sioux City, Nebraska).
Stone State Park, (712) 255–4698, 5 miles north of I–29 on IA 12.

YANKTON, SOUTH DAKOTA

Lewis and Clark Lake/Corps of Engineers, (605) 667–7873, west of town on SD 52.
Lewis and Clark State Recreation Area (Nebraska), (402) 388–4169, northwest of Crofton on Lewis and Clark Lake.
Lewis and Clark State Recreation Area (South Dakota), (605) 668–2985, west of town on SD 52.

PONCA, NEBRASKA

Ponca State Park, (402) 755–2284, 2 miles north of NE 12.

NIOBRARA, NEBRASKA

Niobrara State Park, (402) 857–3373, west on NE 12.

CHAMBERLAIN, SOUTH DAKOTA

American Creek Campground, (605) 734–5151, 2 miles north of I–90 exit 263 on Lake Francis Case.
Cedar Shore Campground, (605) 734–5273, I–90 exit 260.
Oasis Campground, (605) 734–6959, I–90 exit 260.

PIERRE, SOUTH DAKOTA

Downstream Area/Missouri River, (605) 224–5862, north of Pierre below Oahe Dam on Lake Oahe.
Farm Island State Recreation Area, (605) 224–5605, 4 miles east on SD 34.
Griffin Park, 800 East Missouri Avenue. Free camping.
West Bend State Recreation Area, (605) 875–3220, 26 miles east and 9 miles south on SD 34.

GETTYSBURG, SOUTH DAKOTA

Gettysburg City Park, (605) 765–2264.
River Edge Campsite, 10 miles west of U.S. 83 on U.S. 212.

South Whitlock Resort, (605) 765–9762, 8 miles west of U.S. 83 on U.S. 212.
West Whitlock State Recreation Area, (605) 765–9410, 13 miles west of U.S. 83 on U.S. 212, then 9 miles north.

SELBY, SOUTH DAKOTA
Lake Hiddenwood State Park, (605) 765–9410, 2 miles east, then 3 miles north on U.S. 12/83.

MOBRIDGE, SOUTH DAKOTA
Indian Creek, (605) 224–5862, 2 miles east on U.S. 12, then 1 mile south, on Lake Oahe.
Indian Memorial, 3 miles west on U.S. 12, on Lake Oahe.
Kountry Kamping and Kabins, (605) 845–2267, north of town on U.S. 12.

Restaurants

BROWNVILLE, NEBRASKA
Brownville House, (402) 825–4721, 228 Main Street. American food.

AUBURN, NEBRASKA
Darling's Cafe, (402) 274–4125, 520 J Street. Fish, prime rib, Sunday buffet.
Korner Kitchen, (402) 274–3015, "one block east of the stoplight." Weekend breakfast buffet.
The Wheeler Inn, (402) 274–4931, 1905 J Street. Steaks, seafood, salad bar.

NEBRASKA CITY, NEBRASKA
Embers Steak House, (402) 873–6416, junction of U.S. 75 and NE 2. American cuisine with children's menu.

GREATER OMAHA, NEBRASKA/ COUNCIL BLUFFS, IOWA
Ahmad's Persian Cuisine, (402) 341–9616, 1096 Howard Street. Savory food in the Old Market.
Ameristar Casino, (712) 328–8888, I–29 Nebraska Avenue exit (Council Bluffs). Four restaurants.
Bohemian Cafe, (402) 342–9838, 1406 South Thirteenth Street (Omaha). Czech specialties.

Charlie's on the Lake, (402) 894–9411, 144th and F Streets (Omaha). Fresh seafood daily.
Dazy Maze, (402) 346–9342, 521 South Thirteenth Street (Omaha). Vegetarian cafe.
Falling Waters Grill, (402) 346–9000, in the Embassy Suites. Creative Continental dining.
McKenna's, (402) 393–7427, 7425 Pacific Street. Barbecue and live blues music, children's menu.
Tish's, (712) 323–5456, 1207 South Thirty-fifth Street (Council Bluffs).
Upstream Brewing Company, (402) 344–0200, Eleventh and Jackson Streets in Old Market. New American pub food.

ONAWA, IOWA
Casino Omaha Buffet, (712) 423–3700.

SIOUX CITY, IOWA
Belle of Sioux City, (712) 294–5600. Buffet on the Missouri River.
Garfield's Restaurant & Pub, (712) 276–6505, 4400 Sergeant Road. At the Southern Hills Mall.
Sneaky's, (712) 252–0522, 3711 Gordon Drive. Chicken and more.

ELK POINT, SOUTH DAKOTA

Edgar's Ol' Fashioned Soda Fountain, (605) 356–3336, 107 East Main Street. Classic antique ice creamery.

VERMILLION, SOUTH DAKOTA

Buffalo Run Winery, (605) 624–4117, 1500 West Main Street. Creative cuisine.

Recuerdo de Mexico, (605) 624–6445,112 East Main Street. Mexican food.

Whimp's, (605) 624–9973, Burbank (southeast of town). Steaks.

MECKLING, SOUTH DAKOTA

Toby's Lounge, (605) 624–9905, SD 50. Broasted chicken, shrimp, and fish.

YANKTON, SOUTH DAKOTA

The Coffee House & 3rd St. Deli, (605) 668–9575, 300 West Third Street.

JoDean's Steakhouse & Lounge, (605) 665–9884, 2809 Broadway. Wide menu, Sunday brunch.

Quarry Steak House, (605) 665–4337, SD 52 near the lake. Prime rib and nightly specials.

Waterfront Gourmet Grill, (605) 664–5333, 201 Capitol. Large selection of pasta, seafood, and steaks, with daily lunch and dinner specials.

CROFTON, NEBRASKA

Argo Hotel Steakhouse, (402) 388–2400. Downtown Crofton.

Bogner's Steakhouse, (402) 388–4626, U.S. 12 and NE 121.

PLATTE, SOUTH DAKOTA

The Barrister, (605) 337–2580, 311 Main Street. Dinner Monday through Saturday.

GEDDES, SOUTH DAKOTA

Mom's Kitchen, (605) 337–2131, Third and Main. Home cooking and good pie.

CHAMBERLAIN, SOUTH DAKOTA

Al's Oasis, (605) 734–6054, I–90 exit 260. Truck-stop cafe.

Bridges Bar & Grille, (605) 734–6376. At Cedar Shore Resort.

Rainbow Cafe, (605) 734–5481, Main Street in downtown Chamberlain. Home cooking.

LOWER BRULE, SOUTH DAKOTA

Golden Buffalo Casino, (605) 473–5577.

PIERRE, SOUTH DAKOTA

Cattleman's Club, (605) 224–9774, 5 miles east on U.S. 34. Steaks.

Chikadily's Restaurant, (605) 224–7183, 808 West Sioux (next to the bridge). Open twenty-four hours.

Kozy Korner Family Restaurant, (605) 224–9547, 217 East Dakota. Specialties include soups and cream pies.

La Minestra, (605) 224–8090, 106 East Dakota Avenue. Fine dining.

Pizza Ranch, (605) 223–9114, next to the bridge in Fort Pierre.

ONIDA, SOUTH DAKOTA

Fireside Restaurant & Lounge, (605) 258–2377, U.S. 83.

GETTYSBURG, SOUTH DAKOTA

Bob's Steakhouse, (605) 765–2500, at the Lake Oahe bridge. Charbroiled steaks.

MoRest Motel, (605) 845–3668, 706 West Grand Crossing; $48.

Wrangler Motor Inn, (605) 845–3641, U.S. 12; $65–$80.

MOBRIDGE, SOUTH DAKOTA

Dakota Country Restaurant, (605) 845–7495, 122 West Grand Crossing.

The Wheel Family Restaurant, (605) 845–7474, 820 West Grand Crossing. View of Lake Oahe.

5

North Dakota and Eastern Montana

About 5 o'clock this evening one of the wives of Charbonneau (Sacagawea) was delivered of a fine boy. — MERIWETHER LEWIS, FEBRUARY 11, 1805, FORT MANDAN, NORTH DAKOTA.

FORT ABRAHAM LINCOLN STATE PARK

The Lewis and Clark Expedition entered North Dakota on October 14, 1804, and returned to the present North Dakota–South Dakota border twenty-two months later, en route home from the Pacific. All told, the corps spent a total of 212 days in North Dakota. And since the party made its first winter camp there, Lewis and Clark and their men ended up staying longer in North Dakota than in any other state through which they passed.

Fort Yates, headquarters of the Standing Rock Indian Reservation, is the first town travelers see along North Dakota Highway 1806. There really is a "standing rock" on a pedestal near the Missouri River/Lake Oahe shore, and a plaque explains how the reservation got its name: "A famous sacred stone which many years ago came into possession of the Sioux. According to Dakota legend, it is a body of a young Indian woman with her child on her back who were left in camp when she refused to accompany the tribe as they moved south. When others were sent back to find her, she was found to have turned to stone. This stone is held in reverence by the Sioux and is placed here overlooking the waters in the empire once held by the mighty Sioux Nation."

Sacagawea statue on the North Dakota State Capitol grounds, Bismarck.

The corps' camp of October 15, 1804, is now in the middle of Lake Oahe, just northeast of Fort Yates. During the day, the corps saw many Indians on both sides of the river and stopped to eat and trade with about thirty Arikaras. Once camped, Lewis and Clark visited a nearby Arikara village. They scouted the area for a possible wintering location but, finding wood and game scarce, decided to press farther north. We shall do the same; it is about an hour's drive from Fort Yates to Fort Abraham Lincoln State Park, located just south of the town of Mandan. Note that ND 24 swings off to the west about 20 miles north of Fort Yates, but ND 1806 hugs the Missouri River and proceeds north to the park. Few amenities are available along this scenic route, but watch for the Standing Rock Sioux Tribe's Prairie Knights complex, among the region's most deluxe tribal resorts. Standing on a hillside above the plains, Prairie Knights has everything from fine lodging and dining to a Lake Oahe marina and plenty of gaming action, not to mention one of the only gas stations on ND 1806 between Mobridge and Mandan.

The corps camped in the vicinity of what was later Fort Abraham Lincoln on October 20, 1804, and August 18, 1806. During the 1804 visit, Clark wrote: "Camped on the leeward side above a bluff containing coal of an inferior quality. This bank is immediately above the old (deserted) village of the Mandans." Clark marveled at the abundant game he saw, noting that he personally killed three deer and watched gangs of bison and wolves. Although the Mandans had abandoned the villages here by the time the expedition arrived, the park is well worth a stop for its excellent interpretation. The highlight is On a Slant Village, with its earth lodge replicas. The village, sacred to the Mandan people, received its name from the sloping ground on which it was situated. The village included about seven or eight acres of land, and a 1937 survey of the site found ruins of seventy-five earth lodges.

Studies of tree rings in the area indicate the village was occupied from about 1650 to 1750. After that, the Mandan population was reduced by a smallpox epidemic and pressure from other marauding tribes. In 1804, as Clark noted, the village was in ruins and the tribe had moved about 60 miles upriver to the Knife River Villages. The Mandan moved into North Dakota from the south, and other ruins are present from the South Dakota line north to the Fort Berthold Indian Reservation, where Mandan descendants live today.

The village's earth lodge replicas are typical of those used by the Mandans before they were forced onto the reservation. Twenty to 40 feet in diameter, the earth lodges were owned and primarily built by the tribe's women, with some help from the men. The lodges' main supports were 10 to 15 feet high and made of logs from nearby trees. Over the framework, the Indians placed a thick mat of willows followed by a layer of grass and thick layer of earth. A well-constructed earth lodge would last about ten years.

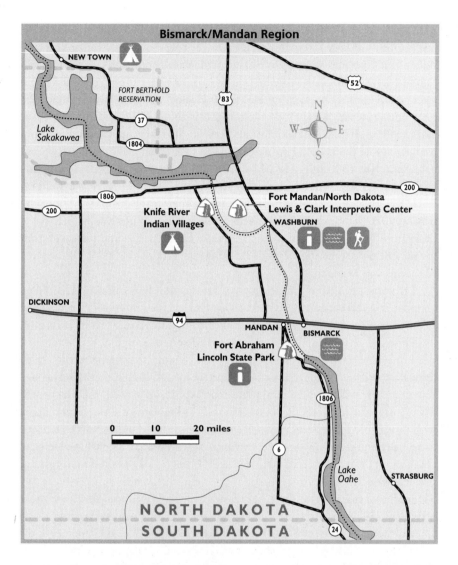

Visitors can walk inside several of the structures. Interpretive panels describe lifestyle, legends, and ceremonies. One lodge shows how such a dwelling may have been furnished, complete with an adult's bed, a small replica of a sweat lodge, and a horse stall.

The Ark of the Lone Man, centrally located in the village, is a special point of interest. According to Mandan legend, the Lone Man saved the Indian nation from a great flood by building a palisade around the village. The ark, a symbolic shrine, became a site for religious ceremonies. A red cedar post represents the lone man, and a circular willow band marks the high water of the flood.

The park's visitor center has interpretation of Lewis and Clark's travels

The Lewis and Clark *riverboat at Bismarck, North Dakota.*

through the area, with a replica elk hide journal, a peace medal, and an espontoon such as the one Lewis carried. Mandan culture is well represented by artifacts ranging from pieces of decorated pottery to projectile points. Other exhibits explain the area's heritage of fur trade, railroading, homesteading, and the military. There's also a boxful of dried medicinal plants. Each specimen includes a drawing of the plant in its native state and possible uses.

Fort Abraham Lincoln itself was in operation from 1872 through 1891, providing protection for railroad workers and survey parties, as well as settlements that sprung up in the area. The infantry soldiers stationed at the post found they were no match for the Sioux, who were excellent horsemen. In response, Congress authorized the addition of a cavalry post, and Lieutenant Colonel George Armstrong Custer arrived with the Seventh Cavalry in the autumn of 1873. From here Custer led expeditions into the Black Hills. When he discovered gold amid the sacred Sioux lands, it marked the beginning of the end for the Sioux way of life.

Tensions rose between the whites and the Indians. Ultimately, it was from Fort Abraham Lincoln that Custer led his troops to the Battle of the Little Big Horn, where he and 265 others were killed by Sioux and Cheyenne warriors led by Sitting Bull and Crazy Horse. Military-oriented exhibits explain the events leading up to the battle, and the trading post offers an excellent selection of the many books written about Custer.

Fort Abraham Lincoln was abandoned in 1891. Most of its original structures were torn down by 1900, with wood from the site reportedly used to construct many buildings in the Bismarck-Mandan area. But several buildings have been reconstructed, including Custer's home.

Fort Abraham Lincoln State Park is open daily from 8:00 A.M. to dusk Central Time all year. The interpretive facilities are open daily from 9:00 A.M. to 7:00 P.M. from Memorial Day through Labor Day. Other hours are as follows: 1:00 to 5:00 P.M. the last two weekends of April; daily from 9:00 A.M. to 5:00 P.M. May 1 to Memorial Day; and from the day after Labor Day through September 30; and daily from 1:00 to 5:00 P.M. through the month of October. Visits can also be made by appointment from November 1 through April 15, except the Custer Christmas weekend, when the fort is open to all.

During the summer months, the Fort Lincoln trolley runs along the Heart and Missouri Rivers between the Third Street Station in Mandan and the state park. You can even get here on bike or on foot; a paved trail runs about 5 miles from Main Street in Mandan to the park.

Park admission in 2002 was $4.00 per vehicle, plus an interpretation fee of $4.00 per adult and $2.00 per student. A modern campground has nearly one hundred sites, two cabins, and river access. For more information call (701) 663–9571.

West River Teamsters, based in Mandan, has plans now through 2006 for annual Lewis and Clark Bicentennial wagon train expeditions. While this blurs the

Mandan earth lodge replica at Fort Abraham Lincoln State Park, North Dakota.

Touring Bismarck–Mandan

Bismarck–Mandan is one of North Dakota's more populous areas, with about 65,000 people calling the two cities home. Bismarck is also the state capital, and several points of interest are found at the capitol complex. The capitol itself is unusual among statehouses: it looks more like an office building than a seat of government. The nineteen-story Art Deco–inspired building is nicknamed the "skyscraper of the prairies." A statue of Sacagawea—or "Sakakawea," as she is known in North Dakota—stands nearby. This statue is set to be replicated and included in Statuary Hall in the U.S. Capitol in Washington, D.C., in 2003.

The North Dakota Heritage Center also makes its home on the capitol grounds. A large main gallery traces the evolution of human and natural history in North Dakota. Exhibits include a mounted grizzly bear, along with this journal entry from Sergeant Gass: "These bears are very numerous in this part of the country and very dangerous as they will attack a man at every opportunity." Amateur ornithologists will love the extensive displays on North Dakota's birds. There's something for everyone here, from a special section called Dakota Kids for the youngsters to an abundance of nostalgia for the older folks. Hours are 8:00 A.M. to 5:00 P.M. Monday through Friday, 9:00 A.M. to 5:00 P.M. Saturday, and 11:00 A.M. to 5:00 P.M. Sunday. The museum is closed Easter, Thanksgiving, Christmas, and New Year's Day.

Bismarck has about 30 miles of public trails, including a path along the Missouri River from the Dakota Zoo area north to Pioneer Park. Look in the local phone book's green pages for a map. Dakota Cyclery at 1606 East Main Avenue rents bikes; call (701) 222–1218 for details. Rates are $15 for a half day or $25 for a full day.

The *Lewis and Clark* riverboat, an all-weather cruise vessel, has sailings most afternoons and evenings Memorial Day through Labor Day. Call (701) 255–4233 for times, special events, and other information. Matah Adventures Canoe Rental & Guide Service in Mandan leads trips and rents gear for people who prefer paddling their own boats. Call (701) 663–0054 for information.

Among the Bismarck area's art galleries are Five Nations Arts, specializing in Native American arts and crafts at 401 West Main Street in Mandan; the Heritage Center museum store; and Bismarck Art and Galleries Association at 422 East Front Avenue in Bismarck. Other attractions include the Dakota Zoo, plenty of golf courses, and several annual powwows. For more information on Bismarck/Mandan, call (800) 767–3555 or visit www.bismarck-mandancvb. org.

Bismarck Travel Tips

Bismarck Municipal Airport (BIS) is served by Big Sky, Northwest Airlines, and United Express. Many car rental companies have offices in town. The Greyhound bus terminal is at 3750 East Rosser Avenue.

lines a bit historically—wagon trains had nothing to do with the Corps of Discovery—it still sounds like a fun way to follow the captains' path across central North Dakota. The five-day treks, set in late July each year, cost $400 in 2003. (A $125 per-day rate is available for people who want to ride a day or two. Family rates are offered as well.) Fees include all meals, guide service, entertainment, and interpretation along the way. For more information call (877) 865–8627, write West River Teamsters, 411 West Main Street, Mandan, North Dakota 58554, or visit www.lewis-clarkwagontrain.com.

From Bismarck/Mandan, U.S. Highway 83 continues north to Washburn, 40 miles away. North Dakota Highway 1804 is a good scenic alternative along the Missouri River much of the way. Double Ditch Indian Village State Historic Site lies along this route about 12 miles north of Bismarck. Lewis and Clark camped in this vicinity on October 22, 1804.

FORT MANDAN

As the expedition moved north through the Dakotas, the need to find a place to spend the winter became acute. Beginning in late October 1804, the journal entries mention bitter winds and snow. On October 26, roughly 1,600 miles from Camp Wood, the Corps of Discovery reached the new villages established by the Mandans, Minitaris (later known as Hidatsa), and Amahamis.

About 4,400 people lived in five separate villages. They greeted the white men warmly, and the captains quickly decided this would be a good place to spend the winter. After several days of searching, a suitable spot was found for a fort. It was there, on the Missouri's east bank about 6 miles below the mouth of Knife River, that Fort Mandan was built.

Construction started November 2, using cottonwood logs cut nearby. Two sides of the V-shaped fort held four rooms each to house the men and their belongings. Each room was 14 feet square, 7 feet high, and equipped with a fireplace. The third side was blockaded by "amazing long pickets." The men occupied the still-unfinished buildings November 16, and the two captains moved into their quarters four days later. The party at that point numbered about forty-five.

The expedition spent a long winter in a variety of pursuits, chief among them finding enough food. Trade with the Indians brought corn, squash, and berries. Meat was obtained by daily hunting parties. Game was abundant, but many of the animals were in such poor shape during the colder months that only the choicest parts—such as buffalo tongue, heart, and liver—could be used. There were many wolves in the area, and harvested animals left overnight without protection were often found completely devoured by the time the men returned to retrieve the game.

They also found themselves expending considerable energy to stay warm: In his journal entry of December 8, Clark reported several cases of frostbitten feet and, in the case of York, a frostbitten male organ. On December 12, he wrote, "We do not think it prudent to turn out to hunt in such cold weather," and on December 13, more of the same: "The thermometer stands this morning at 20 below zero, a fine day." In all, the temperature dipped below zero, once as low as minus 48 degrees Fahrenheit, on forty days during the corps' stay.

Despite the bitter cold, a steady stream of visitors came to the fort all winter long. The captains spent many hours talking with the Mandans, mostly seeking to learn as much as they could about the tribes and the country still to come, but also eager to cement relations for future trading. Lewis, Clark, and company were far from the first white men to arrive in this area. Traders, mostly French, had been operating in the area for perhaps a half century or more, and the captains conferred with some of them during their stay. It was also here the men met Toussaint Charbonneau and Sacagawea, who were to become among the most famous members of the party.

Lewis and Clark had just hired an interpreter, Rene Jessaume, who had moved into Fort Mandan with his wife and child. When Charbonneau offered his services, the captains said they had no need for him. But Charbonneau wouldn't take no for an answer. He finally sold the captains on the idea by promising that Sacagawea could help the expedition communicate with—and perhaps obtain horses from—her people, the Shoshone, once the party reached the Rocky Mountains.

No one knows whether Sacagawea had much say in the matter. Just a few years before, at about age twelve, she had been kidnapped near present-day Three Forks, Montana. She later was either sold to or won by Charbonneau and now, just sixteen or seventeen years old, was about to give birth to her first child. But despite her youth, Sacagawea more than earned her place in history over the next two years as an indispensable member of the expedition, and one of its most controversial.

Much of the controversy surrounds just how to spell and say her name: there are three predominant versions. Scholars generally agree on the spelling—Sacagawea—used throughout this book, pronouncing it "Sah-CAH-ga-we-a." But the spelling Sacajawea, pronounced "Sah-cah-ja-WE-a," is still popular and remains used, especially in her native state of Idaho. The third version is the one

Fort Mandan historic marker.

used most often in North Dakota: Sakakawea, pronounced "Sa-KAH-ka-we-a." A debate is currently under way in North Dakota over whether to adopt the more commonly used Sacagawea.

In addition, Sacagawea is frequently—but erroneously—viewed as the expedition's guide, a myth perpetuated by several books written in the early twentieth century. Although she didn't exactly guide the expedition, Sacagawea's assistance proved invaluable when the party reached the Great Divide of western Montana and Idaho. Here Sacagawea was able to identify landmarks and serve as an intermediary when—in an unbelievable coincidence—the corps came upon the Shoshone village led by Chief Cameahwait, Sacagawea's brother. Sacagawea helped the expedition in other ways, too: Since a war party would not travel with a woman and a baby, she and her baby, Jean Baptiste—or Pomp, as Captain Clark nicknamed him—served as signals of the corps' peaceful intentions. She also gathered plants and herbs for food and medicine.

Washburn is 38 miles north of Bismarck via U.S. Highway 83. The town celebrates its trail heritage each June with Lewis and Clark Days, which include a parade, buffalo barbecue, reenactments, lectures, and demonstrations. Nearby Cross Ranch State Park is one of North Dakota's nicest, with its scenic riverside location. Cross Ranch and an adjacent 6,000-acre nature preserve have more than 15 miles of hiking trails, which become cross-country ski routes in winter. Fishing, camping, and canoe rentals are among the park's other attractions. For a nice lodging alternative, call the state park reservations line at (800) 807–4723 and ask about reserving Cross Ranch's handsome Centennial Cabin.

For a long time, Fort Mandan was among the least-interpreted major sites along the Lewis and Clark Trail. That's no longer the case: The Washburn area is now home to both the North Dakota Lewis and Clark Interpretive Center and a revitalized Fort Mandan replica. Together with the presence of the Knife River Indian Villages and lots of recreation, there's now enough to see and do in central North Dakota that it has become one of the best spots to base a Lewis and Clark adventure.

Start at the interpretive center, where the permanent exhibits include a good overview of the expedition, with special attention paid to the Fort Mandan winter of 1804–1805 and Native American artifacts representing nearly every tribe the explorers encountered on the way west. Visitors can try on a buffalo robe or a weighted cradle board much like that Sacagawea used to carry her baby. You also learn that the corps members routinely ate five to seven pounds of meat per man per day, and that axes made by John Shields during the Mandan winter were quickly traded around the West. (On the corps' 1806 return trip, John Ordway reported seeing a Fort Mandan ax at a Nez Perce village 900 miles away.)

Here, too, is fine commentary on several questions that vex history students—why, for example, the corps ran into such trouble with the Teton Sioux in South Dakota when their dealings with tribes elsewhere went so well. As one exhibit explains, the Teton Sioux chief The Partisan was offended because he had received fewer gifts than his rival chief, Black Buffalo. This incident demonstrated how the captains never really understood tribal ways and methods of leadership. Lewis and Clark wanted to deal with one leader whose word would be law among the tribe, but Indian leaders didn't work that way. The chiefs' power "lay in their ability to persuade others to follow," the exhibit notes. "They needed time to hold councils and talk until the group reached an agreement."

The North Dakota Lewis and Clark Interpretive Center has scored several impressive coups since its 1997 opening. It is one of only a few sites in the world with a full set of prints by Karl Bodmer, the Swiss artist who documented life along the Missouri River in the 1830s. (The originals, as you'll recall, are in the Joslyn Art Museum in Omaha.) The museum has also added a wing to document the history of nearby Fort Clark, an important mid-nineteenth-century fur trading post named for William Clark.

The center is located at the junction of U.S. 83 and North Dakota Highway 200A. From Memorial Day through Labor Day, it is open daily from 9:00 A.M. to 7:00 P.M. Central Time; the rest of the year, hours are 9:00 A.M. to 5:00 P.M. Admission is $5.00 for adults and $3.00 for students (kindergarten through college); members of the North Dakota Lewis and Clark Bicentennial Foundation, which operates the center, are admitted free. For more information call (701) 462–8535.

Interpretive center admission also covers entrance into the reconstructed Fort

Mandan site less than 2 miles away. The replica, approximately 10 miles downstream from the original fort site, was built in the 1970s by local volunteers. It's now run under the auspices of the state bicentennial foundation, which has refurbished and furnished the replica and added year-round living-history demonstrations. Begin at the visitor services center, an earth lodge–shaped building constructed mainly from by-products from the local coal combustion industry. Watch the short orientation film, then wander up the short trail to the fort replica, which showcases the conditions experienced by the Corps of Discovery during the winter of 1804–1805. Interpreters are often on hand to tell stories and give demonstrations; if they're not, a brochure available from the visitor center can help explain what's what. The Fort Mandan replica is open from 9:00 A.M. to 7:00 P.M. in summer and 9:00 A.M. to 5:00 P.M. the rest of the year. The replica grounds are also a nice place for a picnic or easy hike along the Missouri River.

Since Lewis and Clark wintered here, you may wonder whether you might spend a frosty night at Fort Mandan, too. In general, no camping is allowed at Fort Mandan any time of year, but the State Historical Society of North Dakota has been holding special annual winter "Heritage Outbound" weekend campouts in recent years, with plans to continue through the bicentennial. Participants learn winter survival skills and sleep out under the stars (or in a tent, if they prefer). Other activities include cross-country skiing or snowshoeing, winter

Landing a voyageur canoe at the BirdWoman camp near Washburn, North Dakota.

Canoeing the Missouri

The Missouri River flows free from Garrison Dam to south of Bismarck. Here in the vicinity of Washburn, as on the Nebraska–South Dakota border and again in Montana, modern visitors get a rare chance to float a river that still appears much as it did 200 years ago.

BirdWoman Missouri River Adventures is a family-run company that offers canoe trips in its 26-foot-long voyageur canoe and camp stays on riverside land that the Yunker family has lived on since 1945. Named for Sacagawea, the trips aren't strictly Lewis and Clark themed but a historical hybrid incorporating lore from the North Woods voyageurs and the buckskinner era.

Up to eight people can sign on for the excursions, which can last from two hours to two days. Prices start at $40 per person. The trips take place on the same stretch of river where Lewis and Clark spent their long Dakota winter. The setting is splendid, but it's the family's small details that make these trips memorable. Meals are served on china, with cloth napkins and silverware. Becky Yunker Salveson and her children are all talented musicians, and they sometimes play at the nightly campfire. Guests can borrow traditional river clothing to wear on their journey if they choose, and the crew even packs ponchos in the canoe in case of rain.

If you have the chance, be sure to stay in BirdWoman's tepee village, which is probably within a few hundred feet of where Lewis and Clark camped October 25, 1805, shortly before they decided to remain in the area for the winter. Three 18-foot-diameter Sioux-style tepees are comfortably furnished with air beds and quilts for up to six people. Sage bundles hang above the door to keep the spirits happy and provide a fragrant welcome. For more information on BirdWoman River Adventures, call (701) 462–3367 or see www.birdwoman.com.

Another Washburn business, Lewis & Clark Canoe and Kayak Rentals, operates out of the Lewis & Clark Cafe in town. For $30 per day ($25 per kayak), you can paddle in the vicinity of Knife River Indian Village, Fort Mandan, and Cross Ranch State Park. Shuttle service is available for a minimum $10 extra, and box lunches can be included on request. Guided trips may be arranged, too. For more information or a reservation, call (701) 462–3668 or (701) 462–8635 and ask for Dave or Tammy Peyer.

Becky Yunker Salveson and her daughters play at the BirdWoman campfire.

hikes, meals featuring traditional foods, and presentations by historians, naturalists, and people from the nearby Indian nations. A canoe-based summer campout is also available. The two-day events cost about $250 per person. Call (701) 328–2666 for more information.

Fort Mandan was the site of the corps' first Christmas on the trail, and the captains reported their crew spent the day "merrily disposed." "We fired the swivels at daybreak and each man fired one round," wrote Sergeant Ordway. "Our officers gave the party a drink of (rum). We had the best to eat that could be had, and continued firing, dancing, and frolicking during the whole day. The savages did not trouble us as we had requested them not to come as it was a great medicine day with us. We enjoyed a merry Christmas during the day and evening until 9 o'clock—all in peace and quietness."

On February 11, as Lewis noted, Sacagawea gave birth to her son, Jean Baptiste, the newest member of the Lewis and Clark Expedition. "It is worthy of remark that this was the first child which this woman had borne, and as is common in such cases her labor was tedious and the pain violent," Lewis wrote. Jessaume, the interpreter, suggested to Lewis that a small portion of rattlesnake's rattle "never failed to produce the desired effect, that of hastening the birth of the child." Lewis just happened to have a rattle in his possession and gave it to Jessaume. "Whether this medicine was truly the cause or not I shall not undertake to determine, but I was informed that she had not taken it more than 10 minutes before she brought forth."

On April 7, 1805, the keelboat and eleven men were sent back downriver under the command of Corporal Richard Warfington and accompanied by a vast array of specimens for President Jefferson. Items shipped back included Native American artifacts, sixty plant specimens, many animal skins and skeletons, and four living magpies. Later that same day, the captains and the remainder of the party—thirty-three persons in all—resumed the upriver trip in six newly built canoes and the two old pirogues.

KNIFE RIVER INDIAN VILLAGES

From Washburn, it's a short drive west on North Dakota Highway 200A to the Knife River Indian Villages Historic Site, near the small town of Stanton. This site, administered by the National Park Service, offers another haunting hint at what life was like in the area when Lewis and Clark arrived.

Start with a stop at the visitor center, where a short film—shown on request—sets the scene by featuring the words of Buffalo-Bird Woman, one of the last Hidatsa to know the old ways. "Sometimes at evening I sit looking out on the big Missouri. The sun sets and dusk steals over the water," she says. "In the shadows, I seem again to see our Indian village with smoke curling upward from the earth lodges. . . . And in the river's roar, I hear the yells of the warrior, the laughter of little children as of old. It is but an old woman's dream. . . . Again I see but shadows and hear only the roar of the river and tears come into my eyes. Our Indian life, I know, is gone forever."

Gone, perhaps, but not forgotten. A trail from the visitor center winds past what once was the Awatixa Xi'e, or Lower Hidatsa Site. When the earth lodges collapsed, they left circular mounds of earth around hardened, saucerlike floors, surprisingly close together. The Hidatsa had plenty of room to spread out, so the depressions' proximity suggests that the village was quite close-knit, perhaps to offer protection from raiding tribes. About sixty earth-lodge depressions are plainly visible from the air.

The Awatixa abandoned this village sometime around 1780 after a smallpox epidemic but later returned to build a similar village closer to the Knife River. This later village is where Lewis and Clark encountered the Hidatsas when the expedition arrived late in 1804, and it was where Charbonneau and Sacagawea were camped.

Here the trail dips down to the Knife River. If a civilization can be known by its trash, this is where visitors get an even more intimate glimpse at the village. Molehill-like mounds 2 to 4 feet high near the village edge are middens, or garbage heaps, allowing researchers to reconstruct a 3,000-year archaeological profile of the area. Behind the visitor center, a 40-foot-diameter full-scale earth

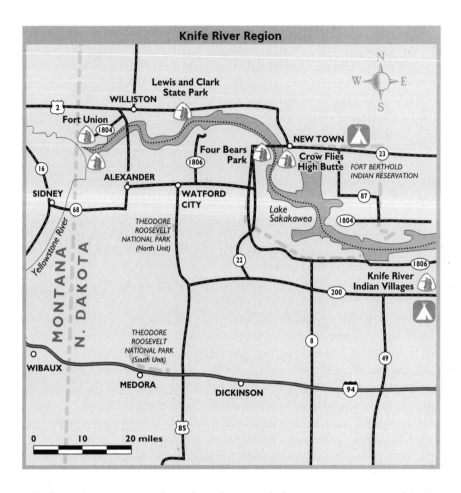

lodge has been constructed. Its furnishings include an impressive reproduction buffalo robe like the one once worn by Four Bears, a Mandan chief. Tours of the earth lodge are offered daily May through September. You can take a virtual tour of the earth lodge at the park's Web site: www.nps.gov/knri.

Knife River Indian Villages Historic Site is on Mountain Time. Hours are from 7:30 A.M. to 6:00 P.M. in summer and daily from 8:00 A.M. to 4:30 P.M. the rest of the year. It's closed Thanksgiving, Christmas, and New Year's Day. Admission is free, although donations are welcome. Call (701) 745–3309 for more information. The park is the site of the Northern Plains Indian Culture Fest held the fourth weekend each July. Ten miles farther north was the Big Hidatsa village, which also is part of the national monument and open to visitors.

Stanton is a tiny town with very basic visitor services and an Indian display at the courthouse. Sakakawea Park offers camping, a boat ramp, a playground, and tennis courts. Many local people work in nearby Beulah, home of the huge

A winter scene from the Knife River in North Dakota inspires awe.

Great Plains Synfuels, where lignite coal is turned into natural gas, or at similar plants in this energy-rich region.

Two good possibilities exist for those seeking a special place to stay in this region. Right on the Lewis and Clark route, consider the history-rich Missouri River Lodge. Diane and Orville Oster have farmed this land since 1968, and their 3,000-acre spread resonates with history. In addition to the Lewis and Clark connection, the ranch harbors several woodland-period Indian sites, a buffalo jump, and badlands bluffs painted by frontier artist George Catlin. There's good hiking, cycling, fishing, hunting, and wildlife viewing on the property, along with a boat ramp and sandy beach. Boat rentals and guided trips are available at a discount from several area outfitters, or you can bring your own watercraft. Horse boarding and rentals are available, as are sleigh rides and cross-country skiing or snowshoeing in winter. Accommodations in the seven guest rooms start at $60 for two persons. Breakfasts (included with overnight stays) are bountiful, and box lunches and gourmet dinners can be arranged. The Missouri River Lodge is 10 miles north of Stanton via county Road 37. For more information call (877) 480–3498 or visit www.moriverlodge.com.

A bit farther afield, near the town of Golden Valley, the Knife River runs through the land of Ron and Lois Wanner, proprietors of Knife River Ranch Vacations. This laid-back, off-the-beaten-path place is an undiscovered treasure

Medora and Theodore Roosevelt National Park

When he first ventured out to North Dakota's Badlands in 1883, Theodore Roosevelt was a sickly young New York State legislator who hoped some time hunting in the Wild West might cure his body and spirit. Like so many before him—and since—Roosevelt fell madly in love with the region and proceeded to spend several years living and ranching in the Dakotas in the mid-1880s before returning to public service as a Spanish-American War hero and, ultimately, as president.

The wealthy French Marquis deMores liked North Dakota, too—so much so that he founded a town on the frontier and named it for his bride, Medora von Hoffman. Within a few years, he had established a brickyard, packing plant, stage line, Catholic church, and several stores and saloons.

Today, the town of Medora serves as the southern gateway to Theodore Roosevelt National Park, and together they are North Dakota's most popular summer vacation destinations. Location hasn't hurt: The town and park sit right along Interstate 94 in the state's southwest corner. Although this is a bit off the Lewis and Clark Trail, it would be easy enough to detour west on I–94 from Bismarck, visit the Medora area and both the south and north units of Roosevelt National Park, then pick up the Corps of Discovery's route at Williston. North Dakota's "Rough Rider" country may also be a viable stop for travelers who return east on Interstates 90 and 94. This route also traverses Captain Clark's homeward journey along the Yellowstone River, a trip examined later in this chapter.

Medora is a very small town totally oriented to tourism. Attractions are numerous, ranging from the Medora Musical, performed nightly during summer at the Burning Hills Amphitheatre, to the Chateau de Mores State Historic Site, where the marquis's twenty-eight-room mansion includes many original furnishings and family possessions. The Medora Doll House claims to have a thousand dolls and antique toys from the eighteenth through twentieth centuries, and the Museum of the Badlands displays exhibits on Native Americans, wildlife, early fur trading, and the pioneer days.

Roosevelt was the best advertisement for one of the area's favorite pursuits: horseback riding. "There are few sensations I prefer to that of galloping over these rolling limitless prairies or winding my way among the barren fantastic and grimly picturesque deserts of the so-called Badlands," he wrote. Medora Stables offers trail rides ranging from one to three hours long from its headquarters on the east side of town (near the Bad Lands Motel), as does

Peaceful Valley Ranch, 7 miles north of town in the national park. Mountain biking is huge here, too, with rentals available in town. Check at the park visitor center for information.

Theodore Roosevelt National Park encompasses more than 70,000 acres in its two major units and at Roosevelt's Elkhorn Ranch, about 35 miles north of Medora. Huge herds of roaming American bison are a major attraction in both the south and north units, and pronghorn antelope, mule deer, elk, bobcats, and coyotes are among the other resident animals. Each unit has a designated scenic drive, a 36-mile loop in the south and a 14-mile route in the north, as well as hiking and nature trails. Early morning and late afternoon are the best time to see the park's legendary colored plateaus, bluffs, and buttes. If you're in the area and have time for just a brief stop, try the Painted Canyon Visitor Center 7 miles east of Medora on I–94.

The park is open year-round, although weather conditions generally close some roads during the winter. Campgrounds are situated in both units, and backcountry camping is also available, by permit.

For more information on Theodore Roosevelt National Park, call (701) 623–4466 (South Unit) or (701) 842–2333 (North Unit). For more information on Medora, call the Medora Chamber of Commerce at (701) 623–4910 or visit www.medorand.com.

where guests can ride horseback, canoe, mountain bike, or just laze in the lodge. It's not a fancy place, but the Wanners are fine hosts. Best of all, with cabins starting at about $55 for 2 persons and reasonably priced activities and meals on request, this is a ranch experience to suit nearly any budget. For more information write Knife River Ranch, RR1 Box 21A, Golden Valley, North Dakota 58541; call (701) 983–4290; or visit www.kniferiverranch.com.

LAKE SAKAKAWEA COUNTRY

Lake Sakakawea, like Lake Oahe, is one of the nation's largest man-made lakes, 178 miles long with a storage capacity of 24.6 million acre-feet and 1,600 miles of shoreline. The lake is the product of Garrison Dam, another of the six Pick-Sloan projects on the Missouri River. Built by the U.S. Army Corps of Engineers from 1947 through 1954 at a cost of $294 million, Garrison is the third-largest earth-filled dam in the United States, after Fort Peck and Oahe. It is 210 feet high and 11,300 feet long. Engineers used 1.5 million cubic yards of concrete in its construction, enough to build a two-lane road 400 miles long.

Despite the superlatives, Lake Sakakawea is relatively easy to break down to a more manageable size, especially along its more accessible northern shores. Secluded bays lure anglers with champion-size walleye, northern pike, smallmouth bass, sauger, chinook salmon, and striped bass. Several state parks, though popular, leave the visitor plenty of room to breathe. North Dakota is one of the smallest western states in total land area—69,299 square miles—but that's still nearly twice the size of Indiana and more than fourteen times the size of Connecticut.

From Stanton, North Dakota Highway 200A (soon ND 200) winds north before turning east at Pick City. Riverdale, 4 miles east, is the headquarters for Garrison Dam. Here in the power plant lobby, visitors can see displays on the dam, along with a 100-square-foot mural of Sacagawea and Pomp, painted by Clarence Cuts the Rope, a Hidatsa Indian. Lake Sakakawea State Park is also nearby, with 300 campsites, several rental cabins, and some of the lake's best salmon fishing.

From Riverdale, drive another 9 miles east to U.S. 83, which heads north, cutting between Lake Sakakawea and the much smaller Audubon Lake. North of the lakes, turn west on ND 37, which, combined with ND 1804, leads all the way to Williston, a distance of about 150 miles. Fort Stevenson State Park is near Garrison, with attractions including a prairie dog town, a 105-site campground, and abundant walleye fishing.

Lake Sakakawea from Crow Flies High Butte near New Town, North Dakota.

The expedition had its share of exciting and dangerous events in this area. On April 13, 1805, the white pirogue—the boat carrying most of the party's valuables, not to mention the two captains, Sacagawea, Charbonneau, and their son—was suddenly struck by a squall of wind and nearly capsized near the mouth of what is now called Van Hook Arm. The next day, Lewis wrote they had attained "the highest point to which any white man had ever ascended" on the Missouri, "except for two Frenchmen (one of whom Lapage was now with us) who having lost their way had straggled a few miles farther though to what place precisely I could not learn."

This same day, April 14, the expedition reached the area of Crow Flies High Butte and camped in the vicinity of Bear Den Bay. The winter had hit this area hard: Clark killed a "meager" buffalo bull, and Lewis shot an elk near Indian Creek, so poor it was unfit for use. But they also saw signs of spring: geese nesting in the trees, magpies, black-tailed prairie dogs, and at least two bears.

Parshall, located just off ND 37 before it turns west to New Town, is home to the noted Paul Broste Rock Museum, which displays rocks, fossils, and a large collection of hand-cut rock spheres. New Town is a good place to stop for fuel and food, since few services are available on ND 1804 for the next 75 miles or so. From New Town, drive about 2.25 miles west to a small interpretive area that tells the story of *Pe-Ri-Tska-Wa-Ku-Re* ("Crow Flies High"), a Hidatsa chief who was a leader on the Fort Berthold Indian Reservation. He lived at Like A Fishhook village until a disagreement with another chief led Crow Flies High and his followers to leave.

About 1870, Crow Flies High and his band of some 140 Hidatsa settled around Fort Buford near Williston, using that area as a winter base camp and ranging back into what is now the Lake Sakakawea area during the summer. For almost twenty-five years, Crow Flies High and his band were self-sustaining, living without government rations. They were forced back on the reservation in 1894, and the chief died of pneumonia in 1900.

The view from Crow Flies High Butte is beautiful, but the butte and its surroundings are also worth a look. Drive over the Four Bears Bridge (or its replacement, set for construction starting in 2004) and look back. A new hiking trail heads west of New Town to access the area.

More than many other Indian nations, the Mandan, Hidatsa, and Arikara people—known collectively as the Three Affiliated Tribes—realize the potential of the Lewis and Clark Bicentennial as an opportunity to tell of their lives before, during, and after the expedition. The tribes plan to build a major new interpretive and cultural center and earth lodge village near the existing Four Bears Park complex, which already includes a casino, hotel, tribal headquarters, and the Three Tribes Museum. New Town will be the site of an August 2006 bicentennial Signature Event (scheduled to mark the Corps of Discovery's 1806 return through the area), but the tribes also plan events in advance of that. For more information call the Three Affiliated Tribes Tourism & Independence office at (701) 627–2870 or visit www.mhanation.com/tourism.

For now the Three Tribes Museum is a good stop, with an abundance of beautiful bead and porcupine quillwork, some of it more than one hundred years old, and an amazing dress decorated with elk teeth. The museum is open daily mid-April through early November from 10:00 A.M. to 6:00 P.M.; admission is $5.00 for adults, $3.00 for seniors and students ages thirteen to eighteen. (Children twelve and under are admitted free.) Call (701) 627–4477 for more information or to arrange an off-season appointment.

Calvin Grinnell, a tribal historian based at the museum, is another good source for guided tours of the area from a native perspective. He offers primitive camping on his land at Saddle Butte, a Lewis and Clark–era landmark. With enough advance notice, he can arrange for tribal dancers and even a sweat ceremony. Call Grinnell at the museum or at (701) 627–4663 to get more information.

It was near here on their return trip that Lewis and Clark reunited on August 12, 1806, after separate explorations along the Missouri (Lewis) and Yellowstone (Clark) Rivers. One day earlier, Lewis had been seriously injured when near-sighted Private Cruzatte mistook the captain's buckskin-clad legs for an elk and shot him through both thighs. "The wounds bled considerably but I was happy to find that it touched neither bone nor artery," Lewis wrote. And the next day, "At 1 P.M. I overtook Captain Clark and party and had the pleasure of finding them all well. As writing in my present situation is extremely painful to me I shall desist until I recover and leave to my friend Captain C. the continuation of our journal."

Although just 19 miles from the town of Williston, Lewis and Clark State Park is rarely crowded. The park features rugged Badlands scenery and a nature trail that winds through one of the largest intact native prairies in the North Dakota state parks system. Camping, fishing, and boating are other popular activities.

Williston has only about 13,500 people, but in this country that's a good-sized town. The traveler will find plenty in the way of motels, restaurants, and shopping, along with several pleasant parks. The Upper Missouri Valley Fair is held just north of town in late June, and the local Frontier Museum's displays include a schoolhouse, medical offices, and a pioneer store. Williston is also the gateway to the North Unit of Theodore Roosevelt State Park (take U.S. Highway 85 south through Watford City), and to the Fort Union and Fort Buford historic sites, which we shall look at in the next section of this chapter. The Lewis and Clark Trail Museum in the small town of Alexander (also located south on U.S. 85) is housed in a 1914 school building, with one room dedicated to a scale model of the explorers' winter camp at Fort Mandan. It's open daily in the summer.

Williston is a stop on Amtrak's Empire Builder line, which runs from Chicago to Portland and Seattle. Amtrak and the National Park Service have teamed up to feature Lewis and Clark lore and other Northern Plains history on the route between Minot, North Dakota, and Shelby, Montana. Interpreters are on board from mid-May through early September. Visit www.amtrak.com for schedules and information.

THE MISSOURI-YELLOWSTONE CONFLUENCE

The Corps of Discovery's excitement grew as they neared the confluence of the Missouri and the Yellowstone, the Missouri's major tributary. The Yellowstone was finally glimpsed on April 25, 1805, by Lewis and four other men walking overland from the Missouri. "When we had proceeded on about 4 miles, I ascended the hills from whence I had a most pleasing view of the country, particularly of the wide and fertile valleys formed by the Yellowstone and Missouri Rivers, which occasionally unmasked by the wood on their borders disclose their meanderings for many miles in their passage through these delightful tracts of country," he wrote. "I determined to camp on the bank of the Yellowstone River which made its appearance about 2 miles south of me. The whole face of the country was covered with herds of buffalo, elk, and antelopes; deer are also abundant, but keep themselves more concealed in the woodland. The buffalo, elk, and antelope are so gentle that we pass near them while feeding without appearing to excite any alarm among them; and when we attract their attention, they frequently approach us more nearly to discover what we are, and in some cases pursue us a considerable distance apparently with that view." True to his word, Lewis and his party did camp on the Yellowstone that night, about 2 miles south of its confluence with the Missouri.

The next day, Lewis walked to the confluence. En route, he heard several shots, "which announced to me the arrival of the party with Captain Clark . . . after I completed my observations in the evening I walked down and joined the party at their encampment on the point of land formed by the junction of the rivers; found them all in good health, and much pleased at having arrived at this long-wished-for spot, and in order to add in some measure to the general pleasure which seemed to pervade our little community, we ordered a dram to be issued to each person; this soon produced the fiddle, and they spent the evening with much hilarity, singing & dancing, and seemed as perfectly as to forget their past toils, as they appeared regardless of those to come."

As they had at the spots that would become Fort Osage and Fort Atkinson, Lewis and Clark thought this confluence would be, as Clark put it, "a handsome situation" for a military or trading post. The explorers noted the riverbanks here had a gravel base and were situated well above flood level. Cottonwood and ash trees were available for construction. The site provided a broad vista, which would prevent approaching Indians from being concealed—and which would let the Indians see any trading post from quite a distance. On his return trip in 1806, Lewis surveyed and charted the land near the confluence.

Several years went by before anyone took advantage of the idea, but in 1828 John Jacob Astor's American Fur Company built Fort Union. Under the supervision of Kenneth McKenzie, the fort's first bourgeois (or superintendent), the new fort became a beacon on the Plains. Indians came to trade: first beaver skins; then tanned buffalo robes, elk, antelope, wolf, otter, hedgehog, and even mice. With these the natives could obtain metal goods, tools, blankets, food, and more. The Assiniboine, Crow, Cree, Gros Ventre, Mandan, Hidatsa, Arikara, Blackfoot, and Hunkpapa Sioux all trekked to Fort Union. Famous white visitors also came to see Fort Union: George Catlin, Prince Maximilian and Karl Bodmer, John Audubon, Jim Bridger, and Father Pierre De Smet were among those who visited the post in its heyday. During those peak years, the fort employed up to one hundred people, including clerks, hunters, craftsmen, herders, and traders. It was always a busy place.

Visitors watch a blacksmith working at Fort Union.

Busy, that is, until about the time of the Civil War. By then, smallpox, white westward expansion, and tensions with the Sioux had altered life on the Plains. In 1864 General Alfred Sully described Fort Union as "an old dilapidated affair, almost falling to pieces." Fort Union's era was almost over, but another era—that of Fort Buford—was about to begin.

Fort Union was located 2 miles from the confluence, but Fort Buford, the new infantry post established in 1866, was built overlooking the river junction. The post eventually housed six companies of infantry and cavalry and served as a vital link in American military strategy of the mid- to late nineteenth century. It was here that Sitting Bull surrendered in 1881; here, too, where Chief Joseph of the Nez Perce was imprisoned after his Montana capture just 42 miles from freedom at the Canadian border. Fort Buford remained in use until 1895, when widespread white settlement of the area made it no longer necessary.

For many decades, Fort Union and Fort Buford were mostly forgotten, but the sites have seen a dramatic upturn in interest and visitation in recent years. Late each April, Fort Union National Historic Site marks Lewis and Clark's arrival at the confluence with a weekend of activities. In midsummer 2003 Fort Buford State Historic Site will open its new Missouri-Yellowstone Confluence Interpretive Center, which explores the area's human and natural history before, during, and after the days of Fort Buford and Fort Union. The building's centerpiece is a striking view of the mighty rivers merging together. Plans also call for a 3.6-mile hiking and biking trail along the Missouri River to Fort Union. The center will be free and open daily year-round, except major winter holidays; tentative hours are 10:00 A.M. to 6:00 P.M. Central Time mid-May through mid-September and 8:00 A.M. to 4:30 P.M. the rest of the year. Fort Buford's grounds are also open for visits. For $4.00 per adult and $1.50 per child, you can take a docent-led tour of the field officers' quarters and the infantry barracks. Call (701) 572–9034 for more information on either the interpretive center or Fort Buford.

Fort Union National Historic Site was a grassy plain when the National Park Service acquired the land in 1966; today, much of the fort has been reconstructed, including the fabulous bourgeois house. Daily tours, living history demonstrations, and special interpretive programs are planned throughout the summer, including the annual Fort Union Trading Post Rendezvous typically held the third weekend of June. The fort is open daily from 8:00 A.M. to 8:00 P.M. Central Time Memorial Day through Labor Day and 9:00 A.M. to 5:30 P.M. the rest of the year except Thanksgiving, Christmas, and New Year's Day. Admission is by donation. For more information call (701) 572–9083.

The Missouri and Yellowstone Rivers meet almost smack-dab on the North Dakota–Montana border. The Corps of Discovery covered more miles in Montana than in any other state. From here Lewis and Clark Trail travelers have several options for proceeding west: retracing Clark's homeward journey along the

Yellowstone River, crossing Montana's most remote country south of the Missouri River, or taking the northern route across the Hi-Line.

HOMEWARD BOUND: CLARK ON THE YELLOWSTONE RIVER

When Lewis and Clark reached the Pacific, their trip was only half over, geographically speaking. And as much country as they'd covered heading west, the captains knew there was much they'd been unable to explore. So even before they left Fort Clatsop, their second winter camp, Lewis and Clark had decided they'd split up near what is now Missoula, Montana, and take separate routes back to the Missouri-Yellowstone confluence.

Clark chose the southerly route, traveling through the Big Hole, over Bozeman Pass, and onto the Yellowstone River—the section we will follow here. This route has little in the way of Lewis and Clark interpretation except for one very notable exception: It was along the Yellowstone, east of present-day Billings, that Clark carved his name at Pompeys Pillar. To this day, it is the only remaining documented physical evidence of the expedition. For that reason this particular side trip—though long—is well worth the traveler's time if it can be included in the itinerary.

Those who live in the East or Upper Midwest may want to make this trip, as Clark did, on their own way home. (In that event, it will be necessary to read this particular section in the reverse direction.) But the side trip may also be done while heading west by detouring from Fort Union to Interstate 94 (via Montana Highways 200 and 16), then on to Pompeys Pillar near Billings. From there the traveler could continue on into Billings and take U.S. Highway 87 north, resuming the corps' westward trek at Great Falls or Fort Benton. Most of the country along the Missouri River west of Fort Peck Dam is inaccessible by motor vehicle, anyway, so this detour, although about 100 miles longer than the alternatives, remains an option. What's a hundred miles in Montana, anyway?

Eastern Montana has a reputation as desolate, barren country. The region's topography certainly differs from the mountainous west, and sheer size and the vast distance between highway exits may be the reason some folks consider it monotonous. But eastern Montana has its own raw beauty and plenty of recreational and historical diversions.

Sidney, Montana, is the major town along the lower Yellowstone Valley. Long an agricultural center, Sidney enjoyed an oil boom in the late 1970s and early 1980s. Sidney's pride is the Mon-Dak Heritage Center, a bright, airy museum with changing art exhibits and a fascinating walk-through streetscape on its lower level. One painting, *Lewis and Clark Arriving at the Confluence* by Barbara

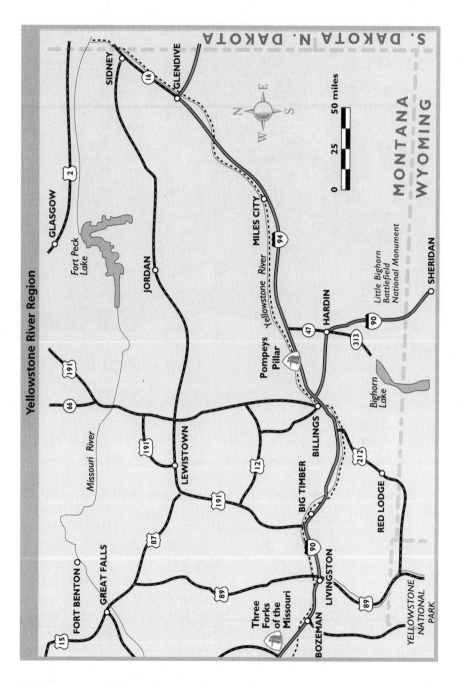

Schaffner, is in the museum's permanent collection. Other exhibits include fossils, dinosaur bones, a gun collection, and numerous photographs.

From Sidney, follow the Yellowstone Valley down MT 16 to Glendive. (If you're in the mood to fish, try your luck at catching the boneless, bottom-

A Lewis and Clark buff's license plate.

dwelling paddlefish, a species unique to this part of the country. You'll need a state license and a copy of the fishing regulations.) Glendive is the gateway to Makoshika State Park, 3 miles south of town in the badlands. Sight-seeing, rock hunting, and hiking are popular activities at Makoshika, and the area has also yielded some major dinosaur fossil finds. Glendive also marks the entrance to I–94.

The next major town, Miles City, is 75 miles west on I-94. Nestled at the mouth of the Tongue River, Miles City relishes its image as a cowboy's town. But this is also a commercial center for southeast Montana, and there are plenty of modern-day visitor amenities. The Miles City Jaycee Bucking Horse Sale, held the third weekend of May, is one of the biggest of its kind: Rodeo folks from many states visit to see and buy some of the wildest broncs this side of Dodge. The Range Riders Museum and historic Montana Bar at 612 Main Street are among Miles City's other attractions. The city park on the west side of town is an excellent place to take a break from the road, with a big playground and squirrels that will eat out of your hand.

Although home to only about 2,500 people, Forsyth is notable for some interesting architecture, especially the Rosebud County Courthouse, a Classical Revival building with a copper dome, murals, and stained glass. It dates from 1911.

The Little Big Horn Battlefield National Monument is accessible via exit 49 from I–94. Follow MT 47 south 30 miles to I–90, then another 15 miles to the battlefield. It was here General George Armstrong Custer and the Seventh Cavalry made their last stand against the Sioux and Northern Cheyenne.

And finally, at long last, Pompeys Pillar National Monument is found at exit 23 on I–94. Clark and his party arrived here July 25, 1806. Looking up at the monolith 200 feet high and 400 paces in circumference, he pronounced it "a remarkable rock" and named it Pompys Tower for Sacagawea's son, who by then was seventeen months old and much attached to Clark. (The affection was mutual).

Approaching the pillar, the visitor can't help but feel a real sense of excitement. Here is one of the few sites where little imagination is required: Captain Clark's signature is right there, plainly visible behind the protective glass casing. Looking at the signature, many visitors wonder: Was Clark that tall? Did someone boost him up to make his mark? Actually, the bluff around the signature has eroded since 1806.

After viewing the signature, continue on to the viewpoint on the pillar's west edge. It's a bit of a climb, but hikers are richly rewarded with a sublime view. Clark likely stood on this exact spot, and it is fun to imagine what the surrounding land may have looked like in his day. No interstate, no neatly plowed rectangles of farmland, no houses, no cars—and certainly no towering grain elevator, a most unfortunate recent development. But some things haven't changed much, chief among them the sprawling horizons and the wild, free-flowing Yellowstone, one of the only great western rivers still unfettered by dams. Clark found two piles of stones placed by Indians at the summit, along with many animals and designs carved on the steep rock faces.

Pompeys Pillar (formation in background) is a highlight on the trail in Montana.

Pompeys Pillar's development as a visitor attraction is something of a recent phenomenon. Montana's first historic marker was a protective grid over the signature, placed by the Northern Pacific Railroad in 1882. The grid did the job, but it also made viewing quite difficult. Some seventy years later, Don C. Foote, the landowner, replaced the grid with bulletproof glass. Ultimately the Footes sold the site to the Bureau of Land Management. The site was dedicated as a National Historic Landmark in 1992 and named a national monument in 2001. The name Pompeys Pillar was first seen upon the publication of the Lewis and Clark journals in 1814.

Several plaques sit at the base of the pillar, among them one dedicating the site to "the vision and spirit of the individuals who passed this way and left an indelible mark on the history of this great nation." The site also includes a riverside picnic area, rest rooms, and a small visitor center, with plans for a larger facility by 2005. Several dugout canoe replicas are also on display, the product of a Lewis and Clark float reenactment a few years back. Anyone unable to climb to Clark's signature will find a replica of his autograph inside the small visitor center.

Pompeys Pillar is accessible all the time. The interpretive staff is there from 8:00 A.M. to 8:00 P.M. Memorial Day weekend through Labor Day weekend, and from 8:00 A.M. to 4:30 P.M. weekdays the rest of the year. Admission during staffed hours is $3.00 per vehicle. Clark Days are held at Pompeys Pillar the last weekend of July. The event usually includes a reenactment of Clark's landing at the site plus demonstrations, nature walks, a pancake breakfast, a buffalo burger

William Clark's signature at Pompeys Pillar near Billings, Montana.

lunch, and more. Contact Pompeys Pillar or visit www.clarkontheyellowstone. org for dates or more information. For more information call (406) 875–2233.

The Yellowstone River is the last free-flowing major waterway in Montana. The section near Billings is a good float for experienced canoeists, but watch out for logjams and other snags. Montana Fun Adventures, based in Billings, can arrange canoe or raft trips on the river; call (888) 618–4FUN or (406) 254–7180 for more information. The same company runs a variety of other guided trips, including hour-long trolley tours in Billings and half-day treks to Pompeys Pillar; the latter cost $34 per person in 2002. Call or visit www.montanafunadventures.com for details. Another Billings company, Montana River Discoveries, offers jetboat trips, bird-watching expeditions, fishing excursions, and dinner cruises on the Yellowstone and Big Horn Rivers. Call (800) 344–0537 or visit www.riverdiscoveries.com for more information.

People touring on their own in Billings will find an array of interesting sites. The Peter Yegen Jr. Yellowstone Country Museum displays a variety of Native American, pioneer, and cowboy artifacts at Billings Logan International Airport, while the Western Heritage Center (2822 Montana Avenue) features changing exhibits on the region's history and culture. The Yellowstone Art Center (located in the original county jail at 401 North Twenty-seventh Street) focuses on contemporary Western works.

For spur-of-the-moment recreation, Billings has a good selection of parks, including Riverfront Park right along the Yellowstone and Lake Elmo, north of town in Billings Heights. The Mustangs, a Cincinnati Reds farm team, play June through August at Cobb Field on North Twenty-seventh Street. Major shopping areas include downtown Billings, with specialty shops and a factory outlet mall, and the West End, home of the Rimrock Mall, Billings' largest, with about ninety stores. Stop by the Billings Chamber of Commerce visitor center at 815 South Twenty-seventh Street for more local information, or call (800) 735–2635.

From Billings, the traveler can either head north on U.S. 87 toward Great Falls and Fort Benton to pick up the westward trek or follow Captain Clark's route in reverse along I–90 all the way to Three Forks—another major junction for the expedition. Highlights of this latter option might include the following:

■ **Park City (exit 426).** It was near here that Clark and his party actually started their Yellowstone River trip, after following the waterway for some distance overland. Near what is now called the Buffalo Mirage Access, Clark finally found some trees suitable for canoe building. The state-run access area offers camping, fishing, boat ramps, and picnic tables. Traveling on I–90, take the Park City exit and follow the signs 13 miles to the site.

■ **Big Timber (exit 377).** Another Yellowstone River access point, although the major attraction here is Big Timber Waterslide, a water-park complex with a half dozen large waterslides, Olympic-size swimming pool, bumper boats, and more. Greycliff Prairie Dog Town State Monument is at this exit, too.

Montana Centennial Trail Drive statue at the Billings visitor center.

■ **Livingston (exit 322)** and **Bozeman (exit 309).** It was between these two towns—helped by Sacagawea, who knew the area from girlhood—that the Clark party crossed Bozeman Pass and descended to the Yellowstone Valley. Both cities are major recreation areas and gateways to Yellowstone National Park (see the side trip near the end of Chapter 6).

The Gallatin County Pioneer Museum at 317 West Main Street in Bozeman has a large collection of books, atlases, and other materials related to Lewis and Clark, donated by Don Nell, a past president of the Lewis and Clark Trail Heritage Foundation, and it's open to public use. There's also a statue of Sacagawea and Pomp by Bozeman's visitor center on North Seventh Avenue.

■ **Three Forks (exit 278).** On their 1804 westward trip, Lewis and Clark finally discovered the Missouri River headwaters here. (See the Three Forks of the Missouri section in Chapter 6 for a complete description of the area.) Eastbound in 1806, the Clark party split up at the Three Forks, with Sergeant Ordway and nine others pushing down the Missouri to rendezvous with Captain Lewis, and Clark and twelve others continuing overland to the Yellowstone.

THE HI-LINE

Now we return to Fort Buford, for travelers who want to follow the corps' westward journey up the Missouri.

Past the Missouri-Yellowstone confluence, it becomes difficult to trace Lewis and Clark's route by land. Two motor routes parallel the Missouri, but neither very closely. Back roads provide access to the river, but these offer little more than a few miles of riverbank driving. The traveler's best bet is to hightail it for Fort Benton, where—if your schedule permits—outfitters can help you backtrack a ways on a stretch of water that closely resembles the waterway Lewis and Clark experienced—the Upper Missouri National Wild and Scenic River.

But first we must get across a huge chunk of northeast Montana, a land so vast that high school sports teams frequently must travel all day to reach their opponents. The two major routes across this part of the state are U.S. Highway 2 and Montana Highway 200/U.S. 87. Often called the Hi-Line, after the Great Northern Railway route it paralleled, U.S. 2 is the more popular and practical of the two.

Urged on by Great Falls founder Paris Gibson and copper baron Marcus Daly, rail magnate James Hill decided that northern Montana was ripe for settling. Towns like Glasgow, Zurich, Havre, and Malta were named in hopes of appealing to would-be European immigrants; in some instances, Great Northern employees reportedly spun the globe, closed their eyes, and jabbed their finger at the whirling sphere. Whatever town they hit, that was the new settlement's name.

Many immigrants arrived between 1910 and 1918, eager to claim their land and start farming. For a while the homesteaders flourished; wet weather and World War I led to inflated grain prices. But a long drought set in about 1918, and many settlers left just as soon as they'd come. These days, however, northeastern Montanans generally do well with wheat, often planted in strips to help control wind erosion.

It's some 350 miles from the North Dakota border to Fort Benton, way too much ground to cover thoroughly when Lewis and Clark lore is the primary objective. So let's take a brief look at highlights of the Hi-Line:

■ When folks think of Montana, many think about cowboys, and several outfitters around the state offer honest-to-goodness working ranch vacations. Montana River Ranch is a bed-and-breakfast lodge coupled with a working 8,000-acre ranch on the north side of the Missouri near Fort Union and Bainville. The Harmon family has been on this spread since 1906, and their land includes the first place in present-day Montana where the Corps of Discovery shot at a grizzly bear, on April 28, 1805. (Lewis wrote that they wounded the

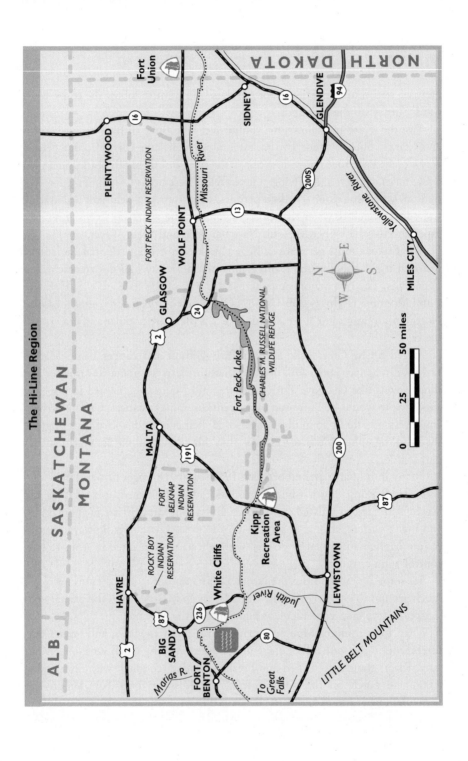

The Hi-Line Region

bear, but it did not die. The hunters actually killed their first grizzly the next day near Culbertson.) Ranch offerings include horseback riding, river rafting, wildlife viewing, and fishing. Activities can be tailored to a guest's interests, and the ranch prides itself on its personal service—90 percent of its business comes from repeat visitors. Package prices run $275 to $325 per person per day, including meals, lodging, and activities; family rates are available. The ranch also welcomes day visitors for canoe trips and sight-seeing; call for rates. For more information phone (877) 277–4084 or visit www.montanariverranch.com. Gene and Marsha Foss of Culbertson, Montana, offer several cattle drives each summer. The five-day rides are geared to people with all levels of riding experience, and the Fosses have guided people from as far away as Hong Kong and Switzerland. For more information write Gene Foss, HC 69 Box 97, Culbertson, MT 59218, or call (406) 787–5559.

■ Poplar is on the Fort Peck Indian Reservation, home to about 6,800 Sioux and Assiniboine people. The Fort Peck Assiniboine and Sioux Culture Center and Museum, open weekdays on the north side of MT 2, has exhibits on Native American culture. Just across the highway, Titoka Tibi ("The Visiting Place") has a good selection of native arts and crafts; the Poplar Museum next door showcases still more local history. Fort Peck Community College runs a week-long Lewis and Clark Upper Missouri River Institute late each June. The seminar includes lectures and field trips to relate the expedition's history with the

American white pelicans on the Missouri River.

Assiniboine and Sioux tribes, and it concludes with a guided float trip from Fort Peck to the Lewis and Clark Bridge 7 miles east of Wolf Point. For more information call (406) 768–5551 or e-mail JoeM@fpcc.cc.mt.us.

■ Wolf Point pays tribute to our heroes at Lewis and Clark Memorial Park, situated several miles east of town on the Missouri River. The town's major event is the Wolf Point Stampede, Montana's oldest rodeo and one of its best. A shared celebration of cowboy and Native American culture, the event takes place the second weekend of July.

■ Nashua and Glasgow, less than an hour west of Wolf Point, are the jumping-off spots for Fort Peck Dam, largest and westernmost of the Pick-Sloan Plan impoundments. The earth-filled dam is more than 21,000 feet long, 3,500 feet wide at its base, and 250 feet high. The dam created Fort Peck Lake, with a storage capacity of nineteen million acre-feet of water and a surface area of 249,000 acres. The lake stretches about 150 miles west, more than the distance spanned between Pittsburgh and Cleveland, while its total shoreline—nearly 1,600 miles—is longer than that of California.

In addition to Fort Peck the dam and Fort Peck the lake, there's Fort Peck the town. Built by the U.S. Army Corps of Engineers to house some of the many thousands who worked on the dam, Fort Peck still boasts some interesting architecture, including the ACOE office, the Fort Peck Hotel, and the popular Fort Peck Theatre, which presents live shows each summer. The new Fort Peck Dam Interpretive Center and Museum, set to open in 2003, will have exhibits on the construction of Fort Peck Dam, Native American culture, homesteading, Lewis and Clark, and paleontology. There also are two new overlooks with Lewis and Clark interpretation on MT 24 near the dam.

■ Glasgow's Valley County Pioneer Museum, just west of town, is one of Montana's better small-town museums. It has several Lewis and Clark exhibits; one tells how Lewis and Clark came to name the Milk River, which the Indians had earlier called "The River Which Scolds at All Others." The expedition reached this largest and most important northern tributary of the Missouri on May 8, 1805. "The water of this river possesses a peculiar whiteness, being about the color of a cup of tea with the admixture of a tablespoonful of milk," Lewis wrote. "From the color of its water we called it Milk River." The museum plans a new panoramic exhibit of the Lewis and Clark at the Missouri-Milk River confluence, featuring a full mount of a grizzly bear, live plants, and a mural by Rocky Boy's Chippewa-Cree artist Jesse Henderson. It will be in place by the end of 2003.

■ Western Montana is full of hot springs, but they're something of a rarity in the state's eastern reaches. Sleeping Buffalo Hot Springs Resort near Saco was named for a group of glacial boulders near the Milk River that, from a distance, resemble a herd of sleeping buffalo. These were held sacred by the Indians, with one rock in particular thought to be the leader. Indians sacrificed possessions at this rock, now part of a roadside monument at the hot springs turnoff. Facilities at the resort include several pools, a water slide, golf course, restaurant, and lodging.

■ Malta sits at the terminus of U.S. 191, the best land route to James Kipp Recreation Area, one of the most popular and accessible spots in the Charles M. Russell National Wildlife Refuge, second largest in the continental United States at 1.2 million acres. Located just east of the designated Upper Missouri National Wild and Scenic River, Kipp Recreation Area is a frequent take-out point for longer river trips through the corridor. Lewis and Clark spent nearly two weeks within the CMR's boundaries on their way west in 1805. Today you can still see much of what they saw: bighorn sheep, pronghorn, deer, elk, and coyotes— everything except grizzly bears and wolves, which now live only in sections of western Montana.

Big as it is, the CMR is difficult to access. The 20-mile CMR Auto Tour Route begins north of the Fred Robinson Bridge, which crosses the Missouri River on MT 191 about 70 miles southwest of Malta. The Missouri Breaks National Back Country Byway, an 81-mile loop, leaves from just south of the Fred Robinson Bridge. For either route, get a good local map, exercise caution, and don't even think of exploring the area's back roads if rain is threatening—the terrain quickly becomes an impassable gumbo when wet.

■ Fort Belknap is the headquarters for the Gros Ventre and Assiniboine Tribes of Montana, with a combined enrollment of about 4,000 people. Together the tribes offer guided tours of a 13,000-acre tribal bison reserve each day between May 1 through September 30. For more information or to reserve a tour, call (406) 353–8473, or stop in the visitor center just south of the corner of U.S. 2 and MT 66. Not far west near Chinook, Chief Joseph of the Nez Perce surrendered on October 5, 1877, with his eloquent "I will fight no more forever…" speech. The site is marked at the Bear's Paw/Chief Joseph Battlefield 16 miles south of U.S. 2. If you're in the area in summer, consider attending Milk River Indian Days (the fourth weekend in July) or the Rocky Boy's Powwow (the first weekend of August). The Rocky Boy's Reservation, home to about 2,500 Chippewa-Cree people, is centered near the town of Box Elder on U.S. 87.

■ Havre is the most populous town on the Hi-Line, home of Northern Montana College and jumping-off spot for Fort Benton, Great Falls, and the rest of the Lewis and Clark route. If you have time, stop by the H. Earl Clack Museum in Havre's Lions Park, where exhibits include some excellent photos of Native American sites and a piece of the Berlin Wall. The park also offers reasonably priced RV and tent sites, as well as tours of nearby Fort Assiniboine and an area buffalo jump. Beaver Creek Park, one of the largest county-run parks in the nation, is south of Havre.

Another alternate route across east-central Montana runs about 400 miles from the Dakota border to Fort Benton, following MT 200 (from Sidney to Grass Range), U.S. 87 (from Grass Range to Stanford via Lewistown), and MT

80 (from Stanford to Fort Benton). This is big, wild country, where a dot on the map doesn't necessarily indicate much. As W. C. McRae and Judy Jewell point out in their *Montana Handbook,* "Between Sidney and Lewistown—a distance of almost 300 miles—Highway 200 passes through only three towns with gas pumps; their combined population approaches 1,500 people. As it connects up these remote enclaves of humanity, Highway 200 intersects a part of Montana often called the Big Lonely. Unpopulated, marginally productive, and often starkly beautiful, this is one of the last vast frontiers left in Montana."

Lewistown is the biggest and most interesting town along this route. Nestled in a valley amid the Judith, Moccasin, and Big Snowy Mountains, this city of about 6,400 was named not for Meriwether Lewis but for an Army officer who established a fort nearby in the 1870s. Lewistown has a handsome downtown area with interesting architecture, notably the Fergus County Courthouse. The Central Montana Museum, in the same building as the chamber of commerce at 408 Northeast Main Street, exhibits pioneer and Native American artifacts.

The Lewistown area's most popular attraction is probably the Charlie Russell Chew-Choo dinner train, which takes a 56-mile, three-and-a-half-hour round-trip between Kingston (about 10 miles northwest of Lewistown) and Denton. The train runs every Saturday night from the last weekend in May through the end of September, with a per-person cost of $85, including a prime rib dinner. The train also makes special runs during the mid-August Montana Cowboy Poetry Festival and for the winter holidays. For reservations call Main Connection Travel in Lewistown at (406) 538–2527.

Lodging

Lodgings, campgrounds, and restaurants listed below are a representative sampling of what is available. Listing in these pages does not imply endorsement, nor is this a complete listing of all reputable businesses. For more complete listings contact the visitor information bureau or chamber of commerce in each town. Room rates were accurate as of summer 2002 but are subject to change.

FORT YATES, NORTH DAKOTA
Prairie Knights Lodge, (701) 258–7000, 46 miles south of Mandan on ND 1806; $65–$120.

BISMARCK/MANDAN, NORTH DAKOTA
Best Western Seven Seas Inn, (701) 663–7401, 2611 Old Red Trail (Mandan); $80.

Bismarck Motor Hotel, (701) 223–2474, 2301 East Main Street; $33–$43.
Expressway Inn, (800) 456–6388, 200 East Bismarck Expressway; $55–$75.
Radisson Inn Bismarck, (701) 258–7700 or (800) 333–3333, 800 South Third Street; $70 and up.
Select Inn, (800) 641–1000, 1505 Interchange Avenue; $50–$65.

*Denotes towns along Clark's 1806 homeward route.

WASHBURN, NORTH DAKOTA

Kroh's Nest Bed & Breakfast, (701) 462–8663, 206 Sixth Street; $60.

ScotWood Motel, (701) 462–8191, 1323 Frontage Road; $42–$50.

STANTON, NORTH DAKOTA

Missouri River Lodge, (879) 480–3498, 10 miles north; $60 and up.

GARRISON, NORTH DAKOTA

Garrison Motel, (701) 463–2858, 0.25 mile east on ND 37; $38–$45.

Indian Hills Resort, (701) 743–4122, ND 1804 west of Garrison on Good Bear Bay. Cabins and condos for rent.

PARSHALL, NORTH DAKOTA

Parshall Motor Inn, (701) 862–3127, North Main Street; $40.

NEW TOWN, NORTH DAKOTA

Cottage Inn, (701) 627–4217, Main Street; $40–$50.

4 Bears Lodge, (800) 294–5454, 4 miles west over bridge; $50–$70.

Sunset Motel, (701) 627–3316, ND 23 East; $40–$55.

West Dakota Inn, (701) 627–3721, ND 23 East; $35–$50.

WILLISTON, NORTH DAKOTA

Airport International Inn, (701) 774–0241, U.S. 2 and U.S. 85 North; $48.

El Rancho Motor Hotel, (701) 572–6321, 1623 Second Avenue West; $50–$55.

Select Inn, (800) 641–1000, 213 Thirty-fifth Street; $48–$52.

Super 8 Lodge, (800) 800–8000, 2324 Second Avenue West; $55.

Travel Host, (701) 774–0041, 3801 Second Avenue West; $40.

*SIDNEY, MONTANA

Lone Tree Inn, (406) 433–4520, 900 South Central; $47–$52.

Park Plaza Motel, (406) 433–1520, 601 South Central; $37.

Richland Motor Inn, (406) 433–6400, 1200 South Central; $62–$67.

*GLENDIVE, MONTANA

Best Western Jordan Inn, (406) 377–5555, 223 North Merrill Avenue; $75–$100.

Budget Host Riverside Inn, (406) 377–2349, I-94 and MT 16; $43–$46.

El Centro Motel, (406) 365–5211, 112 South Kendrick Avenue; $35–$40.

*MILES CITY, MONTANA

Budget Inn, (406) 232–3550, 1006 South Haynes Avenue; $44–$50.

Guest House Inn & Suites, (406) 232–3661, 3111 Steel Street; $70–130.

Holiday Inn Express, (406) 232–1000, 1720 South Haynes Avenue; $90–$100.

*FORSYTH, MONTANA

Best Western Sundowner Inn, (406) 356–2115, 1018 Front Street; $75–$85.

Restwel Motel, (406) 356–2771, 810 Front Street; $45–$50.

*BILLINGS, MONTANA

The Billings Inn, (800) 231–7782, 880 North Twenty-ninth Street; $65–$75.

Hilltop Inn, (800) 878–9282, 1116 North Twenty-eighth Street; $65–$75.

Radisson Northern Hotel, (406) 245–5121, 19 North Twenty-eighth Street; $95 and up.

Ramada Limited, (800) 272–6232, 1345 Mullowney Lane; $85–$100.

Sheraton Billings Hotel, (406) 252–7400, 27 North Twenty-seventh Street; $110.

---

*Denotes towns along Clark's 1806 homeward route.

*COLUMBUS, MONTANA
Riverside Guest Cabins, (406) 322–5066, 44 West Pike Avenue; $45.
Super 8, (406) 322–4101, 602 Eighth Avenue North; $65–$100.

*BIG TIMBER, MONTANA
C. M. Russell Lodge, (406) 932–5244, I–90 exit 367; $45–$55.

*LIVINGSTON, MONTANA
Budget Host Parkway Motel, (406) 222–3840, 1124 West Park; $60–$80.
Del Mar Motel, (406) 222–3120, I–90 business loop; $55–$75.
Murray Hotel, (406) 222–1350, 201 West Park Street; $70–$108.
The River Inn, (406) 222–2429, 4950 U.S. 89; $85–$105.

*BOZEMAN, MONTANA
The Bozeman Inn, (406) 587–3176, 1235 North Seventh Avenue; $70–$80.
Gallatin Gateway Inn, (406) 763–4672, 12 miles southwest on U.S. 19; $135–$245.
Holiday Inn, (406) 587–4561, 5 Baxter Lane; $90–$110.
Howlers Inn Bed & Breakfast, (888) 469–5377, east of Bozeman off I–90; $85–$275. On-premise wolf preserve.
Lewis and Clark Motel, (406) 586–3341, 824 West Main Street; $78–$85.
Royal 7 Motel, (406) 587–3103, 310 North Seventh Avenue; $55–$65.
Voss Inn, (406) 587–0982, 319 South Wilson; $105–$125.

BAINVILLE, MONTANA
Montana River Ranch Country Inn, (406) 769–2127; $275 and up, including meals and activities.

CULBERTSON, MONTANA
Diamond Willow Inn, (406) 787–6218, U.S. 2; $35–$43.
Kings Inn, (406) 787–6277, 408 Sixth Street East; $45–$55.

WOLF POINT, MONTANA
Big Sky Motel, (406) 653–2300, U.S. 2 East; $36–$42.
Homestead Inn, (800) 231–0986, 101 U.S. 2 East; $43–$48.
Sherman Motor Inn, (800) 952–1100, 200 East Main; $47–$52.

GLASGOW, MONTANA
Campbell Lodge, (406) 228–9328, 534 Third Avenue South; $35–$40.
Cottonwood Inn, (800) 321–8213, U.S. 2 East; $60–$70.
La Casa Motel, (406) 228–9311, 238 First Avenue North; $37–$42.

MALTA, MONTANA
Edgewater Inn, (800) 821–7475 (in state) or (406) 654–1302, 101 U.S. 2 West; $50–$60.
Maltana Motel, (406) 654–2610, 138 South First Avenue; $48–$60.

CHINOOK, MONTANA
Chinook Motor Inn, (406) 357–2248, 100 Indiana Avenue; $58–$68.

HAVRE, MONTANA
Super 8, (406) 265–1411, 1901 U.S. 2; $60.
TownHouse Inn, (406) 265–6711, 601 West First Street; $75–$100.

LEWISTOWN, MONTANA
B&B Motel, (406) 538–5496, 520 East Main Street; $50–$55.

*Denotes towns along Clark's 1806 homeward route.

Pheasant Tales Bed & Bistro, (406) 538–7880; $85.

Yogo Inn, (800) 860–9646, 211 East Main Street; $60–$80.

Camping

BISMARCK/MANDAN, NORTH DAKOTA
Bismarck KOA, (701) 222–2662, 3720 Centennial Road.
Colonial Motel and Campground, (701) 663–9824, 4631 Memorial Highway (Mandan).
Fort Abraham Lincoln State Park, (701) 663–9571, south of Mandan on ND 1806.
Mandan Camping Area, (701) 667–3280, 4 blocks west of ND 1806 on Third Street (Mandan).

WASHBURN, NORTH DAKOTA
Fort Mandan Historical Site, (701) 462–8129, west of town.
City Park, free overnight camping.

STANTON, NORTH DAKOTA
Sakakawea Park, (701) 745–3202.

PICK CITY, NORTH DAKOTA
Lake Sakakawea State Park, (701) 487–3315.

GARRISON, NORTH DAKOTA
Fort Stevenson State Park, (701) 337–5576, 3 miles south.
Indian Hills Resort, (701) 463–2102, 31 miles west.

WILLISTON, NORTH DAKOTA
Buffalo Trails Campground, (701) 572–3206, 4 miles north via U.S. 2 and U.S. 85.
Lewis and Clark State Park, (701) 859–3071, 16 miles east on ND 1804.

Lund's Landing, (701) 568–3474, 24 miles east on ND 1804.

*GLENDIVE, MONTANA
Green Valley Campground, (406) 377–1944, I–94 exit 213.
Glendive Campground, (406) 377–6721, I–94 exit 215.
Makoshika State Park, (406) 365–6256, 2 miles southeast on Snyder Avenue.

*MILES CITY, MONTANA
KOA–Miles City, (406) 232–3991, I–94 exit 135.

*BILLINGS, MONTANA
Billings Metro KOA, (406) 252–3104, 547 Garden Avenue.
Yellowstone River RV Park & Campground, (406) 259–0878, I–90 exit 450.

*LAUREL, MONTANA
Pelican RV Park, (406) 628–4324, 11360 South Frontage Road.

*COLUMBUS, MONTANA
Itch-Kep-Pe Park, (406) 322–4505, on south edge of town.

*BIG TIMBER, MONTANA
KOA–Big Timber, (406) 932–6569, I–90 exit 377.

*LIVINGSTON, MONTANA
KOA–Paradise Valley, (406) 222–0992, 10 miles south on U.S. 89.
Livingston Inn & Campground, (406) 222–1122, I–90 exit 333.

*Denotes towns along Clark's 1806 homeward route.

*BOZEMAN, MONTANA
Bear Canyon Campground, (406) 587–1575, I–90 at Bear Canyon Road.
Bozeman Hot Springs KOA, (406) 587–3030, 81123 Gallatin Road. (U.S. 191).
Manhattan RV Park, (406) 284–6930, I–90 exit 288 (Manhattan).
Sunrise Campground, (406) 587–4797, I–90 exit 309.

CULBERTSON, MONTANA
Bicentennial Park, south side of town. Free camping with RV hookups.

WOLF POINT, MONTANA
R.B.W. Campground, (406) 525–3740, 7 miles east on U.S. 2.
Rancho Campground, (406) 653–1940, 1.25 miles west on U.S. 2.

GLASGOW, MONTANA
Shady Rest RV Park, (800) 422–8954, U.S. 2 and Lasar Drive.

Trails West Trailer Park & Campground, (406) 228–2778, 1.5 miles west on U.S. 2 at Skylark Road.

MALTA, MONTANA
Edgewater Campground, (800) 821–7475, U.S. 2 West.

HAVRE, MONTANA
Beaver Creek Park, (406) 395–4565, south of Havre via Fifth Avenue.
Earl Clack Museum & Campground, (406) 265–9913, in Lions Park on U.S. 2.
Evergreen Campground, (406) 265–8228, south of town on U.S. 87.
Fresno Reservoir, (406) 247–7314, 12 miles west of Havre on U.S. 2.
Havre Family Campground, (406) 265–9722, 9 miles east on U.S. 2.
Havre RV Park, (406) 265–8861, 1300 First Street.

LEWISTOWN, MONTANA
Mountain Acres RV Park & Campground, (406) 538–7591, north on U.S. 191. No tents.

Restaurants

FORT YATES, NORTH DAKOTA
Feast of the Rock Buffet at Prairie Knights Casino, (800) 425–8277, 46 miles south of Mandan on Highway 1806.

BISMARCK/MANDAN, NORTH DAKOTA
Little Cottage Cafe, (701) 223–4949, 2513 East Main. Homemade soups, pies, and pastries.
Paradiso, (701) 224–1111, 2620 State Street. Mexican dining.

Peacock Alley Bar & Grill, (701) 255–7917, 422 East Main Street. Dining downtown in a historic setting.
Seasons Cafe, (701) 258–7700; ext. 1850, 800 South Third Street (in the Radisson Inn Bismarck). Featuring regional American specialties.
Space Aliens Grill & Bar, (701) 223–6220, 1304 West Century Avenue. Fun theme restaurant.

WASHBURN, NORTH DAKOTA
Dakota Farms, (701) 462–8175, U.S. 83 bypass. Wide menu with daily specials.

*Denotes towns along Clark's 1806 homeward route.

Lewis & Clark Cafe, (406) 462–3668, 604 Main Street. Breakfast and lunch.

COLEHARBOR, NORTH DAKOTA
83 Cafe, (701) 442–3294, U.S. 83.

GARRISON, NORTH DAKOTA
Lake Road Restaurant, (701) 463–2569, ND 37. Breakfast all day, sack lunches to go.
Stone Inn Supper Club & Lounge, (701) 337–5590, ND 37 East. Nightly specials; prime rib Fridays and Saturdays.

NEW TOWN, NORTH DAKOTA
Lucky's Cafe, (800) 294–5454, at 4 Bears Lodge.
Main Lanes & Café, (701) 627–4494, 204 Main Street. Home–cooked meals.
Scenic 23 Supper Club & Lounge, (701) 627–3949, east of town on ND 23. Steakhouse.

WILLISTON, NORTH DAKOTA
Gramma Sharon's, U.S. 2 and U.S. 85. Open twenty-four hours at the Conoco Truck Stop.
Lund's Landing Restaurant, (701) 568–3474, 24 miles east on ND 1804. Pan-fried walleye and juneberry pie.
Trapper's Kettle, (701) 774–2831, north on U.S. 2 and U.S. 85. Informal American dining.

*SIDNEY, MONTANA
New China Restaurant, (406) 488–6188, 821 South Central Avenue.
South 40 Restaurant, (406) 482–4999, 207 Second Avenue Northwest. Wide menu including entrees, burgers, soup and salad bar.

*GLENDIVE, MONTANA
Twilite Dining & Lounge, (406) 377–8705, 209 North Merrill. Prime rib, steak, chicken, and seafood.

*MILES CITY, MONTANA
Stagecoach Station, (406) 232–2288, 3020 Stower. Local favorite.

*FORSYTH, MONTANA
Bloomin' Onion, (406) 356–2931, 109 South Tenth Avenue.
Speedway Diner, (406) 356–7987, 811 Main. Daily specials, homemade pies, salad bar.

*BILLINGS, MONTANA
Dos Machos, (406) 652–2020, 980 South Twenty-fourth Street West. Mexican-American food.
George Henry's Restaurant, (406) 245–4570, 404 North Thirtieth Street. Food made from scratch in early American atmosphere.
Jake's, (406) 259–9375, 2701 First Avenue North. Steaks, ribs, seafood.
The Rex, (406) 245–7477, 2401 Montana Avenue. Steaks, buffalo, pasta, seafood.
Torres Cafe, (406) 652–8426, 6200 South Frontage Road. Mexican.

*LAUREL, MONTANA
Little Big Men Pizza, (406) 628–8241, 220 First Avenue South. Pizza and more.

*COLUMBUS, MONTANA
Apple Village Cafe, (406) 322–5939, I–90 exit 408. Sunday brunch, salad bar.

*BIG TIMBER, MONTANA
Crazy Jane's Pub & Eatery, (406) 932–4419, I–90 exit 367. Family dining.

*Denotes towns along Clark's 1806 homeward route.

Prospector Pizza Plus, (406) 932–4846, 121 McLeod Street. Pizza, sandwiches, salad, ribs.

*LIVINGSTON, MONTANA
Livingston Bar & Grille, (406) 222–7909, 130 North Main. Montana trout, beef, and buffalo burgers.
Martin's Café, (406) 222–2110, 108 West Park Street. Locally popular home cooking.

*BOZEMAN, MONTANA
John Bozeman's Bistro, (406) 587–4100, 125 West Main. Great American food, generous portions.
O'Brien's, (406) 587–3973, 312 East Main. Local favovrite for breakfast; dinner Tuesday through Saturday.
Spanish Peaks Brewery and Italian Cafe, (406) 585–2296, 14 North Church Avenue. Microbrewery/restaurant featuring brick-oven pizza, pasta, and seafood.

CULBERTSON, MONTANA
M & M's Place, (406) 787–5362, 14 East Sixth. Family restaurant.
Wild West Diner, (406) 787–5374, 20 East Sixth.

WOLF POINT, MONTANA
Old Town Grill, (406) 653–1031, 400 U.S. 2. Mexican food, burgers.

Sherman Motor Inn, (406) 653–1100, 200 East Main. Wide menu.

GLASGOW, MONTANA
Johnnie Cafe, (406) 228–4222, 433 First Avenue. Open twenty-four hours.
Sam's Supper Club, (406) 228–4614, 307 First Avenue North. Here's the beef.

MALTA, MONTANA
Hitchin' Post, (406) 654–1882, U.S. 2. Western home cooking.
Westside Cafe, (406) 654–1555, U.S. 2. West. Wide menu.

HAVRE, MONTANA
Andy's Supper Club and Lounge, (406) 265–9963, 658 First Street West.
Duck Inn Tavern, (406) 265–7891. 1300 First Street.
4B's Restaurant & Black Angus Supper Club, (406) 265–9721, 604 West First Street. Open twenty-four hours with wide menu.

LEWISTOWN, MONTANA
Empire Café, (406) 538–9912, 214 West Main Street. Family dining. Open early for breakfast.
The Whole Famdamily, (406) 538–5161, 206 West Main Street. Homemade sandwiches, salads, soups.

---

*Denotes towns along Clark's 1806 homeward route.

6

Central Montana

The hills and river cliffs which we passed today exhibit a most romantic appearance . . . it seemed as if those scenes of visionary enchantment would never have an end. —MERIWETHER LEWIS, MAY 31, 1805, ON THE UPPER MISSOURI RIVER.

UPPER MISSOURI RIVER BREAKS NATIONAL MONUMENT

The country around Montana's Upper Missouri River Breaks National Monument looks like a blank spot on many maps, but it is far from barren. And with its slow pace and near total lack of modern intrusions, the Missouri Breaks are an excellent place to get a feel for what the Lewis and Clark Expedition really saw and experienced on its journey.

In fact, travelers may want to build their whole Lewis and Clark vacation around a paddle trip on the Upper Missouri National Wild and Scenic River, arguably the most special place left on the Lewis and Clark Trail. This rugged country—377,346 acres surrounding a 149-mile stretch of river—was designated a national monument in 2001. More people float the river now than a decade ago, but you're still unlikely to see more than two or three other parties in a single day. A paddle trip offers views of the river that are all but impossible to experience otherwise. A river trip is just about the only way to see the White Cliffs section, for example. Someone with a four-wheel-drive vehicle could drive down to a few isolated spots on the river but would be unable to get a broad picture of the terrain. A multiday Upper Missouri river trip, preceded or followed by an exploration of the Great Falls area, would make memories for a lifetime. After an overview of this area's history, we'll look at options for seeing it first-hand.

The Lewis and Clark Expedition had its share of excitement during its ascent of the Upper Missouri. May 14 was a particularly eventful day, starting with an-other bear encounter. Six men in the two rear dugout canoes spied a sleeping grizzly—an easy catch, they figured. But this bear proved a beast to kill. Shot first by four of the men, then by the two others, the bear was only enraged by the wounds, and he gave chase to the hunters. "In this manner he pursued two of them separately so close that they were obliged to throw aside their guns and pouches and throw themselves into the river," Lewis wrote. When the bear fi-nally succumbed, "they then took him on shore and butchered him when they found eight balls had passed through him in different directions."

Later that day, the party experienced another near mishap with the boats. As with the incident in North Dakota, Charbonneau—surely one of the world's worst boatmen—was at the helm of the usually stable and steadfast white pirogue. "In this pirogue were embarked our papers, instruments, books, medi-cine, a great part of our merchandise and in short almost every article indispen-sably necessary to further the views, or insure the success of the enterprise in which we are now launched to the distance of 2,200 miles," Lewis wrote. "Suf-fice it to say, the pirogue was under sail when a sudden squall of wind struck her obliquely and turned her considerably. The steersman alarmed, instead of put-ting her before the wind lifted her up into it." Confused, Charbonneau wailed at his misfortune until Cruzatte threatened to "shoot him instantly if he did not take hold of the rudder and do his duty," Lewis recalled. "The waves by this time were running very high but the fortitude, resolution and good conduct of Cruzatte saved her. He ordered two of the men to throw out the water with some kettles that fortunately were convenient, while himself and two others rowed her ashore, where she arrived scarcely above the water." In the next day's journal in-stallment, Lewis also gave credit to Sacagawea, who calmly sat in the back of the pirogue and caught most of the boat's light articles just before they washed over-board. Because of her actions, little of real value was lost.

On May 26 Lewis climbed the river bluffs, "which I found sufficiently fa-tiguing. On arriving to the summit (of) one of the highest points in the neigh-borhood I thought myself well repaid for my labor; as from this point I beheld the Rocky Mountains for the first time . . . These mountains were covered with snow, and the sun shone on it in such manner as to give me the most plain and satisfactory view. While I viewed these mountains, I felt a secret pleasure in find-ing myself so near the head of the heretofore conceived boundless Missouri, but when I reflected on the difficulties which this snowy barrier would most proba-bly throw in my way to the Pacific and the sufferings and hardships of myself

Upper Missouri River Breaks National Monument.

and party in them, it in some measure counterbalanced the joy I had felt in the first moments in which I gazed on them; but as I have always held it a crime to anticipate evils I will believe it a good comfortable road until I am compelled to believe differently."

Lewis's philosophizing makes for evocative reading 200 years later. Alas, the mountains he saw probably weren't the Rockies . . . he was still too far away. He had likely either spied the Bear Paw Mountains near Havre or the Big or Little Belt Mountains south of Great Falls.

On May 28 Lewis and Clark camped near what is now known as Judith Landing, today a major access point to the Missouri River. Many boat trips take out here, and primitive camping is available. There's even a small store selling basic supplies—the only one on the Wild and Scenic stretch beyond the Virgelle Mercantile. The Power Norris Bridge spans the river at Judith Landing, with Montana Highway 236 leading north to Big Sandy and south to Lewistown.

Judith Landing takes its name from the river that runs into the Missouri at the site. At first, Lewis and Clark named it the Big Horn. The next day, however, Clark renamed it the Judith River for his girlfriend in Virginia. Actually, Clark didn't know the young woman all that well: Her real name was Julia Hancock, and her friends called her Judy. Nevertheless, she must have been touched by his tribute, for they later were married.

Lewis and Clark had seen tens of thousands of buffalo by the time they reached this area, but the shaggy beasts were to play prominent roles in their journals over the next few days. On May 29 Lewis wrote, "Last night we were all alarmed by a large buffalo bull which swam over from the opposite shore. . . . (He) . . . ran up the bank in full speed directly toward the fires, and was within 18 inches of the heads of some of the men who lay sleeping." Lewis credited his dog, Seaman, with causing the buffalo to change course, and disaster was averted. Lewis noted the only serious damage done was to a rifle trampled by the buffalo. The gun had been left in the ill-fated white pirogue, and Lewis wrote "it appears that the white pirogue, which contains our most valuable stores, is attended by some evil genie."

Later that day, the explorers found huge mounds of rotting, stinking buffalo. They thought this was evidence of a buffalo jump, a ritual Lewis then described in detail in his journal, but no pishkun has ever been found in the immediate vicinity. Historians now believe the buffalo actually drowned and were washed up at the site on the river's backwater. Nevertheless, this river earned a most unromantic name: the Slaughter River.

Slaughter River is now known as Arrow Creek, an Indian name that actually predated the explorers' trip through the area. It got this moniker from a Blackfeet legend. A poor young man fell in love with a young woman, and they wanted to marry but were discouraged by the man's lack of property. Meanwhile, an evil warrior with many horses, lodges, and wives sought to add the young

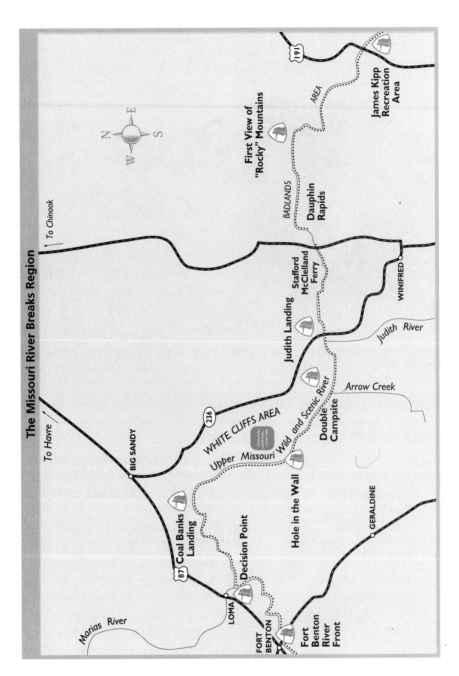

The Missouri River Breaks Region

woman to his harem. Luckily, her father would not sell her to the rich warrior.

As the story goes, the young lovers took a walk up the creek. The evil warrior was waiting to ambush the unsuspecting pair when suddenly they heard a groan. When they investigated, the warrior had been shot with an arrow bearing

Exploring the rugged landscape of unusual rock formations in the Missouri River Breaks, Montana.

feathers from a bird no one had ever seen and a projectile point unlike any other. The tribal elders figured the evil warrior must have been shot by the gods, thus paving the way for the young couple's marriage.

The Slaughter River/Arrow Creek campsite is the lone "double campsite" in Montana, that is, the only place the expedition camped on both its inbound and homeward journeys. The corps stayed here May 29, 1805, and the site was again visited by Lewis and his men on July 29, 1806.

On May 30–31, 1805, the explorers floated through an area now known as the White Cliffs of the Missouri. In one of the journals' most famous passages, Lewis wrote a lengthy description of these fantastic bluffs, noting how water had shaped the rich loam into "a thousand grotesque figures," pyramids, and "lofty freestone buildings . . . their parapets well stocked with statuary . . . so perfect indeed are those walls that I should have thought that nature had attempted here to rival the human art of masonry had I not recollected that she had first begun her work."

In a way, the Upper Missouri's "Wild and Scenic" designation may give people the wrong idea. The river is certainly scenic, but there are very few rapids. "Gentle and Scenic" would be a more apt description. This is a place where it's easy to kick back, daydream, read, ruminate, or do absolutely nothing at all. Modern floaters move downstream—not upstream as the Corps of Discovery did in 1805—making the Upper Missouri an easy paddle for even beginning canoeists and kayakers (see the Floating the Breaks on Your Own section). But travelers interested in a guided trip have ever-increasing options, with far more outfitters working this stretch of the Missouri than any other.

One benefit of taking a guided trip is that outfitters know where the best hikes are. They can help you safely access such sights as Hole in the Wall, tepee rings, and abandoned homesteads. Outfitters usually also provide shuttle service from the take-out back to your original meeting place, which is often a major expense for do-it-yourself boaters. Finally, there's nothing like having someone else do all the cooking and cleanup so that you can have a real vacation.

The Bureau of Land Management annually publishes a list of contact information for authorized outfitters working the upper Missouri National Wild and Scenic River. Get a copy by calling (406) 538–7461 or by writing to the BLM Lewistown Field Office, P.O. Box 1160, Lewistown, MT 59457. In 2002 the list included twenty-one companies doing some sort of outfitted river trips. Contact information for all is given below, and longer descriptions are offered for a few of the more high-profile outfitters—those either based in Fort Benton or running frequent trips in the Breaks.

Although some companies can arrange trips on short notice, it's important to call ahead for reservations; trips sometimes fill weeks or even months in advance. Prices listed applied in 2002 or 2003 and are subject to change. Many outfitters accommodate children at discounted rates.

■ **Adventure Bound Canoe & Shuttle Company** (Michael and Meredith Gregston), P.O. Box 31, Fort Benton, MT 59442; (877) 538–4890; www. montana rivertrip.com. With a storefront location at 1714 Front Street in Fort Benton and lots of canoes and kayaks for rent, sale, and demo, Adventure Bound caters mainly to do-it-yourself floaters. But the Gregstons also do guided canoe and kayak trips ranging from day outings in the Fort Benton vicinity ($80 per person including a meal) to multiday trips priced from $600 for a four-day, three-night float. Family trips include a "kids adventure program" featuring fun activities on Lewis and Clark lore, Native American culture, and more.

■ **Canoe Montana/Montana River Expeditions** (Les Dolezal), 1321 Front St., P.O. Box 591, Fort Benton, MT 5944; (800) 500–4538; www.montanariver.com. Canoe Montana says it specializes in "quiet adventures for discriminating explorers." Like Adventure Bound, it's located right on Fort Benton's Front Street and offers both rental gear and guided trips. In addition to canoes and kayaks, Canoe Montana also runs some trips (including one recent four-generation family reunion) in a large voyageur-style canoe similar in size to Lewis and Clark's pirogues. Multiday trips cost from $850 for a four-day, three-night trip through the White Cliffs section to $1,250 for a six-day, five-night trip covering both the White Cliffs and the Badlands. Shorter trips include sunset tours priced at $70, including a meal. Canoe Montana guides generally pack along a digital camera and offer photos of your trip at no extra charge. Shuttle service is available.

- **Explorations Inc.** (Lorne Riddell), P.O. Box 1303, Trout Creek, MT 59874; (406) 827–3863; www.explorationsmt.com. Experiential wilderness programs for struggling teenagers.
- **Glacier Sea Kayaking** (Bobbie Gillmore), 390 Tally Lake Road, Whitefish, MT 59937; (406) 862–9010; www.montanaweb.com/seakayak. Leisurely five-day sea kayaking trips through the White Cliffs section, with lots of hiking, a trail ride, and gourmet Dutch oven meals.
- **Hawk, I'm Your Sister** (Beverly Antaeus), P.O. Box 9109, Santa Fe, NM 87504; (505) 984–2268; www.womansplace.com. Specialty trips (shamanic arts, astrology, women's wilderness journeys).
- **Hole in the Wall Educational Adventures** (Terry Selph), 731 West Fourth Street, Hardin, MT 59034; (406) 665–3779; www.forevermontana.com. Specialty float and vehicle trips on the Missouri and the C. M. Russell National Wildlife Refuge.
- **Lewis and Clark Canoe Expeditions** (Jim Cummings), P.O. Box 728, Fort Benton, MT 59442; (888) 595–9151 or (406) 622–3698; www.lewisandclark guide.com. This company specializes in flexible, outfitted small-group adventures using both large voyageur-style canoes and smaller craft. Four- to eight-day trips are priced at $175 per person per day if you schedule an "open booking" trip open to others; $225 per person, per day if the trip is your group's alone. Lewis and Clark Canoe Expeditions also offers short trips (a few hours to a full day) priced from $55 to about $100. Cummings is an enthusiastic, personable guide who knows the area's history well (and who has some twisted takes on what *really* happened on the Lewis and Clark Trail). Also ask about guided multiday trips on the Marias and Yellowstone Rivers.
- **Lewis and Clark Trail Adventures** (Wayne and Gia Fairchild), P.O. Box 9051, Missoula, MT 59801; (800) 366–6246 or (406) 728–7609; www.trailad-ventures. com. Lewis and Clark Trail Adventures is the only company licensed on both the Upper Missouri and the Lolo Trail, the Corps of Discovery's route across the Bitterroot Mountains of Idaho. It offers a combination trip priced at $1,105 that combines a three-day trip from Fort Benton to Judith Landing with a three-day hiking or cycling trip on the Lolo. River trips alone (using 17-foot canoes) cost $605 for three days (Fort Benton to Judith Landing) and $1,105 for six days (Fort Benton to Kipp).
- **Missouri Breaks River Company** (Bill Marsik), 2409 Fourth Avenue North, Great Falls, MT 59401; (406) 453–3035; www.missouribreaksriverco.com. As of 2002 this was the only outfitter leading jetboat trips on the Missouri. Trips observe the no-wake, downstream-travel-only regulations on the Wild and Scenic portion of the river from Memorial Day through Labor Day. Other times of the year, upriver travel is possible—like Lewis and Clark, only a lot faster. One popular package, the White Cliffs Cruise, includes two nights' lodging at the Virgelle Merc (see the Missouri River Canoe Company, below), meals, and a day

trip from Coal Banks Landing to Judith Landing for $300 per person, based on four people.

■ **Missouri River Canoe Company** (Don Sorensen and Jim Griffin), 7485 Virgelle Ferry Road North, Loma, MT 59460; (800) 426–2926 or (406) 378–3110; www.canoemontana.com. The Missouri River Canoe Company is just a mile upriver from Coal Banks Landing, the most popular put-in. In addition to canoe and kayak rentals, the company offers trips—all outfitted, some guided—for $150 to $300 per person, per day. Ask about the "Paddles to Saddles" trip pairing a canoe journey with horseback riding along the Breaks. The company's base camp also includes bed-and-breakfast accommodations in the 1912 Virgelle Merc or self-catered (bring your own food) stays in authentic homestead cabins.

■ **Missouri River Outfitters** (Larry and Bonnie Cook), P.O. Box 762, Fort Benton, MT 59442; (406) 622–3295; www.mroutfitters.com. Fort Benton–based Missouri River Outfitters ranks among the most experienced and best-known guides on the Upper Missouri, written about by such authors as Stephen Ambrose and Dayton Duncan. The Cooks offer four- to seven-day outfitted canoe trips and canoe rentals for do-it-yourselfers, but they are probably best known for three- to five-day excursions on motorized, weatherized pontoon boats—the only craft of their kind on the Upper Missouri. Both Cooks are Fort Benton–area natives and former teachers with a genuine love for the river, eager to share their wealth of stories of the Missouri's natural and human history. The motorized trips easily accommodate people of all ages, and the Cooks try to vary each cruise's activities to suit the participants' interests and physical abilities. The cost is $200 per person per day with a three-day minimum.

■ **Montana River Outfitters** (Craig Madsen), 923 Tenth Avenue North, Great Falls, MT 59401; (800) 800–8218 or (406) 761–1677; www.montanariver outfitters.com. Montana River Outfitters offers fully and partially guided White Cliffs trips of varying lengths, as well as gear rental and short-duration floats near Great Falls. (See the end of the Great Falls section for more information.)

■ **River Odysseys West** (Peter Grubb), P.O. Box 579, Coeur d'Alene, ID 83816; (800) 451–6034 or (208) 765–0841; www.rowinc.com. ROW offers five-day Missouri River Expeditions using 34-foot voyageur canoes and smaller outrigger canoes. ROW has luxury camping down pat, from the gourmet meals and attentive guides to the portable, sheltered toilet and sun showers. Trips put in at Coal Banks Landing and travel through the White Cliffs past Judith Landing to the Stafford-McClelland Ferry, offering participants a look at some of the Badlands section. Most trips are accompanied by guest historians who are well versed in Lewis and Clark lore and other area history; at least one departure each summer is geared toward families, with special interpretive activities for children. Lots of time is spent off the river, exploring old homesteads and hiking in sandstone coulees. For 2002 the expeditions cost $1,200 ($1,315 in high summer).

- **Starwest Adventures** (Sid Napier), P.O. Box 227, Lewistown, MT 59457; (877) 538–8670 or (406) 538–8670; www.starwestadventures.com. Starwest runs three- to seven-day trips priced from $650 to $1,400. Smaller groups (of six people or fewer) sometimes make use of a "canoe catamaran"—two attached canoes topped with a sunshade and equipped with a small motor. Horseback riding options are available on some trips.
- **3 Rivers Canoes** (Dale Hankins), P.O. Box 1107, Fort Benton, MT 59442; (406) 622–3486; www.3riverscanoes.com. Trip choices range from a one-day paddle ($95 to $155) to a seven-day float ($995 to $1,085), using either small canoes or a 34-foot voyageur-style craft. The company also offers trips on the Marias River.
- **Upper Missouri River Guides** (Glenn Monahan), 315 West Fourth Street, Anaconda, MT 59711; (866) 266–6519 or (406) 563–2770; www.upper missouri.com. Monahan, coauthor of the *Montana's Wild & Scenic Upper Missouri River* guidebook, offers three- to seven-day trips priced from $625 to about $1,300. Visit his Web site, or see the Floating the Breaks on Your Own section below for information on ordering his book.
- **Upper Missouri River Keelboat Company** (Mike Nottingham), P.O. Box 201, Loma, MT 59460; (800) 721–2133; www.mrkeelboat.com. Mike Nottingham's great-grandfather was a woodhawk and trading post proprietor at Arrow Creek in the 1870s, and Mike now operates the only regularly scheduled keelboat trips anywhere on Lewis and Clark's route. (Of course, the Corps of Discovery dispatched its keelboat downriver from Fort Mandan in 1805, but keelboats plied the upper Missouri River through the mid-nineteenth century.) Nottingham runs one-day trips ($150 per person, including lunch at a Lewis campsite) from Fort Benton to the mouth of the Marias, as well as three- and four-day runs from Virgelle to Judith Landing priced at $250 per person per day. Nottingham also owns M&M River Expeditions, offering one- to seven-day canoe trips on the Missouri and Marias.
- **Wild Rockies Field Institute,** P.O. Box 7071, Missoula, MT 59807; (406) 549–4336; www.wildrockies.org/WRFI. Environmental studies trips (with college credit available), including a two-week Missouri River sea kayak trip as part of the "Montana Afoot & Afloat" course.
- **Wild Rockies Tours** (Matt Thomas or Gail Gutsche), P.O. Box 8184, Missoula, MT 59807; (406) 728–0566; www.wrtours.com. In addition to four- to eight-day Missouri River canoe trips (about $650 to $1,050), Wild Rockies runs the Marias, Yellowstone, Blackfoot, and Jefferson Rivers—all waters traveled by the Corps of Discovery during its time in Montana.
- **Wilderness Inquiry** (Greg Lais), 808 Fourteenth Avenue Southeast, Minneapolis, MN 55414; (800) 728–0719 or (612) 676–9400; www.wilderness inquiry.org. Outfitted trips for people with disabilities.

■ **Wolf Spirit Expeditions** (Mark Smagala), PMB 406, 2401 Brooks Street, Missoula, MT 59801; (800) 241–2615. River trips.

In addition to the water-based outfitters noted above, a few entrepreneurs are offering trips along the river's banks and into the breaks backcountry. White Cliff Tours offers combination hiking-vehicle tours from Fort Benton into the Breaks' most famous section from June through September. The four-and-a-half-hour option ($50 for adults, $45 for children ages six–twelve) includes views from the rim and a hike to Hole in the Wall. Guide Daryl Dammel says he's taken people ages six to eighty-one to the famous landmark. A full-day trip ($85/$75) includes a morning hike through the cliff and sandstone formations of East Mud Spring Canyon, followed by lunch on the rim and a hike to Hole in the Wall. A three-hour, nonhiking option ($40/$35) is available for people who don't care to hike and don't have much time, but who simply want a quick look at what all the fuss is about. For more information or to reserve a trip, call (406) 728–2960 or visit www.skybusiness.com/whiteclifftours.

Gary Darlington's Missouri River Breaks Tours specialize in guided four-wheel-drive excursions across his land, which includes 9 miles of riverfront in the Eagle Creek area, where the corps camped May 31, 1805—the day they floated through the White Cliffs. Darlington's family has been in the area since the early twentieth century, and he takes visitors to many spectacular sights—including petroglyphs and rock formations—that cannot be seen from the river.

Looking at tepee rings on the Missouri River Breaks, Montana.

Darlington's land is accessed via a 20-mile gravel and dirt road drive from Big Sandy, or he can come to pick you up in Big Sandy if you choose. His tours run two to eight hours. Cost is a minimum of $80 for one person for two hours, with a second person half-price and a third person an extra $10 per hour. For a full-day tour, plan on $200 for the first person, $100 for the second, and $80 for the third. Lunch and snacks are included. Darlington may add cabins and backpacking access to his land in the future. For more information call (406) 386–2486 or visit www.fortbenton.com/mrbtours.

Meanwhile, Darlington's neighbor, Glenn Terry, has established Pilot Rock Trail Rides on the land his wife's family has worked since 1898. From horseback, visitors see some of the prettiest sections of the White Cliffs. Terry can take as many as eight people out for $20 per person per hour. Rides can range from a few hours to all day, but there's a four-hour minimum for groups of three or fewer. Terry also has a camp complete with a tepee that sleeps six to eight people. It rents for $50 a night. Many people float in for a horseback ride or overnight stay, but you can also drive in 18 miles from Big Sandy. For more information contact Glenn Terry, P.O. Box 392, Big Sandy, Montana 59520 or call (406) 386-2455. It's best to give either Darlington or Terry at least a few days' advance notice for tours.

THE MARIAS RIVER AND FORT BENTON

When they reached what is now Loma, Montana, on June 2, 1805, the expedition saw a formidable river, one they'd had no warning of. "An interesting question was now to be determined," Lewis wrote the next day, "which of these rivers was the Missouri . . . what astonishes us a little is that the Indians who appeared to be so well acquainted with the geography of this country should not have mentioned this river on (the) right hand if it be not the Missouri." A small interpretive area off U.S. 87 just south of town gives a commanding view of what's now called Decision Point.

From this hillside, it's easy to see why the explorers may have been confused, especially in late spring when both rivers were swollen with runoff. The north fork was whitish brown, very thick and turbid, looking much like the Missouri, while the south fork was transparent. But after exploring the north branch, Lewis was convinced it flowed in too much of a northern direction to be the right path to the Pacific. Further, he reasoned, if the river penetrated the mountains, it would be clearer.

Lewis had an experience here not unlike his adventure at the Tavern Cave way back in Missouri. On June 7, while exploring bluffs in the area, "I slipped at a narrow pass of about 30 yards in length and but for a quick and fortunate

Floating the Breaks on Your Own

n recent years, between 5,000 and 5,750 persons have paddled the Upper Missouri each year—about double the numbers seen in the early 1990s. About 75 percent do the trip on their own, either with personal watercraft or rentals from an outfitter.

The Upper Missouri is a gentle river, with no sizable rapids. It's an easy trip for even the most novice canoeist or kayaker. But it's a wild place, far from civilization, and paddlers must take care to prepare for their trip. Here are some pointers:

Get good local information: Start by obtaining the detailed, mile-by-mile river maps available from the Bureau of Land Management. They're published on two waterproof sheets. One includes maps 1 and 2, covering the river from Fort Benton to Slaughter River. The other, with maps 3 and 4, details Slaughter River to the final take-out at James Kipp Recreation Area. Maps may be purchased at the BLM's Upper Missouri Wild & Scenic Visitor Center at 1718 Front Street in Fort Benton or at any of the staffed river sites (see below). Or you can order them by mail (at $8.00 for the set) by calling (406) 538–7461 (for credit card orders) or by sending a check to P.O. Box 1160, Lewiston, MT 59457.

The BLM, which manages the river, has summer staff stationed at Fort Benton, Coal Banks Landing (the major put-in), Judith Landing (roughly the midway point), and James Kipp Recreation Area (terminus of the designated Wild and Scenic River). Check with them for information on current river conditions. The center in Fort Benton serves as a point of contact in the event of family emergencies. The number is (406) 622–5185. Although it's not mandatory, boaters are asked to register before any trip so that BLM river rangers can find them if necessary. You can register at Fort Benton or any of the put-ins. The BLM is considering a user fee for Upper Missouri paddlers. It won't be implemented by 2003, but paddlers will want to check with the agency before planning trips in the future.

For detailed interpretive information, consider buying *Montana's Wild and Scenic Upper Missouri River,* an excellent mile-by-mile resource from Northern Rocky Mountains Books. It's available at many Montana bookstores or interpretive centers, or you can order it by sending a check for $18.95 to Northern Rocky Mountain Books, 315 West Fourth Street, Anaconda, MT 59711.

Be prepared: Aside from being good information spots, Canoe Montana, 1312 Front Street, and Adventure Bound Canoe & Shuttle Co., 1714 Front

(continued)

Street, in Fort Benton are good places to stock up on last-minute specialized gear for canoeing, kayaking, and wilderness camping. Lehman's True Value Hardware at 1420 Front Street can help with more basic needs like coolers and flashlights.

Bring what you need, because—except for the small store at Judith Landing, which keeps irregular hours, there are no services available along the way. Pay particular attention to drinking water (see below), adequate food, sun protection, and insect repellent. (The bugs tend to get worse toward the lower end of the Upper Missouri, where the river slackens near Fort Peck Reservoir.)

Although weather during the prime Upper Missouri float trip season is usually quite good—hot and sunny during the day, comfortably cool in the evening—storms with heavy rain and hail sometimes occur. Bring good rain gear. Some people even advise taking along a helmet in case of hail! Even in fair weather, you'll encounter plenty of mud along the riverbanks, so bring proper footgear—river sandals or old tennis shoes are good for the boats, while a pair of lightweight hiking boots are best for camp time. (You'll see plenty of prickly pear cactus and perhaps a rattlesnake or two along the Missouri's banks.)

Watch where (and how) you camp: Camping conditions along the river are primitive and serene. There are several marked sites along the route; others have just evolved from word-of-mouth use. Little Sandy, Eagle Creek, Hole-in-the-Wall, Dark Butte, Slaughter River, Judith Landing, Stafford Ferry, and Lower Woodhawk are among the most popular and heavily used sites.

The BLM has erected shelters at Hole-in-the-Wall and Slaughter River. The three-sided log structures are basically just places for canoeists to get out of bad weather. They can sleep up to a dozen people, if necessary.

As the Upper Missouri's popularity grows, it's becoming ever more important to tread lightly on this historic land. Take care to use established sites and fire rings, or use a fire pan. There is no garbage service along the route, so a pack-it-out policy is in effect. Check out the guidelines in the How to Use This Book chapter for more information on minimum-impact camping. Starting in 2003, all parties paddling from Judith Landing to Kipp will be required to carry a portable toilet. The same regulation may apply between Fort Benton and Judith Landing in the future. Check with the BLM for updates.

Nearly two-thirds of the land along the river is privately owned, and some landowners have posted NO TRESPASSING signs. But it's best to avoid even the land that isn't posted and to make camp on public land. Private land is designated on the official river maps.

Watch what you drink: Out here you need plenty of drinking water—a gallon per person per day is a good guideline. The BLM recommends that floaters haul their own drinking water. If you rely on the river water sources, be sure to filter, boil, or chemically treat it before use.

For more information on floating the Upper Missouri, the BLM recommends that you read a copy of its *Hazards and Highlights* brochures. If you have any questions at all, contact the BLM at (406) 538-7461. The BLM's office staff and river rangers are dedicated to ensuring that do-it-yourself paddlers have the information and gear needed for a safe trip on the Wild and Scenic Upper Missouri.

recovery by my espontoon I should have been precipitated into the river down a craggy precipice of about 90 feet." No sooner had Lewis regained his balance than he heard a voice crying for help. It was Private Richard Windsor, who—having slipped and fallen on the same narrow pass that tripped up Lewis—was hanging on for dear life. Lewis slowly talked Windsor down from the cliff, instructing him "to take the knife out of his belt behind him with his right hand and dig a hole with it in the face of the bank to receive his right foot, which he did, and then raise himself to his knees." That night, the captain was exhausted but happy to be alive. After a hearty meal of venison, "I now laid myself down on some willow boughs to a comfortable night's rest, and felt indeed as if I was fully repaid for the toil and pain of the day...."

The party spent nine days at this confluence, trying to figure out which way to go. Both leaders were convinced the south fork was the Missouri, but the rest of the men—including Pierre Cruzatte, probably the expedition's most experienced boatman—wanted to follow the northern fork. On June 11, 1805, Lewis and four others left to seek the Great Falls of the Missouri down the south fork. If they found the falls, they would know they were on the right path. The expedition's continued survival and success rested on making the correct choice. In the meantime, on June 8 Lewis took his turn at flattering womanhood, naming the mystery stream Marias River, in honor of his cousin, Maria Wood. "It is true that the hue of the waters of this turbulent and troubled stream but illy comport with the pure celestial virtues and amiable qualifications of that lovely fair one," he wrote. "But on the other hand it is a noble river; one destined to become in my opinion an object of contention between the two great powers of American and Great Britain with respect to the adjustment of the Northwesterly boundary of the former."

There were once plans for a town named Ophir at the mouth of the Marias. It was 22 miles downriver from Fort Benton, and planners felt that—in low

A drift boat on a section of the Wild and Scenic Upper Missouri, Montana.

water—if steamboats couldn't reach Fort Benton, they could possibly reach Ophir. There was also plentiful timber for building. Moreover, the town was the idea of men with high connections in Montana's territorial government. Ophir seemed destined for success.

Stock in the company was issued on March 24, 1864, and a charter was obtained eleven months later. All went well for a while: A field manager was hired to build the town, a sawmill was established, and 400 lots were laid out. But in May 1865, something went awry. One story goes that nine Blood Indians were killed on the streets of Fort Benton and their bodies thrown into the river. The second story held that during the winter, Charlie Carson, cousin of Kit Carson, was trapping along the Missouri with two buddies when three Bloods stole their horses. Carson and his party pursued the Indians, caught and shot them, and regained their horses. Whatever really happened, a war party of 180 Indians was traveling to Fort Benton for vengeance when they encountered woodcutters building the town of Ophir. Ten whites were killed, and dreams of the town died with them. Nothing remains of the townsite; a few log cabins left over after the attack eventually were used to feed the fires in steamboat boilers. Loma, however, has a smattering of visitor services and a museum specializing in geology.

Fort Benton has many claims to historical fame, but perhaps none so mighty as its reign during the steamboat era, when as many as ten steamboats a day tied up at its waterfront. In its heyday, Fort Benton also boasted what was known as "the wildest block in the West," jam-packed with bars, dance halls, and brothels.

The upriver trip from St. Louis usually took sixty to sixty-five days. Passenger fare averaged $150. During the busy year of 1867, about 1,500 people traveled to Montana on the steamboats. The river route was faster and safer than overland routes, which frequently were closed down by Indians. The riverboats were also important to trade and shipping. The all-time peak of river traffic was in 1879, when forty-seven boats carried 9,444 tons of cargo up the river, but railroads started cutting into the riverboat shipping during the 1880s.

Fort Bentonites are proud their town is home to *Explorers at the Marias,* the official Montana Lewis and Clark Monument. The riverfront statue was created by Bob Scriver to mark the U.S. Bicentennial in 1976. It depicts Sacagawea and her baby, Jean Baptiste, in addition to the captains. Scriver spent a year researching the expedition before starting his work on the statue, trying to ensure the accuracy of the equipment, clothing, body features, and faces. For example, the square compass in Clark's hand was modeled from the actual one he used, and Sacagawea is carrying her baby in a blanket because the packboard he rode in earlier was lost overboard a few days before the party's arrival at the mouth of the Marias River.

The finished product is of heroic proportions: one-sixth larger than life-size. The statue weighs 2.5 tons, is 21 feet high, and sits on an 85-ton granite base given as a gift from Tanner Brothers Quarry near Square Butte, Montana. After its casting at the Modern Art Foundry in New York City, the statue was transported cross-country to Montana upright on the bed of a semitrailer, causing many a head to turn.

A 4-block walking tour along Fort Benton's levee offers a good look at the town's history. Aside from the Lewis and Clark statue, you'll see a monument to the Whoop-Up Trail, a route to western Canada popular before the railroads; a replica of the Mandan keelboat, built for the film The Big Sky; the remains of the Baby Rose steamboat, mired in the Missouri mud below the Lewis and Clark statue; and a monument to the Mullan Road, another famous western route that traveled from Fort Benton to Walla Walla, Washington. Be sure to take a stroll on the pedestrian bridge across the river. You can even pitch a picnic on the table halfway across.

There's also a monument commemorating "Shep." This sheepherder's dog, made famous in Ripley's Believe It Or Not, met every train into Fort Benton for five years after his master's body was taken away by rail. Eventually, Shep was run over by a train, and he was buried on a hillside overlooking the rail depot.

The riverfront tour ends at the Grand Union Hotel, once considered the finest between Minneapolis and Seattle. Long vacant, the hotel finally reopened in 1999 after extensive remodeling by Montana natives Jim and Cheryl Gagnon. It now features twenty-seven guest rooms and public areas done up in elegantly rustic style, with both Western and Victorian touches, along with a restaurant featuring some of the region's best food.

Fort Benton has more than its share of museums. The BLM visitor center at 1718 Front Street has exhibits including an oil painting by Todd Asay of the Eye of the Needle, the Missouri Breaks landmark that was toppled over in 1997. The visitor center is open from 8:00 A.M. to 5:00 P.M. daily, Memorial Day through Labor Day weekends. Admission is free.

Also on Front Street near the boat ramp, the Museum of the Upper Missouri features a wide range of artifacts from the area's past, notably the .44-caliber Winchester rifle Chief Joseph was said to be carrying when he surrendered to the U.S. Army in 1877, ending the Nez Perce War. The museum sits on the same site as old Fort Benton, which is now being reconstructed. Admission to the Museum of the Upper Missouri also includes entrance to the Museum of the Northern Great Plains. This facility focuses on the area's agricultural history, but it also is home to five splendid murals by noted Montana painter Robert Morgan. One, titled Fortunate Meeting, depicts Lewis, Drouillard, and the Fields brothers arriving back on the Missouri River after their July 1806 encounter with Blackfeet Indians on the Two Medicine River.

The Museum of the Northern Great Plains also displays the Hornaday Buffalo. In 1886, when bison had nearly become extinct, taxidermist William Hornaday claimed this big bull—nearly 6 feet tall and more than 10 feet long—to

Statue of Lewis, Clark, Sacagawea, and Pomp at Fort Benton, Montana.

show future generations what the great beasts looked like. It was displayed at the Smithsonian Institution in Washington, D.C. from 1887 through 1957 and served as a model for the buffalo nickel. It's seen here just as it was at the Smithsonian, with several other buffalo mounts. The Museums of the Upper Missouri and the Northern Great Plains are open daily from 10:00 A.M. to 5:00 P.M. mid-May through September, by appointment the rest of the year; call (406) 622–5316. Admission to both is $4.00 for adults and $1.00 for children. Long-time Lewis and Clark buff Bob Doerk, a Fort Benton resident, offers guided tours to area sites associated with the expedition, including Decision Point at the mouth of the Marias and Grog Springs, the June 11, 1805, campsite where Lewis cured his stomachache with chokecherry tea. Doerk usually charges $50 an hour. To arrange a tour call him at (406) 622–5874.

Fort Benton has several motels, a bed-and-breakfast, and about half a dozen restaurants. For more information on Fort Benton, call (406) 622-3864. From here it's an easy 35-mile drive to Great Falls.

HOMEWARD BOUND: CAMP DISAPPOINTMENT, THE TWO MEDICINE FIGHT SITE

As noted earlier, the Marias River had captivated and perplexed the explorers during the 1805 trip through Montana. On his way home in 1806, Lewis was eager to explore the river's upper reaches. His side trip into the area produced some of the most disappointing and dramatic passages of the entire expedition.

Lewis's main purpose in tracing the Marias River was to see if the river reached far enough north to satisfy the northern boundary agreement of the 1783 Paris Treaty between the United States and Great Britain, which ended the American Revolution. This treaty said a line drawn from the northwesternmost point of the Lake of the Woods to the Mississippi River would determine the northwestern boundary of the Northwestern Territory. It was later learned the Mississippi did not reach far enough north to satisfy that article of the treaty, so after the Louisiana Purchase, one of the purposes of the Lewis and Clark expedition was to find a tributary that would fulfill the treaty's requirements. Lewis found that the Marias River didn't reach far enough north, either, and that's how he came to name Camp Disappointment.

Here, Lewis could see that the Cut Bank River was flowing directly from the mountains to the west, meaning—once again—the river did not meander far enough north to help America's claim. The site further earned its name because of the poor weather Lewis and his men experienced here. Beset by rain and clouds, Lewis was unable to complete the celestial observations he hoped would help pinpoint the camp's location.

Guided access to Camp Disappointment is now offered by the proprietors of Meriwether Meadows Campground. For a nominal fee ($5.00 per person in 2002; half-price for campers), owners Kathy and Gene Maggi or Sheryle Bittner will lead you the last 2.5 miles from the campground to the historic site. Passenger cars can make the trip, but in wet weather the road can become impassable to all vehicles.

To access Meriwether Meadows, drive west from Cut Bank on U.S. Highway 2. In 19 miles, turn north on Montana Highway 444, also known as Meriwether Road, and drive 3.7 miles. The campground is near good fishing, hiking, and bird-watching. For more information call (406) 338–2310 or visit www. mericamp.com.

Back on U.S. 2 a short distance west, there's a monument to the Lewis and Clark Expedition's farthest progress north, but it is badly defaced. Continue west to Browning, the center of the Blackfeet Indian Reservation and a gateway to Glacier National Park. (See more information below.) From Browning, head back toward Great Falls on U.S. 89. About 10 miles to the southeast, the road crosses the Two Medicine River. Near here, the Lewis and Clark Expedition had its only armed—and fatal—firefight with Indians.

The Two Medicine Fight Site is even more difficult to find than Camp Disappointment. Moreover, the site is on private land and access is limited. Larry Epstein of Cut Bank, the 2002–2003 president of the Lewis & Clark Trail Heritage Foundation, leads two to three tours each year to both Camp Disappointment and the Two Medicine Fight Site. Call him at (406) 873–2277 to ask about tour dates. The Blackleaf Creek Ranch near Bynum, west of the fight site, also plans tours for guests to its working cattle ranch during the bicentennial years. Call Phyllis Yeager at (812) 923–3822 or e-meal yeager@win.net for reservations or more information.

If you can't time your trip to coincide with one of the tours or don't want a ranch stay, stop at the Cut Bank Area Chamber of Commerce or call the chamber at (406) 873–4041 to check on current policies and conditions. The site is inaccessible in bad weather. If you get a go-ahead—and you have fine weather and a four-wheel-drive vehicle—here's how to find the site:

Near the Two Medicine River on U.S. 89, look for a brown metal shed marked THREE RIVERS TELEPHONE CO-OP on the north side of the road. Turn north here. The road soon parallels a mile-long pishkun (a buffalo jump) and the remnants of the Holy Family Mission, started in 1888 by the Jesuits. The mission was run by the Jesuits and Ursuline nuns until 1939. In the mid-1960s, thirty-five people were killed and the mission grounds inundated when spring floods swept through this area. Most of the bodies were never recovered. The facility no longer operates as a mission, but Catholic services are still held weekly.

This area also is the final resting place of James Willard Schultz. Born in Boonville, New York, in 1859, Schultz moved to Montana at age seventeen. He

View of Camp Disappointment area near Cut Bank, Montana.

worked at Joe Kipp's trading post near what is now Conrad and married a Pie-gan woman. By living with the Blackfeet, Schultz had a ringside seat to the van-ishing West—experiences and impressions he recorded in some three dozen books, including *My Life as an Indian*. Schultz died in 1947 and was buried near the irrigation canal beneath the buffalo jump.

The road eventually turns to gravel, then dead-ends at the paved Valier Road (MT 358). Turn right here and drive south. The road crosses the Two Medicine River again. Another 1.8 miles south, turn right again onto another gravel road at the Stoltz Ranch. This road leads west past three irrigation ditches to a fork about 2.4 miles from the ranch turnoff. After proceeding through (and closing) the gate, bear left to the faint path leading up the ridge. Four-wheel-drive is ad-vised for this ascent.

Once up on the ridge, look for a small rock cairn on the north side of the road. The rocks form an arrow that points directly to the Two Medicine Fight Site. (Look for the telltale clump of trees and a fence erected by area Boy Scouts.) Even if you cannot locate the cairn, the ridge affords an amazing 360-degree view of this wild, forlorn area and the badlands where dinosaurs once roamed.

The high ridge trail proceeds on past a group of tepee rings and another junc-tion. The right fork is extremely rugged and descends into the badlands and a buffalo jump area; the left loops back to the gate. It's possible to hike to the fight

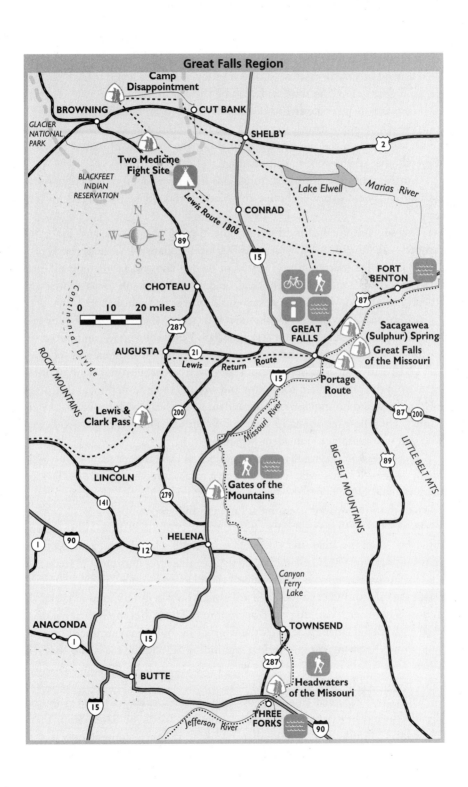

Great Falls Region

Camp Disappointment

BROWNING

CUT BANK

SHELBY

GLACIER NATIONAL PARK

2

Two Medicine Fight Site

BLACKFEET INDIAN RESERVATION

Lake Elwell

Marias River

Lewis Route 1806

CONRAD

FORT BENTON

N
W   E
S

89

15

87

CHOTEAU

Sacagawea (Sulphur) Spring

0   10   20 miles

GREAT FALLS

Great Falls of the Missouri

287

AUGUSTA

21

Lewis Return Route

15

Portage Route

Continental Divide

Lewis & Clark Pass

200

Missouri River

87 200

ROCKY MOUNTAINS

89

BIG BELT MOUNTAINS

LITTLE BELT MTS

LINCOLN

Gates of the Mountains

279

141

HELENA

I 90

12

Canyon Ferry Lake

ANACONDA

TOWNSEND

I

15

287

BUTTE

Headwaters of the Missouri

15

THREE FORKS

Jefferson River

90

site from the right fork; the site may also be approached by returning to the gate, then driving in a north-northwest direction toward the badlands, parking before the land drops off to the river, and walking the rest of the way.

Historians believe the fight occurred here, based on descriptions in Lewis's journals. The hardy narrowleaf cottonwood tree within the fenced area may well be the very one on the site in 1806—or if not the tree, one of its descendants. (Several other cottonwoods mentioned fell to fire about 1980.)

Cuttings from the historic cottonwoods here have found their way to other sites around the country, including the Montana State Capitol grounds in Helena.

The site bears a historical plaque mentioning that Lewis and his party camped here July 26, 1806, with eight Blackfeet Indians with whom they'd nervously counciled that evening. They went to bed late and Lewis took the first guard, relieved later by Reuben Field, and then by Joseph Field. Carelessly, Joseph Field laid down his gun next to his brother's and fell asleep.

At daybreak, the Indians awoke first and, seeing the white men's guns unguarded, quickly made a plan of attack. Joseph Field woke up just in time to see an Indian seize the unattended guns. He hollered for his brother, and together they chased after the Blackfeet, "whom they overtook at the distance of 50 or 60 paces from the camp, seized their guns and wrested them from him, and Reuben Field as he seized his gun stabbed the Indian to the heart with his knife," Lewis wrote. "The fellow ran about 15 steps and fell dead." This was hearsay to Lewis, who was still asleep as the incident began.

In the meantime, Drouillard, too, was locked in a struggle for his gun. This finally awakened Lewis, who realized his own rifle was missing. Lewis reached for his pistol and chased after the Indian who had taken his gun, shouting for the brave to drop the weapon. Sensing failure, the Indian complied.

By this point, the expedition's horses and those of the Blackfeet were galloping away from the scene in two bunches. Drouillard and the Fields brothers chased one group, while Lewis followed the two Blackfeet pursuing the second—straight into a box canyon. Here, one of the Blackfeet jumped behind a pile of rocks; the other turned and took aim at Lewis, who was just 30 steps away. Lewis managed to fire first, striking the Blackfoot in the belly, but the Indian got off a shot, too. "Being bareheaded I felt the wind of his bullet very distinctly," Lewis later wrote. Knowing another Indian was hiding among the rocks and that the others were still in the area, perhaps with reinforcements on the way, Lewis decided to give up his pursuit of the horses.

The party reclaimed enough of its own mounts—plus four owned by the Blackfeet—and beat a hasty retreat from the Two Medicine River. From there they rode 120 miles in little more than twenty-four hours, stopping only to eat, catch catnaps, and let the horses graze. Amazingly, they arrived at the Missouri

Glacier National Park

Meriwether Lewis didn't get to what is now Glacier National Park on his 1806 return trip, but modern travelers may find the park an irresistible detour from their historic travels. Glacier is justly famous for its high-mountain scenery, abundant wildlife, and wide variety of recreation.

From Browning, U.S. 2 skims the park's south edge, while U.S. 89 leads north to the Going-to-the-Sun Road and the heart of Glacier. If you have time for only a day in Glacier National Park, it is perhaps best spent driving at least part of this amazing 50-mile road, deservedly one of the world's most famous. Note, however, that Going-to-the-Sun Road is only open from mid-June to mid-October, and certain vehicle length and width restrictions apply.

Glacier is known as a hikers' park, with more than 700 miles of trails ready for exploration. Some of the most beloved include the Alpine Meadow Walk, which jumps off from Logan Pass on Going-to-the-Sun Road, and Avalanche Lake Trail, an easy path featuring scenic waterfalls. Other activities include backpacking, horseback riding, white-water rafting, open-air bus tours, fishing, and bird-watching.

Glacier visitors can choose from a wide range of accommodations, ranging from designated and backcountry campgrounds to European-inspired lodging at Many Glacier Hotel. For more information on Glacier National Park, call (406) 888–5441 or visit the park's Web site at www.nps.gov/glac/.

River just in time to find the parties led by Sergeant Gass, who had supervised the rest of the Lewis group around the Great Falls portage, and Sergeant Ordway, leading the group Clark sent down the Missouri from Three Forks.

The entire Lewis contingent, thus reunited, traveled down the Missouri, reaching the Yellowstone confluence within nine days of the Clark attachment—good progress, considering the adventure they'd had.

The Two Medicine Fight could have been a disaster for the expedition. Had Lewis and his men been killed, the journals and his accumulated knowledge of the exploration would have been lost forever. The deaths on the Two Medicine were the only casualties the Lewis and Clark expedition inflicted on the West's native peoples during the corps' 2.5-year journey. While it is sad anyone had to die, it is surely to the captains' credit that nearly all the Indian encounters resulted in friendship and cooperation, not animosity and violence.

Return to the Valier Road and drive south. From Valier it is 15 miles east to Interstate 15 and about 70 miles to Great Falls.

The Great Falls of the Missouri River.

Monticello, the home of President Thomas Jefferson. View of the west front and fish pond. President Jefferson played a key role in the Lewis and Clark Expedition.

Photo by R. Lautman/Monticello/Thomas Jefferson Foundation, Inc. Used with permission.

Cahokia Courthouse in Illinois, which was visited by Meriwether Lewis in the winter of 1803–1804.

Near Blackbird Hill, Nebraska.

"Scenes of visionary enchantment" along the Upper Missouri River Breaks, Montana.

White Cliffs, Missouri River Breaks, Montana.

Statue depicting York, Seaman, Lewis, and Clark in Great Falls, Montana.

The Great Falls of the Missouri River, Montana.

Beaverhead Rock, a landmark Sacagawea knew near Dillon, Montana.

Lolo Creek near the Continental Divide, Montana.

View from the Lolo Trail, Idaho.

Tepee camp on the Clearwater River near Orofino, Idaho.

Columbia River near The Dalles, Oregon.

Beacon Rock, Washington.

Ecola State Park on the Oregon Coast.

GREAT FALLS

Lewis and Clark spent thirty-two days in the Great Falls area, more than any other place aside from their winter camps. At Great Falls, the explorers expected to encounter one cascade and a portage of no more than 0.5 mile, easily accomplished in a day. Instead, the corps found five formidable falls and wound up taking nearly two weeks to cover the distance they'd normally travel by water in a single day. The falls, in the order they were reached going up river, were the Great Falls, highest of the series at almost 100 feet; Horseshoe or Crooked Falls; Rainbow or Handsome Falls; Colter Falls, no longer visible, about 0.5 mile upriver from Rainbow Falls; and Black Eagle Falls.

Because of the amount of time the Corps of Discovery spent here, Great Falls has evolved into a major center for modern Lewis and Clark buffs. Here you'll find the Lewis and Clark National Historic Trail Interpretive Center on the bluffs of the Missouri River. Great Falls also is home to the Lewis and Clark Trail Heritage Foundation, and the foundation's local Portage Route chapter is among the nation's most active. For these reasons, the city is a treasure trove of expedition lore and well worth a stop.

The Great Falls of the Missouri are an apt place to begin any visit to the area. To get there, drive north on U.S. 87 and follow the signs to Ryan Dam. The turnoff is about 2 miles north of the town of Black Eagle, just across the river from Great Falls. Remember that Lewis and several others had left the Marias River confluence, intent on making sure this south fork was indeed still the Missouri. Toward noon on June 13, 1805, Lewis and Private Silas Goodrich had walked about 2 miles toward the river when, Lewis wrote, "My ears were saluted with the agreeable sound of a fall of water and advancing a little farther I saw a spray arise above the plain like a column of smoke which would frequently disappear again and an instant caused I presume from the wind which was blowing pretty hard from the southwest. I did not however lose my direction to this point which soon began to make a roaring too tremendous to be mistaken for any cause short of the Great Falls of the Missouri." Today the Ryan Dam day-use area includes several overlooks, picnic tables, and a shelter.

Lewis scrambled down a 200-foot bluff to witness what he called "the grandest sight" he had ever seen. He and his advance party had a good dinner of buffalo and trout and camped overnight at the site. The next day, Lewis sent Joseph Field down the river with word that the south fork was the true Missouri. Later he walked upriver alone 5 miles and found a 19-foot-high waterfall with an irregular rock shelf. He named this cascade Crooked Falls. In another 0.5 mile he discovered what he called in his journal Beautiful or Handsome Falls, now known as Rainbow Falls. A quarter mile farther, he spotted a small falls, Colter; and finally, 2.5 miles more upriver, another large cascade. Nearby, he spied an

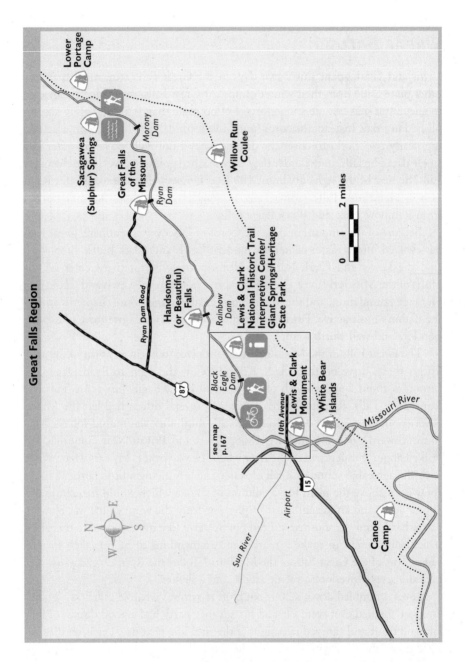

eagle's nest—the very landmark Indians had mentioned the corps would see past the falls.

Meanwhile, as Lewis was exploring the Great Falls, Clark was attending to Sacagawea, who had been ill for about a week. He bled her and tried purges, poultices, and just about every other remedy in the corps' primitive medical

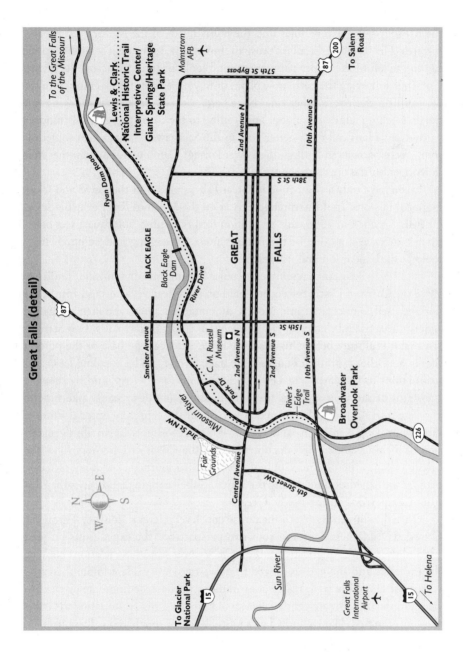

Great Falls (detail)

To the Great Falls
of the Missouri

Lewis & Clark
National Historic Trail
Interpretive Center/
Giant Springs/Heritage
State Park

Malmstrom
AFB

57th St Bypass

87 · 200

To Salem
Road

Ryan Dam Road

2nd Avenue N

10th Avenue S

38th St S

BLACK EAGLE

Black Eagle
Dam

River Drive

GREAT

FALLS

87

Smelter Avenue

C. M. Russell
Museum

2nd Avenue N

2nd Avenue S

10th Avenue S

15th St

River's
Edge
Trail

Broadwater
Overlook Park

Park Dr.

Missouri River

3rd St NW

Fair
Grounds

Central Avenue

6th Street SW

226

N
W E
S

To Glacier
National Park

15

Sun River

Great Falls
International
Airport

15 / To Helena

repertoire, but nothing seemed to work. The situation was dire, for without Sacagawea, the expedition stood much less a chance of getting horses and proceeding peacefully to the coast.

When Lewis returned, he examined Sacagawea and sent for water from a sulphur spring he recalled seeing nearby. She felt better within hours. Today the spring is still known as Sacagawea Springs. It is accessible on the north side of the Missouri via a 1-mile hike atop the bluffs north of the Morony Dam parking area. The unmarked trail isn't easy to find at first; to locate it scramble up the hill to the left of the upper parking area and look for the path across the ravine. Continue following the path, now plain, until you see Belt Creek empty into the Missouri on the river's other side. Near here, a small creek begins flowing due north, smelling faintly of sulphur and leading to the clear springs a few hundred yards away. Plans call for a better trail in the Sacagawea Springs area sometime soon. From Sacagawea Springs, the Lower Portage Camp was about another mile downriver on the opposite shore.

If you have only a short time in Great Falls, spend it at the Lewis and Clark National Historic Trail Interpretive Center on the Missouri River near Black Eagle Falls. Opened in 1998, this $6-million facility (with 5,500 square feet of exhibits) offers visitors one of the nation's most compelling and comprehensive looks at the expedition and its legacy.

The center's entrance resembles a coulee cutting into the hillside, similar to those the Corps of Discovery encountered on the Great Falls portage. Inside, the portage itself is re-created in a life-size diorama that shows the men struggling against the land and elements. (*The Explorers at Giant Springs 1805,* Bob Scriver's last major sculpture before his death in 1999, sits near the base of the portage diorama.) Other exhibits upstairs set the stage for the trip by detailing Jefferson's instructions to the corps and Lewis's preparations for the trip, and by showing the status of the United States in 1803. Before going downstairs, take time to view the thirty-minute film created especially for the center by noted documentary filmmakers Ken Burns and Dayton Duncan—essentially an abridged version of their acclaimed PBS documentary on the Corps of Discovery. The film briefly outlines the explorers' outgoing and return journeys, the array of native peoples the expedition met along the way, and the changing landscapes they saw from Camp Wood to the Pacific Ocean.

Once the film ends, exit to the downstairs level. Here, a "Journey Through a Crowded Wilderness" unfolds from two perspectives: the expedition's on your left and the Native Americans' on the right. Visitors learn how relations between the explorers and the natives ranged from warm to wary. Here, more than anywhere else along the trail, native contributions to the expedition are given their due, and the captains are gently taken to task for not fully appreciating the tribes they encountered. "Lewis and Clark's journals tell us much about these peoples, but the captains' interpretation was sometimes prejudiced by their own culture," one exhibit reads. "They often described only external features and events, neglecting the spiritual or cultural significance of what they saw."

There are plenty of interactive exhibits along the way. Try lashing willow onto an iron boat frame; test your strength by "pulling" a canoe against a current; decide which way to go at the Marias-Missouri confluence; or try to figure out the modern names of some prairie creatures described by Lewis and Clark.

Rainbow Falls at Great Falls, Montana.

Thought-provoking questions abound: When the corps saw no Indians for four months after leaving the Mandan villages, were the natives deliberately avoiding them? (The explorers did see plenty of evidence of tribal activity, including prayer cloth offerings and smoke from distant fires.) The final exhibits examine the expedition's outcome and display some notable reproductions, including a gorgeous recreation of a buffalo robe brought back from the Mandan villages. (The original is at Harvard University's Peabody Museum.)

Downstairs in the Jefferson Commons and outdoors near the river's edge, costumed interpreters give regular talks on such topics as bears, moccasin making, and tepee raising. The interpretive trail leading from the center to the river is delightful, with songbirds darting amid the lush riverside greenery. Other center features include a special exhibit room, a research library, and the headquarters of the Lewis and Clark Trail Heritage Foundation. The Portage Cache gift shop sells books, toys, gifts, and postcards.

To get to the center, follow River Drive, which runs north and east of central Great Falls. Summer hours are 9:00 A.M. to 6:00 P.M. daily, Memorial Day weekend through September 30. October through late May, the center is open from 9:00 A.M. to 5:00 P.M. Tuesday through Saturday and noon to 5:00 P.M. Sunday. Admission is $5.00 for adults, $4.00 for students and seniors sixty-two and over; and $2.00 for children ages six through seventeen. For more information, call (406) 727–8733 or do a Web search for Great Falls Lewis and Clark center.

If possible, time your Great Falls visit with the town's annual Lewis and Clark Festival, held late each June about the same time the explorers arrived. It's one of the best trail-related festivals, with activities including a living-history encampment, noted speakers, float trips, and even a day camp for children. Registration is necessary for many events; contact the interpretive center for exact dates or more information.

Near the interpretive center, Giant Springs/Heritage State Park is also worth a stop. Clark discovered the spring on June 18, 1805, and Lewis later said it was the largest he'd ever seen, perhaps the largest in America. Indeed, Giant Springs lives up to its name with a flow of nearly 8,000,000 gallons per hour. The water comes from the Madison limestone formations lying beneath most of eastern and central Montana. Rainfall and melted snow soak into the limestone to the Great Falls area, where it flows upward about 700 feet through fractures before being pushed out at Giant Springs. This 38-mile trip takes hundreds of years, but the water gains momentum as it travels until it is pumped out at Giant Springs with a force of about 134,000 gallons per minute. The spring also forms the Roe River, the shortest in the world at just over 200 feet.

The springs are rich in calcium, magnesium, bicarbonate, and sulfate. These minerals are all excellent for nurturing trout, and a hatchery is located at the site. Visitors may buy fish food to feed the hatchlings—a great source of cheap entertainment! (Bring nickels!) A playground, picnic tables, and big shade trees make this a very pleasant place to visit. Giant Springs/Heritage State Park is open from dawn to dusk, with the fish hatchery open daily from 8:00 A.M. to 4:30 P.M. For more information call (406) 454–5840. Other good family attractions in Great Falls include Electric City Water Park and the Children's Museum of Montana.

As the interpretive center shows, Great Falls had long been a key spot in Native American travels through the region. Because the confluence of the Missouri and Medicine (now Sun) Rivers boasted the best fording spot for 40 miles in any direction, Indians frequently followed the Medicine River to its mouth here before crossing the Missouri and heading for elk and buffalo hunting grounds on the Plains. Today, this junction is overseen from Broadwater Overlook Park, off Tenth Avenue South. The park's centerpiece is a heroic-sized bronze statue of Lewis and Clark sculpted by Bob Scriver to commemorate the Montana state centennial in 1989. In addition to the captains, it shows York and Lewis's dog, Seaman.

Lewis is pointing—but at what? After finding the remaining falls on June 14, Lewis discovered the Medicine River, which Indians at Fort Mandan had told him to expect. Elated, Lewis decided to kill a buffalo and make camp at the site. He picked his target, shot the beast, and stood watching it die, all the while neglecting to reload his rifle. Suddenly, he saw a grizzly bear walking toward him.

The Corps of Discovery.

Lewis headed off toward a tree where he intended to make camp, but the bear followed him. So Lewis switched directions, heading instead for the river, running in until he was waist-deep in water. He planted his feet, grasped his trusty espontoon, and held it menacingly toward the bear—an action that apparently startled the grizzly. Luckily for Lewis, the bear spun around and ran out of the river, out of sight. This same incident is depicted on a mural titled *The One That Got Away,* painted by John Carlon on the side of the building at Central Avenue and Eighth Street North near downtown Great Falls.

At the upper portage camp at White Bear Islands, Lewis finally had the chance to test the collapsible iron boat he'd had made at Harpers Ferry. The boat was fitted with twenty-eight elk skins and four buffalo hides, then launched into the river. It floated! But after about five hours, the boat started coming apart at the seams. Without pine trees to make pitch, the men had made do with beeswax, tallow, and charcoal, none of which worked as well. "I need not add this circumstance mortified me not a little," Lewis wrote. "I therefore relinquished all further hope of my favorite boat and ordered her to be sunk in the water...." Meanwhile, Clark took some men and proceeded upstream to find trees suitable for making new canoes of the time-tested dugout variety. The iron boat, whether submerged in the river or cached nearby, has never been found.

Lewis was dejected, but other words he wrote during the portage conveyed a

Following the Portage

t's not well marked, but visitors with time and inclination may want to try following the entire Lewis and Clark portage route across the southeast edge of Great Falls. The trek may still be traced with a self-guiding auto-tour tape and map available from the local Lewis and Clark Trail Heritage Foundation chapter. The tapes cost $10 (including a map and compass) and can be purchased at the interpretive center or the Great Falls Visitor Center at Broadwater Overlook Park or by mail to the Portage Route Chapter, P.O. Box 2424, Great Falls, MT 59403.

To outline it briefly, the portage began at what is now known as Belt Creek, located directly across the river from Sacagawea Springs. There the corps built two truck frames with wooden wheels to haul their goods over-land. From the creek, the trail wound up the coulee and on to the prairie bench. (Salem Road now parallels the way.)

Hazards and inconveniences were many. Rattlesnakes were a constant threat all along the portage route, as were prickly pear cactus—the men's soft-soled moccasins were no match for these sharp-spined plants. The expe-dition's pace was also slowed by ruts gouged by the immense hoofprints of thousands of bison. The corps encountered several violent storms, with hail so fierce on one occasion it bloodied several men. Yet despite all the difficulties, Clark noted that "no man complains. All go cheerfully on."

The portage ended at the White Bear Islands, so named because they were teeming with grizzlies. There were three islands when Lewis and Clark camped here, and there are still three today—though not necessarily the same ones the expedition saw. The journals mention that the party drank the last of its spirits here on July 4, 1805. Paris Gibson, the founder of Great Falls, felt the event took place on a knoll north of what is now the Ayrshire Dairy, which overlooks the islands. Gibson commemorated the site with a brass plaque and city park. Both park and plaque are gone now, but the plaque's cement base still stands.

Local historian Don Peterson gives guided tours of the portage route and other regional historic and scenic attractions. He'll ride along in your vehicle for $45 an hour and figures the average portage route tour takes four to six hours; in his vehicle, the cost is $65 an hour. Peterson also talks about Lewis and Clark at the Great Falls KOA most Saturday evenings in the summer. For more information call (406) 268–8403 or e-mail dpete@imt.net.

good deal more hope. The captains had earlier toyed with the idea of sending a boatload of men back East from the Great Falls; they now decided not to do so. The party was still small enough, they reasoned, and all available hands might be needed to deal with the unknown ahead. "We have never hinted to anyone of the party that we had such a scheme in contemplation, and all appear perfectly to have made up their minds to succeed in the expedition or perish in the attempt," Lewis wrote. "We all believe that we are now about to enter the most perilous and difficult part of our voyage, yet I see no one repining. All appear ready to meet those difficulties which await us with resolution and becoming fortitude."

Aside from Lewis and Clark, Charlie Russell is Great Falls's major local hero. The famous Western artist lived much of his life in the area and is buried in Highland Cemetery. Russell's influence seems to loom everywhere—his initials are even carved into a hillside by the Missouri riverbank—but the must-see attraction for Russell buffs is the C. M. Russell Museum Complex, located at 400 Thirteenth Street North. Here visitors can see Russell's home, his original log cabin studio, and one of the largest collections of Russell art and personal effects in any one place. The C. M. Russell Auction of Original

Great Falls Travel Tips

Great Falls International Airport (GTF) is served by Big Sky, Delta, Horizon, and Northwest airlines. Most major car rental companies have offices at the airport. The bus terminal is also at the airport, with service from Rimrock Stages and Intermountain Bus to most major Montana cities. If you travel to Great Falls by air, be sure to check out the mural by Robert Orduno above the main escalators at the airport. Measuring 10 feet by 35 feet, the painting shows the explorers making their portage.

Great Falls Transit runs several routes throughout the city, but none goes close to the Lewis and Clark Interpretive Center, except during the Lewis and Clark Festival each June. Buses typically run from 6:30 A.M. to about 7:00 P.M. Monday through Saturday. For updated schedule information, call (406) 727-0382.

The Great Falls Historic Trolley operates during the summer, with stops at all the major city visitor sites including the Lewis and Clark Interpretive Center and the C. M. Russell Museum. For rates and schedules call (406) 771-1100.

For more information on Great Falls, call (800) 735-8535 or (406) 761-4434, stop by the visitor center at Broadwater Overlook Park, or visit www.greatfallsonline.com.

Portage scene at the Lewis and Clark National Historic Trail Interpretive Center, Great Falls, Montana.

Western Art, held mid-March, is one of Great Falls's biggest annual events.

Paris Gibson Square is another favorite with visitors. The square, at the corner of Fourteenth Street and First Avenue North, includes the Center for Contemporary Arts and the Cascade County Museum, where changing exhibits and a permanent collection of more than 50,000 objects ensure that there's always something new to see. The Museum Cafe here is also one of Great Falls's more interesting places to grab lunch.

Great Falls's biggest recreational asset is the River's Edge Trail, which starts at the Missouri/Sun River confluence and will eventually go all the way out to the Great Falls and Sacagawea Springs. Walkers, strollers, joggers, cyclists, and skaters all enjoy the route, which is being built on a former railroad bed. The trail also passes the site of Lewis's grizzly bear encounter, which likely took place across the river from the tennis courts and horseshoe pits at a site now known as West Bank Park. Every July 4, Great Falls's annual Meriwether Lewis fun run is held to commemorate what must have been the West's fastest 50-yard dash. Sacagawea Island, a kind of nature preserve, is also visible in the river nearby. Cycle rentals ($8.00 for the first hour, $2.00 an hour thereafter) and riding information are available at Knicker Biker, 1123 Central Avenue.

If you didn't get a chance to float the Missouri from Fort Benton, it's not too late to sample it here. Montana River Outfitters offers several short boat trips in the Great Falls area. The Missouri Breaks float heads downriver from Morony Dam past Lewis and Clark's lower portage camp and through some nice white water. The Wolf Creek Canyon float travels along the Missouri south of Great Falls—an area of great beauty, fascinating geology, and lots of wildlife. Either trip can run a half day or whole day; prices start at $39 for adults for the half-day trips and run to $59 for a full-day float with a riverside steak dinner. For anyone really short on time, there's even a two-hour scenic float for just $24 for adults ($19 per child twelve and under). Montana River Outfitters also runs trips on the Upper Missouri, as well as Smith River fishing trips and horseback/float expeditions into the Bob Marshall Wilderness. For more information call (800) 800–8218 or (406) 761–1677.

From Great Falls, it is possible to take scenic MT 200 directly to Missoula, a distance of 167 miles. Doing so will mean missing several key chapters in the Lewis and Clark story, but it will also save about 200 miles and a day or two of rugged travel. MT 200 also takes the traveler close to the route Captain Lewis used on his return journey in 1806 (see the Homeward Bound: Lewis Finds a Shortcut section below for details). Travelers who want to continue following the corps' 1805 route should leave Great Falls south on Interstate 15. It's 76 miles from Great Falls to the Gates of the Mountains, our next major stop.

HOMEWARD BOUND: LEWIS FINDS A SHORTCUT

When the expedition was on its way home in 1806, the captains split up at their Travelers' Rest camp at present-day Lolo, Montana (Chapter 8). From there Clark explored the Big Hole Country and Lewis took the Indian road to the buffalo hunting grounds east of the divide. He crossed the Continental Divide at a point now called Lewis and Clark Pass, something of a misnomer, since Clark never saw the place.

Lewis's route roughly parallels Montana Highway 200 between Great Falls and Missoula, a distance of about 170 miles. Lewis and Clark Pass is near the midway point, and it's a good hike to break up the trip. To get there, look for Forest Road 293 (Alice Creek) on the north side of MT 200, about 8 miles east of Lincoln. This is the turnoff, but you may want to drive on to Lincoln for a stop at the Helena National Forest ranger station (open weekdays), where forest personnel can offer more detailed directions and a map to the site. The ranger station phone number is (406) 362–4265.

Return to FR 293 and head north. Five miles in, a historical sign notes that Lewis and his party stopped in the vicinity for dinner on July 7, 1806. From here the Indian trail they followed closely parallels the forest road. Ten miles from MT 200, a fork in the road marks the trailhead to the pass. Park your vehicle, go

Near Lewis and Clark Pass in the Helena National Forest.

through the gate on the right fork, and start hiking. The 1.5-mile trail has little shade and some moderately steep sections, so bring water and sunscreen. Elevation at the pass, where you'll also find the Continental Divide Trail, is 6,421 feet.

Had Lewis and Clark known heading west what they learned at Travelers' Rest, they could have saved themselves many weeks of tough travel. It took the expedition about two months to cover the route between Great Falls and Travelers' Rest on the outbound trek in 1805; Lewis made the trip in just eight days using the shortcut the following summer, and Indians told the captains it could be done in as few as four days! But perhaps they would not have used the shortcut going westbound even if they'd known about it. After all, President Jefferson had instructed the corps to find the headwaters of the Missouri—a task they would not have accomplished had they followed the more direct route west from Great Falls.

The Lewis and Clark interpretive center in Great Falls typically plans a field trip to Lewis and Clark Pass each July 7. Alice Creek Ranch, halfway to the trailhead on FR 293, is a working guest ranch in summer and a cross-country ski haven on winter weekends; call (406) 362–4810 for details. McDonough Outfitters offers guided pack trips and hunting trips, as well as half-day hikes and horseback rides to Lewis and Clark Pass; the latter cost about $75 per person. They also have a cabin for rent ($50/night) about 2 miles from the pass in the Green Creek area. Call (406) 235–4428 or (406) 235–4205 for more information.

Lincoln is another good spot to spend the night if you're dawdling. The town's Hooper Park has a pavilion with carved, painted figures from the Corps of Discovery. Or drive a half hour west to Ovando, a tiny town that nonetheless has excellent visitor amenities at the Blackfoot Inn B&B and Trixi's Antler Saloon & Fine Dining.

GATES OF THE MOUNTAINS

Driving south of Great Falls, it soon becomes apparent the Montana plains are ending and giving way to the lofty peaks that gave this state its name. ("Montana" is indeed the Spanish word for "mountain.") The ranges surrounding Great Falls—hardly visible in town but prominent once one leaves—are the Highwoods to the east, Little Belts to the southeast, and the Big Belts to the southwest.

The area between Great Falls and Helena is sparsely settled, with the few towns along the way catering to tourism and outdoor activities. Near Ulm (exit 270), the corps camped July 10–14, 1805, and built the dugout canoes needed to replace Lewis's iron boat. Ulm Pishkun State Park preserves a buffalo jump, pictographs, and prairie dog town. Cascade (exit 256) has a free overnight camping park.

Although I–15 is one of the most scenic interstates found anywhere, the traveler can escape it by taking an even more pleasant recreation road that runs closer to the Missouri River. Access this scenic route at Hardy Creek (exit 247). From there, the route can be followed as far south as Spring Creek. Boat ramps and primitive camping areas are plentiful along the way.

Wolf Creek (exits 226–228) is the access point to Holter Lake, the first of several popular lakes located just minutes from the interstate. Wolf Creek is also headquarters for several river and fly-fishing guide services. But the canyon corridor's primary lure for Lewis and Clark buffs is the Gates of the Mountains boat trip. Even the name sounds inviting, a tribute to Meriwether Lewis's poetic imagination. To get there take exit 209 to Upper Holter Lake and follow the signs.

By the time Lewis and Clark arrived in this area in mid-July 1805, it had been months since they had seen any Indians (other than Sacagawea, of course). They were starting to get anxious, knowing the party would need horses to travel over the Continental Divide. Moreover, the captains figured they had to be getting close to Sacagawea's home country, the land of the Shoshones, or Snake Indians, as the white men called them. It was decided they would take turns traveling overland to increase the chances of meeting Indians. Clark and three other men left the canyon on the first expedition, with no clue of the river spectacle they were about to miss.

"This evening we entered the most remarkable cliffs that we have yet seen," Lewis wrote on July 19. "These cliffs rise from the water's edge on either side perpendicularly to the height of 1,200 feet . . . the towering and projecting rocks in many places seem ready to tumble in on us." Lewis also noted that, although it was getting dark, the men had to keep moving, for there was scarcely a spot on shore where "a man could rest the sole of his foot. . . It was late in the evening before I entered this place and was obliged to continue my route until sometime after dark before I found a place sufficiently large to encamp my small party. At length such a one occurred on the larboard side where we found plenty of light wood and pitch pine. This rock is a black granite below and appears to be of a much lighter color above . . . from the singular appearance of this place I called it the gates of the rocky mountains."

The boat tours here last nearly two hours and cover a distance of 6.5 miles on what is now Holter Lake. Guides offer a wealth of information on the canyon's natural and human history, while helping passengers scan the cliffs for bighorn sheep and mountain goats (most likely seen on the right-hand side going into the canyon and the left-hand side going out). Young bald eagles, ospreys,

Gates of the Mountains boat tour.

cliff swallows, and barn swallows live here, too.

Also in evidence are pictographs, probably 200 to 300 years old and of Black-feet origin. And the tours pass by Mann Gulch, where twelve men lost their lives in a wildfire August 1949. The fire spread from 30 acres to 2,000 acres in less than ten minutes when the winds kicked up, and ended up burning 15,000 acres before it was through. The incident made national news and is detailed in *Young Men and Fire,* a book by Montana author Norman Maclean (best known for *A River Runs Through It*).

All trips stop at the Meriwether Picnic Area, believed to be where Lewis and his party found their small campsite. Although these stops are usually brief—just enough time to stretch one's legs and use the rest room—passengers have the op-tion of catching a later boat back to the docks. Those who do so may want to pack a picnic or take the 1-mile trail to Coulter Campground, named after the expedition member but spelled differently for some reason. More ambitious backpackers could stay overnight—or longer—and trek into the Gates of the Mountains Wilderness. One popular destination, Refrigerator Canyon, is an 18-mile round-trip from Coulter Campground.

Gates of the Mountains boat tours run Memorial Day weekend through mid-September. Cruises are offered at 11:00 A.M., 1:00 P.M., and 3:00 P.M. week-days and every hour on the hour from 10:00 A.M. to 4:00 P.M. on Saturday,

Sunday, and holidays during July and August. In June weekday sailings are set for 11:00 A.M. and 2:00 P.M. with weekend and holiday cruises scheduled at 10:00 A.M., noon, 2:00 P.M., and 4:00 P.M. In September tours are at 11:00 A.M. and 2:00 P.M. Wednesday through Friday and 11:00 A.M., 1:00 P.M., and 3:00 P.M. weekends.

Tickets cost $9.00 for adults, $8.00 for seniors (age sixty and over), and $6.00 for kids four to seventeen. Children under four ride free. Plan to arrive about a half hour early to buy tickets. Bring a jacket—even hot days can be breezy on the boat—and binoculars. For more information call (406) 458-5241.

It's a twenty-minute drive from Gates of the Mountains to Helena—Montana's charming capital city. A good way to get oriented here is with an hour-long ride on the Last Chance Tour Train, which departs from the Montana Historical Society on the corner of Roberts and Sixth Avenue just east of the Capitol. The train—and Montana's downtown pedestrian mall, Last Chance Gulch—take their name from "the Georgians," four weary and despondent Southern gold prospectors who, arriving at what is now Helena in 1864, decided to make one more attempt at locating gold. They struck it rich, as did many others: by the late 1880s, there were more millionaires per capita in Helena than anywhere else in the United States.

Tour train guides point out important state buildings (including Montana's decidedly modest governor's residence), the elegant architectural gems on Last Chance Gulch, and the impressive west-side mansion district. Riders also learn that the Helena Masonic Temple has Meriwether Lewis's Masonic apron and that a feisty local pilot once flew between the spires of the lovely Cathedral of St. Helena. In all, it's a very entertaining and informative trip. Trains depart at 10:00 and 11:00 A.M. and 1:00, 2:00, 3:00, 4:00, and 6:00 P.M. daily during July and August. From May 15 to May 30 and during September, trains leave at 11:00 A.M. and 1:00 and 3:00 P.M. In June departures are at 10:00 and 11:00 A.M., and 1:00, 2:00, and 3:00 P.M. Fare is $5.00 for adults and teens, $4.50 for seniors sixty-five and older, and $4.00 for kids ages four to twelve. Call (406) 442-1023 for more information.

Before or after the train ride, stop in the Montana Historical Society. Highlights include the Mackay Gallery of Charlie Russell Art, including several paintings and drawings on the Lewis and Clark theme. *York,* painted by Russell in 1908, is probably the most memorable rendering ever of the African-American man who accompanied his master, Clark, on the expedition. The watercolor, set at the Mandan villages during the winter of 1804–1805, shows two Native Americans touching a towering, bare-chested York to see if he is painted. Others look on in wonder, as smoke from the lodge fire blends magically with light filtering in from above. The Montana Homeland exhibit also has a section on the expedition, featuring three large oil canvases by Robert Morgan: *White Bears and White Cliffs, Decision,* and *At Lemhi.*

The Montana State Capitol, just across Sixth Avenue, also honors Lewis and Clark with grand artworks, including Russell's *Lewis and Clark Meeting the Flathead Indians at Ross' Hole,* at 12 feet by 25 feet his largest work. Other paintings by E. S. Paxson depict the explorers at the Three Forks and Lewis at Black Eagle Falls. The capitol was recently restored to its 1902 appearance, and the free forty-five-minute tour is well worth taking. Memorial Day through Labor Day, tours begin on the hour between 9:00 A.M. and 4:00 P.M. Monday through Saturday and noon to 4:00 P.M. Sunday. Tours are offered weekends only the rest of the year, except during legislative sessions (January through April in odd-numbered years), when they're given daily. Call (406) 444–4789 or visit www.montana capitol.com for more information.

Helena boasts an active cultural scene. On Wednesday evening in summer, downtown comes "Alive at 5," with a wide array of music in a variety of locations. Other hot spots include the Myrna Loy Center for the Performing Arts at 15 North Ewing and the Holter Museum of the Arts at 12 East Lawrence. The city also has a full calendar of annual events, including the Last Chance Stampede in late July and the Western Rendezvous of Art in mid-August. Like Billings, Great Falls, and Butte, Helena fields a Pioneer League baseball team, the Brewers.

Those yearning for more active sports need only look to Mount Helena, where an excellent network of trails offers hiking and mountain biking right out the city's backdoor. To get there take Park Avenue to the Reeders Alley trailhead. Spring Meadow State Park, on the north side of town between Euclid Avenue and Country Club Drive, has good fishing, swimming, and bird-watching. For more information on Helena, call (800) 743–5362 (out of state) or (406) 442–4120 or visit www.helenachamber.com.

A bit out of town, but still close by, Frontier Town is an Old West–theme village on the Continental Divide built almost entirely by one man, John Quigley. Aside from an outstanding view, Frontier Town offers a museum, a shop, and a restaurant—even a wedding chapel. Hiking trails thread through the nearby forest. Frontier Town is located 15 miles west of Helena on U.S. Highway 12.

From Helena, the Lewis and Clark Trail bends to the southeast, following U.S. 12 to Townsend, then U.S. 287 to Three Forks. En route, travelers may want to stop at Canyon Ferry Recreation Area, one of Montana's most popular. The original Canyon Ferry Dam was completed in 1898 to provide power to the booming town of Helena. The present dam, completed in 1954, is 225 feet high and impounds the 25-mile-long Canyon Ferry Lake.

Canyon Ferry Village has a visitor center that is open from noon to 4:00 P.M. Sunday, Monday, Wednesday, and Friday and noon to 8:00 P.M. on Saturday during the summer. If the center isn't open, you can still get information at a nearby shelter. Interpretive panels tell about the dam and describe an 85-mile auto tour through the nearby Helena National Forest.

There is scant Lewis and Clark interpretation. A picnic area on the lake's west shore is named for our heroes, but no camping is allowed. To get there from Canyon Ferry Village, take Montana Highway 284 southeast, across the dam, and bear left at the Yacht Basin Marina area. The community of York near Canyon Ferry was named for New York City, not the York of Lewis and Clark fame.

Canyon Ferry's congested campgrounds seem better suited to RVers than tent campers, although a few decent tent sites may be found in the Court Sheriff area's back loop and at Hellgate. Showers are available at some of the nearby commercial establishments including Kim's Marina. Boats, windsurfing gear, and other water toys are available for rent at Yacht Basin Marina.

Canyon Ferry Lake's southern stretch reaches nearly to U.S. 12 north of Townsend. The Indian Road Campground just north of town has a great little fishing pond designed for children under twelve and handicapped anglers. The Missouri River flows into the Canyon Ferry impoundment here, and a boat ramp is available. Townsend, 29 miles south of Helena, is an agricultural hub and tourist-oriented community. The Broadwater County Museum at 133 North Walnut Street has displays of pioneer artifacts and information on the area's mining history. From Townsend it is 31 miles to Interstate 90 and the Missouri headwaters.

THREE FORKS OF THE MISSOURI

As they moved up the Missouri past the Gates of the Mountains, Lewis and his party suddenly had reason to celebrate. Sacagawea recognized the land through which they were passing! "This piece of information has cheered the spirits of the party who . . . console themselves with the anticipation of shortly seeing the head of the Missouri yet unknown to the civilized world," Lewis wrote.

Clark and his contingent reached the Three Forks of the Missouri first, on July 25, and explored the surrounding area while waiting for Lewis. They looked everywhere for Indians, but there were still none to be seen. The rest of the party arrived July 27, and the expedition camped in the area through July 30, 1805, largely to allow time for rest. Clark in particular was well worn-out, his feet throbbing painfully from the many miles of overland travel over prickly pear cactus. More than ever, the expedition realized its need for horses. But again, Sacagawea offered reason for hope, recognizing this as the place of her kidnapping some five years earlier. She had been camped at the forks with her Shoshone family when the band was attacked by Hidatsa Indians, killing four men and taking a number of prisoners, "though I cannot discover that she shows any emotion of sorrow in recollecting this event, or of joy in being restored to her native country," Lewis wrote.

Here the captains had to decide which of the three forks would lead them toward the Continental Divide and the Pacific watershed. Although the streams were roughly similar in size, it wasn't an especially tough puzzle. They soon settled on the westernmost of the rivers, which they named the Jefferson in honor of "the author of our enterprise," as Lewis put it. The middle fork was named for then–Secretary of State James Madison, and the easternmost stream honored Albert Gallatin, Jefferson's Secretary of the Treasury (and a strong supporter of the Louisiana Purchase).

Missouri Headwaters State Park now commemorates the expedition's arrival, as well as the area's importance to Indians, trappers, traders, and settlers. The park is located 6 miles northeast of the town of Three Forks on Montana Secondary Route 285. Within the park, a short trail leads to the riverbank and a sign marking the headwaters.

An excellent interpretive display elsewhere in the park tells about the many aspects of Three Forks history. The visitor learns, for example, that the headwaters later served as the setting for a dramatic episode involving two former members of the expedition, John Colter and John Potts. In 1808 the two men were trapping on the Jefferson River. A band of Blackfeet, angered by previous encounters with whites, attacked both men.

Potts was killed right away, but Colter's fate seemed even worse: He was stripped and told to run for his life. Colter tore barefoot across the cactus-laden plains, outrunning all but one of his pursuers for about 6 miles. Despite his exhaustion, Colter turned on the Indian and killed him. He continued on into the Jefferson River and hid under a snag, eluding the other Blackfeet. Later, naked and weaponless, Colter headed for Manuel Lisa's fort on the Big Horn River. He made the 200-mile trip in seven days.

In 1810 Lisa, of the Missouri Fur Company, sent thirty-two trappers to establish a post at the headwaters. They found good beaver trapping, but grizzly bears and Blackfeet killed several of the frontiersmen, including George Drouillard, another Lewis and Clark alumnus. "Popular history has surrounded the mountain man with glory and adventure," one interpretive panel reads. "But reality was often short rations, bitter cold, boredom and even sudden death." The idea of a permanent post was soon abandoned, although trappers continued to work the headwaters region until the 1840s. By that time, the beaver had nearly become extinct, and silk had replaced fur as the hat material of choice.

As Sacagawea would attest, the Three Forks area had long been an important hunting ground for the region's Indians. An 1855 treaty between the natives and whites declared the headwaters region to be a common hunting ground for ninety-nine years, supposedly guaranteeing all people "equal and uninterrupted

Yellowstone National Park and Nearby Attractions

Although only a sliver of Yellowstone National Park lies in Montana, the Treasure State claims three of the park's five entrances. The choices are West Yellowstone, south of Bozeman on U.S. 191 or south of Three Forks via U.S. 287; Gardiner, south of Livingston by way of U.S. 89; and Cooke City/Silver Gate, reached by way of the famous Beartooth Highway, U.S. Highway 212, southwest from Laurel near Billings.

Yellowstone was the world's first national park, so declared by an act of Congress in 1872. Known for its geysers, waterfalls, and wildlife (not to mention the 1988 fires that burned more than a third of the park), Yellowstone is among the most frequently visited national parks, so it can be crowded. Still, Yellowstone is a big place, with more than a thousand miles of trails. Solitude is available for those who seek it.

Yellowstone boasts so many spectacular sights that it's hard to know where to begin. Artist Point and Inspiration Point offer vistas of the Grand Canyon of the Yellowstone River and its famous falls. Old Faithful is but one example of the park's intense thermal activity, all triggered by an immense volcanic eruption 600,000 years ago. Norris Geyser Basin and the Fountain Paint Pots area offer the park's most concentrated displays of these steaming, gurgling natural features.

Sight-seeing is definitely the main attraction at Yellowstone. But other opportunities available include fishing, backcountry camping and hiking, and canoeing (especially on Shoshone Lake). A permit is required to fish in Yellowstone, and there is a fee for anglers age sixteen and up. Powerboaters are permitted on Yellowstone and Lewis Lakes.

While at Yellowstone, don't forget its less famous but equally scenic sister park, Grand Teton National Park. Few people forget their first sight of the Tetons, which are among the youngest mountains in North America. These soaring, craggy peaks provide the setting for some of the greatest hiking in the world.

The Cascade Canyon Trail is among the most popular Teton treks, and the hikes to Hermitage Point or on the Paintbrush Trail often reward visitors with wildlife views. Mountain climbing instruction and guides are available. It's difficult to pull your gaze away from the mountains, but the lakes and the Snake River are lovely, too. Activities include scenic boat trips, boat rentals, sailboarding on Jackson Lake, and floats down the Snake. Horseback riding, fishing, and camping offer still more pleasures.

The town of Jackson sits south of Grand Teton National Park. Like other mountain resort towns, Jackson has gone through a lot of changes in recent decades. It no longer qualifies as a "typical" Western town, but it certainly is a fun place to visit. Jackson crackles with energy, from its creative restaurants to its lively nightlife (don't miss the famous Million Dollar Cowboy Bar on the main square downtown), superb shopping, and active arts scene.

Another northwest Wyoming town, Cody, is famous for the Buffalo Bill Historical Center, widely considered to be the best overall Western museum in the United States. The five-part complex includes the Buffalo Bill Museum, which documents Colonel William Cody's colorful life; the Whitney Gallery of Western Art, featuring original works by such famous names as Russell and Remington; the Plains Indian Museum, with extensive displays on the life and times of the region's great tribes; the Cody Firearms Museum, which includes guns from throughout history; and the new Draper Museum of Natural History, a great place to learn more about the Yellowstone ecosystem. Cody is 80 miles east of the Fishing Bridge junction at Yellowstone National Park.

For more information contact Grand Teton National Park at (307) 739-3300 or www.nps.gov/grte; Yellowstone National Park at (307) 344-7381 or www.nps.gov/yell; the Jackson Hole Area Chamber of Commerce at (307) 733-3316; or www.jacksonholechamber.com; or Buffalo Bill's Yellowstone Country at (800) 393-2639 or www.pctc.org.

---

privileges" in the area. But rapid settlement by the whites brought the treaty to its knees less than a decade later.

Native vegetation in the park remains much the same as when Lewis and Clark visited. Plants include buckwheat brush, big sagebrush, pincushion cactus, saltbrush, prickly pear cactus, and bluebunch wheatgrass. A short trail leads to an overlook that points out key features of the landscape in all directions, including the Tobacco Root, Madison, and Gallatin Mountain ranges.

Missouri Headwaters State Park has a small but appealing campground, with a handful of choice secluded sites. Day-use visitors and campers alike enjoy facilities for picnicking, as well as fishing and boating access to the three rivers. Ranger-led tours of the park are offered at 11:00 A.M. and 1:30 P.M. daily spring through fall. Meet at the picnic area. At 7:00 P.M. each Saturday evening in summer, the park presents a speaker (often on a Lewis and Clark theme), followed by a social with free s'mores. A 7-mile run commemorating John Colter's sprint takes place here the second weekend in September. For more information on park activities, call (406) 994-6934.

For an off-the-beaten-path look at the Headwaters area, consider booking a tour with the Yellowstone Safari Company. Guide Ken Sinay, a wildlife biologist by training, takes small parties of up to six people out on a stretch of the Jefferson River that runs far from the road. Reading from the Lewis and Clark journals and consulting the expedition's maps, Sinay strives to compare what we see today with what the expedition encountered 200 years ago. Then as now, antelope, sandhill cranes, bald eagles, and beaver are among the many species living along the river.

Sinay takes people out in a hard-bottomed boat outfitted with comfortable chairs. (He can even accommodate wheelchairs.) Cost for a full-day safari runs from $420 for one person to $790 for seven, including lunch, snacks, and transportation. In the off-season (December to mid-May), Sinay is often available to lead half-day tours of the Headwaters/Gallatin Canyon area for $80 per person. He's also known for his wildlife-viewing trips to and around Yellowstone National Park, and he'll custom-design itineraries elsewhere in Montana by request. For more information or to plan a trip, call (406) 586–1155 or visit www.yellow stonesafari.com.

Montana River Expeditions runs scenic canoe and kayak trips on both the Madison and Jefferson Rivers; call (800) 500-4538 for information. Canoe rentals, shuttles, and fly-fishing trips also are available from the Canoeing House and Guide Service at (406) 285-3488.

Three Forks is an interesting little town in a picturesque setting. Visitors can shoot a round at the scenic Headwaters Public Golf Course or hire a river guide for a day of fly-fishing or river running. The Headwaters Heritage Museum at the corner of Main and Cedar is an appealing small-town history museum with two full floors of fascinating exhibits. The most interesting thing on view from a Lewis and Clark perspective is an anvil dating to 1810, the only artifact remaining from Manuel Lisa's short-lived Fort Three Forks. Though no one can be sure, John Colter and George Drouillard may have been among those using the anvil since both spent time at the fort that year. Three Forks holds an annual Children's Festival of Discovery on the fourth Saturday of July. Fun activities include a parade, crafts, barbecue, and a play.

For more local information on Three Forks, stop by the caboose visitor center at the entrance to town. It's open from 10:00 A.M. to 5:00 P.M. Wednesday through Sunday in the summer. Or call the Three Forks Chamber of Commerce at (406) 285–4753.

From Three Forks, proceed west on MT 2. Dillon is about 90 miles away via Montana Highways 2, 55, and 41.

Statue of Sacagawea in Bozeman, Montana.

Lodging

Lodgings, campgrounds, and restaurants listed below are a representative sampling of what is available. Listing in these pages does not imply endorsement, nor is this a complete listing of all reputable businesses. For more complete listings, contact the visitor information bureau or chamber of commerce in each town. Room rates were accurate as of summer 2002 but are subject to change.

LOMA, MONTANA
Virgelle Mercantile, (800) 426–2926. Cabins and bed-and-breakfast accommodations; $60–$120.

FORT BENTON, MONTANA
Grand Union Hotel, (406) 622–1882, 1 Grand Union Square; $99–$159.
Fort Motel, (406) 622–3312, 1809 St. Charles; $50–$75.
Long's Landing Bed and Breakfast, (406) 622–3461, 1011 Seventeenth Street; $50.
Pioneer Lodge, (406) 622–5441, 1700 Front Street; $50–$75.

*CONRAD, MONTANA
Conrad Super 8, (800) 442–4667, 215 North Main; $60–$70.

*SHELBY, MONTANA
Crossroads Inn, (406) 434–5134, U.S. 2; $60–$70.
O'Haire Manor Motel, (800) 541–5809, 204 Second Street South; $50–$65.

*CUT BANK, MONTANA
Corner Motel, (406) 873–5588, 1201 East Main Street; $50.
Cut Bank Super 8, (406) 873–5662, 609 West Main Street; $67–$77.
Glacier Gateway Inn, (406) 873–5544, 1121 East Railroad Street; $56–$64.

*BROWNING, MONTANA
Blackleaf Creek Ranch, (406) 469–2294 or (812) 923–3822, 50 miles south on MT 89. (Guest ranch; minimum stay may apply, call for rates.)
War Bonnet Lodge, (406) 338–7610, MT 89; $59.
Western Motel, (406) 338–7572, 121 Central Avenue East; $60–$90.

GREAT FALLS, MONTANA
Best Western Heritage Inn, (800) 548–0361, 1700 Fox Farm Road; $90–$100.
Charlie Russell Manor Bed & Breakfast, (877) 207–6131, 825 Fourth Avenue North; $80–$145.
Collins Mansion Bed & Breakfast, (877) 452–6798, 1003 Second Avenue Northwest; $89–$99.
Fairfield Inn, (406) 454–3000, 1000 Ninth Avenue South; $65–$85.
Great Falls Inn, (800) 454–6010, 1400 Twenty-eighth Street South; $60–$70.
Holiday Inn, (406) 727–7200, 400 Tenth Avenue South; $70–$100.
Old Oak Inn, (888) 727–5782, 709 Fourth Avenue North; $55–$95.

CASCADE, MONTANA
Badger Motel, (406) 468–9330, 132 First Street North; $49.
Fly Fishers' Inn, (406) 468–2529, 2629 Old Highway 91. Upscale lodge and guide service.

*Denotes town on Lewis's explorations of the Marias River region in 1806.
**Denotes town on Lewis's return route over the Continental Divide in 1806.

WOLF CREEK, MONTANA
Blacktail Ranch, (406) 235–4330, 4440 South Fork Trail; $150–$175. (Three-night minimum.)
The Bungalow Bed & Breakfast, (406) 235–4276, 2020 U.S. 287; $110–$125.
Frenchy's Motel, (406) 235–4251; $40–$45.
Holter Lake Lodge, (888) 235–4331, 1350 Beartooth Road; $78.
Montana River Outfitters, (800) 800–4350, 515 Recreation Road; $40–$80.

HELENA, MONTANA
Budget Inn Express, (800) 862–1334, 524 North Last Chance Gulch; $42–$47.
Comfort Inn, (406) 443–1000, 750 North Fee Street; $70–$90.
Jorgenson's Inn & Suites, (800) 272–1770 (in state) or (800) 521–2743, 1714 Eleventh Avenue; $60–$100.
Knight's Rest Motel, (888) 442–6384, 1831 Euclid Avenue; $50–$75.
Shilo Inn, (406) 442–0320, 2020 Prospect Avenue; $60–$110.
The Sanders—Helena's Bed & Breakfast, (406) 442–3309, 328 North Ewing; $95–$125.

**LINCOLN, MONTANA
Alice Creek Ranch, (406) 362–4810. Working ranch with lodging.
Leepers Ponderosa Motel, (406) 362–4333, MT 200; $47–$55.

**OVANDO, MONTANA
Blackfoot Inn Bed & Breakfast, (406) 793–5555; $55–$75.

TOWNSEND, MONTANA
Lake Townsend Motel, (406) 266–3461, 413 North Pine; $40–$45.
Mustang Motel, (406) 266–3491, 412 North Front; $38–$45.

THREE FORKS, MONTANA
Broken Spur Motel, (406) 285–3237, 124 West Elm; $46–$60.
Bud Lilly's Anglers Retreat, (406) 285–6690, 16 West Birch; $60–$165.
Fort Three Forks Motel, (406) 285–3233, I–90 at U.S. 287; $65–$80.
Sacajawea Hotel, (888) 722–4210, 5 North Main Street; $75–$105.

Camping

BIG SANDY, MONTANA
Coal Banks Landing, 11 miles south on U.S. 87, then south at sign for Upper Missouri Wild and Scenic River. Primitive sites.
Judith Landing, 44 miles southeast on Secondary Route 236, on the Upper Missouri Wild and Scenic River. Primitive sites.

FORT BENTON, MONTANA
Benton RV Park, (406) 622–5015, 2411 St. Charles.
D&S RV Park, (406) 622–5104, 316 Franklin.

*CONRAD, MONTANA
Sunrise Trailer Court, (406) 278–5901, 4 blocks east of stoplight.

*Denotes town on Lewis's explorations of the Marias River region in 1806.
**Denotes town on Lewis's return route over the Continental Divide in 1806.

*SHELBY, MONTANA
Lake Shel-oole Campground, (406) 434–5222, 0.5 mile south on I–15 business bypass.
Lewis and Clark RV Park, (406) 434–2710, I–15 exit 364, 1575 Oilfield Avenue.

*CUT BANK, MONTANA
Meriwether Meadows Campground, (406) 338–7737, 19 miles West of Cut Bank, then north on MT 444.
Shady Grove Campground, (406) 336–2475, 6 miles west on U.S. 2.

*BROWNING, MONTANA
Sleeping Wolf Campground, (406) 338–7933, 0.5 mile west on U.S. 89.

GREAT FALLS, MONTANA
Dick's RV Park, (406) 452–0333, I–15 exit 278, west of river on Tenth Avenue South.
Great Falls KOA, (406) 727–3191, 1500 Fifty-first Street South.

CASCADE, MONTANA
Atkinson Park, (406) 468–2808, adjacent to I–15 in town.

WOLF CREEK, MONTANA
Holter Lake, (406) 235–4314, I–15 exit 226, left 3 miles to lake. Primitive sites.

HELENA, MONTANA
Canyon Ferry Reservoir, (406) 475–3128, 10 miles east on U.S. 12/287, then 12 miles north on County Road 284.
Helena Campground & RV Resort, (406) 458–4714, 5820 North Montana Avenue.
Kim's Marina and RV Resort, (406) 475–3723, 10 miles east on U.S. 12/287, then 10 miles north on County Road 284.
Lincoln Road RV Park, (406) 458–3725, I–15 exit 200.

**LINCOLN, MONTANA
Aspen Grove, (406) 362–4265, 7 miles east on MT 200. Primitive sites.
Spring Creek RV Park, (406) 362–4140, west edge of town on MT 200.

TOWNSEND, MONTANA
Indian Road, (406) 475–3128, 1 mile north on U.S. 12/287.
Silos RV Park, (406) 266–3100, 7 miles north on U.S. 12/87, then east on Silos Road.

THREE FORKS, MONTANA
Missouri Headwaters State Park, 6 miles northeast on Secondary Road 286. Primitive sites.
Three Forks KOA, (406) 285–3611, 1 mile south of I–90 exit 274.

Restaurants

LOMA, MONTANA
Ma's Loma Cafe, (406) 739–4000, U.S. 87. Home cooking.

FORT BENTON, MONTANA
The Banque Club, (406) 622–5272, 1318 Front Street. Popular steakhouse.

Bob's Riverfront Restaurant, (406) 622–3443, 1414 Front Street. Good food, local gathering place.
Union Grille, (406) 622–1882, in the Grand Union Hotel. Innovative fine dining.

Denotes town on Lewis's explorations of the Marias River region in 1806.
**Denotes town on Lewis's return route over the Continental Divide in 1806.

*CUT BANK, MONTANA

Village Dining and Lounge, (406) 873–5005, Northern Village Shopping Center.

*BROWNING, MONTANA

Browning Cafe, (406) 338–7478. Burgers, soups, steaks. Open twenty-four hours.

GREAT FALLS, MONTANA

Baker Bob's Big Stack Bakery & Delicatessen/Back Alley Pub, (406) 727–5910, 110 Central Avenue.

Bert and Ernie's Saloon and Eatery, (406) 453–0601, 300 First Avenue South. Charbroiled burgers, big selection of imported draft beer. Also in Helena.

Dante's Creative Cuisine, (406) 453–9599, 1325 Eighth Avenue North. Casual fine dining.

Eddie's Supper Club, (406) 453–1616, 3725 Second Avenue North. Popular local steakhouse.

Jaker's Steak Ribs & Fish House, (406) 727–1033, 1500 Tenth Avenue South.

3D International, (406) 453–6561, 1825 Smelter Avenue (Black Eagle). Chinese-American-Mongolian fare overlooking Missouri River.

Penny's Gourmet to Go, (406) 453–7070, 815 Central Avenue. Healthy food to eat in or take out.

Willow Creek Steakhouse, (406) 761–1900, 1700 Fox Farm Road. In the Best Western Heritage Inn.

CASCADE, MONTANA

Badger Cafe, (406) 468–2777, 132 First Street North. Homemade specialties.

Osterman's Missouri Inn, (406) 468–9884, 2474 Old Highway 91.

WOLF CREEK, MONTANA

Holter Lake Lodge, (406) 235–4331, on Holter Lake.

Oasis Bar and Cafe, (406) 235–9992.

Wolf Creek Cyber Stop, (406) 235–4097. In-town Internet cafe.

HELENA, MONTANA

Benny's Restaurant, (406) 443–0105, 108 East Sixth Avenue. Breakfast, lunch, live music Friday evenings.

Country Harvest, (406) 443–7457, 2000 Prospect Avenue. Twenty-four-hour family restaurant.

The Rialto, (406) 442–1890, 52 North Last Chance Gulch. Famous burgers.

The Stonehouse Restaurant, (406) 449–2552, 120 Reeder's Alley. Wide, imaginative menu.

The Windbag Saloon, (406) 443–9669, 19 South Last Chance Gulch. Burgers, steaks, and colorful atmosphere.

Yacht Basin Restaurant, (406) 475–3125, 7025 Canyon Ferry Road. Overlooking Canyon Ferry Lake.

TOWNSEND, MONTANA

The Creamery, (406) 266–5254, 108 North Front Street. Casual dining.

THREE FORKS, MONTANA

Custer's Last Root Beer Stand, (406) 285–6713, 23 West Date Street.

Historic Headwaters Restaurant, (406) 285–4511, 105 South Main Street. Creative food. Lunch and dinner Wednesday–Saturday; brunch Sunday.

Sacajawea Hotel, (406) 285–6515, 5 North Main Street. Lunch and dinner daily.

Denotes town on Lewis's explorations of the Marias River region in 1806.
**Denotes town on Lewis's return route over the Continental Divide in 1806.*

7

Western Montana and Idaho

I have been wet and as cold in every part as I ever was in my life, indeed I was at one time fearful my feet would freeze in the thin moccasins I wore. —WILLIAM CLARK, SEPTEMBER 16, 1805, ON THE LOLO TRAIL IN PRESENT-DAY IDAHO.

THE JEFFERSON AND BEAVERHEAD VALLEYS

From the Three Forks area, follow Montana Highway 2/U.S. Highway 287. When U.S. 287 branches off south toward Yellowstone, stay on the Lewis and Clark Trail by continuing west on MT 2.

The entrance to Lewis and Clark Caverns State Park is just west of this junction. This was Montana's first state park, but before that it was a national monument, and President Theodore Roosevelt is credited with naming the park in honor of the captains. It's true the corps followed the Jefferson River right through this area, but there is no evidence the captains were aware of the caverns' existence.

A steep, winding, 3-mile road leading from the highway reaches the caverns, considered among the best in the Northwest. Trailers may be left in the lower parking lot at their owners' discretion, but park staff say all sorts of big rigs have made the drive with no trouble. Two-hour guided tours of the caverns are avail-

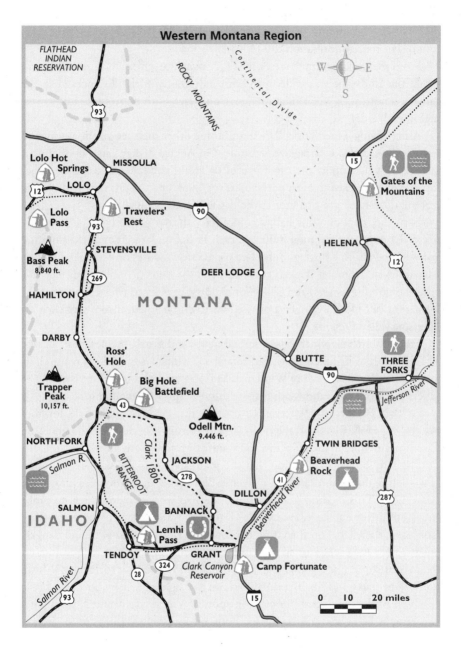

Western Montana Region

FLATHEAD INDIAN RESERVATION

ROCKY MOUNTAINS

Continental Divide

93

Lolo Hot Springs

MISSOULA

12 LOLO

Lolo Pass

93

Travelers' Rest

90

Bass Peak 8,840 ft.

STEVENSVILLE

269

DEER LODGE

HAMILTON

MONTANA

HELENA

12

Gates of the Mountains

DARBY

Ross' Hole

BUTTE

90

THREE FORKS

Trapper Peak 10,157 ft.

Big Hole Battlefield

43

Odell Mtn. 9,446 ft.

Jefferson River

NORTH FORK

BITTERROOT RANGE

Clark 1806

JACKSON

278

TWIN BRIDGES

Beaverhead Rock

Salmon R.

41

Beaverhead River

287

SALMON

IDAHO

BANNACK

DILLON

Lemhi Pass

TENDOY

324

GRANT

Clark Canyon Reservoir

Camp Fortunate

28

Salmon River

93

15

0   10   20 miles

able May 1 through September 30. The visitor center has additional information and displays, and food and gifts are offered for sale during summer months. The scenic road also winds past two shady picnic areas and an overlook of the Jefferson River valley.

Aside from cavern connoisseurs, the park draws its share of cyclists, anglers, hikers, canoeists, and wildlife watchers. Those who want to stay overnight have their choice of camping or cabins; the latter are available by reservation year-round. For more information call (406) 287–3541.

From the park, continue west on MT 2. North of Three Forks, travelers will recall, the landscape was wide open with mountains in the distance. Here the canyon is not much wider than the Jefferson River, with impressive cliffs towering on each side.

After leaving Three Forks, Lewis and three other men set out in advance to resume the search for Sacagawea's people. On August 1 they came upon a herd of elk near what is now the tiny town of La Hood and killed two for lunch before moving on, leaving most of the meat for Clark and the rest of the party. The rear guard reached the site later in the day and made camp.

Near the town of Whitehall, a community theater group is staging a "Journey of Discovery" pageant at 8:00 P.M. each Friday and Saturday night from the last weekend in June through July. The production focuses on Lewis and Clark's adventures in Montana. Tickets cost $12.00 at the door ($10.00 in advance) for adults, $8.00 for seniors, and $4.00 for children ages six to twelve. For more information call (406) 287–5664 or visit www.whitehall-ledger.com and click on Jefferson Valley Presents.

From Whitehall, which boasts several Lewis and Clark–themed murals, take MT 55 south to its junction with Montana 41, which leads all the way into Dillon. About 10 miles south of Whitehall, MT 55 passes through three counties—Jefferson, Silver Bow, and Madison—within the space of about a mile.

At Twin Bridges, the Jefferson River splits into two forks, the right fork being the Big Hole River and the main stem becoming the Beaverhead (the Ruby River, meanwhile, branches off to the southeast a few more miles south). Concluding after a day's exploration that the main stem was still the correct route, Lewis left a note for Clark on a green willow pole and proceeded down the Beaverhead. This method of communication had worked before with no problem, but this time a beaver gnawed down the willow and made off with the note. Confused, the Clark contingent set off down the Big Hole—a swift and dangerous stream. One canoe turned over and two others filled with water, resulting in the loss of some trade goods and gunpowder and an injury to Private Whitehouse. The party was finally turned back on the right course by Drouillard.

Twin Bridges is a good jumping-off spot for Virginia City and Nevada City, two famous Montana mining towns. Both are accessible via MT 287. Virginia City harbored 10,000 prospectors in the 1860s, and the town soon became a hotbed of lawlessness. A local group of vigilantes eventually took matters in their own hands, hanging the outlaws (along with the scofflaws' leader, the sheriff). Today Virginia City has a population of only 150 or so, but it's still the seat of Madison County and a big hit with the tourists. Nevada City, 1 mile downriver, has nearly a hundred buildings restored to preserve the air of an early mining camp. The Alder Gulch short-line steam railroad runs between the two towns.

Twin Bridges has a small riverside park. There's no camping, but a display board posts several large Forest Service maps. It's a good place to get your bearings and plot the rest of the day's travels. Twin Bridges is also home to the Madison County Fair each August, and to the R. L. Winston Rod Company, purveyors of top-notch fly-fishing gear. From here continue south toward Dillon.

Seeing Beaverhead Rock from MT 41, the traveler's first thought is, "Boy, those Shoshone Indians must have had vivid imaginations." Supposedly the rock resembles the head of a swimming beaver, and Sacagawea had no trouble recognizing the landmark when the corps arrived in the area. A historical marker about 0.5 mile south of the Beaverhead County line tells the tale: In August 1805 members of the expedition sighted what Clark called a "remarkable cliff" to the west. Both Lewis and Clark agreed on the resemblance and noted it in their journals, adding that Sacagawea said it meant her homeland was on a river just over the mountains to the southwest.

Area historians say that Beaverhead Rock looks most like its namesake from the east, backlit by a setting sun. But there is some controversy in southwest Montana over which rock is the Beaverhead Rock. Most folks agree it is the one north of Dillon, but some feel it is an area otherwise referred to in the journals as Rattlesnake Cliffs—an area located south of Dillon at Interstate 15, Exit 56. From the modern highway angle, however, Rattlesnake Cliffs looks a lot like a buffalo, not a beaver's head.

Beaverhead Rock is important because Sacagawea knew that near here, her people customarily crossed the Continental Divide. "The Indian woman recognized the point of a high plain to our right which she informed us was not very distant from the summer retreat of her nation on a river beyond the mountains which runs to the west," Lewis wrote on August 8, 1805. "She assures us that we shall either find her people on this river or the river immediately west of its source, which from its present size cannot be distant. As it is now all important with us to meet with those people as soon as possible, I determined to proceed tomorrow with a small party to the source of the principal stream of this river and pass the mountains to the Columbia, and down that river until I find the Indians." About 9 miles south of Beaverhead Rock, the expedition reached its 3,000-mile mark.

Dillon is a major trade center for southwest Montana, as well as the home of the University of Montana—Western. Stop by the 1909 Union Pacific Depot at 125 South Montana Street to load up on local travel information and see an impressive diorama depicting Lewis's departure for Lemhi Pass. Once featured in the Montana Historical Society Museum in Helena, the diorama sat in storage for many years before being reconstructed in Dillon. Next door, the Beaverhead

County Museum has an extremely helpful staff and interesting exhibits from all aspects of life in early Dillon.

By now you've probably noticed many Montana towns mark their communities by painting letters on a nearby hillside. In Dillon the letter is "B," which might seem strange until you learn it can stand for either Beaverhead or the Bulldogs of UM—Western. Dillon has an excellent variety of stores for a town its size. It's a good place to get fuel or stock up for a trip over Lemhi Pass or into the Big Hole country. This is also major fly-fishing country, with many outfitters available to guide a trip on the Big Hole or Beaverhead Rivers.

Clark's Lookout, just northwest of Dillon, is locally known as Lover's Leap. Clark—again bringing up the rear after Lewis and party had gone on ahead— reportedly ascended this bluff to survey the surrounding country and get his bearings before moving on. To get there turn west at the sign for the Frontage Road/Old U.S. Highway 91 north. After about 0.3 mile, the road goes underneath the overpass to the interstate. At 0.6 mile it crosses the Beaverhead. After the bridge, turn left and cross a set of railroad tracks. Clark's Lookout is on the right.

The area is under the state parks department's jurisdiction, but it has not been developed. The only way to know you're in the right place is by the small sign on the log fence, noting that the site is property of the Montana Department of Fish, Wildlife and Parks. Perch atop the lookout for a picnic; then head for the interstate to continue following the explorers' trail.

The Dillon-based Great Divide Wildlands Institute offers several guided trips in the area. The most popular trip is a one-day trek that includes Beaverhead Rock, Clark's Lookout, Camp Fortunate, and Lemhi Pass. Along the way participants see such sites as Native American pictographs and an Indian campsite with more than twenty tepee rings; the trip can also include a visit to Bannack State Park for some gold-panning and ghost town history. This tour costs $125 per person, with a two-person minimum; lunch costs an extra $5.00 per person. Overnight treks into Idaho's Lemhi Valley and horseback rides also are available. Guide Dan Pence spent thirty-five years with the USDA Forest Service, and he's been a Lewis and Clark buff since childhood. Call (406) 683–4669 for more information, or visit www.greatdividetours.com.

Jim's Guide Service also leads tours in the Dillon-Big Hole-Lemhi Pass area. Jim Boetticher is a longtime Lewis and Clark aficionado and resident of Jackson, Montana, who charges $35 an hour (with a four-hour minimum outside a 10-mile radius of Jackson) to ride in your vehicle and serve as a guide to the local sights. Call (406) 834–3186 to learn more or arrange a trip.

County Road 278 (at exit 59, Dillon) is the gateway to the Big Hole Valley, as well as a shortcut over the Divide for motorists unwilling or unable to try Lemhi Pass. CR 278 gives access to the ghost town of Bannack (Montana's first capital), the quintessentially Montanan ranching towns of Jackson and Wisdom, the Big Hole National Battlefield, and the Bitterroot Valley via Chief Joseph Pass. William Clark followed this route east on his trip home in 1806; highlights will be described in a separate section (Homeward Bound: Clark Explores the Big Hole) later in this chapter.

CAMP FORTUNATE AND LEMHI PASS

Once back on Interstate 15, drive south to exit 44 (Clark Canyon Dam).

Camp Fortunate was inundated by the reservoir, but a lookout on the lake's west side offers an approximate view of this important site. It was here the expedition was assured of help in its passage across the Continental Divide, and here that Sacagawea's presence proved especially beneficial. (There's a monument to her at the campground on the northeast shore of Clark Canyon Reservoir.)

Lewis arrived in the area first, coming to a fork at the head of the Beaverhead River on August 10, 1805. After examining both forks, he and the advance party decided to follow the right stream, Horse Prairie Creek, although geographers later determined that the left fork—Red Rock River—led to the true Missouri River headwaters. Nevertheless, Lewis's instincts proved correct, as we shall soon see.

The next day, Lewis spotted a Shoshone on horseback—the first Indian the expedition had seen in the whole of what is now Montana. Thrilled, he moved toward the Indian, shouting "tab-ba-bone." Earlier, Lewis had asked Sacagawea the Shoshone word for "white man." She must have misunderstood, however, for the word "tab-ba-bone" actually meant "stranger." To make matters worse, John Shields continued moving toward the Indian, who—frightened by Lewis's calls and Shields's action—took off into the mountains, "and with him vanished all my hopes of obtaining horses for the present," Lewis wrote. "I now felt quite as much mortification and disappointment as I had pleasure and expectation at the first sight of this Indian." Lewis fixed an American flag to a pole as a symbol of peace, and his party spent the rest of the day trying to track the Indians, to no avail.

On August 12 the party moved on up into the mountains, following what Lewis called a "large and plain Indian road. . . . I therefore did not despair of shortly finding a passage over the mountains and of tasting the waters of the great Columbia this evening." Another 4 miles on, Lewis and his men reached the head of Trail Creek, which Lewis dubbed "the most distant fountain of the mighty Missouri in search of which we have spent so many toilsome days and restless nights. Thus far I had accomplished one of those great objects on which my mind has been unalterably fixed for many years." With great gusto, Lewis drank the water. Meanwhile, Private Hugh McNeal "had exultingly stood with a foot on each side of this little rivulet and thanked his god that he had lived to bestride the mighty and heretofore deemed endless Missouri."

Plenty of excitement for one day, but there was more to come—and a bit of disappointment, too. "After refreshing ourselves we proceeded on to the top of the dividing ridge [Lemhi Pass] from which I discovered immense ranges of high mountains still to the West of us with their tops partially covered with snow," Lewis continued. "I now descended the mountain about three-quarters of a mile which I found much steeper than on the opposite side, to a handsome bold running creek of cold clear water. Here I first tasted the water of the great Columbia River."

Lewis had crossed the divide, but the sight of those "immense ranges of mountains" made it clear there was still no easy way to the Columbia. It was already mid-August, and who knew how far they had to go? The men made their first camp in what is now Idaho, determined to contact the Shoshone the next day—which is exactly what happened.

On August 13 the advance party made its way into the valley and finally, about a mile ahead, saw two women, a man, and some dogs. Lewis and his men kept walking as the Shoshone stood still; when they came within 0.5 mile, Lewis asked the others to wait as he moved ahead, unfurling the flag and still calling out "tab-ba-bone." These Indians soon disappeared, but a mile down the road, the white men saw three more women. Giving them presents and painting their cheeks with vermillion, a sign of peace, Lewis asked them to alert their village that the white men came in peace. "We had marched on about two miles when we met a party of about 60 warriors mounted on excellent horses who came in nearly full speed," Lewis wrote. "The chief and two others who were a little in advance of the main body spoke to the women, and they informed them who we were and exultingly showed the presents which had been given them. These men then advanced and embraced me very affectionately . . . both parties now advanced and we were all caressed and besmeared with their grease and paint til I was heartily tired of the national hug. I now had the pipe lit and gave them smoke."

Lewis's next task was to convince the Shoshone to accompany him back over the divide. He told how Clark and the others were waiting over the mountains with their baggage, and that they needed horses to make the trip. At first Lewis's pleas were met with resistance, for some of the Shoshone feared the white men might be in league with their enemies, the Pahkees. But Lewis finally convinced Cameahwait, the Shoshone chief, and a number of others to go with him. They arrived back at the forks of the Jefferson, with Clark nowhere to be found. Lewis feared the Indians, feeling tricked, would leave. But most stayed, and Clark and his contingent arrived the next day, August 17.

Nicholas Biddle, in his 1814 history of the expedition, related the meeting this way: "On setting out at 7 o'clock, Captain Clark with Charbonneau and his wife walked on shore, but they had not gone more than a mile before Clark saw Sacagawea, who was with her husband 100 yards ahead, begin to dance and show every mark of the most extravagant joy." As the parties drew closer, "a woman made her way through the crowd toward Sacagawea, and recognizing each other, they embraced with the most tender affection." The two women, it turned out, had been childhood friends. Sacagawea hadn't seen her since girlhood. The other child had slipped into the water to escape capture at Three Forks, which is how she got her name—Jumping Fish.

The captains and Indians exchanged greetings and made preparations for council. Sacagawea was set to help interpret the Shoshone message. "She came into the tent, sat down, and was beginning to interpret, when in the person of Cameahwait she recognized her brother," Biddle wrote. "She instantly jumped up, and ran and embraced him, throwing over him her blanket and weeping profusely. The chief was himself moved, though not in the same degree. After some conversation between them, she returned to her seat, and attempted to interpret, but her new situation seemed to overpower her, and she was frequently interrupted by tears."

Despite her emotion, Sacagawea was successful in helping the expedition negotiate for horses. Here at the newly named Camp Fortunate, the corps also cached canoes and supplies for the return trip, and prepared to begin their overland journey.

Today just about any vehicle can travel over Lemhi Pass from June through October, although the Idaho side (more steep and narrow than the Montana

Horse Prairie Ranch near Lemhi Pass.

Real Western Ranch Life

T ravelers looking for an authentic working ranch experience along the Lewis and Clark Trail will want to check into a stay at the Horse Prairie Ranch near Grant, Montana. It was on this very ground that Lewis first spotted the Shoshone boy on horseback. Today ranch personnel can show guests such landmarks as the "elevated situation" where Lewis awaited further signs of Indians.

The HPR, in business under various names since the late nineteenth century, is a true cattle ranch that just happens to have some of Montana's most comfortable accommodations. Summertime guests stay for four or six nights, typically spending much of each day on horseback (though no previous riding experience is required; visitors go through a complete orientation at the beginning of their stay). When they're not helping wranglers move cattle, guests can take treks to such nearby historical sites as Lemhi Pass, the Big Hole National Battlefield, and Bannack. Other leisure activities include hayrides, fishing, line dancing, and campfires.

Horse Prairie Ranch does a great job of blending the ranch experience with fine amenities. The cabins—which sleep one to eight persons—feature modern furnishings, down comforters, and porches for enjoying the mountain views all around. There's no TV reception out here, but each cabin has a VCR, and guests can choose from a big library of tapes (by the Creekside Lodge's fireplace, beneath the Charlie Russell painting of *Lewis & Clark Meeting the Shoshones,* on loan from the State Bank & Trust in Dillon). Mealtimes are a real highlight, with plenty of creative comfort food and lighter fare on each menu. Rates for a six-night stay start at $1,620 per person. (A minimum four-night stay is also available, with prices starting at about $1,140 per person.) For an authentic ranch adventure in an unbeatable historic location, Horse Prairie Ranch may well be Montana's last best place. For reservations or more information, call (888) 726–2454; write to Horse Prairie Guest Ranch, 3300 Bachelor Mountain Road, Dillon, MT 59725; or visit www.ranchlife.com.

side, as Lewis noted) isn't recommended for large motor homes or vehicles towing trailers, with a maximum vehicle length of 26 feet. There's also a possibility Lemhi Pass will be open to one-way, east-to-west traffic only during peak periods of the Lewis and Clark Bicentennial. Before setting out, it's a good idea to contact the local Forest Service offices (the Beaverhead-Deerlodge National Forest at 420 Barrett Street in Dillon at (406) 683–3900 or the Salmon-Challis National Forest along Idaho Highway 28 in Leadore at (208) 768–2500 to check on road conditions and construction. You can also follow the Lewis and Clark link from the Beaverhead Deerlodge Forest Web site at www.fs.fed.us/rl/b-d/.

To reach Lemhi Pass, take Highway 324 west from Clark Canyon Dam and drive 22 miles. About 9 miles past the small settlement of Grant, turn right onto Lemhi Pass Road. The new Shoshone Ridge interpretive site here has pull-through parking areas, picnic tables, a brochure box, and a rest room. Signs include a "mountain finder" to help visitors locate Lemhi Pass and other landmarks. This is a good spot to leave your RV, if you have a separate car to access the pass. If you're traveling from southern Idaho, it's also possible (and a bit faster) to get to the Lemhi Pass junction via Bannack Pass northeast of Leadore, Idaho. In that case, just watch for the turnoff on your left 12 miles north of Bannack Pass.

From the turn it is 12 miles of gravel road to the pass. The road passes through the Bar Double T ranch, and drivers may well encounter cattle on the road. Past the ranch houses, the road narrows to a single lane. Watch for oncoming traffic and use the turnouts. A few miles farther, you'll pass a road on your left to Frying Pan Creek. Stay on the main way; it's just 3 more miles to the pass.

Another road to the left approaching Lemhi Pass from Montana leads 0.2 mile to Sacajawea Memorial Camp. (The Indian woman's name is still steadfastly spelled and pronounced *Sac-a-ja-WE-a* in these parts.) This used to be a primitive campground, but it is open for day use only during the bicentennial years of 2003–2006. It's a beautiful spot, nestled in the forest and sheltered from the wind. The area is known for its abundant wildflowers in June and July, and lucky visitors may see mule deer, moose, or other wildlife. There are picnic tables, fire rings, toilets, and interpretive signs. Near the camp, you can visit the "Most Distant Fountain" spring, which flows from the mountain and on down to join Trail Creek at the headwaters of the Missouri River.

A new parking area is planned for 2003 on the Montana side just shy of the pass. From here it's a short stroll up to the divide. At 7,373 feet, Lemhi Pass National Historic Landmark is the high spot on the Lewis and Clark Trail. It's a splendid place to imagine the mixture of emotions Lewis must have felt when he saw the same thing visitors see today: range after range of mountains.

From Lemhi Pass there are two ways to get down the mountain to Tendoy and Idaho Highway 28; together, they make a loop known as the Lewis and Clark National Backcountry Byway and Adventure Road. (The actual route taken by the expedition lay mostly between the two present-day roads.) The route straight ahead, Agency Creek Road, is a sharp, steep descent with many tight curves. Via Agency Creek, it's 13 miles to Tendoy. The other route, on your right if you're facing into Idaho, is the Warm Springs Wood Road. It's exactly twice as long—26 miles—as the Agency Creek Road, but it's the better choice for larger vehicles up to 26 feet long or cars with minimal clearance. It's best to avoid both roads in bad weather.

We'll begin with a look at Agency Creek Road. Be alert for oncoming traffic, and remember that vehicles traveling uphill have the right of way. A sign a few miles down the road marks the corps' first Idaho campsite, which can be reached by hiking 0.75 mile from the road. Other signs explain later facets of area history. If you think modern vehicles have it tough, imagine what this route must have been like for the Red Rock Stage, which ran between Salmon, Idaho, and Red Rock, Montana, daily from 1866 until 1910. Several holdups occurred near Lemhi Pass, and it wasn't unusual for a stage or freight wagon to overturn on the treacherous road.

The area also saw some mining activity, most notably at the Copper Queen Mine, which operated sporadically from 1883 to 1940. The BLM's small Agency Creek campground about 7.5 miles from the summit has a toilet and picnic tables. Eleven miles west of Lemhi Pass, a sign on the left-hand side notes the nearby grave of Chief Tendoy, who was a well-respected and influential Lemhi Shoshone leader. The site is sacred to Native Americans, and visitation by the general public is not considered appropriate. At 12 miles, the traveler comes to a T in the road. Turn right, then left to get to the hamlet of Tendoy.

The other route from the pass, the Warm Springs Wood Road, is also known as Forest Road 185. About 0.8 mile down the road, there's a sign for WESTWARD VIEW interpretive area. This is a good place to stop if the parking lot just below Lemhi Pass is full, since this site, too, has a trail leading to an overlook of "the immense ranges of high mountains still to the West" and the route followed by Lewis and Clark in 1805. Just past the interpretive area, the Warm Springs Wood Road forks. Stay to the left.

The first half of the Warm Springs Wood route travels mostly through forested areas, but the terrain opens up about 14 miles from Lemhi Pass. Pull over at about the 16-mile mark (at the junction of Forest Road 186, Kenney Creek Road) for a tremendous view up and down the Lemhi Valley. Here, even more than at Lemhi Pass, it's possible to get a sense of what must have been going through the corps' minds before they were certain they'd get horses. The entire western horizon is blocked by mountains, some covered by snow even in late summer.

From here the Warm Springs Wood Road gets steeper and more winding, so be attentive, use pullouts, and yield the right of way to any uphill traffic you encounter. Watch on your left for the sign indicating the FLAG UNFURLING interpretive site commemorating Lewis's first display of the U.S. flag west of the Continental Divide on August 13, 1805. Farther down the road on your right, there's an interpretive kiosk heralding the homeland of Sacagawea. As the road enters Tendoy, several monuments and signs pay homage to Sacagawea and to Fort Lemhi, a Mormon outpost in the area from 1855 to 1858 and site of the first irrigation project in the Northwest.

The Tendoy Store on Idaho Highway 28 sells gas, food, and a good selection of groceries and hardware. It's usually open daily from about 7:00 A.M. to 7:00 P.M. in summertime and 8:00 A.M. to 6:00 P.M. the rest of the year. Long-time owner Viola Anglin has all kinds of great stories about the wide range of Lewis and Clark buffs who inevitably stop in after traversing Lemhi Pass—including the man who rolled out his sleeping bag half in Montana, half in Idaho, to spend the night literally on the Continental Divide. That sort of thing's not allowed during the bicentennial—but hold the thought for 2007, when camping will again be allowed at Lemhi Pass.

> ### Salmon Travel Tips
>
> Salmon is accessible via Salmon Air, which offers scheduled round-trip flights to and from Boise Monday through Friday year-round. Round-trip cost is about $200 per person. Scenic chartered flights of the area also are available. For reservations, call (800) 448–3413 or (208) 756–6211. The nearest major airports are at Missoula (142 miles) and Idaho Falls (161 miles).

From Tendoy, it's a quick and scenic 22 miles north to Salmon, the major town in these parts. Idaho Highway 28 parallels the Lemhi River through a valley that was Sacagawea's true homeland, the area in which she was born and grew up until that ill-fated trip to the Three Forks.

The Salmon National Forest office on U.S. Highway 93 south of Salmon has an interesting exhibit showing several researchers' opinions on the route Lewis and Clark took over Lost Trail Pass in September 1805. On an area topographic map, the known trail is traced through the September 2 campsite near Deep Creek north of Gibbonsville. From there, however, no one is sure of the exact route taken.

Salmon is celebrating its status as the Corps of Discovery heroine's childhood home with the new Sacajawea Interpretive, Cultural, and Education Center. Located a mile east of town on ID 28, the grounds feature a small indoor visitor center and a mile-long self-guided outdoor interpretive trail with such features as a tepee encampment and sweat lodge. A statue of Sacajawea is here, too; it's the second of two castings of a statue that can also be seen in front of the Idaho Historical Museum in Boise. From June through August the center is open from 9:00 A.M. to 5:00 P.M. daily. In May, September, and October, it's open 9:00 A.M. to 5:00 P.M. Tuesday through Saturday. Admission is $3.00 per person or $9.00 per family; children under six are admitted free. Call (208) 756–1188 for more information. The third weekend of August, Salmon holds its annual Sacajawea Heritage Days festival, an event that will expand to ten days in 2005 for its bicentennial. Each year, look for Native American dancers and artisans, a dutch-oven cook-off, concerts, and children's activities.

Salmon is a prime launching point for pack and float trips into the Central Idaho Rockies. The Salmon River, which originates in central Idaho not far from Sun Valley, is the longest American free-flowing and undammed river running entirely within one state. It parallels U.S. 93 north and south of Salmon, and numerous fishing and recreation points dot the way.

Salmon-based Idaho Adventures offers an interesting twist on the Lewis and Clark river tour—a three-hour ride down a gentle stretch of the Salmon River on a 30-foot scow, a replica of the same craft that plied the river one hundred or more years ago. Visitors hear about Lewis and Clark and later river history while enjoying the scenery and homemade snacks. The cost is $35 for adults, $29 for children ages four to sixteen. (Kids must be at least four to take the trip.) The company also runs raft trips on this scenic stretch and on the white-water stretch of the Salmon described below, as well as a three-day Lewis and Clark trip that combines travel on the explorers' river and land routes. Call (800) 789–WAVE or visit www.idahoadventures.com for more details.

Near what is now North Fork, Idaho, Clark and an advance party—including his newly hired Shoshone guide, Toby—explored the Salmon River several miles downstream to see if it might provide the hoped-for route to the Pacific. It's possible to retrace their reconnaissance by motor vehicle along Forest Road 30 west of North Fork. Between 2 and 4 miles in, the party encountered what Sergeant Patrick Gass described as "dreadful narrows, where the rocks were in some places breast high, and no path or trail of any kind." The next day, Gass wrote that the river—by this point about 6 miles from North Fork—"is not confined by the mountains that it is not more than 20 yards wide, and very rapid. The mountains on the side are not less than 1,000 feet high and very steep." The party turned back between Spring Creek and Squaw Creek. Toby told Clark that no one from his tribe had ever ventured farther down the river. Clark, surveying the roiling, churning waters of Pine Creek Rapids, agreed they appeared entirely impassable.

Maybe so, but the Salmon Wild and Scenic River—often called "the River of No Return"—is now a favorite among white-water rafters. How can modern boaters go where Lewis and Clark and their Native American forerunners could not? For one thing, the Civilian Conservation Corps dynamited part of Pine Creek Rapids to build the road from North Fork. (Before the blasting, Pine Creek Rapids were almost certainly Class V.) For another, today's self-bailing white-water rafts are technologically superior to the dugout canoes of Lewis and Clark's day.

North Fork is the jumping-off spot for float trips ranging from five hours to several days, making this an ideal place to fit some white-water action into your travel plans. Kookaburra Guided Whitewater Trips offers a full-day trip includ-

Touring the Salmon Area

Salmon is one of the most remote places in the contiguous United States, but it's starting to emerge as a center of Lewis and Clark Trail tourism. Already, several local businesses are taking people on guided tours of the area. The excursions all are rooted in the idea that here in the high country, it's best to leave the driving to someone else.

Martin Capps's father homesteaded in the Salmon area in the early 1930s, and Capps—a licensed outfitter since 1954—has led trips into the nearby wilderness for many years. Recently, he's also been driving people over Lemhi Pass, in either their own vehicle or Capps's van. Cost is about $55 per person, with a four-person or $200 minimum. Lunch is extra. Capps also offers horseback-riding trips to several locations (including the Continental Divide Trail); combination van and float trips down the Salmon River; and working ranch vacations. Prices vary; call (208) 756–3954 or write Happy Hollow Vacation, 1035 Highway 93 South, Salmon ID 83467 for details.

Keating Outfitters, based in Gibbonsville north of Salmon, has a combination Lewis and Clark horseback/river trip available. The package, priced in 2002 at $250 per person, includes a one-day white-water float on the Salmon River, overnight accommodations in the rustic cabins at Broken Arrow Resort, and a one-day horseback ride to a high-mountain lake. Call (208) 865–2252, or visit www.21a-idaho-outfitters.com.

Two Salmon-area bed-and-breakfasts—one traditional, the other contemporary—offer optional guided Lewis and Clark tours to their guests. Greyhouse Inn Bed & Breakfast, 12 miles south of Salmon on U.S. 93, is one of the nicest in central Idaho, with a scenic setting in the Salmon River Canyon and gracious hospitality from Sharon and David Osgood. Greyhouse's five-hour tour travels up the Warm Springs Wood Road, stopping for lunch at Sacajawea Memorial Camp before traveling back down Agency Creek Road. Cost is $75 per person. Overnight rates in the Greyhouse Inn's four cozy Victorian-style rooms, carriage house, or Lewis and Clark cabins run $70 to $90 in the summer, including breakfast. The Osgoods' hundred-year-old-plus house is itself historic; it was originally the hospital in Salmon before being moved upriver. For reservations or more information, call (800) 348–8097 or (208) 756–3968; write to HC-61, Box 16, Salmon, ID 83467; or visit www.greyhouse inn.com.

Lewis and Clark tours also are possible from 100 Acre Wood Bed & Breakfast Resort, located 25 miles north of Salmon. This contemporary three-story

(continued)

log home has seven comfortable rooms priced from $55 to $120, including breakfast. Activities include fishing and boating, horseback riding, wildlife viewing,
and dining at the resort's highly regarded restaurant. The resort's typical Corps
of Discovery trek involves a full-day loop up Agency Creek to Lemhi Pass, returning via the Warm Springs Wood Road. The cost is $100, including lunch; package
deals including lodging and dinner are available. The resort also sits within an
easy stroll of Trail Gulch, terminus of the hiking and horseback trail that begins
at Wagonhammer Springs south of North Fork. For more information or to book
a room or tour, call Jon and Nancy Cummings at (208) 865–2165; write 100 Acre
Wood, P.O. Box 202, North Fork, ID 83466; or visit www.100acrewoodresort.com.

Rawhide Outfitters, based in Ssalmon, recently received a permit from the
Bureau of Land Management to offer guided tours in the Lemhi Pass area. Although full details weren't available at presstime, Rawhide will be offering van
tours and trail rides to Lemhi and other local landmarks. The outfitter also leads
fishing trips and Salmon River floats, some including tours of abandoned gold
mines. For more information call (208) 756–4276; write Rawhide Outfitters, 204
Larson Street, Salmon, ID 83467; or visit www.rawhideoutfitters.com.

ing lunch for $85 per person. The adventures include Pine Creek Rapids and
other Class III water, along with plenty of historical and natural interpretation
and a gourmet lunch. Kookaburra also has Lewis and Clark specialty tours that
include a one-day drive on the Lewis and Clark Backcountry Byway to Lemhi
Pass, one day of river tripping (either scenic or white water), three nights' lodging at the Greyhouse Inn, and all meals for $1,230 for a family of four. If time
is short, consider the half-day scenic Sacajawea Discovery Trips. Call (888)
654–4386 or visit Kookaburra's Web site at www.raft4fun.com for reservations
or information.

Silver Cloud Outfitters is marking the Lewis and Clark Bicentennial with
special expeditions in August 2004 and 2005 that will include visits to Lemhi
Pass and the Sacajawea Interpretive Center, as well as a five-day white-water trip
on the Main Salmon. Historical actor Tim McNeil, known for his portrayal of
Meriwether Lewis, will be on the trips, which cost about $1,500 per person. Call
(877) 756–6215 or visit www.silvercloudexp.com for details.

Many other outfitters run longer trips farther down the Salmon, beyond
where Clark journeyed. For a complete list of outfitters, contact the Idaho Outfitters and Guides Association at (208) 342–1438, or visit www.ioga.org. Plan on
spending about $1,100 to $1,500 per person for a five- to six-day Main Salmon
float.

 The North Fork area also has a stretch of hiking trail where travelers can
take the same path trod by Lewis and Clark. To get there, park at the Wag-

onhammer Springs area on the right side of U.S. 93 northbound near milepost 324. Follow the 2-mile trail up Wagonhammer Creek to the mouth of Thompson Gulch. From there, take a left onto the marked trail that leads to Trail Gulch, which meets U.S. 93 about 3 miles north of North Fork. Total trail distance is about 6 miles. This is a strenuous hike with many ups and downs. Be sure to carry water and wear sunscreen.

Once it became apparent the Salmon River was impassable, Clark sent Lewis a message outlining three possible options. The first involved obtaining one horse for each man and, using Toby as a guide, proceeding by land to a navigable river. The second plan would divide the men into two groups. One party would attempt to navigate the Salmon River, while the other would travel by horseback. The third idea also involved splitting the corps into two parties, with one going over the mountains to the north while the other returned to Great Falls for supplies that had been cached there before traveling, via the Sun River to the land of the Flatheads near present-day Missoula.

Clark recommended the first, noting that if the Indians and their women and children could make it, it would be a snap for his trail-hardened men. When Lewis received the message, however, he had learned the Shoshone didn't have enough horses to spare one for each of the white men. Lewis wrote back and asked Clark to come anyway and get the twenty-two horses he had been able to buy. Clark negotiated for another two animals. Reunited, the parties started their ascent toward Lost Trail Pass.

HOMEWARD BOUND: CLARK EXPLORES THE BIG HOLE

On his return trip in 1806, Clark explored what is now one of Montana's most isolated and beautiful areas: the Big Hole. To follow his route today, head east on Montana Highway 43 at Lost Trail Pass. Clark, coming from the north, actually traversed Gibbons Pass, also nearby. This way is navigable, but the road is not much better than the one Clark found almost 200 years ago. An interpretive marker between mileposts 12 and 13 on MT 43 mentions that Clark passed through the area in July 1806.

From the pass, Clark and his party traveled down into the Big Hole, southeast toward what is now Jackson, to Bannack and to the Beaverhead River at what would become Armstead, a town now inundated by Clark Canyon Reservoir. From there they followed the Beaverhead and Jefferson Rivers to the Three Forks. Sacagawea, familiar with all this country, continued to help find the way.

Big Hole National Battlefield, 10 miles west of Wisdom, is definitely worth a stop. Start in the visitor center, where a slide show is projected on

Big Hole National Battlefield near Wisdom, Montana.

a screen just above a panoramic window that looks out on the battlefield. The presentation explains just why and how the Nez Perce War of 1877 got started, while other exhibits tell of key Indian and white players in the battle. Many of the photos are accompanied by quotes.

Before the war, the Nez Perce prided themselves on never killing a white settler. In fact, the tribe was instrumental in helping Lewis and Clark complete their journey, as we shall see. By 1855 the Nez Perce were convinced to move onto a reservation, albeit one that preserved most of their original homelands. But with the discovery of gold on the reservation in 1860, whites wanted to redraw the boundaries to exclude the mining lands. In 1863 the U.S. government proposed a reservation just one-tenth the size originally agreed on. President Andrew Johnson signed the treaty in 1867, and the government started a campaign to get the Nez Perce onto the new reservation.

Some agreed to the move, but others did not. By 1877 the nontreaty Nez Perce were told they would be forcibly moved to the reservation if they did not go on their own. The major band of nontreaty Nez Perce lived in Oregon under Old Joseph—but Old Joseph's son, Young Joseph, wanted a peaceful solution and prepared to move the band to the reservation by the June 14 deadline. On June 13, however, three young Nez Perce men, angered by the forced move and seeking revenge for the murder of one of their fathers by a white man, killed four settlers. Over the next two days, the group—joined by seventeen others—killed fourteen or fifteen whites. The Nez Perce War was on.

By the time they reached the Big Hole, Chief Joseph and the Nez Perce had fought several battles in Idaho—one a crushing defeat of General Oliver O. Howard at White Bird Canyon and others that proved inconclusive. Chief Joseph decided to take five nontreaty bands of some 800 persons and 2,000 horses into Montana and on, they hoped, to refuge at the Canadian border. They arrived at the Big Hole August 7, sure they were far ahead of Howard and his troops. They did not know, however, that a second force led by Colonel John Gibbon had joined the chase and was closing in. The battle of August 9–10, 1877, resulted in the deaths of some sixty to ninety Nez Perce, only thirty of whom were warriors, the rest women and children, and twenty-nine U.S. soldiers.

Three short hikes from a lower parking lot lead to key sites in the battle. The trails aren't long, but they are largely out in the open, so sunscreen and water are advised. It's 1.5 miles to the Nez Perce camp, 0.75 mile along a level trail to the siege area and 0.75 mile uphill to the howitzer site. (The original howitzer now sits inside the visitor center.) Picnic tables are available at the lower parking lot.

Memorial observances take place on the battlefield every year on the weekend closest to the battle anniversary. Once held separately, the white and Native American observances have now been combined. The public is welcome, but no picture taking is permitted.

Clark camped within 1.5 miles of the battlefield, but no one is exactly sure where. Big Hole Battlefield itself has no campground, but May Creek Campground—about 8 miles east of Chief Joseph Pass—attracts many park visitors. Park service staff sometimes conduct interpretive campfire programs there on summer evenings.

Big Hole National Battlefield is open 8:30 A.M. to 6:00 P.M. late May through Labor Day and 9:00 A.M. to 5:00 P.M. the rest of the year. Admission is $3.00 per person or $5.00 per family during the summer and free otherwise. For more information call (406) 689–3155.

The Big Hole is just as its name implies: wide 360-degree views rimmed everywhere you look by towering mountains. This is the haystack capital of the world—"valley of 10,000 haystacks," many call it. Wisdom and Jackson, 10 and 30 miles, respectively, east of Big Hole National Battlefield, are the area's two major towns (although each is actually quite tiny). Although it is home to just 175 persons, Wisdom boasts the noted Wisdom River Gallery, specializing in Western and wildlife art. Jackson, meanwhile, is best known for its hot springs—Clark and company not only soaked their weary bones here in 1806, but they also cooked dinner in the water! These days, boiling meat is probably off-limits in the pools at Jackson Hot Springs Resort, but you can still get a home-cooked meal, along with a comfy cabin.

Bannack State Park commemorates another famous Montana ghost town (and seat of the first territorial capital). You can reach Bannack either from County Road 278 west of Dillon or via 16 miles of good gravel road from Grant on the route to Lemhi Pass. Remains of several original buildings may be viewed, along with a visitor center that offers more information and photos on the nineteenth-century mining boom in Bannack.

LOST TRAIL PASS AND THE BITTERROOT VALLEY

The Corps of Discovery had one heck of a time getting over Lost Trail Pass—largely because their hapless guide, Toby, lost the trail to the pass. On September 2, 1805, Clark wrote: "We were obliged to cut a road over rock hillsides where our horses were in danger of slipping to their certain destruction." Several horses fell. One was crippled, and two gave out.

Toby led the explorers over a trail more than a thousand feet higher than the current route, U.S. Highway 93, which generally follows the path of least resistance. A small visitor center at the pass offers information on attractions in both Montana and Idaho. From the pass it is 31 miles to Darby, the first sizable town along U.S. 93 in Montana's Bitterroot Valley.

Once they negotiated the mountains, the explorers had a relatively easy time of it in the Bitterroot Valley. Soon after descending, they came upon an area later known as Ross's Hole for Alexander Ross of the Hudson Bay Company, who ranged far and wide over these parts. He camped here with 55 Indian and white trappers, 89 women and children, and 392 horses in 1824 en route from Spokane to the Snake River. They spent nearly a month trying to break across the pass to the Big Hole, and Ross wound up naming the basin "the valley of troubles." For Lewis and Clark, however, this area brought their first meeting with the Flathead (or Salish) Indians and an opportunity to trade for more horses.

Montana's Bitterroot Valley is one of the nation's fastest-growing areas. The boom is most evident in the towns nearest Missoula, but even the smaller settlements have been converted from sleepy little timber towns to bustling burgs complete with espresso machines and offbeat shops. A taste of the past isn't impossible to find, however. The Sula Ranger Station rents out its historic East Fork Guard Station, 16 miles east of town, on a year-round basis. Stop by the ranger station weekdays or call (406) 821-3201 for more information. The village of Sula has a small store, campground, and cabins.

Lewis and Clark camped about 2 miles downstream from the present-day Spring Gulch Campground north of Sula, and everyone went to bed wet and

Touring Missoula

Missoula, just 11 miles north from Traveler's Rest and Lolo, is indisputably one of the Rocky Mountain region's most interesting, lively towns. This city of about 57,500 persons makes a fine place to overnight and resupply before heading out over the Lolo Trail.

Five valleys converge in the Missoula area, so it's not surprising this has long been a way station for travelers. Lewis and party camped near the confluence of the Rattlesnake and Clark's Fork Rivers on July 3, 1806, before leaving east on their shortcut across the Great Divide. Before that, Native Americans used the area as a thoroughfare to hunting grounds east of the mountains.

The valley floor here was once covered by Glacial Lake Missoula to a depth of 2,000 feet, about 500 feet higher than the "M" above the University of Montana campus. Formed about 15,000 years ago during the most recent Ice Age, geologists estimate the lake filled and drained at least six times during its existence. The big valley makes for a fairly moderate climate (for Montana, at least), but the topography also tends to make Missoula susceptible to air inversions and pollution—again, at least by Big Sky standards.

The Historical Museum at Fort Missoula is the city's most interesting relic from the past. Federal troops arrived at the site in 1877, just in time to try stopping Chief Joseph and the Nez Perce from traveling down Lolo Creek. Failing that, they joined Colonel Gibbon at the Battle of the Big Hole. The fort's buildings were built soon after, and three of the original structures still remain. Later, the fort was home to an unusual experiment in American military history: a bicycle corps. (Missoula remains a big cycling community, home of an extensive trails network and bike shops galore.)

The fort grounds are now home to a historical museum with permanent exhibits on Missoula history and changing displays on other aspects of early settlement in the area. Military reserve units and the USDA Forest Service also have offices here. Don't miss climbing the fire lookout. Fort Missoula is open 10:00 A.M. to 5:00 P.M. Monday through Saturday and noon to 5:00 P.M. Sunday, Memorial Day through Labor Day. The rest of the year the museum is open noon to 5:00 P.M. Tuesday through Sunday. Admission is $3.00 for adults, $2.00 for seniors, and $1.00 for students. Children under age six are free.

Missoula is perhaps best known as home of the University of Montana, and as a primary cultural capital between Minneapolis and Seattle. In recent years, Missoula has become a real writers' and readers' center, with an

(continued)

abundance of fine bookstores and an active literary community. Don't miss the University bookstore, Fact and Fiction, or Garth's Book Shop, among others. The city also has active theatrical and visual arts scenes, not to mention the wonderful old Wilma Theatre movie palace. Needless to say, the recreation minded have it made in Missoula. Aside from the city's own network of riverside trails and the ever-popular hike to the "M" (a 1.5-mile round-trip), residents and visitors can take their pick of the Rattlesnake National Recreation Area and Wilderness to the north, Pattee Canyon Recreation Area to the southeast, and Blue Mountain Recreation Area to the southwest, all within a few miles of downtown.

Missoula has a full calendar of special events, especially during the summer. The city's big Fourth of July bash takes place out at Fort Missoula. In town, people go "Out to Lunch at Caras Park" on the riverfront every Wednesday June through August. Other regular events include an active farmers' market (Tuesday evening and Saturday morning) and Wednesday-night band concerts at Bonner Park late June through August. For more information on Missoula, call (800) 526–3465, visit www.exploremissoula.com, or stop by the visitor bureau office on the downtown side of the Van Buren Street footbridge.

hungry. Clark wrote: "It rained this evening. Nothing to eat but berries. Our flour out and but little corn. The hunters killed two pheasants only."

U.S. 93 parallels the East Fork Bitterroot River, which runs along the highway from Sula to Conner, picking up the main stem there. The Bitterroot is noted for its rainbow and cutthroat trout. Several fishing access points are easily accessible near the road. Conner is also the turnoff point to Trapper Peak—at 10,157 feet, the highest in the Bitterroots.

The Bitterroot National Forest ranger station in Darby doubles as a historic center, offering displays and books. Five miles north of town, watch for the road to Lake Como. This popular and beautiful lake offers another great view of Trapper Peak, along with fishing, boating, camping, and hiking.

Hamilton—about halfway to Missoula from Lost Trail Pass—is the main trade center for the Bitterroot Valley. This was home to the Rocky Mountain Laboratory, which researched Rocky Mountain Spotted Fever, first detected here in 1873. "Neither cause nor cure was known and mortality was high," a historic marker reads. By 1906 scientists determined that the disease was spread by a tick and were finally able to prevent and treat the fever via vaccinations and medicine. A modern federal laboratory has replaced the tents, log cabins, woodsheds, and abandoned schoolhouse that served the first researchers, and the center still studies infectious diseases.

At Hamilton, it's possible to get off the beaten path of U.S. 93 and tool along on the Eastside Highway (also known as Montana Highway 269). Simply turn east instead of west at the signs for Hamilton's city center. The famous Daly Mansion is the back road's first landmark. Marcus Daly came to America from Ireland as a poor immigrant. He liked mining and was soon attracted to camps of the West, where he quickly learned the trade. He rapidly grew rich and was a powerful force in Montana business and politics for many years.

A splendid Georgian Revival–style dwelling, also called Riverside, served as the summer home for the Daly family. Its forty-two rooms are filled with exquisite furnishings. Privately held for many years, Riverside was acquired by the state in 1987 and is now open for tours mid-April through mid-October. Cost is $6.00 for adults, with youth and senior discounts available. Visitors may tour just the grounds for $1.00 per person. Hours are 11:00 A.M. to 4:00 P.M.

The Lee Metcalf National Wildlife Refuge, north of Stevensville, offers a close-by oasis of calm in the increasingly urban Bitterroot Valley. The refuge is primarily a home for birds and waterfowl, including blue-winged teal, osprey, Canada geese, and many others. For another great hiking opportunity, try the Bass Creek Trail into the Bitterroot range. To get there, drive north from Stevensville on U.S. 93 and watch for a sign on the west side of the road marking the turnoff to the Charles Waters Campground and Recreation Site. There's good fishing along the Bitterroot, too, although the stretch from Tucker Crossing to Florence Bridge is catch-and-release only. Look for other regulations posted near the many fishing access spots.

The Lewis and Clark expedition camped near the confluence of the Bitterroot River and Lolo Creek, at what is now the town of Lolo on September 9 and 10, 1805, and again on June 30 through July 2, 1806. The site they named Travelers' Rest was also a longtime Native American campsite. Long on private property, Travelers' Rest is now a Montana state park located just south of Lolo and west of U.S. 93, at 6550 Mormon Creek Road. Although interpretation is still being developed, guided tours are now available on a regular basis; call (406) 273–4253 or check www.travelersrest.org for times and more details. Also ask about the annual reenactments at the site, timed to coincide with the expedition's two visits.

Travelers' Rest tells the stories of Lewis and Clark as well as the Native Americans who camped here for centuries before the Corps of Discovery and the pioneers who followed soon after. Some of the tales are still unfolding; in summer 2002 archaeologist Dan Hall and his team from Missoula found traces of mercury in the soil, helping them pinpoint the location of what was likely the Lewis and Clark campsite latrine. (The mercury would have come from excretion of Dr. Rush's Thunderbolts, a cure-all "medicine" often administered by Lewis.) The Travelers' Rest site is still unusually pristine for an area so close to two major highways, and visitors sometimes see osprey, deer, fox, and other wild things. It's a pleasant place to stop and picnic or stroll.

It was here the captains learned they could have taken a shortcut west from the Great Falls, rather than the arduous route they had just completed. That was disappointing news, especially now, with still more mountains to cross and winter quickly drawing nigh. There was little time to waste, and on September 11 the party started up the Lolo Trail—a march that would prove the most taxing part of the entire trip.

U.S. HIGHWAY 12

Lewis and Clark expected to cross one mountain range in the Bitterroots. Instead they found ridge after ridge. By the time the expedition arrived in what is now northern Idaho, corps members were a hardened, gristled lot—mountain men, really. Still, nothing could have prepared them for what they encountered on the Lolo Trail.

Patrick Gass, who would survive longer than any other expedition member, called the Idaho Bitterroots "the most terrible mountains I ever beheld." For his part, Captain Clark—at thirty-five one of the oldest members of the corps—had long lived the military life and wasn't one to complain. But over and over as his men crossed these mountains, he said he'd never been colder, never been wetter.

Today's travelers have a choice of routes across this rugged land. U.S. 12 winds through the Lochsa-Clearwater canyon at the base of the Bitterroots. It's a good, paved scenic route officially marked as the Lewis and Clark Trail, but the corps followed only a portion of it. Most of the time they were high on the ridge to the north: the real Lolo Trail, used for centuries beforehand by the Nez Perce and Salish peoples. The canyon below—which had to be extensively blasted just to make room for the two-lane U.S. 12—was far too narrow in 1805–1806 to allow passage by land, and the rivers were unnavigable. U.S. 12 itself wasn't even completed until 1962, which gives some indication of just how rough things were.

Which route to take? U.S. 12 is the best route for enjoying the scenery and for making time, but the Lolo Motorway (Forest Road 500) gives the traveler a better firsthand feel for the hardships the expedition endured. During the Lewis and Clark Bicentennial years of 2003–2006, the Clearwater National Forest expects to have a permit system to manage access to the Lolo Motorway and its approaches—roads that aren't meant to handle a lot of traffic. According to forest officials, visitors must pick up a free permit at the Lolo Pass Visitor Center, Lochsa Ranger Station, or forest supervisor's office in Orofino (open daily) or the Powell, Kooskia, or Kamiah ranger stations (open Monday through Friday) and

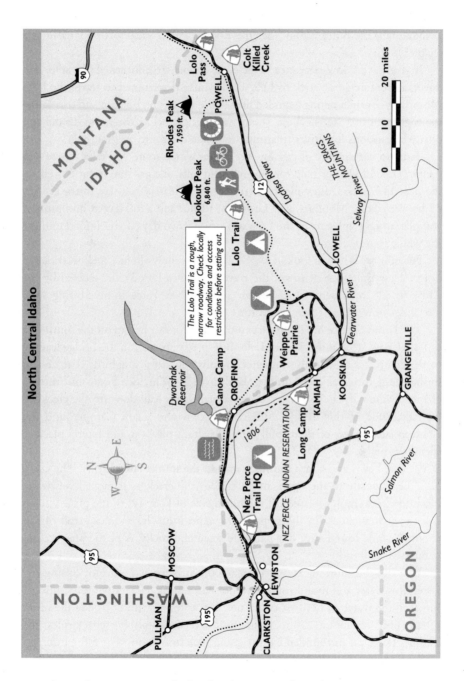

complete a short orientation before heading up to the Lolo Motorway. A permit lottery may be held 2004 through 2006. If you plan to travel the trail in those years, call (208) 926–4274 for updated permit information. Lolo Trail travel permits will not be necessary for people who have rental reservations at Castle Butte

Lookout and Liz Butte Cabin. (See the Rooms with a View section later in this chapter.)

If you have a low-clearance vehicle, or if you are concerned about break-downs in remote areas, stick to U.S. 12. If you're determined to travel the Lolo Motorway, consider taking a guided horseback, mountain bike, or van trip across the high country. See the Lolo Motorway section below for more details and plenty of cautions for drivers planning to tackle the route on their own.

Tank up with plenty of gasoline no matter which route you take. There's no fuel on U.S. 12 west of Lolo for 50 miles and only one gas station (at Powell) in the next 115 miles! Allow plenty of time, too: at least a half-day to travel U.S. 12 between Lolo, Montana, and Lewiston, Idaho, and a full day at minimum if you plan to take any part of the Lolo Motorway (two days if you intend to drive the whole route).

For now we'll have a look at U.S. 12, which follows Lolo Creek west out of Lolo. A few miles out of town, the traveler reaches Fort Fizzle, erected by the Army to try to prevent Chief Joseph and the Nez Perce from crossing Lolo Creek. It's now a Forest Service Historic Site.

The Forest Service has named a campground for our heroes on the south side of Lolo Creek, 15.5 miles west of Lolo. Interpretive panels on the bridge leading to the campsites explain the presence of tiny migratory songbirds that nest in bushes along the creek each summer. Birds to look for include Swainson's thrush, greenish willow flycatcher, and yellow warbler. Trails lead down to the creekbed on either side of this bridge. Altogether, Lewis and Clark Campground has eighteen sites, a few of them pull-throughs. It's a pleasant and handy place to spend the night.

Alas, Lewis and Clark did not camp in the immediate vicinity. The corps kept mostly to the open, north side of the creek as it moved westward. Howard Creek Trail, accessed off the north side of U.S. 12, is one place visitors still can follow closely in the steps of the expedition. It's a quick stroll of just about 0.5 mile round-trip, but parts are steep and rocky. A picnic area accompanies the trailhead.

U.S. 12 continues its steady climb, soon arriving at Lolo Hot Springs. "I tasted this water and found it hot and not bad tasting," Clark wrote. "I put my finger in the water and at first could not bear it for a second." Today the resort offers a pool, restaurant, casino, campground, tepee rentals, horseback rides, and bumper boats, all surrounded by intriguing rock formations. For more information call (406) 273–2290 or visit www.lolohotsprings.com. Next door, the Lolo Trail Center offers lodge-style motel rooms and an exhibition center of Lewis and Clark replica artifacts, Native American lore, and related displays. Call (406) 273–2201 or check www.lolotrailcenter.com for details. Although the businesses are unrelated, together they make Lolo Hot Springs a good base camp or family reunion site.

A mile and a half past Lolo Hot Springs, another Forest Service campground, Lee Creek, serves as trailhead for a 5-mile path to Lolo Pass. Like the shorter trail at Howard Creek, Wagon Mountain Trail 300 parallels the route taken by Lewis and Clark. Lee Creek campers can also enjoy a 2.5-mile interpretive loop trail that traverses the immediate area. Day-use facilities at the campground include rest rooms and picnic tables.

From Lolo Hot Springs, it is 7 miles to the Idaho border. West of the resort, a sign reads: WINDING ROAD NEXT 77 MILES. More than on any other highway along the trail since the hill country of Missouri, motorists need to be alert while traveling U.S. 12. It's curvy, it's narrow, it's heavily used by logging and grain trucks, and it's one long deer-crossing zone.

The highway crosses the Montana-Idaho border and the Mountain-Pacific time zone line at Lolo Pass, elevation 5,233 feet. The expedition crossed the Lolo divide about a mile east of the present pass and camped near Glade Creek. Packer Meadows near here are especially pretty in mid- to late June, when the fields turn purple with blooming camas. A new visitor center at the pass explains the area's significance, and it's a good spot to stop for local travel information.

The Glade Creek area was recently transferred from the Plum Creek Timber Company to the Idaho Department of Parks and Recreation via the Idaho Heritage Trust, which raised $255,000 for the land acquisition. Still, there are no plans for development at the site. Packer Meadows and the Lolo Pass area already are very popular with winter-sports enthusiasts, with more than 100 miles of marked snowmobile trails and more than 30 miles of cross-country ski trails, including some groomed paths.

A picnic area near milepost 165 on U.S. 12 is of more than passing interest to avid Lewis and Clark buffs. This is the DeVoto Memorial Cedar Grove, a cool green cathedral named in honor of Bernard DeVoto, noted writer, historian, and editor of the Lewis and Clark journals. DeVoto used to camp here among the western red cedar while preparing his edition of the journals. Some say DeVoto's spirit still lingers in the area—his ashes were scattered over the grove after his death in 1955.

On September 14 the party reached what is now the Powell Ranger Station. Toby, their guide, had mistakenly left the main Lolo Trail and descended to the Lochsa—or Koos Koos Kee—River. By now, nearly all their food supplies were exhausted, and game was nowhere to be seen. Lewis broke out his food of last resort, an experimental "portable soup" he had obtained from the Army as emergency rations. It was barely edible, and the corps was forced to more extreme measures. "Here we were compelled to kill a colt for our men and selves to eat for the want of meat and we named the south fork Colt Killed Creek," Clark wrote. "The mountains which we passed today (were) much worse than yesterday . . . our men and horses much fatigued." By walking to the rear of the Powell Ranger Station complex, you can be sure you are standing near where the

DeVoto Memorial Cedar Grove along U.S. Highway 12, Idaho.

expedition camped, "opposite a small island at the mouth of a branch on the right side of the river which at this place is 80 yards wide, swift and stony," Clark wrote.

The Powell Ranger Station and nearby Lochsa Lodge are the last real outposts of civilization on U.S. 12 until Lowell about 50 miles west. In addition to gasoline, Lochsa Lodge offers several cabins and motel-type rooms and a restaurant with a big fireplace. Nearby, the ranger station also serves as home to the local post office and the Powell Public Library—several cardboard boxes filled with books. Self-guiding cassette tour tapes of U.S. 12 are available at the ranger's office here. Pick one up and drop it off down the road at the Forest Service office in either Kooskia or Orofino.

For a nice hike with good fishing opportunities, take White Sand Trail 50, which begins 2 miles east of the ranger station, off Beaver Meadows Road (Forest Road 368) near the White Sand Campground. Forest Road 569—Parachute Hill Road—is located on the north side of U.S. 12 just east of the Powell Ranger Station road. This is probably the best access road to the eastern reaches of the Lolo Motorway, and it will be a main entrance area for permit holders during the bicentennial years.

On September 15 the corps trudged another 4 miles down the Lochsa River. Toby had finally figured out that he had lost the trail, and he determined the party should climb a steep ridge to regain the route. So the party started up Wendover Ridge, located across U.S. 12 from the present-day Wendover-Whitehouse campgrounds (the latter named for expedition member Joseph Whitehouse). It was no picnic, particularly for the horses. "Several horses slipped and rolled down steep hills which hurt them very much. The one which carried my desk and small trunk turned over and rolled down a mountain for 40 yards," Clark wrote. The field desk was smashed, but the horse managed to survive "and appeared but little hurt," according to Clark. After a rest of two hours, the party continued on to the Lolo Trail, where they found snow. There, the men supped on the portable soup, made a bit more palatable with some leftover colt. "From this mountain I could observe high rugged mountains in every direction as far as I could see," Clark added.

It's possible to hike part of the Wendover Ridge today, from U.S. 12 to the Wendover-Badger Road. It takes a moderately fit person about forty minutes to hike from the highway to the road, and about a half hour to come back. From the Wendover-Badger Road, the trail continues, but it becomes faint and the air gets thin. The second leg goes to Wendover Ridge Rest Site and the third to the Lolo Motorway at Snowbank Camp.

Colgate Licks and Jerry Johnson Hot Springs, both located not far west of the Wendover-Whitehouse campgrounds, are among the most popular stops along U.S. 12. At Colgate Licks, deer, elk, and other animals are attracted to the springs by their salty content. A loop trail winds from the parking lot past the springs. The Jerry Johnson Hot Springs are accessed by a mile-long trail up Warm Springs Creek.

West of the hot springs, the traveler can make a little better time while enjoying the river canyon scenery. That's not to say the distractions fade completely, however: The Lochsa Historical Ranger Station has one of the West's best collections of Forest Service memorabilia. Forest Service retirees staff the ranger station, located across U.S. 12 from the Wilderness Gateway campground, all summer. Forest Road 107—the Saddle Camp Road and another good access point to and from the Lolo Motorway—is located midway between Colgate Licks and the Lochsa Ranger Station. Wilderness Gateway Campground is a base of operations for several outfitters who lead horse-packing trips into the Selway-Bitterroot Wilderness south of U.S. 12.

Twenty-five miles west of the historical station, U.S. 12 finally reaches Lowell and, just beyond it, Syringa. Lowell serves as gateway to the Selway River; together, the Selway and Lochsa become the Clearwater River west of here. A 23-mile back road parallels the Selway, a river well known to white-water enthusiasts. In fact, the Lochsa, Selway, and Clearwater all present challenging rafting and kayaking opportunities. Area businesses can provide more information, as can the Idaho Outfitters and Guides Association at (208) 342–1438.

From Lowell, it's 23 miles to Kooskia (pronounced KOO-skee), a pretty little town surrounded by hills. Check out the Lewis and Clark mural on the side of Pankey's Grocery Store, depicting members of the Corps of Discovery on a hill near Nez Perce longhouses. The Kooskia National Fish Hatchery near the junction of U.S. 12 and Idaho Highway 13 raises more than one million salmon each year. Kamiah (KAM-ee-eye), a slightly larger town with good visitor services, is 7 miles north on U.S. 12.

As we've already seen, the history of the Nez Perce people is closely intertwined with that of the Lewis and Clark Trail, and we're now entering an area offering many opportunities to explore this tribe's history and present. The Nez Perce sites are well worth visiting, both because of the tribe's important contributions to the expedition and the Nez Perces' own proud past.

One such site is a basaltic formation on the outskirts of Kamiah that for centuries has been known as the "Heart of the Monster." According to Nez Perce legend, Coyote slew a great monster near here. The Nez Perce and other tribes sprang forth, each from where parts of the monster fell. The site is located across the road from the Lewis-Clark Resort RV park and motel just south of Kamiah on U.S. 12.

On their return trip east in 1806, Lewis and Clark spent twenty-seven days camped in the Kamiah area while waiting for snow to melt along the Lolo Trail. Here the expedition members hunted, fished, and learned more about the Nez Perce, with whom the whites had become good friends. "Those people have shown much greater acts of hospitality than we have witnessed from any nation or tribe since we have passed the Rocky Mountains," Clark wrote. The site of the Long Camp, also sometimes called Camp Chopunnish, is noted with a state historical marker on U.S. 12 not far from the Heart of the Monster. The Long Camp also was the jumping-off spot for an eight-day side trip undertaken by Sergeant John Ordway, who led a small party from the Kamiah area to the Salmon and Snake Rivers in search of salmon to bolster the expedition's meager food supply. Their route probably passed near the modern-day towns of Nezperce (where a historic marker details the corps' spring 1806 travels in the area) and Cottonwood. The latter community also is home to both the fine Historical Museum at St. Gertrude and Dog Bark Park, a whimsical business based on the canine folk art of Dennis Sullivan and Frances Conklin, who have been known to carve a Seaman figure or two. By summer 2003 an interpretive kiosk featuring Ordway's journey will be atop Craig Mountain west of here. Maps and brochures of the route (mainly on dirt and gravel back roads) will be available; ask for one at the Lewiston office of the Idaho Department of Fish and Game at 1540 Warner Avenue.

Longtime Idaho river outfitter and Lewis and Clark buff John Barker has spent years trying to reconstruct the Ordway party's route. His findings informed the kiosk and brochure project, and they also serve as part of a four-day Lewis and Clark Experience tour of North Central Idaho. The package includes a chartered small-airplane overflight of the region (including the Lolo Trail corridor)

Heart of the Monster Nez Perce site near Kamiah, Idaho.

from Missoula to Lewiston; exploration of the Ordway route by van and on foot; a rafting day trip on the Clearwater; and nightly seminars featuring history faculty from Lewis-Clark State College. The cost is about $1,800 per person, including lodging and all meals. Call (800) 353–7459 for more information. Barker River Trips also offers the one-day Clearwater float separately for $75 per person.

Kamiah has a vaguely Victorian flavor and a full calendar of annual events. The Nez Perce celebrate Mata-Lyma, a root feast and powwow, the third weekend each May and Chief Looking Glass Days the third weekend in August. The local business community throws a free barbecue over Labor Day Weekend, complete with dances, games, and the crowning of the Barbecue Queen. Kamiah's Riverfront Park has a boat ramp and free RV camping for no more than forty-eight hours.

From Kamiah, it's 23 miles northwest on U.S. 12 to Orofino, site of the expedition's Canoe Camp. But before we proceed, let's take a better look at the Lolo Motorway, the difficult but rewarding alternate route across the Bitterroot Mountains, and the Weippe Prairie, where the Corps of Discovery finally descended from the mountains in the fall of 1805. Kamiah is the western gateway to this route. If you decide to explore the motorway from here, be sure to stop by the local Clearwater National Forest office for more information and a map.

THE LOLO MOTORWAY

Indians, trappers, military men, and settlers have used what is now known as the Lolo Trail as the main way across northern Idaho. But the corps were almost certainly the first white men to travel the route. Much of their path is paralleled by present-day FR 500, the Lolo Motorway. The "motorway" designation may conjure up images of men in snappy driving caps and women in smart scarves breezing through the countryside in a convertible, but don't be misled: This motorway is no joy ride. Moreover, it follows the Lewis and Clark Trail exactly only in a few places.

U.S. 12 is open year-round, but the Lolo Motorway is typically accessible only from mid-July through mid-September. Four-wheel drive isn't essential, but good clearance is a must. Make sure tires, belts, and so on are in good shape (and carry full-size spare tires; small "donut" type spares are inadequate for this road). Needless to say, there are no services of any kind. The bottom line may be this warning from a recent Forest Service brochure: "Tow truck service can take days to arrange and can cost $250–$500."

Check with the Forest Service on current conditions before setting out. It's also wise to carry an ax (or chain saw) and shovel, since downed trees and iso-

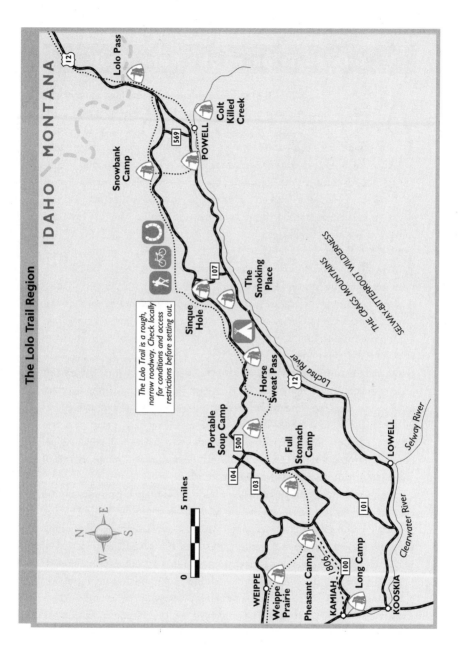

The Lolo Trail Region

The Lolo Trail is a rough, narrow roadway. Check locally for conditions and access restrictions before setting out.

lated patches of snow aren't uncommon on the motorway even in high summer. If you camp overnight (there are no formal campgrounds along the way), try to choose a site that has been used previously, and be sure to pack out your garbage. Finally, get a copy of the Clearwater National Forest map (available at the Lolo Pass Visitor Center or area ranger stations) before exploring the back roads.

Guided Trips on the Lolo Trail

Along with the Missouri Breaks of Central Montana, Idaho's Lolo Trail ranks as one of the most remote stretches of the Lewis and Clark Trail. And although it is possible to travel the Lolo on your own, it can be more fun—and safer—to take a guided trip. This is especially true because, as expected, the Clearwater National Forest has begun requiring permits for travel on the Lolo Trail Corridor in the trail bicentennial years (2003–2006). If you travel with an outfitter, you won't need a permit, and you won't be hassled by transportation concerns, cooking, or cleanup. Here are some of the options available:

  If you want outfitted journeys on both the Lolo Trail and the Missouri Breaks, your best bet may be Lewis & Clark Trail Adventures' combination Missouri Breaks/Lolo Trail trip. For $1,105 per person, participants get a three-day canoe trip from Fort Benton, Montana, through the Breaks' famous White Cliffs section, plus a three-day mountain biking or hiking trip on the Lolo Trail. The company offers a wide range of options on the Lolo Trail, including one- to three-day biking, hiking, or van trips; these are priced at $139 to $605 for hikers, an extra $25 per day for cyclists. There's also an annual Lolo Trail Commemorative Hike each September on the anniversary of the same days the expedition traveled the trail. This challenging trek begins with the famous 8-mile Wendover Ridge-to-Snowbank Camp hike, the hardest leg of the trip. The six-day, vehicle-supported hike cost $995 in 2002. For more information on Lewis & Clark Trail Adventures' offerings, call (800) 366–6246 or visit www.trailadventures.com.

Western Spirit is another company offering mountain biking trips on the Lolo. Its five-day trek starts and ends in Missoula and includes about 75 miles of pedaling and a few hikes, including stops at several Lewis and Clark campsites and important Native American sites. The trip cost $895 in 2002. Call (800) 845–2453 or check www.westernspirit.com for current information.

The Corps of Discovery spent most of their Lolo Trail time on horseback, and you can do the same by booking a trip with Harlan and Barbara Opdahl of Triple O Outfitters. The Opdahls have been leading trips on the Lolo since the mid-1980s, with Stephen Ambrose and Ken Burns among their satisfied customers.

The most popular Triple O trip is a week-long adventure that includes four days of riding in the backcountry. The trips meet in Lewiston, Idaho, and visit the Nez Perce National Historic Park museum in Spalding and the Canoe Camp in Orofino before spending the first night at Lochsa Lodge. Then it's on up to the Lolo Trail, with stops at all the highlights: Rocky Point Lookout, Indian Post Office, the Smoking Place, Sinque Hole, and Spirit Revival Ridge. Participants also enjoy fun evenings around the campfire, often with storytellers or singers.

Triple O charges $1,650 per person for the trip described above. They also have a five-day "Combination Lewis & Clark Expedition" offered in conjunction with the Clearwater River Company that includes a van tour, one-day horseback ride on the Lolo Trail, and two days on the Clearwater River, priced about $1,700. If these trips don't suit your needs or pocketbook, talk with the Opdahls about a shorter trip or a customized adventure. They've done horseback trips as short as two days, van-supported trips for hikers, and snowmobile excursions in winter. For a fee they'll even help you plan a do-it-yourself adventure if you're determined to brave the Lolo on your own. For more information on current trip dates and rates, call (208) 464–2349 or (208) 464–2761 or visit www.tripleo-outfitters.com.

Lewis Clark Idaho Road Tours offers a five-day "Crossing the Bitterroots with Lewis & Clark" tour a few times each summer. The trek, priced in 2002 at $1,100 per person, includes both the Lolo Trail and the surrounding area: Lolo Pass, Canoe Camp, Long Camp, the Weippe Prairie, and more. Participants travel by van (with a few short hikes to expedition campsites), camp two nights on the Lolo, and spend the other nights indoors at area inns or lodges. Call (208) 926–7875 or check www.lewisclarkidaho.com for more details. Tour operators Linwood Laughy and Borg Hendrickson are coauthors of *Clearwater Country: The Traveler's Historical and Recreational Guide,* which is packed with information about North Central Idaho. It's available from the Web site noted above.

Weitas Creek Outfitters offers one-day trail rides ($125 per person) May through September and three-day backcountry trips on the west end of the Lolo Trail, including some stretches you can get to only on horseback. The three-day trips cost $1,295 to $1,695 per person. Call (888) 983–WEST for information. Lost Lakes Outfitters, experienced in backcountry hunting trips, plans to add one- to three-day van, horseback, and combination trips in the Lolo Trail corridor during the bicentennial, including rides up Wendover Ridge. Details weren't set at press time, but you can call outfitter Al Hatch at (208) 926–4988 for details.

The outfitters mentioned above were the only ones licensed to guide visitors along the Lolo Trail as of 2003. For updated information contact the Clearwater National Forest offices in Orofino (208–476–4541), Powell (208–942–3113), Kooskia (208–926–4274), or Kamiah (208–935–2513).

Be sure to get the latest version of the map. An earlier edition, published in 1992, has one major Lolo Trail mistake; the junction labeled PETE FORKS on the western reach of the trail is actually Boundary Junction. Pete Forks is a few miles north at the junction of FR 104 and 500.

Use caution and courtesy when driving the Lolo Motorway or any of the roads that access it. Vehicles traveling uphill have the right-of-way; if you meet another vehicle while traveling downhill, you may need to back up as much as a quarter mile to let the other vehicle pass. You may want to avoid driving shortly after sunrise (if you're heading east) or just before sunset (if you're driving west), because the sun's low rays—combined with road dust—wreak real havoc with visibility. Take special care to get your bearings at intersections. Many logging roads enter the motorway, often at odd angles, and it's easy to get turned around.

If you have any doubts about your vehicle's ability to handle the Lolo Motorway, it's best not to chance the trip. As an alternative, consider exploring the route's western end, accessible via Forest Road 100 from Kamiah. This is the least taxing part of the route, but it has several sites of interest to Lewis and Clark buffs. See the end of this section for details.

As you travel along the Lolo Motorway—or anywhere on the Lewis and Clark Trail, for that matter —it's important to remember that the historic route is seldom something you can follow precisely. The corps passed through only briefly and left no evidence of its visit. Rather than dwelling on locating the exact campsites or precise trail tread, relax and enjoy the spirit of the place and the scenery.

After they climbed the Wendover Ridge and regained the Lolo Trail on September 15, Lewis, Clark, and company camped at what is now referred to as the Snowbank Camp. The next morning they awoke to find their beds covered with 4 inches of fresh snow. All day, the snow kept falling, obscuring the trail and making everyone miserable. It was this day Clark pronounced he was "wet and as cold" as he'd ever been in his life. And on this night, camped at what's now called Lonesome Cove, the party had to kill yet another colt to keep from starving. Clark had tried to shoot a deer—one of very few the men saw in this area—but his gun apparently misfired.

A few miles west of the SNOW BANK CAMP sign, FR 500 comes to Cayuse Junction. Head less than a mile north from here on FR 581 to reach Cayuse Creek. Once you cross the bridge over the creek, look to your right for some prime possible campsites along this lovely stream. Back on the motorway and another few miles west, the road nears the June 27, 1806, eastbound campsite, where Clark reported they ate bear's oil and boiled roots for dinner.

On September 17 the party probably passed—but did not mention—Indian Post Office, several rock cairns marking the highest point on the Lolo Trail at

At the Smoking Place on the Lolo Trail, Idaho.

7,033 feet. A short trail leads to the cairns; from there, walk a little way east along the ridge for one of the area's best sunset-viewing sites.

Past Indian Post Office, the corps left the main ridge and followed a more northerly route for about 12 miles. The trails converge again past FR 107, also known as Saddle Camp Road, a good route back to U.S. Highway 12. Within a few miles west of FR 107, FR 500 reaches the Sinque Hole camp of September 17, 1805, and the Smoking Place of June 27, 1806, where the returning expedition stopped to share a pipe with its Nez Perce guides. The Indian Post Office and Smoking Place—indeed, the whole Lolo Trail—has had spiritual and cultural significance for the Nez Perce people for centuries, and it's important to treat the area with the utmost respect. You can backtrack from here to FR 107 or proceed on the motorway—but be aware that west of here you're committed to many more hours of rough travel.

The Dry Camp of September 18, 1805, marks the spot where Captain Clark moved ahead with six hunters to look for game. Left behind, Lewis and the rest suffered a particularly toilsome night. There was scant water, and supper consisted once again of leftover colt, portable soup, "a little bears oil and about 20 pounds of candles from our stock of provisions." Candles! Could matters possibly get worse?

From here, however, things finally looked up—literally. From nearby Sherman Peak, first Captain Clark and later Captain Lewis glimpsed prairies in the

Rooms with a View

There are no motels along the Lolo Motorway, but four Forest Service rental cabins are within short (albeit bumpy) drives of the route. The best is Castle Butte, just 1 mile from the motorway. Castle Butte is a former working fire lookout about 15 feet square, perched on a stone foundation about 20 feet high. A catwalk extends around the lookout, and lightning rods at each corner give visitors a feeling of vulnerability and safety at the same time. Sweeping vistas are impressive in all directions, but especially to the south where the Selway-Bitterroot Wilderness—among the largest in the continental United States—lies sprawled beyond the Lochsa River. The river, for its part, may barely be seen, a slim and silvery ribbon far below your feet.

The lookout is furnished with a double bed, single cot, table with two chairs looking out toward the west (perfect for sunset dinners), propane stove, and several chests of drawers. A looseleaf-bound visitors' guide logs past renters' reactions, which range from deeply religious ("Thank you God for your marvelous creation") to anger at government policies that endanger the surrounding wild country. ("It would be a shame to come back to Castle Butte in five years to be surrounded by clearcuts," one guest wrote in 1992.)

Castle Butte is a marvelous place to nap, write, paint, make music, learn to use the firefinder, or read: The visitors' book also contains a copy of The Smokechaser, a memoir by Carl A. Weholt, who tells of his days in the fire lookout and of the many colorful characters he met during his Forest Service career. It's also fun to rummage through items left by past occupants: an October 1965 Reader's Digest, a deck of cards, and a Western dime novel. For information on how to rent Castle Butte, contact the Clearwater National Forest's Lochsa Ranger District office, Route 1, Box 398, Kooskia, ID 83539, or call (208) 926–4275. It's typically available only mid-July through late September, at a cost of $30 per night with a two-night minimum and a seven-night maximum stay.

Castle Butte may be the rental facility most convenient to the Lolo Motorway, but it's not the only one near the route. Not far to the west, Liz Butte Cabin is situated 3 miles off the motorway. Weitas Butte Lookout, about 3 miles north of Rocky Ridge Lake and Weitas Meadows, is perched on a 53-foot tower, making it unsuitable for families with small children. Austin Ridge, another high tower, lies 8 miles from the Lewis and Clark Trail, but it's available earlier in the season—usually by late June. For information on renting Liz Butte, Weitas Butte, or Austin Ridge, contact the Lochsa Ranger District in Kamiah, Route 2, Box 191, Kamiah, ID 83536, or call (208) 935–2513.

distance. True, the plains were still about 40 miles off, but the end of the mountains was finally in sight. The corps called this place Spirit Revival Ridge.

At Horse Sweat Pass, the Lewis and Clark Trail again leaves the main divide, regaining it 12 miles to the west. The motorway continues on due west, passing Rocky Ridge Lake and Weitas Meadows, a popular campsite and a good picnic stop with an actual pit toilet—a real luxury in these parts! Another few miles west, the motorway reaches Pete Forks Junction. You can jump off here, but if you've come this far, you may well want to stay on the motorway, which will soon be regaining the Lewis and Clark Trail a few miles to the south near Boundary Junction. If you've had enough, drive 1 mile west on Forest Road 104 from Pete Forks to reach FR 103 at Beaver Dam Saddle. From here it's 30 miles west to Weippe via FR 103 and FR 100.

The western reach of the Lolo Motorway near the Canyon Junction/Mex Mountain area is a good gravel section of road, much more easily traveled than the rough dirt track to the east. This area also has the best, most accessible hiking along the remote route, with about 15 miles of continuous, easy-to-follow trail with moderate-to-steep grades. Taking off from the motorway between Boundary Junction and Canyon Junction, Trail 25 travels 5 miles to Salmon Trout Camp. From there, after crossing the Dollar Creek Bridge, the trail proceeds about 7 miles to Lewis and Clark Grove and another 3 miles to the trailhead at Lolo Campground along Idaho's Lolo Creek—not to be confused with the one in Montana, on the east side of the Lolo Trail.

Lewis and Clark Grove marks the spot where Clark and his advance party spent the night of September 19, 1805. It had been another rough day in which they'd traveled 22 miles over several mountains and through plenty of fallen timber. But it would be their last night on the Lolo Trail; from here Clark and the advance guard would soon reach flat land. From the Lolo Campground, drivers can follow FR 100 either north to Weippe (via the gravel road at Petersons Corners) or south to Kamiah.

WEIPPE PRAIRIE

An Indian had told Lewis and Clark the Lolo Trail crossing could be made in five days. It had taken the corps twice that. But on September 20, 1805, Clark and his advance party of six other men finally stumbled out of the Bitterroots and onto the Weippe (pronounced WE-ipe) Prairie.

As he and his men walked across the open plain, Clark saw three Nez Perce boys at a slight distance. Frightened, the boys hid in the grass as the white men approached. Clark found two of them and, after reassuring them, asked the boys to lead him and the others to their village.

Once again, many of the village leaders were away on a hunt. The nearest one, Twisted Hair, was at a fishing camp 20 miles down the Clearwater. Clark decided to go meet the chief the next day, but in the meantime bartered for some dried salmon, berries, and camas roots for his party and for the starving men still back in the mountains. He then dispatched Reuben Field and a Nez Perce guide to bring food back to Lewis and the others, who arrived at the Nez Perce camps on September 22.

Within a day, all the white men were sick as dogs. The reason, all thought, was the sudden change in diet from near-starvation rations to the rich salmon and camas roots. The Nez Perce could have easily taken advantage of this situation to kill the ailing explorers; in fact, tribal oral history indicates that the warriors who met Clark and his advance party intended to do just that. But providence intervened in the person of Watkuweis, a Nez Perce woman who had been kidnapped by Blackfeet several years before. Alone among the Nez Perce, Watkuweis knew of the whites; she had been sold to a white trader and lived among whites in Canada before returning to her homeland. "These are the people who helped me," Watkuweis told the warriors. "Do them no hurt." As Stephen Ambrose recounted in *Undaunted Courage*: "First Sacagawea, now Watkuweis. The expedition owed more to Indian women than either captain ever acknowledged." In fact, without these two women, the Lewis and Clark Expedition would probably not have succeeded at all.

Weippe Prairie, Idaho, where the expedition first met the Nez Perce Indians.

The site where expedition members first met the Nez Perce may be viewed southeast of Weippe, about 3 miles from the historical marker on Idaho Highway 11 west of Weippe. To get there, turn south on Fourth Street South 100 (just east of the elementary school but on the opposite side of the road). Drive south and turn left (or east) about 0.4 mile past the Weippe Cemetery. The site is another 0.4 mile east on the south side.

Weippe Prairie is a designated National Historic Landmark. A historical marker here notes: "For the Nez Perce, this meeting meant the beginning of change for their way of life. For the members of the Lewis and Clark Expedition, it meant survival." Once again, native people had saved the Corps of Discovery from bitter defeat.

The Retreat at Someday Ranch is a memorable place to stay on the Weippe Prairie. Proprietors Ed and Marge Kuchynka welcome Lewis and Clark buffs, wildlife-watching enthusiasts, and solitude seekers to a private cabin with its own stocked kitchen. It costs $60 for one or two persons, including food for breakfast. There's also a tepee that can sleep four or five persons for $35, with cots, sleeping bags, and a Dutch oven breakfast available for a small extra charge. The retreat is open May through October at 2021 Musselshell Road, 0.5 mile east of town. Call (208) 435–4362.

Whether you stay over in Weippe or just pass through, be sure to see the new Weippe Discovery Center. The community building on Idaho Highway 11 has exterior exhibits (open twenty-four hours a day) showing the Lewis and Clark Expedition's progress from Travelers' Rest to the Canoe Camp. From Weippe, head west on ID 11 to return to U.S. 12 and the Clearwater corridor. En route, motorists are treated to dazzling views while descending a magnificent, winding grade. At U.S. 12 turn right to proceed west toward Orofino.

THE CANOE CAMP AND THE CLEARWATER

After more than a month's search, Lewis and Clark had finally found a westward river to take them to the Pacific Ocean. Their next task was locating a campsite where they could make new canoes. They found the spot just west of what is now Orofino, Idaho. A roadside park along U.S. Highway 12 marks the approximate spot.

Interpretive panels at Canoe Camp recap the expedition's route through the Bitterroots and its meeting with the Nez Perce, as well as their labors at the Canoe Camp. They arrived in the area on September 26, 1805, and camped on the river's south side. Just days before, the men had been freezing in the mountains.

Now the weather was hot, and it sapped the men's already frail health. But by October 6 the party had built five new canoes to complete the run to the Pacific. The following day the corps proceeded downriver with two new guides: Twisted Hair and Tetoharsky, both Nez Perce chieftains.

Look northeast across the river from Canoe Camp to see Dworshak Dam. This mighty structure is the highest straight-axis concrete dam in the West. Completed in 1973, it rises 717 feet and backs up a popular 53-mile-long reservoir with some of Idaho's best steelhead fishing. Dworshak Reservoir is also known for its boat-accessed minicamps: eighty scenic spots scattered along the shoreline that together provide 125 sites for camping and day use. To visit the dam or the town of Orofino proper, backtrack east from the Canoe Camp site and take the bridge across the Clearwater.

The Clearwater National Forest supervisor's office is just east of the Canoe Camp park, on the opposite side of U.S. 12. Stop by for recreation information or a look at the displays, which include a wildlife diorama and an interesting relief map of the region.

Clearwater River Company runs a variety of voyages along this stretch of river. Opportunities range from half-day paddles priced at $60 to overnight trips costing about $195. Clearwater River Company uses the big voyageur-style canoes that have become so popular along the rivers of Lewis and Clark. Although the trips run right along U.S. 12 (with traffic nearly always in view), the company's big plus is its riverside tepee village, where trip participants can spend the night and learn primitive skills, including fire making, basket weaving, archery, and hide tanning. Several Native Americans are on staff to add their perspectives. The food is tasty, too, with such offerings as garlic and herb–basted chicken or buffalo burgers. The offerings are fun for families, and they're a great choice for business team-building outings. The company also runs year-round drift-boat float and fishing trips. For more information contact Clearwater River Company at (208) 476–9199 or visit www.clearwatertrips.com.

Going upriver as they did east of the Rockies, Lewis and Clark frequently traveled as few as 15 miles a day. But now the current was with them, and it wasn't unusual to complete 30 or 40 miles in a day. In many places, however, the party encountered dangerous rapids—on October 8 Sergeant Gass's canoe struck a rock and sank, necessitating a day's stop for repairs.

U.S. 12 hugs the Clearwater from Orofino all the way to Lewiston. On the way, watch the terrain change from forested river canyon to the grassy steppes of the Inland Northwest. For the next 200 miles, this arid landscape of velvety, undulating green-and-gold hills will be the dominant visual feature along the Lewis and Clark route.

This also remains the heart of the Nez Perce country, and a visitor center at Spalding serves as headquarters for the various units of Nez Perce National Park.

Canoe Camp along the Clearwater River, Orofino, Idaho.

The center is reached via a short jog south from U.S. 12 on U.S. 95. Lapwai, 3 miles south of Spalding, serves as Nez Perce tribal headquarters.

Spalding is named for the Presbyterian missionary Henry Spalding, who sincerely believed it was his duty to Christianize the Indians. "What is done for the poor Indians of this Western world must be done soon," he said. "The only thing that can save them from annihilation is the introduction of civilization."

The Nez Perce Visitor Center chronicles and exhibits many of the changes—good and bad—this philosophy brought to the Indians. A Book of Matthew printed in Nez Perce is among the items on display in the center. Other exhibits include a case full of beautiful beadwork, as well as a silk ribbon and silver friendship medal presented to the Nez Perce from Lewis and Clark. The center is open daily 8:00 A.M. to 5:30 P.M. Pacific Time in summer and to 4:30 P.M. the rest of the year. Call (208) 843–2261 or visit www.nps.gov/nepe for more information.

The large factory on the south side of the Clearwater River near Lewiston is the Potlatch paper mill. Lewiston has its share of industry (and occasionally fragrant air to match), but it is also an educational center and major retail hub—and possibly the public art capital of the Lewis and Clark Trail. Visitors entering town from the north will see about two dozen sculpted figures near the interchange of U.S. Highways 95 and 12. These works by David Govedare and Keith Powell show the Corps of Discovery and the Nez Perce from many perspectives:

an Indian and an expedition member in a horse race, George Drouillard returning from a hunt, and so on. Across the Clearwater River below the Red Lion Inn,
look for bronze statues of Lewis, Clark, and Sacagawea by J. Shirly Bothum.
These works were all new in 2003.

Your next stop might be the Lewis-Clark State College campus. Park at the
corner of Ninth Avenue and Sixth Street and walk onto the campus's Centennial
Mall, where artist Doug Hyde has created a beautiful collection of statues: Lewis
and Clark conferring with Nez Perce chief Twisted Hair, a woman picking huck-
leberries, and another woman showing a girl how to find camas roots. A replica
dugout canoe is on view nearby, and the college library has a bronze relief of the
expedition, as well as a good collection of books and publications related to
Lewis and Clark.

Next, head for the interpretive shelter overlooking the confluence of the
Clearwater and Snake Rivers. To get there, park at the Lewiston Levee Parkways
Center on the northwest side of downtown (on D Street) and walk over the
footbridge. The center's entrance is graced with the sculpture *Tsceminicum,*
meaning "meeting of the waters" in Nez Perce. Designed by Nancy N. Dreher,
the artwork depicts a variety of wildlife and the symbolic Earth Mother.

Displays in the shelter note that when Lewis and Clark arrived here, they
thought they'd found the Columbia River. Six days later, after a difficult journey

**Near the confluence of the Clearwater and Snake Rivers, Lewiston–Clarkston,
Idaho–Washington.**

across the eastern Washington desert, they actually did reach the Columbia. While here, the corps camped on the north bank of what was then named Lewis's River—the Snake—on October 10, 1805.

Lewiston's historical center, the Nez Perce County Museum, also has exhibits of interest to Lewis and Clark buffs. It's located at Third and C Streets and is usually open from 10:00 A.M. to 4:00 P.M. Tuesday through Saturday, March through mid-December. Hours can vary, however, so call (208) 743-2535 before making a special trip. In addition to these sites, several local murals include Lewis and Clark themes, including those on the north side of the Lewis-Clark Center for Arts and History at Fifth and Main Streets downtown; the district health department building at 215 Tenth Street; and even the Lewis Clark Auto Superstore showroom, 1005 Warner Avenue in the Lewiston Orchards area on the plateau above downtown. Finally, don't miss the Sacagawea statue at the Fountain in Pioneer Park along Fifth Street, first placed there in 1911 and rededicated in 1990 for the Idaho Centennial.

Hells Gate State Park, just south of Lewiston on the Snake River, will open a new interpretive center by fall 2003. Its theme will be "From the Mountains to the Sea," and its interpretation will focus on the Corps of Discovery's interactions with Idaho's natural environment. Highlights will include a mural showing the expedition making its canoes for the trip to the Pacific. Hells Gate has good camping, swimming (with a beach), fishing, and other recreation. It's also a launching spot for many jet-boat trips into Hells Canyon; see The Snake River section at the start of the next chapter for more information.

Lewiston is blessed with a mild climate most of the year (although summer days can be scorchers). Because of that, local residents enjoy some recreational pursuits other Idahoans cannot: golfing twelve months a year, for example. Lewiston and its sister city, Clarkston, also have more than 15 miles of paths for joggers, cyclists, walkers, and strollers. Many of these trails are on the Lewiston Levee, which was constructed by the U.S. Army Corps of Engineers to protect Lewiston after the completion of Lower Granite Dam downriver. Look for historical interpretive panels along the trail at Kiwanis Park, south of the confluence along Snake River Avenue.

From Lewiston, continue west on U.S. 12 into Clarkston and Washington State. It's all downriver from here.

Lodging

Lodgings, campgrounds, and restaurants listed below are a representative sampling of what is available. Listing in these pages does not imply endorsement, nor is this a complete listing of all reputable businesses. For more complete listings, contact the visitor information bureau or chamber of commerce in each town. Room rates were accurate as of summer 2002 but are subject to change.

WHITEHALL, MONTANA
Chief Motel, (406) 287–3921, 303 East Legion; $42–$47.
Rice Motel, (406) 287–3895, 7 North A Street; $28–$38.
Super 8 Motel, (406) 287–5588, 515 North Whitehall Street; $60.

TWIN BRIDGES, MONTANA
Hemingway's Lodge, (888) 434–5118, 409 North Main Street; $50–$75.
King's Motel, (800) 222–5510, 307 South Main Street; $50–$60.
The Old Hotel Bed & Breakfast, (406) 684–5959, 101 East Fifth Avenue; $125.

DILLON, MONTANA
Best Western Paradise Inn, (406) 683–4214, 650 North Montana Street; $60–$85.
Centennial Inn Bed & Breakfast, (406) 683–4454, 122 South Washington; $80.
Creston Motel, (406) 683–2341, 335 South Atlantic; $50–$60.
Horse Prairie Guest Ranch, 3300 Bachelor Mountain Road. (Guest ranch; minimum stay may apply.)
Sacajawea Motel, (406) 683–2381, 775 North Montana; $40–$45.
Sundowner Motel, (800) 524–9746, 500 North Montana; $45–$50.

SALMON, IDAHO
Greyhouse Inn Bed & Breakfast, (800) 348–8097, 12 miles south on U.S. 93; $70–$90.

Heritage Inn Bed & Breakfast, (208) 756–3174, 510 Lena Street; $35–$45.
Solaas Bed & Breakfast, (208) 756–3903, south of town on ID 28 in Baker; $45–$50.
Stagecoach Inn Motel, (208) 756–4251, 201 U.S. 93 North; $60–$75.
Suncrest Motel, (208) 756–2294, 705 Challis Street; $33–$40.
Wagons West Motel, (208) 756–4281, 503 U.S. 93 North; $60.

NORTH FORK, IDAHO
100 Acre Wood Bed & Breakfast Resort, (208) 865–2165, U.S. 93; $55–$120.
North Fork Motel, (208) 865–2412, U.S. 93; $40–$47.
River's Fork Inn, (208) 865–2301, U.S. 93; $63.

*WISDOM, MONTANA
Nez Perce Motel, (406) 689–3254; $50.
Sandman Motel, (406) 689–3218; $38.

*JACKSON, MONTANA
Jackson Hot Springs Lodge, (406) 834–3151; $32–$75.

SULA, MONTANA
Broad Axe Lodge, (406) 821–3878, 1237 East Fork Road. Cabins.
Lost Trail Hot Springs Resort, (406) 821–3574, U.S. 93 south of Sula; $55–$85.

*Denotes town on Clark's return route through the Big Hole, 1806.

CONNER, MONTANA

Rocky Knob Lodge, (406) 821–3520, U.S. 93; $42.

DARBY, MONTANA

Alta Meadow Ranch, (406) 349–2464, 9975 West Fork Road. (Guest ranch; minimum stays may apply.)

Bud & Shirley's Motel, (406) 821–3401; $50–$75.

Pepperbox Ranch, (406) 349–2920, 9959 West Fork Road. (Guest ranch; minimum stays may apply.)

Wilderness Motel, (406) 821–3405, 308 South Main Street; $45–$70.

HAMILTON, MONTANA

Best Western Hamilton Inn, (800) 426–4586, 409 South First Street. (U.S. 93); $70–$100.

Bitterroot Motel, (406) 363–1142, 408 South First Street; $45–$48.

Comfort Inn, (800) 442–4667, 1113 North First Street; $65–$100.

Deer Crossing Bed & Breakfast, (406) 363–2232, 396 Hayes Creek Road; $90–$150.

LOLO, MONTANA

Days Inn, (406) 273–2121, 11225 U.S. 93; $75–$90.

MISSOULA, MONTANA

BelAire Motel, (800) 543–3184, 300 East Broadway; $50–$75.

Best Inn—South, (406) 251–2665, 3803 Brooks Street; $80–$90.

City Center Motel, (406) 543–3193, 338 East Broadway; $45–$55.

Goldsmith's Inn Bed & Breakfast, (406) 721–6732, 809 East Front Street; $100–$140.

Holiday Inn–Missoula Parkside, (800) 399–0408, 200 South Pattee Street; $90–$100.

Red Lion Inn, (406) 728–3300, 700 West Broadway; $82–$92.

LOLO HOT SPRINGS, MONTANA

Lolo Trail Center, (406) 273–2201, U.S. 12; $67–$117.

POWELL, IDAHO

Lochsa Lodge, (208) 942–3405, U.S. 12; $38–$85.

LOWELL, IDAHO

Ryan's Wilderness Inn, (208) 926–4706, U.S. 12; $45–$50.

Three Rivers Resort, (208) 926–4430, U.S. 12; $50–$100.

KOOSKIA, IDAHO

Bear Hollow Bed & Breakfast, (800) 831–3713, U.S. 12; $75–$125.

Reflections on the Clearwater (formerly Looking Glass Inn), (208) 926–0855, U.S. 12; $75–$85.

WEIPPE, IDAHO

The Retreat at Someday Ranch, (208) 435–4362, 2021 Musselshell Road; $60.

KAMIAH, IDAHO

Clearwater 12 Motel, (208) 935–2671, U.S. 12; $45–$50.

Lewis–Clark Resort, (208) 935–2556, U.S. 12; $40–$60.

OROFINO, IDAHO

Konkolville Motel, (208) 476–5584, 2000 Konkolville Road; $50–$65.

Riverside Motel, (208) 476–5711, 10560 U.S. 12; $33.

*Denotes town on Clark's return route through the Big Hole, 1806.

White Pine Motel, (208) 476–7093, 222 Brown Avenue; $45.

LEWISTON, IDAHO
Carriage House Inn Bed & Breakfast, (208) 746–4506, 504 Sixth Avenue; $80–$140.
El Rancho Motel, (208) 743–8517, 2240 3rd Avenue North; $38–$48.

Inn America, (800) 469–4667 or (208) 746–4600, 702 Twenty-first Street; $65–$75.
Red Lion Hotel, (208) 799–1000, 621 Twenty-first Street; $100–$120.
Sacajawea Select Inn, (800) 333–1393 or (208) 746–1393, 1824 Main Street; $60–$65.
Super 8, (208) 743–8808, 3120 North South Highway; $50.

Camping

THREE FORKS, MONTANA
Lewis & Clark Caverns State Park, (406) 287–3541, west on MT 2. Campground and cabins.

WHITEHALL, MONTANA
Whitetail Creek Motel & RV Park, (406) 287–5315, 516 East Legion Avenue.

TWIN BRIDGES, MONTANA
Hemingway's RV Park, (406) 684–5648, 409 North Main Street.
Jefferson River Camp, (406) 684–5262, MT 41 between Silver Star and Twin Bridges.

DILLON, MONTANA
Armstead Campground, (406) 683–4199, I–15 exit 44, at Clark Canyon Reservoir.
Clark Canyon Reservoir, I–15 exit 44.
Dillon KOA, (406) 683–2749, 735 West Park Street.
Sacajawea Memorial Camp, at Lemhi Pass. Closed to camping until 2007.
Southside RV Park, (406) 683–2244, I–15 exit 62, then right on Poindexter.

SALMON, IDAHO
Century II Campground, (208) 756–2063, U.S. 93.
Salmon Meadows Campground, (208) 756–2640, U.S. 93 at St. Charles Street.

NORTH FORK, IDAHO
North Fork Campground, (208) 865–2412, U.S. 93.
Wagonhammer Campground, (208) 865–2477, U.S. 93.

GIBBONSVILLE, IDAHO
Broken Arrow Campground, (208) 865–2241, U.S. 93.
Twin Creek, (208) 865–2383, U.S. 93. Primitive sites.

*WISDOM, MONTANA
May Creek, (406) 689–2431, west of Big Hole National Battlefield on MT 43.

*JACKSON, MONTANA
Jackson Hot Springs Lodge, (406) 834–3151, on County Road 278.

*BANNACK, MONTANA
Bannack State Park, (406) 834–3413, 4 miles south of County Road 278.

*Denotes town on Clark's return route through the Big Hole, 1806.

SULA, MONTANA
Lost Trail Hot Springs Resort, (406) 821–3574, U.S. 93 south of Sula.
Spring Gulch Campground, north of Sula on U.S. 93. Primitive sites.
Sula Store & KOA, (406) 821–3364, U.S. 93.

HAMILTON, MONTANA
Angler's Roost RV Park, (406) 363–1268, 4 miles south on U.S. 93.
Bitterroot Family Campground, (406) 363–2430, 9 miles south on U.S. 93.
Black Rabbit RV Park, (406) 363–3744, 1.5 miles north on U.S. 93.

LOLO, MONTANA
Lee Creek, (406) 329–3814, 26 miles west on U.S. 12. Primitive sites.
Lewis and Clark Campground, (406) 329–3814, 15 miles west on U.S. 12. Primitive sites.

MISSOULA, MONTANA
Missoula KOA, (406) 549–0881, Reserve Street to Tina Avenue.
Outpost Family Campground, (406) 549–2016, north of town on U.S. 93.

LOLO HOT SPRINGS, MONTANA
Lolo Hot Springs RV Park & Campground, (800) 273–2290, U.S. 12.

POWELL, IDAHO
Jerry Johnson, (208) 942–3113, west on U.S. 12. Primitive sites.

Wendover-Whitehouse, (208) 942–3113, west on U.S. 12. Primitive sites.

LOWELL, IDAHO
Apgar, (208) 926–4275, east on U.S. 12. Primitive sites.
Knife Edge, (208) 926–4275, east on U.S. 12. Primitive sites.
Three Rivers Resort, (208) 926–4430, U.S. 12.
Wild Goose, (208) 926–4275, east on U.S. 12. Primitive sites.
Wilderness Gateway, (208) 926–4275, east on U.S. 12. Primitive sites.

WEIPPE, IDAHO
Timberline Cafe, RV Park and Cabins, (208) 435–4763, 1022 North Main Street.

KAMIAH, IDAHO
Lewis-Clark Resort RV Park, (208) 935–2556, U.S. 12.

OROFINO, IDAHO
Canoe Camp RV Park, (208) 476–7530, 14224 U.S. 12. Across from Nez Perce/Lewis and Clark Canoe Camp site.

LENORE, IDAHO
Dworshak State Park, (208) 476–5994, 1 mile north of town to Cavendish, then 10 miles east.

LEWISTON, IDAHO
Hells Gate State Park, (208) 743–2363, 4 miles south on Snake River Avenue.

Restaurants

WHITEHALL, MONTANA
Crzy Bear Pizza, (406) 287–9202, 7 West Legion Avenue.

Land of Magic Too Supper Club, (406) 287–5252, 27 West Legion. Steaks and seafood.

---

*Denotes town on Clark's return route through the Big Hole, 1806.

TWIN BRIDGES, MONTANA
Blue Anchor Bar and Cafe, (406) 684–5655, 102 North Main.

DILLON, MONTANA
Centennial Inn, (406) 683–4454, 122 South Washington.
Crosswinds Restaurant, (406) 683–6370, 1008 South Atlantic. Breakfast all day, prime rib on weekends.
Longhorn Saloon & Grill, (406) 683–6839, 8 North Montana Street. Breakfast, lunch, and dinner.
Papa T's, (406) 683–6432, 10 North Montana. Family-oriented restaurant featuring burgers, pizza.
Western Wok, (406) 683–2356, 17 East Bannack. Chinese and American food.

SALMON, IDAHO
Bertram's Brewery, (406) 756–3391, 101 South Andrews. Brewpub and fine dining.
Cabbage Patch Restaurant, (208) 756–3337, 206 Van Dreff Street. Casual lunches, fine dining at night.
Granny's Steakhouse, (208) 756–2309, 1403 East Main Street. Burgers, pies, cinnamon rolls.
Shady Nook Restaurant, (208) 756–4182, U.S. 93. Specialties include prime rib and seafood.

NORTH FORK, IDAHO
100 Acre Wood, (208) 865–2165, north of town on U.S. 93. Fine dining.
North Fork Cafe, (208) 865–2412, U.S. 93. Hearty food popular with river rats.
River's Fork Inn, (208) 865–2301. Riverside dining featuring steaks and seafood.

GIBBONSVILLE, IDAHO
Broken Arrow, (208) 856–2241, U.S. 93. Mexican food.

*WISDOM, MONTANA
Big Hole Crossing, (406) 689–3800. Home cooking.
Fetty's Bar & Cafe, (406) 689–3260. Specialties include shakes and burgers.

*JACKSON, MONTANA
Jackson Hot Springs Lodge, (406) 834–3151.
Rose's Cantina Cafe, (406) 834–3100. Breakfast, lunch, and dinner.

SULA, MONTANA
Lost Trail Hot Springs, (406) 821–3574, U.S. 93. Steaks and more.

CONNER, MONTANA
Rocky Knob Restaurant, (406) 821–3520, between Sula and Conner on U.S. 93. Hickory-smoked ribs.

DARBY, MONTANA
Outpost Restaurant, (406) 821–3388. Between Sula and Darby on U.S. 93.
Trapper's Family Restaurant, (406) 821–4465, 561 Main.

HAMILTON, MONTANA
A Place to Ponder Bakery & Cafe, (406) 363–0080, 166 South Second Street. Baked goods, lunch specials.
Banque Club, (406) 363–1955, 225 West Main. Steaks, chicken, ribs.
Coffee Cup Cafe, (406) 363–3822, 500 South First Street. Popular for breakfast.
The Grubstake, (406) 363–3068, 1017 Grubstake Road. Mountainside dining with a wide menu.

---

*Denotes town on Clark's return route through the Big Hole, 1806.

Stavers Tavern, (406) 363–4433, 163 South Second Street. Steaks, seafood, fine beer and ales on tap.

VICTOR, MONTANA
Cantina La Cocina, (406) 642–3192, U.S. 93. Homemade Mexican food.

STEVENSVILLE, MONTANA
Fort Owen Inn, (406) 777–3483, U.S. 93. Steaks and beef.
Marie's Italian Cafe, (406) 777–3681, 4040 South U.S. 93. Closed in winter.

FLORENCE, MONTANA
Glenn's Cafe, (406) 273–2534, U.S. 93. Famous for pie.

LOLO, MONTANA
Guy's Lolo Creek Steakhouse, (406) 273–2622, U.S. 12. Western-style steaks, chicken.
Lolo Trail Cafe, (406) 273–6580, U.S. 93.

MISSOULA, MONTANA
Black Dog Cafe, (406) 542–1138, 138 West Broadway. Vegetarian and organic fare.
The Bridge, (406) 542–0638, 515 South Higgins. Bistro fare, popular for pizza.
The Depot, (406) 728–7007, Railroad & Ryman. Steaks, salad bar, desserts.
McKay's On the River, (406) 728–0098, 1111 East Broadway. Steaks, seafood, burgers.
Tipu's Tiger, (406) 542–0622, 531 South Higgins. Indian, vegetarian, and vegan selections.
The Shack, (406) 549–9903, 222 West Main. A breakfast favorite, patio dining.
Zimorino's, (406) 549–7434, 424 North Higgins. Popular for pizza and pasta.

LOLO HOT SPRINGS, MONTANA
Lolo Hot Springs, (406) 273–2290, U.S. 12. Steaks and ribs.

POWELL, IDAHO
Lochsa Lodge, (208) 942–3405, U.S. 12. Fireside dining.

LOWELL/SYRINGA, IDAHO
Three Rivers Resort, (208) 926–4430, U.S. 12. Wide menu three meals a day.
Wilderness Inn, (208) 926–4706, U.S. 12.

KOOSKIA, IDAHO
Idaho Backroads Cafe, (208) 926–4304, 118 South Main.

KAMIAH, IDAHO
Jilinda's, (208) 935–1158, U.S. 12. Family dining with great view of the Clearwater River.
Kamiah Cafe, (208) 935–2563, 714 Third Street. Homemade food.
Syringa Lounge & Steak House, (208) 935–0960, 501 Fourth Street. Steaks and salad bar.

WEIPPE, IDAHO
Timberline Cafe, (208) 435–4763, 1022 North Main Street. Breakfast, lunch, and dinner daily.
Weippe Pizza & Cafe, (208) 435–4823, 118 North Main. Creative pizzas and more. Closed Monday and Tuesday.

OROFINO, IDAHO
Becky's Burgers, (208) 476–7361, 105 Michigan Avenue.
Ponderosa Restaurant, (208) 476–4818, 220 Michigan Avenue.

*Denotes town on Clark's return route through the Big Hole, 1806.

LEWISTON, IDAHO

The Helm Restaurant, (208) 746–9661, 1826 Main. Family dining.

Jonathan's, (208) 746–3438, 1516 Main Street. Casual fine dining.

Meriwether's Restaurant, (208) 799–1000, in the Red Lion Hotel. Fine dining.

Thai Taste, (208) 746–6192, 1410 Twenty-first Street.

Waffles Cafe, (208) 743–5189, 1421 Main. Popular for breakfast, close to motels.

Zany's, (208) 746–8131, 2006 Nineteenth Avenue. Sandwiches and barbecue in fun atmosphere.

---

*Denotes town on Clark's return route through the Big Hole, 1806.

8

Washington and Oregon

Men appear much satisfied with their trip, beholding with astonishment the high waves dashing against the rocks and this immense ocean. —WILLIAM CLARK, NOVEMBER 18, 1805, ON THE PACIFIC COAST.

THE SNAKE RIVER

When most travelers think of the Northwest, they think of evergreen forests, snowcapped Cascade peaks, and copious amounts of rain. All those qualities are true of western Washington and Oregon, but the Inland Northwest could not be more different. East of the Cascades, Washington is dominated by arid, rolling hills and bisected by deep river canyons—none deeper than Hells Canyon on the Washington-Oregon-Idaho border. This impressive gorge is deeper than even the Grand Canyon, because the Snake River runs smack-dab against Idaho's towering Seven Devils mountain range. When Congress created Hells Canyon National Recreation Area in 1975, it saved some of the best white-water rapids in the United States by protecting 67 miles of the Snake River. Congress also set aside 215,000 acres as the Hells Canyon Wilderness, with an outstanding network of trails open only to hikers and horseback riders.

Abundant in fish, wildlife, and geologic splendor, Hells Canyon is a sight to see. Sturgeon up to 12 feet long swim the depths of the Snake. Elk, mule deer, bighorn sheep, cougar, bobcat, bear, and smaller mammals patrol the mountainsides. About thirty outfitters offer float, jet-boat, or white-water trips through

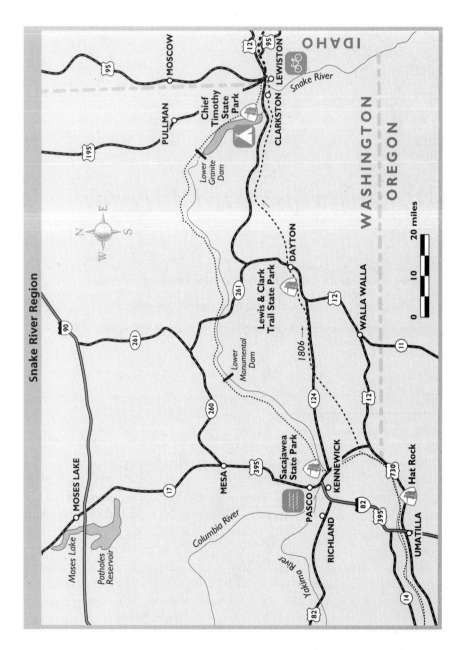

the canyon. For a list contact the Hells Canyon National Recreation Area head-quarters in Clarkston at (509) 758–0616, or stop by the office at 2535 Riverside Drive, where you can also get information on private boat trip permits. Swallows Park, near the Hells Canyon NRA office, is a great day-use park with a paved riverside path, swimming beach, boat ramp, picnicking, and a playground.

The Clarkston area is slated to be one of four sites in Washington State to have a new sculpture by famed architect Maya Lin, best known as designer of the Vietnam Veterans Memorial in Washington, D.C. By 2005 four Lin works will be installed at the major confluences Lewis and Clark visited in the Northwest: at the Clearwater/Snake, Snake/Columbia, Willamette/Columbia, and the Columbia at the Pacific. All will incorporate themes of the tribes the explorers met at these junctions.

Before leaving the Clarkston area, stop by Hells Canyon resort at 1550 Port Drive to see the 300-foot Lewis and Clark Timeline detailing highlights of the expedition. The resort also includes a marina, restaurant, and store. The Snake River here is actually Lower Granite Lake—first of a series of lakes backed up by dams along the Snake and Columbia Rivers.

Chief Timothy State Park, 8 miles west of Clarkston on U.S. Highway 12, closed in fall 2002 due to Washington State budget cutbacks. At press time, negotiators were trying to find a way to reopen the park and its Alopwai Interpretive Center before the bicentennial. Get project updates at www.parks.wa.gov, or call (360) 902–8844.

Alpowai (pronounced Al-POW-ee) was a major Nez Perce settlement at the junction of Alpowa Creek and the Snake River. The town was led by Chief Timothy and Chief Red Wolf, who—like many Washingtonians after him—ran an apple orchard. In the 1860s, when the second treaty with the U.S. government drastically reduced the size of the Nez Perce reservation, Alpowai found itself outside the reservation boundaries. White settlers flowed into the area, and by the late 1880s the small town of Silcott overshadowed Alpowai, only to deteriorate by the 1920s and eventually disappear. In 1975 Lower Granite Dam's gates were closed, and water covered the Nez Perce village site.

After a steep climb up U.S. 12, the panorama shifts again, this time to rolling fields of grain. This is the edge of the Palouse, one of the nation's most beautiful and productive wheat-growing areas. An interpretive sign mentions that on their way home May 3, 1806, the Lewis and Clark expedition camped at a grove of cottonwoods near the present-day highway after a tedious 28-mile journey up Pataha Creek. Supper that night included scant rations of dried meat and dog. Throughout their travels in the Northwest, the party turned frequently to dog meat to help extend their rations—a phenomenon that had to unnerve Lewis's steadfast companion, Seaman, at least a little. The next morning, they followed a branch of the Indian trail they had followed up the creek. The trail can still be faintly seen on the north side of the highway across from the historic marker.

By now, today's traveler has lost the river Lewis and Clark worked so hard to find. Ledgerwood Road, just west of the rest area at Alpowai Summit, leads to Lower Granite Dam, as does Mayview Road (just west of the THREE FORKS INDIAN TRAILS sign). Back roads along the impounded Snake River parallel the Lewis and Clark route of 1805; U.S. 12 roughly follows the expedition's return route of 1806.

The corps traveled the Snake River westward in 1805 and homeward in 1806.

Pomeroy is a major agricultural hub for Garfield County. The city park has a pool, lots of shade, and even a small golf course. Columbia Street boasts a lovely garden, planted for the one-hundredth anniversary of Washington's statehood.

Twenty-two miles west of Pomeroy, Washington Highway 261 leads to Lyons Ferry State Park, nestled at the confluence of the Snake and Palouse Rivers. The expedition had earlier named the Palouse River for George Drouillard, misspelling it as usual "Drewyer." Throughout the journals, Drouillard was praised as a hunter, scout, and interpreter. He was a good friend to Lewis and is considered one of the two or three most valuable enlisted members of the expedition.

Like Chief Timothy State Park, Lyons Ferry has closed due to budget cuts. But visitors can still travel to nearby Palouse Falls State Park, which seems entirely out of place in this denuded landscape. You're driving through a landscape with no water in sight when suddenly a gorge opens up and a 190-foot waterfall plunges majestically into a small pond. There's no easy way down to the pool, but trails along the ledge offer super views. Camping is available. From Palouse Falls, travelers can either follow back roads along the Snake River to the Tri-Cities (check a detailed state map to plot your route) or backtrack to U.S. 12 to have a look at part of Lewis and Clark's homeward route via Dayton and Walla Walla, a route explained a bit later—albeit in reverse, the way the explorers encountered it.

MEETING THE COLUMBIA

Travelers approaching the Tri-Cities on Washington Highway 124 will find a wealth of camping opportunities along the lower reaches of the Snake River. These mostly come courtesy of the U.S. Army Corps of Engineers. Areas include Fishhook, Charbonneau, and Hood parks, each boasting a swimming beach, boat launch, and trailer dump station. As with other public campgrounds in eastern Washington, lawns at these parks are irrigated on a daily or nightly basis. Tenters should take care to make sure their shelter is placed far from sprinkler heads.

A Lewis and Clark interpretive sign at the intersection of Columbia Center Boulevard and Columbia Drive in Richland marks the farthest point upriver on the Columbia reached by the Corps of Discovery. But the main point of interest in the Tri-Cities is Sacajawea State Park and its fine, small interpretive center at the confluence of the Snake and Columbia. The center was built by the Work Projects Administration in 1939. It uses the spelling "Sacajawea," which, although considered inaccurate by many scholars, is definitely the most common spelling popularly used in the Northwest. A plaque notes that "Sacagawea" is now the preferred scholarly spelling, and that is the one used in most of the center's displays.

Sacagawea's contributions to the expedition are extensively and accurately explained. Other exhibits praise the pairing of Lewis and Clark. "Both men were experienced leaders and seasoned wilderness travelers. Lewis had commanded a frontier fort; Clark had dealt extensively with Indians. The skills one man lacked, the other possessed," one display reads. "In temperament, this was also true. Lewis was intellectual, speculative, and moody. Clark was pragmatic, extroverted, and even-tempered. Most important of all, Lewis and Clark worked together so harmoniously that it is difficult to believe the expedition actually had two individual leaders."

Viewed from the center, the Snake River is on the left and the Columbia River is on the right. The corps arrived in the area October 16, 1805, to a hearty welcome from the Columbia River Indians—mostly Wanapums and Yakamas. Clark wrote: "After we had our camp fixed and fires made a chief came at the head of about 200 men singing and beating on their drums. They formed a half-circle around us and sung for some time. We gave them all smoke and spoke to their chief as well as we could by signs." By that night, the Corps of Discovery had logged 3,714 miles from Camp River Dubois.

The explorers had become used to the sight and taste of salmon long before this point, but they were astounded at the spectacle they met at the junction of the Snake and Columbia. They arrived at the height of fall chinook runs, and the men wrote of the immense quantities of salmon jumping from the rivers. Clark seemed frustrated at being unable to describe the sight. The corps were also confused by the vast numbers of dead salmon on the riverbanks. They didn't yet know that Pacific salmon, unlike Atlantic varieties, die after spawning, so they spurned the natives' offer of fish in favor of purchasing still more dogs.

The expedition camped at the confluence two nights, during which time the men made celestial observations, updated their journals, mended clothes, and bought at least forty dogs. Clark also explored the Columbia several miles upstream, during which time he met with more Indians and was shown the mouth of the Yakima—or Tapteel—River. On October 18 a council was held, and in the afternoon the expedition at long last moved onto the Columbia River.

Sacajawea State Park is open April through October from 6:30 A.M. to dusk, and the interpretive center is generally open from 1:00 P.M. to 5:00 P.M. Friday through Tuesday, although it's wise to call ahead to check. To get to the park from WA 124, turn right at the intersection for U.S. Highway 12. Immediately after crossing the Snake River, get into the left-hand lane. Signs point to the park, which is 2 miles from the intersection. For more information call (509) 545–2361.

From the park, Lewis and Clark's route is most closely followed by taking U.S. 12 south to Wallula, where the traveler picks up U.S. 730 southwest to Umatilla, Oregon. This is the route we will follow next, but first you might want to pause awhile in the Tri-Cities, which together—with a population of about 130,000—make up the major urban center for southeastern Washington. The East Benton County Historical Museum at 205 Keewaydin in Kennewick has exhibits on the pioneers who followed Lewis and Clark to the region. The Columbia River Exhibition of History, Science, and Technology at 95 Lee Boulevard in Richland plans an exhibit of scientific instruments used by Lewis and Clark.

With three rivers at their disposal, Tri-Cities residents enjoy all kinds of water sports, from boating and fishing to swimming and water-skiing. A bit farther afield, Columbia River Journeys offers daily river cruises on the Columbia's free-flowing Hanford Reach, now a national monument. Trips run May through mid-October; in 2002, the cost was $45 for adults and $35 for children four through eleven. Wine tours are offered, too. For more information or reservations, call (888) 486–9119 or visit www.columbiariverjourneys.com. Other recreational attractions in the Tri-Cities include the new, 22-mile Sacagawea Heritage Trail along the Columbia River and the Playground of Dreams and Family Fishing Pond at Columbia Park in Kennewick. For more information on the Tri-Cities, call (888) 254–5824 or visit www.VisitTri-Cities.com.

If you have an extra half day, consider a side trip from here up the Yakima River Valley, famous for its fruit orchards and wineries. Follow either Interstate 82 or the Yakima Valley Highway that winds between the region's small towns. The Yakama Nation Cultural Center in Toppenish, about an hour's drive from the Tri-Cities, features excellent interpretation of the tribe's colorful past and present. Toppenish also has about sixty murals on a range of historic themes. From Toppenish it's a 60-mile drive south on U.S. 97 to the Columbia River and Interstate 84 or WA 14 (see The Columbia Plateau and The Dalles section later in this chapter).

HOMEWARD BOUND: THE LAND ROUTE

On their way back east in the spring of 1806, Lewis and Clark decided to try an overland shortcut from the mouth of the Walla Walla River northeast to the confluence of the Clearwater and Snake and the land of the Nez Perce—a trek roughly followed by U.S. Highway 12 through Walla Walla, Waitsburg, and Dayton.

The jumping-off spot was present-day Wallula, a small town south of the Tri-Cities. Near here, the Corps of Discovery spent three days camped with the friendly Walla Walla Indians and their leader, Chief Yellept, whom they had met on the way west and promised to visit again. "He appeared much gratified at seeing us return, invited us to remain at his village three or four days, and assured us that we should be furnished with a plenty of such food as they had themselves, and some horses to assist us on our journey," Lewis wrote.

Madam Dorian Memorial Park is located just north of the junction of U.S. 12 and U.S. 730, with camping, picnicking, fishing access, and an RV dump station. The park is named for Marie Dorian, an Iowa Indian who—if it weren't for Sacagawea's amazing adventures—may have become the most famous Native American woman in history.

Dorian traveled west with the Wilson Price Hunt party of Astorians in 1811. The Astorians had left Missouri to establish trading posts along the Columbia and arrived at Wallula in January 1812. Later, members of the Dorian party trekked to the Snake River country to trap. There the men were killed by Bannack Indians. Remarkably, Marie and her two young children survived the winter, hiding in the Blue Mountains. She managed to get her children to safety in the spring and lived the rest of her years in Walla Walla and the Willamette Valley.

From Wallula it's a half-hour drive east on U.S. 12 to the town so nice they named it twice. Walla Walla, meaning "many waters" or "small rapid stream," is worth a visit for several reasons, including Fort Walla Walla Museum and the Whitman Mission National Historic Site, both key outposts in the history of U.S. westward expansion.

Whitman Mission National Historic Site, 7 miles west of Walla Walla off U.S. 12, tells one of the saddest tales from the saga of westward expansion. Marcus

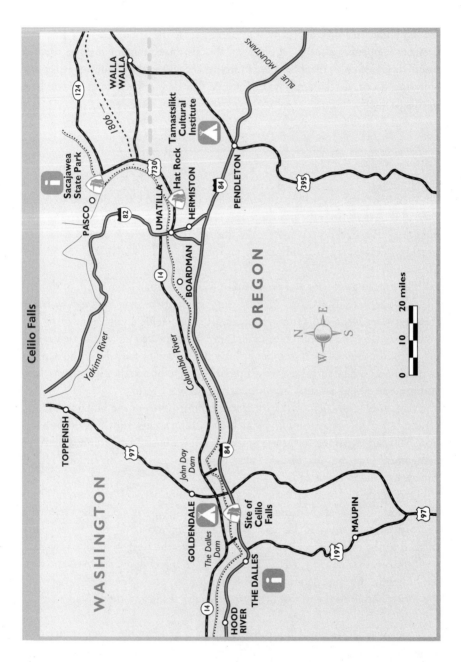

and Narcissa Whitman traveled west together in 1836 to found Waiilatpu, "Place of the Rye Grass," on the banks of the Walla Walla River. For the next decade they would serve as missionaries, teachers, and friends to the Cayuse. Still, cultural differences remained and—with the coming of ever more whites— deepened. In 1847 immigrants brought a measles epidemic that spread rapidly among the Cayuse, who had no resistance to the disease. Soon, half the tribe was dead. When Dr. Whitman's medicine helped whites but not Indians, many Cayuse believed they were being poisoned to make way for the pioneers. On November 29, 1847, a band of Cayuse attacked the mission and killed the Whitmans and eleven others.

Through its exhibits, the Whitman Mission clearly shows the collision between the native people of the West and those who pursued religious zeal and America's "manifest destiny." A small interpretive center tells the story from both sides. Other sites at the Whitman Mission include a great grave in which the massacre victims were buried and an excavated area where early mission buildings are outlined. Visitors can get a good view of the entire grounds by taking the short, steep walk to the Whitman Memorial Shaft. From the top you can see all Waiilatpu, as well as the Blue Mountains. Living-history demonstrations featuring pioneer and Native American crafts are given on summer weekends.

Whitman Mission is open daily from 8:00 A.M. to 6:00 P.M. June through August and from 8:00 A.M. to 4:30 P.M. the rest of the year. The cost of admission is $3.00 per person, or $5.00 per family group. Call (509) 522–6360 for more information.

A few miles farther east at 755 Myra Road, Fort Walla Walla Museum is a comprehensive facility focusing on every aspect of the area's history. A Lewis and Clark diorama on display in the hilltop Penner Exhibit Building features a "hide-and-seek" game for children, who are asked to find objects included in the scene. Kids will also be impressed with two early-twentieth-century playhouses that are among the collection of historical buildings moved to the site.

Fort Walla Walla Museum is open 10:00 A.M. to 5:00 P.M. daily April through October. Admission is $6.00 for adults, $5.00 for students and seniors, and $2.00 for children ages six to twelve. The museum sponsors an annual Lewis and Clark Days event the first weekend in June, which includes interpretation not just of the Corps of Discovery but also of the fur-trade era and area Native American lore. It's followed a few weeks later by a one-day Lewis and Clark Kids Camp for children entering grades four through six. The camp is open to the public, but slots fill quickly. Call (509) 525-7703 for more information.

Walla Walla, a pleasant small city, is home to several colleges, beautiful parks, and a thriving downtown. From here it's a 40-mile drive south via Oregon Highway 11 to the Tamastslikt Cultural Institute outside Pendleton, Oregon—another good place to gain the Native American perspective on westward expansion. Operated by the Confederated Tribes of the Cayuse, Umatilla, and Walla Walla, the institute is open daily except Thanksgiving, Christmas, and New Year's Day. Call (541) 966–9748 for more information. The tribes also run the adjacent Wildhorse Resort & Casino.

U.S. 12 continues east through Waitsburg to Lewis and Clark Trail State Park near the town of Dayton. The site's heavy woodsiness is in extreme contrast to many of southeastern Washington's other state parks. The preserve sits on both sides of U.S. 12, with the campground located on the northwest side and a day-use picnic area (and Lewis and Clark marker) situated on the southeast. The marker explains how, in this area, the corps ate cow parsnip and dog for lack of better food. Again, they were on their way home, and camped west of present-day Dayton on May 1, 1806, and east of town May 2.

Each Saturday evening from Memorial Day through Labor Day, the park presents living history programs on aspects of the Lewis and Clark Expedition. The forty-five-minute programs begin at 8:00 P.M.; call the park at (509) 337–6457 for a list of upcoming topics. Cost is a $1.00 donation per person. Bring a flashlight and lawn chairs.

THE COLUMBIA PLATEAU AND THE DALLES

U.S. Highway 730 starts its run alongside the Columbia River at the Wallula Gap just a few miles north of the Oregon state line. From here the highway hugs the Columbia, offering splendid vistas. A turnout about 2 miles south of the U.S. 12 junction tells the Cayuse legend of "Two Sisters," who may still be seen in rock on the cliffs above the road.

Lewis and Clark didn't mention the Two Sisters in their journals, but they did write of Hat Rock; Clark, in fact, is credited with giving the landmark its name. The Hat Rock State Park entrance is just west of the junction of U.S. 730 and Oregon Highway 37. The road that leads east at the Hat Rock State Park entrance sign winds up in a private subdivision; instead, take the road to the left, which leads to an absolutely gorgeous little day-use park area with big shade trees, picnic tables, and a pond filled with ducks and geese eager for handouts.

The Lewis and Clark historical marker is located at the upper parking lot. It notes the captains passed and named this point on October 19, 1805. Clark climbed to the top of the landmark and said that from its summit, a snow-covered mountain could be seen to the northwest. He first thought it was Mount Saint Helens, but it was really Mount Adams, Washington's second-highest peak at 12,307 feet. Homeward bound, the expedition passed Hat Rock again on April 27, 1806.

There is no camping in the park itself, but a private campground is located just outside the site boundaries. Other activities include swimming and boating. Climbing Hat Rock is no longer permitted.

From Hat Rock, continue west on U.S. 730 to Umatilla, home of McNary Dam, the first of four on the Oregon-Washington border. A bit farther west, the Corps of Discovery camped October 19, 1805, on a now-submerged island not

Hat Rock along the Columbia River near Umatilla, Oregon.

far from what is now the city park in Irrigon, Oregon. The park has interpretation of the encampment, and the communities of Irrigon and Boardman throw a party each year on the Sunday closest to October 19 to commemorate the occasion. A 12-mile recreational trail links Boardman and Irrigon.

Two highways parallel the Columbia River the length of the Washington-Oregon border from Umatilla west. Washington Highway 14 is a two-lane road with few services that generally sits higher above the river with better views. Interstate 84 (accessible via U.S. 730 to Boardman) allows the traveler to really make some time.

Either way, plan to stop at the remarkable Maryhill Museum of Art, located just west of U.S. 97 on the Washington side of the river.

Somewhat eccentric railroad magnate Sam Hill built Maryhill (as well as the nearby replica of Britain's Stonehenge). Lewis and Clark buffs will be most interested in the museum's extensive collection of Native American artifacts, representing many of the tribes the expedition met on its route, as well as a Lewis and Clark Overlook on the grounds. (The expedition camped nearby in 1805 and traversed the land on its return journey in April 1806.) Other permanent exhibits include many Rodin sculptures, Russian icons, unique and historic chess sets, and personal possessions of Queen Marie of Romania, who was a close friend of Hill's.

The museum plans a special art exhibit, "Reflecting on Lewis & Clark: Contemporary American Indian Viewpoints," mid-July through mid-November 2003, and it holds an annual Lewis and Clark lecture each April. Maryhill Museum is open daily from 9:00 A.M. to 5:00 P.M. March 15 through November 15. Admission is $7.00 for adults, $6.00 for seniors, and $2.00 for children ages six to twelve. The Museum's Cafe Maryhill, open 10:00 A.M. to 4:00 P.M. daily, is a good spot to have lunch. For more information on events or programs, call (509) 773–3733 or visit www.maryhillmuseum.org. Nearby Maryhill State Park is a pleasant place to camp and a popular destination for sailboarders.

After visiting Maryhill, you may want to take a short side trip to the town of Goldendale, Washington, 11 miles up U.S. 97, if for no other reason than to see the splendid mountain panorama on the plateau above the river gorge. If the weather is clear, the mountains may be "out," which is Pacific Northwest lingo for the peaks being visible. From south to north they are Mount Hood (elevation 11,235 feet), Mount Saint Helens (8,365 feet), Mount Adams (12,276 feet), and Mount Rainier (14,410 feet). Goldendale has the full range of visitor services, as well as the nation's largest telescope open to the general public at Goldendale Observatory State Park.

Horsethief Lake State Park is a satellite area of Maryhill State Park, and it is famous for its excellent Indian petroglyphs, including Tsagaglalal ("She Who Watches"), 10,000 years old and perhaps the most famous native drawing in the Northwest. Sadly, the rock art area was closed to the public after vandalism, but

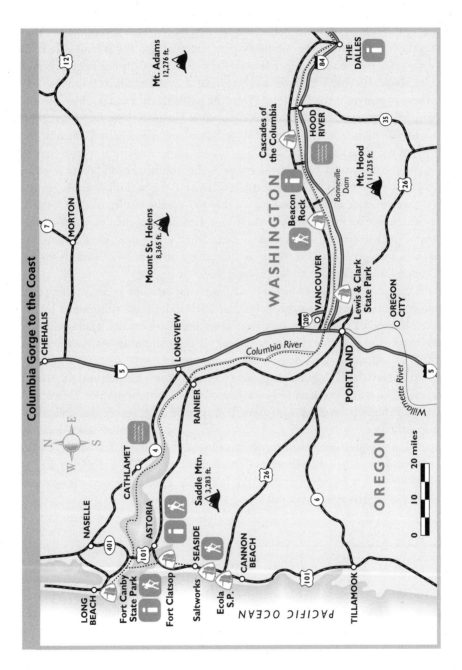

tours are still available by reservation on Friday and Saturday April through October at 10:00 A.M. For information contact the park staff or call (509) 767–1159.

On the Oregon side, the Columbia takes the starring role, even though it is little more than a lake. As have the Missouri and Snake Rivers, the Columbia has been greatly changed by the dams along its length. It's scarcely possible to imagine the raging, churning Columbia encountered by Lewis and Clark in 1805–1806. On the plus side, however, the U.S. Army Corps of Engineers provides abundant visitor facilities and recreational access at all its locations. The centers downriver at the Bonneville Dam are probably the most popular, but visitors may also want to visit the McNary Dam at Umatilla, John Day Dam (with the world's highest lock lift, 110 feet) at Rufus, and The Dalles Dam near the town of the same name.

On the Columbia Plateau, the traveler joins another historic route in addition to the one taken by Lewis and Clark. During the mid-nineteenth century, tens of thousands of Americans passed this way on the last leg of their journey to the fertile river valleys of western Oregon. Remnants of the Oregon Trail may still be seen in several locations near Interstate 84, the most notable near the town of Biggs at exit 104. Drive west from Biggs on U.S. 30 and watch for the Oregon Trail marker on the road's south side.

Celilo, not far west of Maryhill and Biggs, was once the greatest fishing area and gathering point along the Columbia River and a place still revered by the tribes who called this river gorge home. Lewis and Clark reached a falls—the first of four major obstacles they encountered on the Columbia—on October 22, 1805, and spent two days negotiating the barrier.

At Celilo, the Columbia swept into several narrow channels and dropped a total of 38 feet. The men had to portage around the greatest drop of 20 feet, and found themselves besieged with fleas. "Every man of the party was obliged to strip naked during the time of taking over the canoes, that they might have an opportunity of brushing the fleas off their legs and bodies," Clark wrote. Celilo Falls were inundated by the waters of The Dalles Dam in 1957, changing the Indians' way of life forever. Travelers who have been proceeding west on I-84 will also get their first view of Mount Hood around this area.

THE COLUMBIA RIVER GORGE

No sooner had Lewis and Clark made it through Celilo Falls than the corps was faced with The Dalles, where the river again narrowed and spilled over a great series of rapids. Here the white men amazed the local Indians by riding their canoes and much of the cargo straight through the Short Narrows. Three miles farther downriver, the party reached the Long Narrows and again shot the rapids. The exhausted corps then camped several nights at the "Rock Fort" site now surrounded by The Dalles's riverfront industrial area. To get there, take Webber Street on the west side of town north to First Street. Turn right and follow First Street to the site, which still bears much resemblance to Clark's description of "a

Dueling Interpretive Centers

The Columbia River Gorge has two major interpretive centers, set about 45 miles and a river apart. Both are worth seeing—perhaps one on your way west and another coming home.

The Dalles is home to the Columbia Gorge Discovery Center. Its many kid-friendly exhibits make this a marvelous place for families, but even grown-ups will want to "hang ten" on the see-yourself-sailboard exhibit. Look for "Cargo: The Equipment and Supplies of the Lewis and Clark Expedition" on exhibit through the bicentennial years.

You can see a vintage newsreel about the creation of the Bonneville Dam or ask questions of local Native American artists, who often spend weekends at the center demonstrating their skills. The center also includes the Wasco County Historical Museum, which has an exhibit telling how in this area, Lewis witnessed an annual ritual known as the "first salmon" ceremony. When the natives caught the first salmon of the spring, "this fish was dressed and being divided into small pieces was given to each child in the village," Lewis wrote. In this way, the natives gave thanks for the fish and hoped to ensure that the salmon would return each spring.

The Columbia Gorge Discovery Center is an impressive place, from its stunning entrance hall to its screened-in Basalt Rock Cafe and gift shop. Hours are 10:00 A.M. to 6:00 P.M. daily March 15 through December and 10:00 A.M. to 4:00 P.M. Tuesday through Sunday the rest of the year. Admission is $6.50 for adults, $5.50 for senior citizens, and $3.50 for ages six to sixteen. (Children age five and under are admitted free.) For more information call (541) 296–8600 or visit www.gorgediscovery.org.

At Stevenson, Washington, the Columbia Gorge Interpretive Center is best recommended for its occasional appearances by storyteller Merna De-Bolt, who portrays Meriwether Lewis's mother. DeBolt, a teacher by training, explains in entertaining style how Lucy Meriwether Marks taught her son the many uses of medicinal plants and herbs—knowledge he later put to use on the expedition. On a more moving note, she also shares Lucy's thoughts on whether Lewis's untimely death in 1809 was murder or suicide. Call ahead to find out when she will be performing.

Elsewhere in the center, a Lewis and Clark tapestry rug ranks among the most impressive exhibits. Created over eleven years by Gretchen Leiberg of Cheshire, Oregon, the rug includes 1.2 million stitches, including pieces from

(continued)

the suits of prominent Oregon state and U.S. officials. The tapestry is on in-definite loan from its owner, Bruce Meland of Bend, Oregon. Other exhibits at the center include a replica fish wheel (now illegal along the Columbia, for it was way too efficient in scooping up salmon) and a pit house similar to that used by the tribes Lewis and Clark encountered in the region. Take time for the impressive twelve-minute slide show, which utilizes five projectors to tell the geological story of how the gorge was formed. Center hours are 10:00 A.M. to 5:00 P.M. except New Year's Day, Thanksgiving, and Christmas. Admis-sion is $6.00 for adults, $5.00 for students and seniors, and $4.00 for children ages six to twelve. Call (509) 427–8211 for more information.

high point of rocks." A mural at 401 East Second Street in The Dalles offers an artist's interpretation of the explorers' visit.

Once they passed the Short and Long Narrows of The Dalles, Lewis and Clark had just one major obstacle remaining: the Cascades of the Columbia. On the way there, the party enjoyed several days of relatively calm waters between The Dalles and Hood River. But although the water was placid, relations with the region's Indians were not; in fact, tensions rose higher here than in any place since the Teton Sioux country back in South Dakota.

Unlike the friendly bands at the confluence of the Snake and Columbia, many of the Indians farther downriver partook in thievery, deception, and beg-ging, perhaps influenced by their past experiences with early white traders near the mouth of the Columbia. (It was in the mid-Columbia region that Lewis and Clark first saw wool clothing and blankets, powder flasks, and guns, all signs of other whites preceding them from the west.) Moreover, many of the Columbia River people were infested with fleas or lice, afflictions they passed on to the newcomers. As the corps moved through the Celilo-Dalles stretch, either Twisted Hair or Tetoharsky of the Nez Perce heard a rumor that one of the local tribes planned to attack the white men. This story may have sprung from the Nez Perce's own mistrust of the Columbia River tribes—both men decided to leave the corps and return home after the passage through The Dalles—but the cap-tains decided not to take any chances. With the local Indians watching, the men made a great show of examining their stores of weapons and ammunition, mak-ing sure all were in proper working order.

The Corps of Discovery successfully made it through the last water barrier, the Cascades of the Columbia, on November 1–2, 1805. The rapids here were known as the Upper and Lower Cascades; Clark came to call the upper rapids "the Great Chute." The baggage was portaged through this area, but the empty canoes once again made it through the rapids unscathed. Soon after the passage, Clark noted in his journal the presence of "a remarkable high rock . . . about 800

Columbia Gorge Discovery Center at The Dalles, Oregon.

Portland Travel Tips

Portland International Airport (PDX) is served by most major airlines and rental car companies. Amtrak serves Portland's Union station at 800 Northwest Sixth Avenue; Greyhound is at 550 Northwest Sixth Avenue.

Portland has excellent public transportation via buses (Tri-Met) and light rail (MAX), with passengers riding free in "Fareless Square" (most of the downtown area) and for $1.55 or less to other destinations, including the airport. For schedules and other information, visit the Tri-Met office at Pioneer Courthouse Square, Portland's main downtown gathering place at Broadway and Yamhill, call (503) 238–7433, or visit www.trimet.org.

feet high and 400 yards round." He named it Beacon Rock, and it is among the world's largest freestanding rock monoliths.

The Dalles area marks the traveler's entrance into the Columbia River Gorge National Scenic Area, the first region so designated in the United States. Quite simply, the gorge is an area of sublime scenic splendor and recreational choices so abundant it would take weeks to exhaust the possibilities. Once again, the traveler has a choice of driving Oregon's I-84 or WA 14 through the gorge (with the U.S. 197 bridge at The Dalles offering the last free river crossing until the Portland-Vancouver metropolitan area). Both sides have plenty to offer. We'll look at I-84 first.

Hood River is unofficial gorge headquarters, and the town has changed dramatically with the influx of sailboarders, rock climbers, bungee jumpers, and other (mostly) youthful adventurers. Hood River plays host to some of the world's premier sailboarding competitions (notably Wind Fest in late June and the Gorge Games in late July), as well as a full calendar of events such as the Hood River Valley Harvest Festival each October. Hood River also serves as a gateway to Mount Hood, with OR 35 south of town traversing the south shoulder of Oregon's highest peak.

Cascade Locks is home port for the stern-wheeler *Columbia Gorge,* a pleasure boat that offers two-hour sightseeing cruises each afternoon in summer. Each sailing includes narration about the Lewis and Clark Expedition and the Oregon Trail. The stern-wheeler is a good way to get to know the gorge, or at least a small part of it. Tickets cost $15.00 for adults and $9.00 for children. Call (800) 643–1354 or visit www.sternwheeler.com for current times or information on Bonneville Locks dinner cruises, champagne brunch sailings, or other specialty trips.

A natural bridge once spanned the Columbia River near what is now Cascade Locks. Indian legend traces this "Bridge of the Gods" to Ka'nax, a chief who ruled the tribes on both sides of the Columbia. Ka'nax used the bridge to carry on love affairs with two different princesses: Wy'east (Mount Hood) and Pahto

Horsetail Falls, Columbia River Gorge.

(Mount Adams). Ultimately the gods of these two mountains destroyed the natural bridge, ending both the romances and Ka'nax's reign. Scientists explain it a bit differently, but with similar results. Around A.D. 1100, a massive landslide crumbled the bridge and created several sets of rapids within a 5-mile stretch of the Columbia River—the same rapids that slowed Lewis and Clark's passage in 1805.

If you visit only one dam on your Lewis and Clark journey, Bonneville Dam is a good choice. It has visitor facilities on both the Washington and Oregon sides, and each tells the important role hydropower plays in the Northwest economy. The Washington-side visitor center also has an exhibit explaining the archaeological dig of villages noted in the Lewis and Clark journals of October 1805. But the centers' most popular exhibits are doubtless the fish-viewing windows. Children especially enjoy watching salmon swim through the mazelike fish ladders that have been erected to help fish past the dams. People employed as fish counters sit by a window all day and keep tabs on how many fish swim by. This close to the Pacific, the numbers are high. But the salmon have many more dams to pass before they reach their spawning grounds upriver. For wild salmon, life in the Columbia River is more than ever an uphill struggle for survival.

Just west of Bonneville, I-84 travelers have the opportunity to leave the freeway and drive the Columbia River Scenic Highway, a 22-mile masterpiece of en-

Native American fishing platforms along the Columbia River.

Touring Portland and Vancouver

T wo great metropolitan areas anchor the Lewis and Clark Trail: St. Louis, Gateway to the West, and Portland, Gateway to the Pacific. Oregon's largest city is growing by leaps and bounds but still manages to preserve the Northwest outpost character that so endears it to residents and visitors alike.

Several Portland sights are of special interest to the Lewis and Clark aficionado. A striking statue of Sacagawea by sculptress Alice Cooper sits in the city's Washington Park. A trompe l'oeil mural at the Oregon Historical Society, corner of Park and Madison in downtown Portland, depicts an almost-lifelike Lewis, Clark, York, Sacagawea, Pomp, and Seaman. Inside the center, the Historical Society offers permanent and changing exhibits on Northwest history. (The museum is closed for renovations through summer 2003 and will reopen in September 2003.) Finally, the lobby of the Governor Hotel at 611 Southwest Tenth downtown features several murals honoring the Lewis and Clark Expedition.

Naturally, many Portlanders spend their free time fleeing town to the slopes of Mount Hood or the beaches of the windswept Oregon Coast. But anyone deciding to stay and explore the city itself has plenty of options from which to choose. Portland is a city of parks, with 4,700-acre Forest Park on the west side leading the way. This beauty spot boasts hiking trails and picnic grounds with spectacular views of the city. It is also close to Washington Park, home of the Metro Washington Park Zoo, the World Forestry Center, and an impressive Japanese Garden. Alder Creek Kayak & Canoe, right on the Columbia at 250 Northeast Tomahawk Island Drive, doesn't currently lead any Lewis and Clark–oriented trips, but the company rents gear and offers classes. Call (503) 285-0464, or visit www.aldercreek.com.

Weekends between March and December, the Portland Saturday Market beneath the Burnside Bridge offers wares from more than 250 artists, craftspeople, and fresh produce sellers. Food to eat on the premises and a wide array of entertainment are also available, and the market is open Sunday as well as Saturday. Families flock to the acclaimed Oregon Museum of Science and Industry (OMSI) at 1945 Southeast Water Avenue for its interactive exhibits, planetarium presentations, and OMNIMAX Theater shows.

Special events in Portland include the Rose Festival, which takes place annually each June and lasts several weeks. Downtown Portland is known for its public gathering places and eclectic architecture. Northwest Twenty-third

(continued)

Avenue is another interesting area, full of shops and strolling people. For more information on Portland-area attractions, call the Portland/Oregon Visitors Association at (877) 678–5263 or (503) 275–8355 locally, visit www.pova.com, or stop at the visitor center at Pioneer Courthouse Square.

Vancouver, the oldest city in Washington State, has a population of about 127,000. It sits right across the river from Portland, offering its residents what may be the best of both worlds: life in a large metropolitan area combined with Vancouver's lingering small-city feel and easy access to recreation. Because of these attributes, Vancouver has twice been named an "All-American City." The Clark County Fair, held early each August, is one of the nation's ten largest.

In the years following Lewis and Clark's explorations, Fort Vancouver became an important way station for trappers, traders, and immigrants on their way to the Oregon country. The fort was established by the Hudson's Bay Company in 1824, which hoped to secure Britain's claim to Oregon by moving its Northwest headquarters inland from the mouth of the Columbia. But by 1846 Britain's hopes of claiming Oregon were dashed when the Northwest Territory was divided along the forty-ninth parallel (the current United States–Canada boundary), not the Columbia River, as the British had hoped.

Fort Vancouver is now a national historic site. Its stockade and several major buildings have been reconstructed on their original locations. Visitors are welcome from 9:00 A.M. to 5:00 P.M. daily March through October and from 9:00 A.M. to 4:00 P.M. the rest of the year. Admission is $3.00 per person or $5.00 for a family. This is the site of a gala Fourth of July celebration often cited as one of the Northwest's best. For more information on Vancouver, contact the Vancouver/Clark County Visitor and Convention Bureau at (206) 693–1313.

gineering that provides close-up access to the famous gorge waterfalls as well as to Crown Point, a promontory 733 feet above the river.

Each set of falls has its own character and beauty. Horsetail Falls unfurls like a banner, while Wahkeena Falls cascades in a mass of curlicues. Multnomah Falls is world-famous and easily accessed from the interstate, as is Bridal Veil Falls. And that's just the start. Other falls can be reached by trails. The gorge is a hiking paradise, with a multitude of paths snaking through shady side canyons and up mountain grades. For hiking information stop by any Forest Service office. A few favorites include the Eagle Creek Trail to Punch Bowl Falls (exit 41); Dog Mountain Trail, a challenging hike that starts between Bingen and Stevenson on the Washington side; and the Oneonta Gorge. Rooster Rock State Park near Troutdale is popular with swimmers and windsurfers, with a separate nude sunbathing area designated about a mile to the east. Lewis and Clark named Rooster Rock and camped in the area on November 2, 1805, and April 7–8, 1806.

The scenic route ends at Troutdale just east of Portland. Nearby is Lewis and Clark State Park, where a self-guiding nature trail showcases the local plants chronicled by the expedition. The small state park is near the Sandy River, where the expedition stopped November 3 on their final push to the Pacific. They found the river silty and shallow, and when Clark tried to wade across, he found the bottom like quicksand. So the captains named the waterway "Quicksand River" and explored along its shore for about 1.5 miles before returning to make camp on Government Island in the Columbia. On the trip home the corps again camped near the mouth of the Sandy, and several men explored about 6 miles up the river. They learned from local Indians that they had already passed the major tributary of the Columbia they had been seeking—the Willamette River—so Clark and several men backtracked to explore 10 miles up the Willamette from modern-day Portland.

On the Washington side, WA 14 remains an absolute delight, dominated by interesting little towns and stupendous views of Mount Hood. The Cascades are strikingly different from the Rocky Mountains, and they must have seemed strange to Lewis and Clark. The corps had grown used to the jagged, sawtooth contours of the Rockies, which frequently stretched out one ridge after another. The Cascade peaks, on the other hand, stand alone. These snowy sentinels seem almost to hover in midair, dwarfing everything around them. (Remember the average elevation in the valleys here is less than 100 feet above sea level, unlike the high valleys of the Rockies, where towns sit at 3,000 to 5,000 feet.) Mount Hood and its Cascade cousins are, of course, volcanic in nature, thus their conical shapes and isolated placement.

If the Columbia River Gorge is the nation's top sailboarding area, then Doug's Beach State Park east of Lyle, Washington, is the sport's epicenter. Hood River, the hip town downriver, may be where people work, eat, and sleep, but Doug's Beach is where they play. People interested in learning sailboarding will find several Gorge-area businesses eager to help. And although Doug's Beach is the place to see and be seen, many other less-crowded areas are better bets for novice sailboarders as well as for people who crave a more solitary sailing experience.

The twin towns of Bingen and White Salmon sit right across the river (and a toll bridge) from Hood River. Bingen has a winery, Mont Elise, with tours and tastings. The White Salmon River is popular for rafting, kayaking, and fishing. Both towns boast a number of German-style buildings, including the Glockenspiel Tower in White Salmon.

Carson is a gateway to Mount Saint Helens, as well as the site of Carson Hot Springs. Here visitors are treated to hot mineral baths, massages, and towel wraps. Lodging, meals, and RV hookups are available. The best time to visit is on a weekday; folks from Portland and even Seattle crowd in on the weekends.

Beacon Rock in the Columbia River Gorge.

Bonneville Dam's Washington-side visitor center is situated between Stevenson and North Bonneville. The latter is a planned community in every sense of the word: The entire town was moved to its present location before construction began on Bonneville Dam's second powerhouse. The new town was dedicated in 1978.

Beacon Rock, just west of Bonneville Dam, is truly immense, to use one of the captains' favorite words. It was here Lewis and Clark first saw the effects of the tide as it rolled in from the Pacific. They didn't yet know they were still 142 river miles from the coast!

The remnants of a volcanic core, Beacon Rock is composed of basalt and has been eroded for years by the river. As the Oregon territory was settled, the 848-foot monolith was for years known as Castle Rock, but it has reclaimed its previous name. Interestingly enough, Henry J. Biddle, a descendant of Nicholas Biddle, early editor of the Lewis and Clark journals, once owned the rock. Biddle built the first trail to its top, completing it in 1918 after two years of work.

Today's trail is 4,500 feet long with a 15-percent grade and handrails lining most of the way. It's possible to hike to the top in about a half hour, but the trek isn't recommended for people wary of heights. Advanced rock climbers are also welcome to try an ascent off the trail, but all climbers must register, and no technical climbing is allowed on the south face during falcon nesting season (February 1–July 15). Required equipment for climbers includes a hard hat, two

150-foot climbing ropes, clothes for any change in the weather, a standard rack for fifth-class climbing, rappelling equipment, proper footwear, and a headlamp for the longer routes.

Beacon Rock State Park actually overlooks the rock from the north side of WA 14. It has a small campground and picnic facilities, as well as several hiking trailheads. The picnic area just down the road from the campground affords a good view of Beacon Rock, particularly at sunrise and sunset.

For more information on activities and attractions in the Columbia River Gorge, call (509) 427-8911 (Skamania County, Washington); (800) 366-3530 (Hood River); or (800) 255-3385 (The Dalles). From Beacon Rock continue west on hilly and winding WA 14, or backtrack to Stevenson, cross the Bridge of the Gods, and proceed west via I-84 or the Columbia River Scenic Highway.

TO THE PACIFIC

From Vancouver or Portland, the traveler has three major options for getting to the Washington and Oregon coasts, the final westbound destination of our heroes. The fastest choice by far is U.S. Highway 26—the Sunset Highway—best accessed via the Interstate 405 beltway around downtown Portland. This route strays the farthest from Lewis and Clark's river route, but it is the best option if time is of the essence. U.S. 30 out of northwest Portland stays close to the river on a two-lane crawl through heavy forests and small towns, winding up in Astoria. Washington Highways 4 and 401 also take their time meandering along the river west from Longview/Kelso to the Long Beach Peninsula, although travelers choosing this option get a jump on things by taking I-5 north from Vancouver to Longview.

For travelers desiring a scenic approach or the closest route to that of Lewis and Clark, the best approach is probably a hybrid of the slower options: I-5 to Washington 432 (at exit 36), then west to WA 433 (Oregon Way), which crosses the Columbia to U.S. 30 via the Lewis and Clark Bridge between Longview, Washington, and Rainier, Oregon. Kayakers and canoeists have yet another option: taking to the river along the Lewis and Clark Columbia River Water Trail (see below). This route follows the free-flowing Lower Columbia from Bonneville Dam to the coast (or at least as far as Gray's Bay, where the dangerous Columbia River bar looms and small boaters need to bail out). Whichever way you choose, try to preserve historical order in your coastal explorations by starting on the Washington side, as the Corps of Discovery did.

As the Corps of Discovery pressed down the last stretch of the Columbia River, the captains noted more sightings of Indians who already possessed white men's trade goods. They also marveled at the natives' large, ornate, and high-prowed canoes, much more suited to the turbulent Columbia than the explorers' dugouts. But most of all they spoke and wrote of unceasing rain—a phenomenon that would prove the hallmark of the corps' winter on the coast.

On November 7, 1805, the party camped near Pillar Rock, a site just east of the small modern-day town of Altoona, Washington. "Great joy in camp," Clark reported. "We are in view of the ocean, this great Pacific Ocean which we have been so long anxious to see, and the roaring or noise made by the waves breaking on the rocky shores (as I suppose) may be heard distinctly." Historians long believed that Clark wasn't quite right. They reasoned that his view of the ocean would have been blocked and he was actually only seeing Gray's Bay, named for American ship captain Robert Gray, who in 1792 became the first Euro-American to explore the mouth of the Columbia. But local historian Rex Ziak makes a strong case that the modern-day jetty that today blocks the distant vista from Pillar Rock didn't exist in 1805, so the expedition would have indeed been "in view of the ocean." Ziak details the expedition's stay on the Washington coast in his book *In Full View*, published in 2002 by Moffitt House Press.

Many Lewis and Clark buffs are intrigued by the idea of paddling part of the expedition's final stretch toward the ocean, and this is possible on the newly mapped Lower Columbia River Water Trail. (See the Bike It or Boat It section in Chapter 2.) According to Keith Hay, author of a guidebook to the route, the trail splits at Skamokawa (see below), with the southern route following the Oregon coast to Astoria. This south-side stretch is safe for most paddlers under good weather conditions, since it stays out of the main channel of the river and is largely protected by the islands of the Lewis & Clark National Wildlife Refuge.

The northern route following the Washington shore is for experienced open-water paddlers only. It's subject to strong winds and ship wakes, and there are no protected bays or sloughs, nor are there any camping areas or road access points until Gray's Bay and Deep River. Paddlers planning to take this route need to be experienced in self-rescue and able to read navigational charts to stay out of the way of shipping traffic. Unguided boaters should also wear a wet suit to prevent hypothermia in the event of capsize.

Skamokawa (pronounced Ska-MOCK-away), Washington, about 20 miles from the ocean, is the hub of canoeing and sea kayaking action on the Lower Columbia. The small town is close to both the Julia Butler Hansen National Wildlife Refuge on the Washington side and the Lewis & Clark National Wildlife Refuge, with 35,000 acres of mudflats, tidal marshes, open water, and islands on the Oregon side. Skamokawa Paddle Center rents canoes ($50/full day), kayaks ($35–50/day), and bicycles ($12/day). The center also has half-day tours starting about $60, which are great for beginners, and overnight trips ($178 per person, double occupancy). Many Elderhostel programs are held here, and lodging is available. Call (888) 920–2777 or visit www.skamokawakayak. com for details.

Columbia River Kayaking, also based in Skamokawa, offers a variety of four-to-six-day sea kayaking tours—some camping out each night, others featuring overnight stays at bed-and-breakfast inns or motels. Trips were priced in 2002 from $649 to $1,119 per person. All tours feature American Canoe Association–approved instruction in sea kayaking. Call (360) 795–8300 or visit www.columbiariverseakayaking.com for more information on upcoming trips. The Web site also has a comprehensive section on how to plan a do-it-yourself trip on the Lower Columbia.

Skamokawa also is home to the River Life Interpretive Center in an 1894 building once used as a schoolhouse and fraternal lodge. It now has exhibits on the river's natural and human history, along with a great view of the Columbia from the bell tower. West of town, Skamokawa Vista Park has camping and a great vantage point for seeing ships cross the Columbia River Bar.

From Gray's Bay, progress down the river was slow, no doubt much slower than the captains would have liked. On November 8 the corps pulled over to shore after finding the waves so high "that we thought it imprudent to proceed," Clark wrote. The next day, "monstrous trees" set afloat by a high afternoon tide nearly smashed the party's beached canoes. On November 10 the corps advanced all of 2 miles before high winds returned, compelling them to once again make camp. "We are all wet as usual and our situation is truly a disagreeable one," Clark wrote on November 11. On November 15, noting the eleventh straight day of rain, Clark railed: "…the most disagreeable time I have ever experienced…. I can neither get out to hunt, return to a better situation, or proceed on."

Yet later that same day, the winds abated and the party pressed on. Again, the captains made but a few miles, but it was far enough. Now there was no doubt: they had reached the Pacific Ocean. Noting the sweeping tide and immense waves, "I concluded to form a camp on the highest spot I could find in the marshy bottom, and proceed no further by water as the coast becomes very dangerous for crafts of the size of our canoes," Clark wrote, adding that "the ocean is immediately in front and gives us an extensive view of it from Cape Disappointment to Point Adams." Camp was made, and the corps stayed put November 15-24, 1805, while various parties went off to explore the coast.

"Station Camp" is now marked at a roadside picnic area about 2 miles west of the bridge from Astoria, Oregon, on U.S. 101. The area includes a historic marker and a large wooden statue of the captains looking out to sea. It's a fairly scruffy site for now, but major improvements are planned by 2005. Look for a realignment of U.S. 101 and better interpretation of the expedition's long stay on the Washington coast. To learn more about developments in the area, visit the Pacific County Friends of Lewis and Clark's Web site at www.lewisandclarkwa. com.

U.S. 101 proceeds through the towns of Chinook and Ilwaco. At Ilwaco, WA 103 heads up the Long Beach Peninsula, while a spur route provides access to

Fort Canby State Park and its Lewis and Clark Interpretive Center on Cape Disappointment. The center has always done a superb job detailing the expedition, but renovations set to be done by summer 2003 will include new displays with more interactive elements and a stronger focus on the corps' time along the Columbia River and on the coast.

The center has a good collection of artifacts related to Patrick Gass, including such items as his family Bible, expense account journal, metal flask, and a razor box believed to been carved and given to Gass by Sacagawea. The exhibits culminate at a picture-perfect, floor-to-ceiling window view of the Columbia River Bar and the Pacific Ocean beyond. It was likely near this spot that Clark stood with his men on November 18, 1805, and viewed with wonder "the high waves dashing against the rocks and this immense ocean." Lewis and a separate party explored the area earlier and probably saw this exact view.

The interpretive center is open from 10:00 A.M. to 5:00 P.M. daily year-round. A small admission fee will be charged once the renovations are complete. For more information call (360) 642–3029.

Following a visit to the center, be sure to explore more of the grounds. Cape Disappointment was named by British sea captain and fur trader John Meares, who visited the area in 1788 in an attempt to confirm the presence of a large river in the vicinity. Failing to do so, he named the promontory Cape Disappointment. Although others had speculated on the river's existence, it took American Robert Gray four more years to cross the Columbia River Bar and explore nearly 100 miles upriver.

A trail leads to the Cape Disappointment Lighthouse, built in 1856 and the oldest one remaining in use along the West Coast. The lighthouse isn't generally open to the public, but it's easy to look in, and personnel on duty are happy to step out and answer visitors' questions. Ask about the treacherous Columbia Bar or the Coast Guard's Motor Lifeboat School, where students learn to conduct rescue operations on the world's most predictably rough surf. Another commonly asked question is: "Where does the river stop and the ocean begin?" The truth is, the river current is detected several miles out into the ocean at a spot the Coast Guard calls Buoy 2, while brackish seawater is often found upriver all the way past Cathlamet, so pinpointing a precise dividing line is just about impossible.

The lighthouse vicinity also affords a good view of the rest of Cape Disappointment, including the bluff on which the visitor center sits and the Pacific Ocean beyond. It all makes a fine picture from this angle. The lighthouse trail also boasts a short, steep side trail leading to a scenic beach called Dead Man's Hollow tucked in a tiny bay—a perfect place for a picnic, despite the grisly name. Other places worth exploring within the park include lovely little Waikiki Beach and the North Head Lighthouse, which is open for tours daily. Two lighthouse keepers' residences at North Head can be rented. Each has three bedrooms, one bath, a full kitchen, and living and dining rooms. Prices vary with the season. To make a reservation up to a year in advance, call park headquarters at (360) 642–3078.

Fort Canby State Park has a large campground with about 250 sites, but it is dwarfed by Fort Stevens State Park across the Columbia in Oregon, which has more than 600 sites. Despite these parks' gargantuan proportions, visitors can forget about just driving in and finding a site during summer. In fact, it's essential to make reservations for any state park campgrounds on the Pacific Coast well before peak vacation season. Fort Stevens State Park has yurts available for rent, too, but these go especially fast, so call well ahead of time. For more information on reserving a campsite on the coast, call (888) CAMPOUT in Washington or (800) 452–5687 in Oregon. Private campgrounds often are less crowded, but it's still wise to call and secure a spot in advance.

Washington's Long Beach Peninsula is heavily oriented to tourists. Visitors will find plenty of restaurant choices and legions of motels and campgrounds, although many will be full on summer weekends, especially during the kite festival in mid-August. The town of Long Beach is the peninsula's largest, a quintessential beach community. Stop amid the bustle of its main drag (Highway 103, also called the Pacific Highway) to admire a statue that shows Clark marking his name on a tree. The World Kite Museum at 112 Third Street Northwest is the only one of its kind anywhere, with exhibits that trace 2,000 years of kite-flying history and a kite-making table for kids. It's open daily Memorial Day through Labor Day and Friday through Monday the rest of the year.

Long Beach also has a great boardwalk with exhibits that explain the many shipwrecks that have occurred along the Columbia River Bar, where clouds, sandbars, and ceaseless drizzle all wreak havoc with navigation. In all, about 2,000 boats have been wrecked or sunk and some 700 lives lost.

A new Discovery Trail winds along the oceanfront, paralleling the coastal explorations of Lewis and Clark. A 2-mile segment is in place now, and plans call for it to eventually wind from Long Beach to Fort Canby State Park.

Ilwaco is another peninsula town worth a few hours of exploration. More subdued than Long Beach, it has a small but growing collection of shops and restaurants (plus a fun Saturday Market) in its port area. There's some Lewis and Clark interpretation at the Ilwaco Heritage Museum, 115 Southeast Lake Street, where you'll also find a fascinating exhibit and film on Gerald d'Aboville's 134-day solo kayak trip across the Pacific from Japan to Ilwaco. The museum is open daily in summer and Monday through Saturday in winter; call (360) 642–3446. For more information on Long Beach Peninsula activities and attractions, call (800) 451–2542 or visit www.funbeach.com.

Secluded beach at Cape Disappointment, Fort Canby State Park, Washington.

FORT CLATSOP NATIONAL MEMORIAL

By late November, it had become clear that the corps would not be able to stay on the Washington side of the coast. There was little game, and the explorers were sick of eating salmon and roots—goods they had to purchase from the local Indians at a high price. Moreover, there was the interminable rain and rotting clothing, bedding, and spirits.

Lewis and Clark had heard game was more plentiful on the south shore of the Columbia and hoped that a suitable camp might be established close to both a freshwater river, which they'd had difficulty finding on the north side, and a seawater source from which they could make salt. Moreover, by staying close to the ocean, they increased their chances of meeting any trading ships that pulled into the Columbia harbors. Jefferson had instructed Lewis to send two men and a copy of his notes back by sea if a suitable vessel could be found—though the likelihood of seeing such a ship in winter was small.

Still, many members of the expedition had other ideas. Sick of the damp weather, they talked of moving back up the Columbia to spend the winter in a drier climate. Eager to reach a consensus before winter, the captains decided to put the matter to a vote on November 24, 1805, extending the franchise to York and Sacagawea as well as to the enlisted men. As Stephen Ambrose noted in *Undaunted Courage:* "It was the first time in American history that a black slave had voted, the first time a woman had voted." Based on scouting reports from Lewis, who'd gone over to examine the options, the party agreed to check out the south shore and stay there if enough game was available. The decision made, the party moved back to the vicinity of Pillar Rock and prepared to cross to the other side. Before they left, Clark carved his name in a tree, adding "December 3rd 1805. By Land. U. States in 1804-05."

The Corps of Discovery had a dangerous paddle across the Columbia to reach its new winter camp at the site of present-day Fort Clatsop National Memorial. Today the trip is as easy as driving over the 4-mile-long bridge from Megler, Washington, to Astoria, Oregon. To get to Fort Clatsop from Astoria, follow the signs for Warrenton and Seaside. Both U.S. Highway 101 and the 101 business loop lead there, and both routes are marked. (Motorists taking U.S. 101 should get into the left-hand turn lane as soon as possible after crossing Youngs Bay from Astoria to Warrenton.) Turn left onto Marlin Avenue, then left at the next stop sign.

Fort Clatsop is among the very best interpretive sites along the Lewis and Clark route. Exhibits, short hiking trails, and living-history programs combine to give visitors a comprehensive picture of the expedition's winter on the Pacific Coast. It's an especially interesting place for kids, who really delight in the summer living history programs (and are often invited to take part). Don't miss the fort replica, lovingly furnished in detail and staffed by National Park rangers who will answer any and all questions. The first Fort Clatsop rotted within ten to fifteen years of its occupancy, reclaimed by the soggy coastal climate. The wood in the replica is now treated every year to make sure the fort escapes the fate of its predecessor.

In 1901 the Oregon Historical Society started searching for the original fort site. But it wasn't until the expedition's 150th anniversary in 1955 that the replica was built, its construction based on floor plan drawings and descriptions from the expedition journals. Archaeologists (including, most recently, Ken Karsmizki of the Columbia Gorge Discovery Center and Julie Stein of the University of Washington) have not pinpointed the fort's exact location, but they are certain it was near the current replica.

During most of the journey, the captains and their corps shared very similar conditions. Here at Fort Clatsop, however, rank had its privileges. The fort measured about 50 feet square, with two rows of huts separated by a parade ground. One row had three small rooms, two of which measured 16 feet by 15 feet, with the other 15 feet by 18 feet. These were the enlisted men's quarters, each housing eight men. The other row held four rooms, the largest of which was the captains' quarters. Charbonneau, Sacagawea, and Pomp had another room for their own. An orderly room housed the sergeant of the guard and his three men, a rotating assignment. It's not known exactly where York lived, but he may have slept in the orderly room, too. The fourth room was used for smoking and storing meat.

There were also differences in the daily routine. After the voyage's original shakedown period, all the men generally pulled together, everyone more or less equal. But when they arrived at Fort Clatsop, the captains realized they would have to restore a level of military discipline. Sentries were always posted. Weapons were cleaned and inspected each day. Without some regimentation, the men may have started deserting to go live with the Indians after just a few weeks at their soggy outpost.

And it was rainy. In fact it rained 94 days that winter, all but 12 days of their stay. Of the 106 days spent at the site, only 6 were sunny. The men spent their time in various ways: hunting, updating maps and journals (and plotting their return routes), and sewing elk-hide moccasins for the trip home. Each man made about ten pairs of shoes during the winter's stay. That may sound like a lot of moccasins, but each pair typically lasted only ten days before wearing out.

There was game, but it was of dubious quality. On Christmas Day 1805 Clark wrote: "We would have spent this day the nativity of Christ in feasting, had we anything either to raise our spirits or even gratify our appetites. Our dinner consisted of poor elk, so much spoiled that we ate it through mere necessity, some spoiled pounded fish, and a few roots." Dogs, too, remained part of the diet. The men were also plagued by fleas—all but Lewis. Sally Freeman, a ranger

Historic interpretive program at Fort Clatsop National Memorial near Astoria, Oregon.

at Fort Clatsop, theorizes that Lewis's canine companion, Seaman, may have deflected the pests from his master.

All in all, it was a difficult winter. But again, the captains were able to gain information from the nearby Indians who, although reportedly prone to thievery, were friendly. And there were occasional diversions, such as the trip Clark and others made to see a beached whale on the ocean shore, and of other sorts: Lewis reported on January 27, "Goodrich has recovered from the Louis Veneri which he contracted from an amorous contact with a Chinook damsel. I cured him as I did Gibson last winter by the use of mercury." (Interestingly, since the men excreted the insoluble mercury, finding high mercury levels in the soil may help archaeologists pinpoint the location of the privy, if not Fort Clatsop itself.)

Save some time to stop inside the park's visitor center. One display right by the visitor center entrance describes exactly where the Corps of Discovery was in its voyage during any given day you might visit. Another records the pay level of each expedition member, the roles each played in the mission, and comments from the captains on each. Drouillard was paid $833, Charbonneau earned $490, but Sacagawea received nothing. Most of the comments made about the men were complimentary, but Charbonneau proved an exception. "A man of no particular merit. Was useful as an interpreter only," Lewis wrote, perhaps remembering the near-disastrous episodes with the white pirogue on the Missouri River. Clark was more kind, saying: "You have conducted yourself in such a

Dugout canoe replica at Fort Clatsop.

manner as to gain my friendship." Of Sacagawea, Clark added to Charbonneau, "Your woman on that long, dangerous, and fatiguing route deserved a better reward than we had in our power to give her." And of Pomp, he said, "As for your little son, my boy Pomp, you well know my fondness for him and my anxiety to take and raise him as my own child." Pomp was indeed adopted by Clark, educated in St. Louis and Europe, worked as a frontier interpreter and guide, and died in Oregon in 1866. He is buried in eastern Oregon's Jordan Valley.

The corps originally planned to leave April 1, but hunting became difficult weeks earlier as the elk moved back to the mountains. Moreover, the warming temperatures gave the men a good case of spring fever, so they departed Fort Clatsop March 23, 1806. On that day Clark wrote in his journal: "At this place we had wintered and remained from the 7th of December 1805 to this day and have lived as well as we had any right to expect."

Fort Clatsop is open daily from 8:00 A.M. to 6:00 P.M. mid-June through Labor Day and 8:00 A.M. to 5:00 P.M. daily the rest of the year. The park is closed on Christmas. Admission is $3.00 per person with a maximum of $5.00 per family. Admission tickets are good for a week. For more information call (503) 861–2471 or visit www.nps.gov/focl.

Astoria is a fascinating historic town worth a look either before or after Fort Clatsop. The Astoria Column atop Coxcomb Hill pays tribute to Lewis and Clark and others who led American westward expansion. A 164-step circular stairway leads to the top of the 125-foot column and great views of the area. The drive to Coxcomb Hill gives visitors a good glimpse of the Victorian architecture of Astoria, the first American settlement in the Northwest.

The Columbia River Maritime Museum is one of the best of its kind. In addition to seeing exhibits on seafaring history, visitors can tour the lightship *Columbia,* which not so long ago was the last seagoing lighthouse on the West Coast. Union soldiers at nearby Fort Stevens guarded the mouth of the Columbia during the Civil War, and in 1942 Fort Stevens became the only American military installation in the continental United States to be fired upon by foreigners since the War of 1812. A Japanese submarine fired seventeen shells at the fort. There was no damage.

If you're caught in Astoria on a rainy day, consider spending some time at the city's Aquatic Center at 1997 Marine Drive. This year-round facility has everything from wading pools to water slides—even a river channel. (Betcha you can't float it just once.) If the weather's fine, head instead to Youngs River Falls, a 65-foot cascade found by one of the Corps of Discovery's hunting parties. The falls are along the Youngs River Loop Road south of U.S. 101 between Astoria and Warrenton. Other outdoor highlights in the area include the Lewis & Clark National Wildlife Refuge/Twilight Creek Eagle Sanctuary east of Astoria on U.S. 30 and Sunset Beach on the Pacific Ocean south of Warrenton. For more information on Astoria and Oregon's north coast, call (800) 875–6807 or visit www. oldoregon.com.

Pacific Wave Kayak at 21 U.S. 101 in Warrenton rents kayaks and canoes and is a good source of information on local paddling. Although none of its standard tours is specifically related to Lewis and Clark, they do offer several excursions on the Lower Columbia and other nearby rivers. They can also outfit you for an easy trip up the Lewis & Clark River past Fort Clatsop. For more information call (888) 223–9794 or visit www.pacwave.net.

From Astoria or Fort Clatsop, continue south on U.S. 101 to Seaside, home of the expedition's saltworks, and to the picturesque Oregon coastline of Cannon Beach.

SEASIDE AND ECOLA STATE PARK

By the time it reached the Pacific, the expedition had long since run out of salt for preserving and flavoring food, so shortly after the party's arrival at Fort Clatsop, Captain Lewis ordered that a salt cairn be established near the camp. After a search of five days by Clark, a suitable location was found in what is now the town of Seaside, about 14 miles south of Fort Clatsop. (There will soon be a hiking trail following Clark's route from the fort to the ocean.)

The operation was established on January 2, 1806, by the expedition's three saltmakers: Joseph Field, William Bratton, and George Gibson. They remained on the site until February 20 and were able to produce about four bushels of salt by boiling seawater day and night, laboriously walking back and forth the 100 paces to and from the ocean. Sampling an early batch on January 5, Lewis pronounced it "excellent, fine, strong, and white. This was a great treat to myself and most of the party . . . I say most of the party for my friend Captain Clark declares it to be a mere matter of indifference with him whether he uses it or not; for myself I must confess I felt a considerable inconvenience from the want of it."

A replica of the saltworks remains in its original location. To get there, take Avenue G west off U.S. Highway 101 to South Beach Drive and follow the signs. (Better yet, since parking is at a premium, walk down the South Prom from central Seaside and turn left on Lewis and Clark Way.) The site is now officially part of Fort Clatsop National Memorial. Several weekends each year, Fort Clatsop sends a living-history team to the coast to reenact the salt makers' camp on the ocean a few blocks from the replica. Visitors are greeted by a sign which reads YOU ARE NOW ENTERING THE YEAR 1806 and by gung-ho interpreters who will regale you with lots of tales of camp life—but who won't know a thing about whatever happened beyond that year.

You Are Now
Entering the
Year 1806

The living history camp at Seaside, Oregon, is fun for all ages.

End-of-the-trail monument at Seaside, Oregon.

Seaside is the most commercial town on the north Oregon coast, with lots of shopping, several good restaurants, and all kinds of entertainment ranging from an aquarium to carnival rides and lots of nightlife. Surprisingly, however, morning may be the best time to explore the coastal towns of Oregon and Washington. The beaches and boardwalks are nearly empty, allowing perfect conditions for a leisurely stroll. Moreover, almost every town has a great local bakery or coffee shop where you can pick up a cup of java and a snack for the trip.

Seaside's main commercial drag ends near the beach at what is called "the turnaround." A statue of Lewis and Clark shows the captains gazing off at the ocean, an exhausted Seaman lying at their feet. Other scenes from the expedition circle the monument's base. This statue, like one at Fort Clatsop, is by former Astoria artist Stanley Wanlass.

In early January 1806 the corps heard of a great whale that had washed up on a nearby beach. Clark led a contingent of fifteen persons (including Sacagawea and Pomp) to seek the whale, which was pretty well picked over by the local Indians by the time the visitors arrived. Nevertheless, Clark succeeded in negotiating for the purchase of some 300 pounds of blubber and a few gallons of whale oil. "Small as this stock is I prize it highly; and thank providence for directing the whale to us; and think him much more kind to us than he was to Jonah, having sent this monster to be swallowed by us instead of swallowing of us as Jonah's did."

Oregon Coast at Ecola State Park near Cannon Beach, Oregon.

There are few places along the Lewis and Clark Trail where modern travelers can be certain they're hiking nearly the same route used by the explorers. Tillamook Head Trail is one of them. The trailhead is just south of Seaside; take Avenue U west from U.S. 101, then south on Edgewood Drive and Sunset Boulevard. It's a moderately strenuous 6-mile trek one-way to Indian Beach or 7 miles to Ecola Point, if you can arrange a shuttle. A 12- or 14-mile round-trip would take the better part of a day to complete, but a hiker campsite is available for folks who want to make an overnight of it.

Venture Outdoors includes the Tillamook Head hike in a six-day Lewis and Clark multisport adventure that also features sea kayaking and other coastal hikes. The cost was $1,595 in 2003. Call (800) 528–5262 or visit www.venout. com for details.

From Seaside the trail climbs steadily for its first few miles before winding about the top of the headlands. Up there, it's mostly mud and thick rain forest–like vegetation, but at least there is a trail of sorts. Clark, describing his trek, wrote: ". . . at one place we were obligated to support and draw ourselves up by the bushes and roots for near 100 feet, and after about two hours labor and fatigue we reached the top of this high mountain, from the top of which I looked down with astonishment to behold the height which we had ascended." The area marked Clark's viewpoint is overgrown these days, but another spot just a bit farther on has a wide ocean vista.

At the 4-mile mark, the trail reaches a backcountry campsite outfitted with several picnic tables (one under a modest shelter), fire rings, and an outhouse. Nearby viewpoints afford hikers views of Tillamook Rock Light. The remaining stretch to Indian Beach descends gradually amid moss-draped trees and graceful ferns on a more open path. After a series of switchbacks near the 5-mile mark, look for a clearing that overlooks the Indian Beach area and Haystack Rock beyond. The trail winds up near the rest rooms at Indian Beach.

If a long hike doesn't fit your schedule, simply drive to Ecola State Park, where short pathways lead to wonderful vistas of Haystack Rock and the rugged coastline. Just head south from Seaside on U.S. 101 and watch for the Cannon Beach turn. (It's somewhat sudden on the right-hand side.) Follow the signs to Ecola State Park, and take care driving the winding entrance road. The park charges a small day-use fee, $3.00 in 2002. Bring exact change, because it may be necessary for the automatic permit-dispensing machine if the park entrance booth is not staffed.

Another Cannon Beach site, Les Shirley Park, offers further interpretation of the Lewis and Clark story. To get there, continue on the road into Cannon Beach instead of turning right toward Ecola State Park. The park, almost immediately on the left, has picnic grounds and another fine Haystack Rock view. Wherever you wind up, take time to savor the ocean sights and sounds and reflect on the journey of Lewis and Clark—one of the greatest adventures the world has ever known.

Lodging

Lodgings, campgrounds, and restaurants listed below are a representative sampling of what is available. Listing in these pages does not imply endorsement, nor is this a complete listing of all reputable businesses. For more complete listings, contact the visitor information bureau or chamber of commerce in each town. Room rates were accurate as of summer 2002 but are subject to change.

CLARKSTON, WASHINGTON
Hacienda Lodge, (509) 758–5583, U.S. 12; $40–$46.
Highland House Bed & Breakfast, (509) 758–3126, 707 Highland Street; $55–$85.
Motel 6, (509) 758–1631, 222 Bridge Street; $48.
Quality Inn, (509) 758–9500, 700 Port Drive; $85–$105.

POMEROY, WASHINGTON
Pioneer Motel, (509) 843–1559, 1201 Main; $40–$50.

*DAYTON, WASHINGTON
Blue Mountain Motel, (509) 382–3040, 414 Main Street; $44–$49.
Dayton Motel, (509) 382–4503, 111 South Pine Street; $35–$65.
Weinhard Hotel, (509) 382–4032, 235 East Main Street; $70–$125.

*Denotes town along the expedition's homeward route, 1806.

TRI-CITIES, WASHINGTON
Budget Inn, (509) 546–2010, 1520 North Oregon Street (Pasco); $44.
Clover Island Inn, (509) 586–0541, 435 Clover Island (Kennewick); $60–$80.
DoubleTree Hotel, (509) 547–0701, 2525 North Twentieth Avenue (Pasco); $100–$180.
Super 8, (509) 736–6888, 626 Columbia Center Boulevard (Kennewick); $65.
Vineyard Inn, (509) 547–0791, 1800 West Lewis Street (Pasco); $50–$55.

*WALLA WALLA, WASHINGTON
Capri Motel, (509) 525–1130, 2003 Melrose; $50–$55.
Green Gables Inn Bed & Breakfast, (509) 525–5501, 922 Bonsella; $110–$140.
Marcus Whitman Hotel, (509) 525–2200, 6 West Rose Street; $115–$225.
Walla Walla Travelodge, (509) 529–4940, 421 East Main; $60–$65.

UMATILLA, OREGON
Desert River Inn, (541) 922–1000, 705 Willamette Avenue; $81.
Tillicum Motor Inn, (541) 922–3236, 1481 Sixth Street; $45.

BOARDMAN, OREGON
Dodge City Inn, (541) 481–2451, First and Front Street; $47–$51.
Riverfront Lodge Hotel, (888) 988–2009, 6 Marine Drive; $99.

THE DALLES, OREGON
Best Western River City Inn, (541) 296–9107, 112 West 2nd; $65–$90.
Comfort Inn, (541) 298–2800, I–84 exit 87; $60–$140.

Shilo Inn, (541) 298–5502, 3223 Bret Clodfelter Way; $60–$110.
The Inn at The Dalles, (541) 296–1167, 3550 Southeast Frontage Road; $45–$55.

HOOD RIVER, OREGON
Columbia Gorge Hotel, (541) 386–5566, 4000 Westcliff Drive; $179–$299.
Hood River Hotel, (541) 386–1900, 102 Oak; $69–$169.
Meredith Gorge Motel, (541) 386–1515, 4300 Westcliff Drive; $60–$80.
Panorama Lodge Bed & Breakfast, (541) 387–2687, 2290 Old Dalles Drive; $60–$100.
Riverview Lodge, (541) 386–8719, 1505 Oak; $62–$215.
Vagabond Lodge, (541) 386–2992, 4070 Westcliff Drive (I–84 exit 62); $55–$90.

WHITE SALMON, WASHINGTON
Inn of the White Salmon Bed & Breakfast, (800) 972–5226; $106–$143.

STEVENSON, WASHINGTON
EconoLodge, (509) 427–5628, 40 Northeast Second Street; $70–$75.
Skamania Lodge, (800) 221–7117, 1131 Skamania Lodge Drive; $170–$385.

CASCADE LOCKS, OREGON
Best Western Columbia River Inn, (541) 374–8777, 735 WaNaPa Street; $79–$134.
Bridge of the Gods Motel, (541) 374–8628, U.S. 30; $54–$60.
Econo Inn, (541) 374–8417, U.S. 30; $45–$55.

PORTLAND, OREGON
Cameo Motel, (503) 288–5981, 4111 Northeast Eighty-second Avenue; $40–$50.

---

*Denotes town along the expedition's homeward route, 1806.

Governor Hotel, (503) 224–3400, 611 Southwest Tenth; $185 and up.

DoubleTree Hotel Columbia River, (503) 283–2111, 1401 North Hayden Island Drive; $130–$150.

Holiday Inn–Convention Center, (503) 235–2100, 1021 Northeast Grand Avenue; $120–$155.

Hostelling International—Northwest Portland, (503) 241–2783, 1818 Northwest Glisan Street.

Hostelling International—Portland, (503) 236–3380, 3031 Hawthorne Boulevard Southeast.

River's Edge Bed & Breakfast, (503) 621–9856, 22502 Northwest Gillihan Road (Sauvie Island); $85.

Sleep Inn, (503) 618–8400, I–84 exit 13 (Gresham); $70–$80.

VANCOUVER, WASHINGTON

Best Inn & Suites, (360) 696–0516, 7001 Northeast Highway 99; $65–$75.

Ferryman's Inn, (360) 574–2151, 7901 Northeast Sixth Avenue; $60–$65.

Heathman Lodge, (888) 475–3100, 7801 Northeast Greenwood Drive; $89 and up.

Salmon Creek Motel, (360) 573–0751, 11901 Northeast Highway 99; $48–$60.

LONGVIEW, WASHINGTON

Hudson Manor Inn, (360) 425–1100, 1616 Hudson Street; $46–$55.

KELSO, WASHINGTON

Best Value Inn, (360) 636–4610, 505 North Pacific; $38–$44.

Comfort Inn, (360) 425–4600, 440 Three Rivers Drive; $72.

ST. HELENS, OREGON

Village Inn, (503) 397–1490, 535 South U.S. 30; $50–$55.

RAINIER, OREGON

Rainier Budget Inn, (503) 556–4231, 120 "A" Street West; $58.

CLATSKANIE, OREGON

Northwoods Inn, (503) 728–4311, 945 East Columbia River Highway; $60–$100.

CATHLAMET, WASHINGTON

Bradley House of Cathlamet B&B, (360) 795–3030, 61 Main Street; $99–$130.

The Farm at RiverMile39, (360) 431–2746, Ostervold Road, on Puget Island; $150.

Nassa Point Motel, (360) 795–3941, 851 East WA 4; $40.

Redfern Farm B&B, (360) 849–4108, 277 Cross Dike Road, on Puget Island; $65.

SKAMOKAWA, WASHINGTON

Skamokawa Inn, (888) 920–2777, WA 4; $70–$190.

NASELLE, WASHINGTON

Hunter's Inn, (360) 484–9215, WA 4; $50.

Naselle Village Inn Motel, (360) 484–3111, WA 4; $50.

Sleepy Hollow Motel, (360) 484–3232, WA 4; $40.

ILWACO, WASHINGTON

Heidi's Inn, (360) 642–2387, U.S. 101; $48–$85.

SEAVIEW, WASHINGTON

Shelburne Inn, (360) 642–2442, 4415 Pacific Way; $119–$159.

---

*Denotes town along the expedition's homeward route, 1806.

Sou'wester Lodge, (360) 642–2542, Thirty-eighth Place. Bed and make-your-own breakfast; $55–$149.

LONG BEACH, WASHINGTON
The Breakers, (800) 219–9833, 1.25 miles north via Highway 103; $70–$225.
Edgewater Inn, (360) 642–2311; $75–$140.
Shaman Motel, (360) 642–3714 or (800) 753–3750, 115 Third Street Northwest; $60–$100.
Super 8 Motel, (360) 642–8988, 500 Ocean Beach Boulevard; $70–$135.

ASTORIA, OREGON
Astoria Dunes Motel, (503) 325–7111, 288 West Marine Drive; $70–$90.
Astoria Inn Bed & Breakfast, (503) 325–8153, 3391 Irving Avenue; $70–$85.
Bayshore Motor Inn, (503) 325–2205, 555 Hamburg; $65–$80.
Crest Motel, (503) 325–3141 or (800) 421–3141, 5366 Leif Erickson Drive; $65–$110.
Franklin Street Station Bed & Breakfast, (503) 325–4314, 1140 Franklin Avenue; $75–$135.
Red Lion Inn, (503) 325–7373, 400 Industry Street; $90–$125.

WARRENTON, OREGON
Shilo Inn Suites, (503) 861–2181, 1609 East Harbor Drive; $70–$180.

GEARHART, OREGON
Gearhart Ocean Inn, (503) 738–7373, 67 North Cottage Street; $45–$120.

SEASIDE, OREGON
Best Western Ocean View Resort, (503) 738–3334 or (800) 234–8439, 414 North Prom; $155–$275.
Ebb Tide Motel, (503) 738–8371 or (800) 468–6232, 300 North Prom; $130–$160.
Hostelling International–Seaside, (503) 738–7911, 930 North Holladay Drive.
Riverside Inn Bed & Breakfast, (503) 738–8254 or (800) 826–6151, 430 South Holladay Drive; $70–$110.
Royale Motel, (503) 738–9541, 531 Avenue A; $50–$70.

CANNON BEACH, OREGON
Blue Gull Inn, (503) 436–2714 or (800) 507–2714, 487 South Hemlock Street; $65–$110.
Cannon Beach Hotel Lodgings, (503) 436–1392 or (800) 238–4107, 1116 South Hemlock; $50–$170.
Hallmark Resort, (503) 436–1566 or (888) 448–4449, 1400 South Hemlock; $80 and up.
McBee Motel Cottages, (503) 436–2569 or (800) 238–4107, 888 South Hemlock; $35–$135.

Camping

STARBUCK, WASHINGTON
Palouse Falls State Park, (509) 646–3252, WA 261. Primitive sites.

*DAYTON, WASHINGTON
Lewis and Clark Trail State Park, (509) 337–6457, 4 miles east on U.S. 12.

*WALLA WALLA, WASHINGTON
Fort Walla Walla Campground, (509) 527–3770, west of town at Fort Walla Walla Museum complex.

*Denotes town along the expedition's homeward route, 1806.

TRI–CITIES, WASHINGTON

Arrowhead RV Park, (509) 545–8206, 3120 Commercial (Pasco).

Charbonneau Park, (509) 547–7781, off of WA 124 east of Pasco.

Columbia Park Campground, (509) 585–4529, 6601 Southeast Columbia Drive (Kennewick).

Desert Gold Motel & RV Park, (509) 627–1000, Columbia Drive west of I–182 exit 3 (Richland).

Fishhook Park, (509) 547–7781, off of WA 124 east of Pasco.

Hood Park, (509) 547–7781, 3 miles east of Pasco on Highway 12E.

UMATILLA, OREGON

Hat Rock Campground, (541) 567–4188, east on U.S. 730 opposite Hat Rock State Park.

Umatilla Marina and RV Park, (541) 922–3939, north of U.S. 730. No tents.

GOLDENDALE, WASHINGTON

Horsethief Lake State Park, (509) 767–1159, west on WA 14. Primitive sites.

Maryhill State Park, (509) 773–5007, near junction of U.S. 97 and WA 14.

Peach Beach, (509) 773–4698, at Gunkel Orchards adjacent to Maryhill State Park.

THE DALLES, OREGON

Deschutes River Recreation Area, 17 miles east on I–84. Primitive sites.

Lone Pine Travel Park, (541) 506–3755, I–84 exit 87.

Memaloose State Park, 11 miles west on I–84.

WHITE SALMON, WASHINGTON

Bridge RV Park, (509) 493–1111 or (888) 550–7275, 65271 WA 14.

HOOD RIVER, OREGON

Tucker Park, (541) 386–4477, 4 miles south on OR 281. Mostly tent sites.

Viento State Park, (541) 374–8811, 8 miles west on I–84.

CASCADE LOCKS, OREGON

Bridge of the Gods RV Park, (541) 374–8628, U.S. 30.

Cascade Locks KOA, (541) 374–8668, U.S. 30.

STEVENSON, WASHINGTON

Hidden Coves Campground, (509) 427–8098, WA 14.

NORTH BONNEVILLE, WASHINGTON

Beacon Rock Resort, (509) 427–8473, west on WA 14.

Beacon Rock State Park, (509) 427–8265, 3 miles west on WA 14.

Lewis and Clark Campground, (509) 427–5982, west on WA 14.

GRESHAM, OREGON

Oxbow Park, (503) 663–4708, 3010 Southeast Oxbow Parkway.

PORTLAND, OREGON

Jantzen Beach RV Park, (503) 289–7626 or (800) 443–7248, 1503 North Hayden Island Drive. No tents.

Reeder Beach Resort RV Park, (503) 621–3098, 26048 Northwest Reeder Road on Sauvie Island. No tents.

RIDGEFIELD, WASHINGTON

Big Fir Campground & RV Park, (360) 887–8970 or (800) 532–4397, I–15 exit 14.

---

*Denotes town along the expedition's homeward route, 1806.

WOODLAND, WASHINGTON
Columbia Riverfront RV Park, (360) 225–8051 or (800) 845–9842, I–5 exit 22.
Lewis River RV Park, (360) 225–9556, I–5 exit 21.
Paradise Point State Park, (360) 263–2350, south via I–5.

KALAMA, WASHINGTON
Camp Kalama RV Park, (360) 673–2456, I–5 exit 32.

KELSO, WASHINGTON
Brook Hollow RV Park, (360) 577–6474, I–5 exit 39.
The Cedars RV Park, (360) 274–5136, I–5 exit 46.

CATHLAMET, WASHINGTON
County Line Park, east on WA 4 at the Cowlitz/Wahkiakum county line.

CHINOOK, WASHINGTON
Chinook County Park, (360) 777–8442, U.S. 101.
Mauch's Sundown RV Park, (360) 777–8713, 4 miles east on U.S. 101.
River's End Campground, (360) 777–8317, west of town on U.S. 101.

ILWACO, WASHINGTON
Fort Canby State Park, (360) 642–3078, 2.5 miles southwest of U.S. 101.

Ilwaco KOA, (360) 642–3292, 2 miles south on U.S. 101.

LONG BEACH, WASHINGTON
Andersen's RV Park on the Ocean, (360) 642–2231, 1400 138th Street.
Driftwood RV Park, (360) 642–2711, 1512 North Pacific Way.
Pegg's Oceanside RV Park, (360) 642–2451, north on WA 103.
Pioneer RV Park, (360) 642–3990, WA 103 and Pioneer Road.

ASTORIA, OREGON
Astoria-Warrenton-Seaside KOA, (503) 861–2606, 1100 Northwest Ridge Road (Hammond).
Fort Stevens State Park, (503) 861–1671, west on U.S. 101.
Kampers West, (503) 861–1814, 1140 Northwest Warrenton Drive.
Sunset Lake Resort & RV Park, (503) 861–1760, 850 Lewis Avenue.

SEASIDE, OREGON
Circle Creek RV Park & Campground, (503) 738–6070, U.S. 101.

CANNON BEACH, OREGON
Oswald West State Park, (503) 368–5154, 10 miles south via U.S. 101.
RV Resort at Cannon Beach, (503) 436–2231, Elk Creek Road. No tents.

Restaurants

CLARKSTON, WASHINGTON
Bamboo Gardens, (509) 758–8898, 907 Sixth Street. Mandarin and Szechuan cuisine.
Bridge Street Connection, (509) 758–3141, U.S. 12. Prime rib, daily specials.

Rooster's Landing, (509) 751–0155, 1550 Port Drive. Popular place on the river.

POMEROY, WASHINGTON
Donna's Drive-In, (509) 843–1510, Fourteenth and Main.

*Denotes town along the expedition's homeward route, 1806.

*DAYTON, WASHINGTON

Panhandler's Pizza & Pasta, (509) 382–4160, 404 West Main.

Patit Creek Restaurant, (509) 382–2625, 725 East Main. French cuisine in an unlikely small-town setting. Lunch Wednesday–Friday; dinner Wednesday–Saturday.

Weinhard's Espresso Cafe, (509) 382–2091, 235 East Main Street. Breakfast and lunch.

*WAITSBURG, WASHINGTON

Farmer's Cafe, (509) 337–6845, 216 Main.

TRI-CITIES, WASHINGTON

Aioli's Restaurant & Wine Bar, (509) 942–1914, 94 Lee Boulevard (Pasco).

Cedars Restaurant, (509) 582–2143, 555 Clover Island (Kennewick). Steak and seafood with riverside seating.

Rattlesnake Mountain Brewing Company, (509) 783–5747, 2696 Columbia Center Boulevard (Richland). Riverside dining.

Roy's Western Smorgy, (509) 735–8539, 2602 North Columbia Center Boulevard (Richland). One-price buffet.

T. S. Cattle Company Steakhouse, (509) 783–8251, 6515 West Clearwater (Kennewick). No ties allowed.

*WALLA WALLA, WASHINGTON

The Homestead Restaurant, (509) 522–0345, 1528 East Isaacs. Lunch and dinner specials daily.

Jacobi's Train Car Cafe, (509) 525–2677, 416 North Second. Wide menu, vegetarian dishes.

Pastime Cafe, (509) 525–0873, 215 West Main. Italian and American food.

THE DALLES, OREGON

Cousins, (541) 298–2771, at the Quality Inn. Ribs, pot roast, other home-style fare.

Lone Pine Restaurant, (541) 296–5333, I–84 at U.S. 197. Family dining, breakfast all day.

Windseeker, (541) 298–7171, 1535 Bargeway Road. Riverfront restaurant with deck seating.

HOOD RIVER, OREGON

Columbia Court Dining Room, (541) 387–5409, in the Columbia Gorge Hotel. Elegant dining and "famous farm breakfast."

The Mesquitery, (541) 386–2002, 1219 Twelfth Street. Gourmet grilling with mesquite wood.

6th Street Bistro & Loft, (541) 386–5737, Sixth and Cascade. New American cuisine featuring local foods.

Sage's Café & Coffee House, (541) 386–9404, 202 Cascade Street. Salads, sandwiches, baked goods.

Stonehedge Inn, (541) 386–3940, 3405 Cascade Drive. Elegant dining amid wooded surroundings.

LYLE, WASHINGTON

Country Cafe, (509) 365–3883, WA 14. Burgers, omelettes, homemade pie.

BINGEN, WASHINGTON

Fidel's, (509) 493–1017, 120 East Steuben. Mexican food.

CASCADE LOCKS, OREGON

Charburger Restaurant, (541) 374–8477, 714 Southwest WaNaPa. Breakfast specialties, chili, chicken.

---

*Denotes town along the expedition's homeward route, 1806.

Sam Hill's River Room & Patio, (541) 374–8477, 745 WaNaPa. Northwest cuisine.

STEVENSON, WASHINGTON
Big River Grill, (509) 427–4888, WA 14. Tasty food in historic building.
Dee's Kich-Inn, (509) 427–4670, 10 Northwest Second Street. Home cooking three meals a day.
Skamania Lodge, (509) 427–2508, in the Skamania Lodge. Several dining options, breakfast buffet.

TROUTDALE, OREGON
McMenamin's Edgefield Power Station, (503) 669–8610, just off I–84. Movie theater/bistro/B&B/hostel.
Tad's Chicken 'n Dumplins, (503) 666–5337, east on Crown Point Highway (Troutdale). Dining on the Sandy River.

PORTLAND, OREGON
Avalon Restaurant, (503) 227–4630, 4630 Southwest Macadam Avenue. French-Asian fusion fare.
Byways, (503) 221–0011, 1212 Northwest Glisan Street. Retro travel theme. Closed Monday.
Hamburger Mary's, (503) 223–0900, 239 Southwest Broadway. A funky local favorite.
Jake's Famous Crawfish, (503) 226–1419, 401 Southwest Twelfth Street. Wide seafood menu.
Jake's Grill, (503) 220–1850, 611 Southwest Tenth Avenue. Steaks and more in the Governor Hotel.
Macheezmo Mouse, (503) 248–0917, 723 Southwest Salmon and other locations. Heart-smart Mexican fare.

Saigon Kitchen, (503) 281–3669, 835 Northeast Broadway. Locally popular Vietnamese restaurant.
Zell's: An American Cafe, (503) 239–0196, 1300 Southeast Morrison. Breakfast and lunch.

VANCOUVER, WASHINGTON
Hudson's Bar & Grill, (360) 254–3100, 7801 Northeast Greenwood Drive. Northwest seasonal comfort food in the Heathman Lodge.
Juanita's Mexican Restaurant, (360) 834–5856, 231 Third Avenue (Camas). Daily specials.
Peach Tree Restaurant and Pie House, (360) 693–6736, 6600 Northeast Highway 99. Family dining.

KALAMA, WASHINGTON
Romer's Restaurant, (360) 673–2800, 698 Northeast Frontage.

LONGVIEW, WASHINGTON
Charlie's, (360) 636–5661, 1826 First Avenue. Family dining, wide menu.
Hart C's, (360) 425–6292, 3171 Ocean Beach Highway. Thai and American cuisine.
The Masthead, (360) 577–7972, 1210 Ocean Beach Highway. Seafood, burgers, chicken.

CATHLAMET, WASHINGTON
Ranch House Restaurant, (360) 795–8015, Third and Una.

SKAMOKAWA, WASHINGTON
The Duck Inn, (360) 795–3655, WA 4.

CHINOOK, WASHINGTON
Sanctuary Restaurant, (360) 777–8380, U.S. 101. Seafood and Scandinavian food in 1906 church.

*Denotes town along the expedition's homeward route, 1806.

SEAVIEW, WASHINGTON

The Depot, (360) 642–7880, Thirty-eighth and L Place. Casual gourmet fare, Thursday burger nights.

42nd Street Cafe, (360) 642–2323, Forty-second Street and Pacific Highway. Chicken, pot roast, seafood, steaks.

Shoalwater Restaurant, (360) 642–4142, WA 103 at Forty-fifth Street. One of the region's best.

LONG BEACH, WASHINGTON

Chuck's Restaurant, (360) 642–2721, Nineteenth and Pacific. Chicken-fried steak, seafood, prime rib.

The Lightship Restaurant & Lounge, (360) 642–3252. Casual ocean-view dining in the Edgewater Inn.

CLATSKANIE, OREGON

Northwoods Inn Restaurant, (503) 728–4311, 945 East Columbia River Highway.

ASTORIA, OREGON

Andrew & Steve's Cafe, (503) 325–5762, 1196 Marine Drive. Greek specialties and seafood, open since 1916.

Cafe Uniontown, (503) 325–8708, 218 West Marine Drive. Steaks, seafood, pasta. Closed Monday.

Columbian Cafe—Fresca Deli, (503) 325–2233, 1114 Marine Drive. Friendly place.

Pig 'n Pancake, (503) 325–3144, 146 West Bond. Breakfast anytime. Also in Seaside and Cannon Beach.

Ship Inn, (503) 325–0033, Second Street at Marine Drive. Fish-and-chips, other pub fare.

GEARHART, OREGON

Pacific Way Bakery & Café, (503) 738–0245, 601 Pacific Way. Famous croissants, pasta, seafood.

SEASIDE, OREGON

BeeBop Burgers, (503) 738–3271, 111 Broadway. Clam chowder, burgers, fish-and-chips.

Bell Buoy, (503) 738–2722, 1800 South Holladay. Seafood since 1946.

Dooger's Seafood Grill, (503) 738–3773, 505 Broadway. Clam chowder, steak, salads. Also in Cannon Beach and Long Beach.

Pudgy's, (503) 738–8330, 227 Broadway. Seafood and steaks with outdoor dining.

CANNON BEACH, OREGON

Heather's Cafe, (503) 436–9356, 217 North Hemlock. Soup, sandwiches, decadent desserts.

Wayfarer Restaurant & Lounge, (503) 436–1108, Ocean Front and Gower. Wide menu.

---

*Denotes town along the expedition's homeward route, 1806.

Epilogue

It took Lewis and Clark eighteen months to reach the Pacific Ocean on their outbound trip. But like any travelers eager to get home, they made much better time on the return journey, arriving in St. Louis September 23, 1806, six months to the day after leaving Fort Clatsop. A newspaper account reporting the occasion read thus: "Mssrs. Lewis and Clark arrived here about one hour ago. Three cheers were fired. They really have the appearance of Robinson Crusoes, dressed entirely in buckskins."

In the years following the expedition, many of its members went on to fame and fortune. Even before the party arrived home, John Colter asked to be allowed to return west as a trapper. "We agreed to allow him the privilege provided no one of the party would ask or expect a similar permission," Clark wrote on August 16, 1806. Soon Colter became known as the first white man to explore the area around what is now Yellowstone and Grand Teton National Parks.

George Shannon, the enlisted party's youngest man, became a congressman from Kentucky. York was eventually freed (albeit grudgingly) by Clark. Patrick Gass, the first corps member to publish his journals, was a bit slower to establish his personal life. At age sixty, he finally married Maria Hamilton, a woman one-third his age. He died shortly before his one-hundredth birthday, outliving his young wife by more than a decade. He also lived longer than anyone else who had been on the expedition, including Sacagawea's son, Jean Baptiste.

As for Clark, he enjoyed a stellar postexpedition career. He was appointed Superintendent of Indian Affairs in 1807 and served in that role until his death in 1838. In 1813 he was also appointed governor of the newly established Missouri Territory and was reappointed three times, holding the office until Missouri became a state in 1821 (although he failed to win the post in the first state election). But it was in his position as Indian Superintendent that he won his greatest acclaim. "In this role, he broadened the base of goodwill the Lewis and Clark Expedition had established, and probably did more to help the Indians than any of his successors," wrote Roy E. Appleman in his National Park Service survey. "Their friend, protector, and advocate, who always tried to obtain as much justice as possible for them, he was fondly known as the 'Red-Headed Chief.'" Clark also had a happy personal life, marrying his sweetheart Julia Hancock in 1808. They had five children, naming the firstborn Meriwether Lewis Clark. Julia died in 1821, but Clark then married Harriet Kennerly Radford, a widow with three children. Together they went on to have two more sons. Clark died in 1838 at age sixty-eight.

And what of Lewis? Sadly, fate was not as kind. Despite his keen intellect and bright record of service, Lewis had difficulty establishing himself after the expedition, either professionally or personally. Things started well enough: Lewis was appointed governor of the Louisiana Territory and made plans for publication of the expedition's journals. But long given to brooding and mood swings, Lewis was not an especially adept politician. He also suffered financial problems, particularly after the U.S. War Department refused to honor drafts Lewis had signed to provide for the safe return of an Indian party that had accompanied the corps back east at Jefferson's request. Lewis was held personally responsible for the debt, and it appeared he would have to sell title to the 1,600 acres of land he was rewarded for his part in the expedition.

In the fall of 1809, Lewis set off for Washington to plead his case in person. On the night of October 9, two of his party's packhorses escaped, and Lewis dispatched his companion, Maj. James Neelly, to search for them. On October 11, Neelly found Lewis dead of two gunshot wounds. He was just thirty-five years old. To this day, no one has proven conclusively whether the captain's death was murder or suicide, but his memory is honored at a park along Tennessee's Natchez Trace. The park's centerpiece is a broken column that stands in mute testimony to Lewis's untimely death.

But even tragedy could not blunt the expedition's impact nor dull the sense something great had been accomplished. "The expedition of Mssrs. Lewis and Clark for exploring the River Missouri and the best communication from that to the Pacific Ocean has had all the success which could have been expected," Jefferson said in his report to Congress in December 1806. "They have traced the Missouri nearly to its source, descended the Columbia to the Pacific Ocean, ascertaining with accuracy the geography of that interesting communication across our continent, learned the character of the country, of its commerce and inhabitants, and it is but justice to say that Mssrs. Lewis and Clark and their brave companions have by this arduous service deserved well of their country." Long after their death, the legacy left by Lewis and Clark ensured the future of America as a world power and, even more important, as a nation that ever dares to dream—and to discover.

Lewis and Clark Bicentennial Signature Events

The National Council of the Lewis and Clark Bicentennial has announced this calendar of events that will serve as "exclamation points" in the 2003–2006 commemoration. For details or updates, contact event organizers or visit the council's Web site at www.lewisandclark200.org.

January 14–19, 2003
Bicentennial Inaugural: Jefferson's West
Charlottesville, Virginia (434)
   984–9822
www.monticello.org

October 14–26, 2003
Falls of the Ohio
Louisville, Kentucky, and Clarksville,
   Indiana
(502) 292–0059
www.fallsoftheohio.org/lewisand
   clark.html

March 12–14, 2004
Three Flags Ceremony
St. Louis, Missouri
(314) 516–6884
louisianapurchase.umsl.edu

May 13–16, 2004
*Expedition's Departure: Camp River
   Dubois*
Hartford and Wood River vicinity,
   Illinois
(618) 467–2288
www.lewisandclarkillinois.org

May 14–23, 2004
*St. Charles: Preparations Complete, the
   Expedition Faces West*
St. Charles, Missouri
(800) 366–2427
www.lewisandclarkstcharles.com

July 3–4, 2004
Heart of America: A Journey Forth
Kansas City area, Missouri/Kansas
(800) 767–7700
www.visitkc.com

July 31–August 3, 2004
First Tribal Council
Omaha, Nebraska, area
(402) 471–3368
www.visitnebraska.org

August 27–28, 2004
Oceti Sakowin Experience:
  Remembering and Educating
Dakota/Lakota/Nakota Tribes and
  the State of South Dakota
(605) 473–0561
www.travelsd.com

October 22–31, 2004
Circle of Cultures, Time of
  Renewal and Exchange
Bismarck, North Dakota, area
(701) 663–4758
www.fortlincoln.com

June 2–July 4, 2005
Explore the Big Sky
Great Falls, Montana
(406) 455–8451
www.explorethebigsky.org

November 24–27, 2005
Destination 2005—The Pacific
Lower Columbia River, Washington
  and Oregon
(503) 861–2471
www.nps.gov/focl

June 14–17, 2006
Among the Nez Perce
Lewiston/Lapwai, Idaho, area
(208) 843–2253
www.nezperce.org

July 25, 2006
Clark on the Yellowstone
Pompeys Pillar/Billings, Montana
(406) 256–8628
www.clarkontheyellowstone.org

August 17–20, 2006
Home of Sakakawea
New Town, North Dakota
(701) 627–2870
www.mhanation.com

September 23, 2006
The Return of Lewis and Clark
St. Louis, Missouri, area
(314) 655–1600
www.nps.gov/jeff/overview.htm

All the Signature Events will be accompanied by "Corps of Discovery II: 200 Years to the Future," a traveling museum sponsored by the National Park Service and other agencies. Corps II will also travel to other cities on and off the trail between Signature Events. Check the Park Service's Lewis and Clark Web site at www.nps.gov/lecl for schedules and updates.

Selected Annual Events

Here are some major events held annually along the trail. Dates can change; please call ahead to confirm. For more complete listings of Lewis and Clark–related events, visit www.lewisandclarktravel.info.

Third weekend in May
Lewis & Clark Heritage Days
St. Charles, Missouri
(636) 947–3199

First weekend in June
Lewis & Clark Days
Washburn, North Dakota
(701) 462–8535

First weekend in June
Lewis & Clark Days
Walla Walla, Washington
(509) 525–7703

Second weekend in June
Lewis & Clark Festival
Onawa, Iowa
(712) 423–2829

Late June
Lewis & Clark Festival
Great Falls, Montana
(406) 727–8733

Last weekend in July
Lewis and Clark Festival and White Catfish Camp
Council Bluffs, Iowa
(712) 366–4900

Third weekend in August
Sacajawea Heritage Days
Salmon, Idaho
(208) 756–1188

Late September
Lewis & Clark Goosefest
Pierre, South Dakota
(800) 962–2034

Late October
Falls of the Ohio Lewis & Clark River Festival
Clarksville, Indiana, and Louisville, Kentucky
(502) 292–0059

Early November
"Ocean in View" Weekend
Pacific County, Washington
(800) 451–2542

Index

About the Author

Photo: Byron Fanselow

Julie Fanselow was born in Illinois and grew up in Bethel Park, Pennsylvania. She earned a bachelor's degree in journalism at Ohio University.

After ten years as a reporter and editor for daily newspapers in Ohio, Idaho, and Washington state, Fanselow became a full-time independent writer specializing in travel. Her other books include *Traveling the Oregon Trail* (Falcon), *Texas* (Lonely Planet), and *Idaho Off the Beaten Path* (Globe Pequot). She also writes regularly for magazines and serves as a guest interpreter for outfitters traveling the Lewis and Clark Trial.

Fanselow is a member of the Society of American Travel Writers, the American Society of Journalists and Authors, and the Lewis and Clark Trail Heritage Foundation. She now lives in Idaho with her family.